LAW, COURTS, AND POLICY

Mitchell S. G. Klein

Prentice-Hall, Inc., Englewood Cliffs, N.J. 07632

Library of Congress Cataloging in Publication Data

Klein, Mitchell S. G.
   Law, courts, and policy.

   Includes bibliographies and index.
   1. Justice, Administration of—United States.
2. Courts—United States.   3. Law—United States.
4. Sociological jurisprudence.   I. Title.
KF8700.K63   1984   347.73   83-9540
ISBN 0-13-526079-5   347.307

To my mother, Gloria Klein,
and my brother, Sydney.

Editorial/production supervision and
   interior design: Dee Amir Josephson
Cover design: Mark Benghash
Manufacturing buyer: Ron Chapman

Printed in the United States of America

10 9 8 7 6 5 4 3 2 1

ISBN 0-13-526079-5

Prentice-Hall International, Inc., *London*
Prentice-Hall of Australia Pty. Limited, *Sydney*
Editora Prentice-Hall do Brasil, Ltda., *Rio de Janeiro*
Prentice-Hall Canada Inc., *Toronto*
Prentice-Hall of India Private Limited, *New Delhi*
Prentice-Hall of Japan, Inc., *Tokyo*
Prentice-Hall of Southeast Asia Pte. Ltd., *Singapore*
Whitehall Books Limited, *Wellington, New Zealand*

CONTENTS

PREFACE

This book introduces you to the subject of the American judiciary. In clear and understandable prose, it tells you about the full range of interests, ideas, and research in this subject area. It tries to do this in a way that will sensitize you to how the courts influence the achievement of values in our society.

A vast array of concerns are relevant to the judiciary. A few of these include crime-fighting by police, jury nullification, equal protection of the law, no fault auto insurance, and plea bargaining. The eight chapters of this book deal with the full range of concerns in law and politics and put each in its proper place. Each chapter summarizes the past research and prevailing theory from political science, legal studies, and the other social sciences. It is simply stunning to learn just how many books and research articles have been published on the subject of the judiciary.

Chapter 1 provides you with a general introduction to Law and Society. This includes a discussion of law and the legal system. The chapter points out that law has two basic roles in society. First, it provides guidelines to help you avoid disputes or deal with the disputes that you become involved in. You should be aware, however, that only a small portion of the disputes occurring in our society ever enter the courtroom. Most are dealt with through private, informal negotiations or some other means. A second role of the law is to select among competing values. Among the most important of these values are liberty, equality, procedural justice, democracy, effectiveness, and social order. Clearly, the criminal laws of our country represent an effort to achieve some degree of social order. They aim to regulate people's conduct, steering them from certain kinds of behavior and punishing transgressions that are discovered. As you will see, the law also seeks to achieve other important social values. Under certain circumstances, the law can act as a powerful source of social change.

The next four chapters discuss the leading participants in the courtroom. These chapters (2–5) include Police, Lawyers, Judges, and the Public. This last chapter will include consideration of litigants, witnesses, juries, interest groups, the new media, and scientists. Common themes are examined in each of these chapters. Thus, the chapters generally include some consideration of the personal characteristics of the legal participants, then effectiveness in carrying out various roles, their decision-making processes, ethics, and public relations. A continuing theme in each of these chapters is the extent to which the courtroom participants promote or impinge upon various values.

The final three chapters of this book (Chapters 6–8) treat the policies of the American judiciary. Chapter 6 focuses on the procedures and substance of civil law. You will learn the characteristics of property law, contracts, torts, and human relations law. For each area of civil law there are some specific examples. For instance, when discussing domestic relations, divorce cases and civil commitment are discussed. Chapter 7 analyzes criminal justice. This will include sections on the nature of crime, causes of crime, criminal justice process, and penal justice. Some important social values are at stake in both the civil and criminal courts. Finally, Chapter 8 analyzes constitutional law. Discussions of the notion of judicial review, the substance of Supreme Court decisions, and the impact of the courts are included. Although critics charge that the courts are undemocratic and incompetent, this book indicates that the case against the courts has been badly overstated.

I am very grateful to four people who commented on an earlier version of this book. Peter Galie has been a very conscientious and helpful reader. He examined nearly all that follows and saved me from numerous errors of fact and judgment. In addition, on selected chapters, a number of similarly helpful comments were made by Stephen Halpern (Chapters 2, 3, and 8), Henry Langer (Chapters 3, and 7), and H. Laurence Ross (Chapter 1). I am also grateful to my editor, Stan Wakefield, and the entire team at Prentice-Hall, including Dee Josephson, Audrey Marshall, David O'Brien, and the fine group of reviewers: Edward V. Heck, University of New Orleans; Richard P. Claude, University of Maryland; Karl Andresen, University of Wisconsin; William P. Mc-Lauchlan, Purdue University; and Roger C. Schaefer, Texas Tech. University. Finally, I am indebted to the libraries of the State University of New York at Buffalo.

1
LAW AND SOCIETY*

PREVIEW

Chapter 1 discusses the nature of law, its roles, and its impact on society. The chapter consists of four sections:

Law and the legal system
Dispute processing
Law and social values
The impact of law

The first section discusses law and the legal system. A law is a ground rule backed by the coercive power of government. As you will see, laws in the United States result from a complex decision-making process involving separated institutions sharing power. The decisions of elected representatives are heavily influenced by organized interest groups and are often constrained by constitutional provisions as interpreted by judges. The second section treats the role of law in dispute processing. A person may at any time become involved in a dispute with a relative, friend, businessperson, government offi-

*Full citations for cases discussed herein appear at the end of each chapter under "Supreme Court Rulings."

cial, or complete stranger. While most disputes are handled in a less formal manner, people may turn to the law to process their disputes. The third section examines law and social values. It is a critical role of the law to influence the distribution of values in our society. Such values include procedural justice, liberty, equality, social order, effectiveness, and democracy. The fourth section of the chapter analyzes the impact of law. While some view the law as virtually omnipotent in producing social change, others consider the law rather impotent. Surely, the effectiveness of law lies somewhere in between these extremes. It will also be stressed that the law has a greater impact upon society when certain circumstances prevail.

LAW AND THE LEGAL SYSTEM

Nature of Law

Defining law has been a leading preoccupation of legal scholars (Ford, 1970, pp. 1–31). It seems as if the three favorite activities of law professors are assigning cases, asking students questions about cases, and writing new definitions of "law." I will not present a lengthy discussion of alternative definitions here. It may be most useful simply to think of law as a ground rule backed by the coercive power of government. The legal system has two basic purposes in establishing these ground rules. First, such rules help people to avoid disputes and deal with the disputes that occur in their daily lives: Legal ground rules tell people how they must act when they are involved in certain kinds of disputes. Second, law is used by government to influence the distribution of values in society. By permitting some kinds of behavior and outlawing others, government promotes certain values and impinges on others. For example, an affirmative action law may seek to further *equality* between the races and sexes. However, the same law may also constrain the *liberty* of employers to hire whomever they wish to fill a job vacancy.

Although law is a ground rule, it is surely not the only type of ground rule that exists. In the home parents may establish a host of rules regulating the behavior of their children. For example, there may be rules about finishing homework, staying up late at night, or watching television. (Fortunately, few parents have established rules against reading political science textbooks.) There are many ground rules at the work place as well: for example, on the number of coffee breaks, the amount of payment for overtime work, and the taking of personal phone calls. Ground rules are even present in the games people play. For example, baseball is played with nine people per team, football with eleven, and basketball with five. Intricate rules regulate the playing of these games, with penalties imposed for any violations detected by referees or umpires.

Legal ground rules can be distinguished from the other ground rules existing in society (Kelsen, 1978; Hart, 1961; Hogan and Henley, 1972). Uniquely, laws are established by government and backed by its coercive sanctions. Possible violations of the law may be detected by ordinary citizens, private organizations, police officers, and lawyers. Legal ground rules may then be enforced by judges (or sometimes by public administrators). In a very real sense, therefore, law is "the formal means of social control that involves the use of rules that are interpreted, and are enforceable, by the courts of a political community." (Davis, 1962, p. 41) Similarly, law may be seen as "a series of commands about how people in a society ought to behave." (Casper, 1972a, p. 145) Apart from law, there are other forms of social control, such as ostracism, shaming, and gossip. Only law is backed by government's coercive force (Jeffery, 1962, p. 264). Custom has the sanction of group disapproval; religion has a supernatural sanction; and morality has the sanction of conscience. The formal control of law is needed to a greater extent in complex, heterogeneous societies such as the United States in order to deal with disputes and avert disorder (Felstiner, 1974).

Five sources of law in the United States are generally cited.[1] Constitutional law involves the interpretation and application of the United States Constitution to specific concerns. It is a major focus of the Supreme Court. Constitutional law is primarily concerned with determining how much power should be exercised by each institution of government and what rights should be possessed by individuals. Statutory law consists of law passed by a legislature—whether by Congress, a state legislature, or a city council. The scope of statutory law has greatly broadened in the course of United States history.

Common law is judge-made law based on precedent (that is, on prior court decisions). It consists of the totality of decisions made by judges in past cases. Despite the great increase in the number of statutes, common law is still applied by judges in a vast number of cases. Equity guides judicial decisions where common law does not apply. It enables judges to order that something be done or not done in order to prevent a harm from taking place. A well-known example of equity law is a court injunction. Administrative law consists of ground rules established by bureaucracies. Congress has granted bureaucracies the power to issue regulations that are binding on people and organizations. Those displeased with an administrative decision may appeal the matter to the regular federal court system.

In addition to the five sources of law discussed above, we find also international law. Indeed, Article VI, section 2, of the Constitution states that treaties, like the Constitution, are part of the "supreme law of the

---

[1]For example, see David V. Edwards, *The American Political Experience* (Englewood Cliffs, N. J.: Prentice-Hall, 1979), pp. 283–284.

land. . . ." The treaties entered into by the president, and confirmed by the Senate, may have an important bearing upon domestic matters.[2]

Legal rules permeate complex, heterogeneous societies such as the United States (Friedman, 1973; B. Schwartz, 1974). Any aspect of social relationships may be brought within the scope of the law. For example, laws define some behavior as criminal and subject to government penalties such as imprisonment. The 1976 edition of the United States Code (1977) contains sixteen huge volumes and the annual supplements are quite lengthy. The various "titles" of the Code focus on a wide range of subjects, including banks and banking (Title 12), crimes and criminal procedure (Title 18), and judiciary and judicial procedure (Title 28). Title 18 identifies an enormous number of federal crimes. As regards counterfeiting, section 471 of Title 18 reads: "Whoever, with intent to defraud, falsely makes, forges, counterfeits, or alters any obligation or other security of the United States, shall be fined not more than $5,000 or imprisoned not more than fifteen years, or both" (Vol. 4, p. 1060). Moreover, it should be noted that most of the criminal laws of our nation are promulgated at the state level rather than at the federal level. The range of criminal laws in our country is quite broad, including areas such as murder, theft, price fixing, treason, and driving while intoxicated.

There also exists a large number of noncriminal laws. These civil laws have broad coverage—protecting and limiting the right to property, regulating the enforcement of contracts, requiring compensation for damages inflicted, and governing domestic relations. Laws provide a framework for social and economic life in our society. By providing this framework, laws promote a regularity and predictability in relationships among people.[3]

When disputes enter the legal system, they may do so as either civil or criminal cases. Civil judicial procedure is used to deal with disputes between two parties (Mayers, 1973). It is incumbent upon one of the parties in a dispute to bring the matter to the attention of the legal system and act as the plaintiff. Courts in the United States are passive and reactive—they will not seek out civil disputes to resolve. Instead, the courts rely upon a complainant to take a legal claim to the courtroom. When a civil dispute is brought forward, the judge is obliged to rule on the basis of law rather than on personal beliefs. In theory only the legality of a claim is considered in the courts. To have a claim

---

[2]Article VI, section 2, states, in part: "This Constitution, and the laws of the United States which shall be made in pursuance thereof; and all treaties made, or which shall be made, under the authority of the United States, shall be the supreme law of the land. . . ." The Supreme Court has long held that valid treaties have domestic applicability. See, for example, *Ware v. Hylton,* 3 Dall. 199 (1796); *Geofroy v. Riggs,* 133 U. S. 258 (1890); and *Missouri v. Holland,* 252 U. S. 416 (1920). Of special relevance is the potential development of international human rights standards which would be applicable in the United States. See Judge Irving Kaufman's circuit court decision in *Filartiga v. Pena-Irala,* 630 F. 2d 876 (1980). See also issues of *The Human Rights Quarterly.*

[3]For example, see Harry C. Bredemeier, "Law as an Integrative Mechanism," William M. Evan, ed., *Law and Sociology* (New York: Free Press, 1962).

affirmed, there must be a rule of law in one's favor. Many disputes occur for which there are no legal remedies. For example, a professor who believes that he or she has been unfairly denied tenure will not necessarily have legal recourse (Kaplin, 1978). Only under specific circumstances—such as cases of discrimination or violations of academic freedom—might a court intervene in the dispute.

Criminal cases are not merely the province of the party that has been wronged but also are the concern of government (Fitzgerald, 1962, Ch. 1).[4] In civil cases it is the victim who decides whether to use the law to deal with the wrongdoer. In the criminal courts a cooperative victim is important; however, it is the police and prosecutors who decide whether to press the matter. A second distinction between civil and criminal cases is the way in which those found guilty are dealt with. Individuals convicted of a criminal offense are branded "criminals" and subject to punishment administered by government. This may even include the loss of liberty through imprisonment. Those who have committed a civil wrong may be obliged to compensate the victim, but they are not punished per se or held in disrepute.

We generally expect people to obey the law even if they disagree with it. In fact, obedience to most laws most of the time is the norm in the United States (Friedman, 1975, Chaps. 3, 4, 5; Anderson, 1979, pp. 113–122). Noncompliance does occur, but it is the exception rather than the rule. For example, we stop our cars at a red light even if it is 3:00 A.M. and no other cars are in sight. This is habitual behavior that is ultimately grounded not only in a fear of sanctions but also in an acceptance of the legitimacy of government to issue binding rules. Of course, some evasion of the law does occur. For self-serving reasons people sometimes disobey the law quite intentionally. Prime examples include evasion of tax laws, drug laws, and prostitution ordinances. We also find the phenomenon of civil disobedience (Schur, 1968, pp. 60–62; King, 1967; Rawls, 1975). A leading tactic of the civil rights movement, for example, was to violate discriminatory laws intentionally in order to publicly dramatize a social injustice. Still, while dissent from the law has a place in our society, government necessarily has a stake in protecting law-abiding citizens and in safeguarding the legitimacy of laws that are constitutionally valid. Despite our nation's concern for personal liberty, one does not have the right to disobey a valid law simply because it is unappealing.

While we may disagree about the proper substance of the law, it is possible that there are some characteristics we would want all laws to have. Lon Fuller has attempted to spell out some criteria of "internal morality" (1969, Ch. 2). This notion refers to the procedural characteristics embodied in the law in order to preserve its integrity. Fuller spells out eight requirements for internal morality. First, he suggests that there must be general rules. If dis-

---

[4]Note that government sometimes acts as a plaintiff or defendant in civil cases. Then too, the police sometimes initiate certain civil actions such as civil commitment.

putes are settled on an ad hoc basis, government will have failed to guide the conduct of individuals. Fuller is especially critical of administrative agencies for their failure to create a system of general rules. Second, Fuller argues that rules must be made known. While it would not be possible to educate every citizen as to the meaning of every law, there ought to be some way for the citizen to know the nature of existing rules. Third, laws must not be retroactive. While it is impossible for government to foresee all the misconduct it would want to prohibit, a citizen needs to know the rules in advance so that he or she can act on them. In fact, a provision of the Constitution provides that no ex post facto law shall be passed in the criminal sphere. Fourth, laws must be reasonably clear. Certainly, it would be very difficult to obey an incomprehensible law. It is important that laws be stated in such a way that they can be understood.

Fuller's fifth requirement for internal morality is that laws must not be contradictory. An act cannot be both commanded and forbidden at the same time. Surely, it would be unfair for government to require that a person do something and then punish that person for doing it. Sixth, laws should not require either the impossible or the extremely difficult. For example, the legal system does not attempt to compel people to have particular religious or political beliefs, since these beliefs are held involuntarily. Seventh, Fuller argues that as far as possible, laws should be constant over time. A law that changes every day may be worse than no law at all. While there is some room for changing objectionable laws, people depend on a general constancy in the law in order to make plans for the future. Finally, Fuller suggests that legal rules and the way in which the law is administered should not be in conflict. Discrepancies may arise from a variety of factors, including misinterpretation, inaccessibility of the law, bribery, prejudice, indifference, stupidity, and the drive for personal power. Still, a basic ideal of the judiciary is to ensure, on a case-by-case basis, that laws are carried out as intended.

The Legal System

Laws are neither self-generating nor self-executing. Consequently, the United States necessarily has a legal system responsible for creating, interpreting, and implementing laws. The basic contours of our legal system are contained in the Constitution. This document was drafted in 1787 by fifty-five delegates to a constitutional convention held in Philadelphia. While we often consider our system of government to be democratic ("rule by the people"), the Constitution clearly did not create a "direct democracy" in which policy decisions were to be made by majority votes of the populace. A basic fear of the framers was that popular majorities would not be respectful of the interests of minorities—a key minority being the few who were wealthy. Indeed, even as many states now permit voters to approve state legislation through referendums and initiatives, there are no similar mechanisms for direct democracy at the national level.

Distrustful of the tyranny of majority rule, the Constitution created the beginnings (*but only* the beginnings) of a representative democracy in which officials elected by the people would be responsible for policymaking. It was believed that elected representatives, while generally responsive to the public, would resist irresponsible policies. Nevertheless, constitutional roadblocks were still placed in the way of a fully representative democracy. Initially, only the members of the House of Representatives were selected through popular elections. Direct election of senators was not instituted until 1913, with the ratification of the Seventeenth Amendment. Even today it is the electoral college that chooses the president, although presidential electors almost never exercise the discretion intended by the framers. Finally, it is also true that federal judges and the key personnel of the federal bureacracy are not elected but instead are appointed by the president.

Despite these roadblocks to unrestrained majority rule, it is possible for a popular majority to gain control of the leading institutions of government. Even here, however, the Constitution restrains public officials. In some sense ours is a "constitutional democracy." The Constitution seeks to guarantee certain rights from intrusion by legislators or executives (Friedman, 1971; Scheingold, 1974). Some rights are procedural (for example, trial by jury), while others are substantive (for example, freedom of speech). The provisions of the Constitution, as interpreted by judges, stand above other forms of law. Any law or action that is inconsistent with the Constitution can be declared null and void. Given the broad scope of the Constitution and the requirement that three-quarters of the states are needed to ratify amendments, the Constitution can sometimes act as a very real constraint on majority rule.

If the framers had little faith in popular majorities, they clearly were distrustful of government as well. A significant feature of the American legal system is the presence of "separated institutions *sharing* powers." (Neustadt, 1960, p. 33) Institutions are separated to prevent the abuse of power by any individual or institution. The framers of the Constitution greatly feared the corrupting influence of power. Consequently, they were drawn to the idea of dividing authority among several institutions and setting each of these institutions against the others. Horizontally, power is shared by the executive branch, the legislature, and the judiciary. In practice no branch of government is clearly and consistently superior to the others. Vertically, there is a sharing of power among the national government, fifty state governments, and thousands of local governments. The framers invented the notion of federalism, where authority over people is exercised simultaneously by both the national government and state governments. In addition, private institutions such as interest groups, political parties, and the news media are allowed to thrive in our nation and exert substantial influence on government and its policies.

The concept of "checks and balances" is also closely connected to our system of government. Each branch at the national level not only has certain independent powers but also exercises a series of "checks" on the other branches of government. The notion here is that some mixing of power is essential to keep the parts of government in proper balance and to prevent tyranny by any one branch. For example, Congress has the sole power to pass laws, but the president has the authority to veto legislation. However, if Congress can muster a vote of two thirds in both the Senate and House of Representatives, it can override the president's veto. Checks and balances between the president and Congress also govern the enactment of treaties and the appointment of leading executive officers.

The judiciary is also implicated in the system of checks and balances. Courts are the authoritative interpreters of the law. However, Congress has some (as yet undefined) constitutional authority to limit the scope of the Supreme Court's appellate jurisdiction.[5] In addition, the courts depend on the executive branch to enforce judicial decisions. Moreover, federal judges—including Supreme Court justices—are appointed by the president and confirmed by the Senate. The justices of the Supreme Court are not even authorized to choose their own Chief Justice. When a vacancy occurs, the power of appointment resides with the president, subject to confirmation by the Senate.

Of course, the judiciary is not powerless in its dealings with the other institutions of government. Indeed, the presence of separated institutions sharing power provides the foundation for a critical function of the Supreme Court. The High Court is responsible for resolving conflicts of authority between the president and Congress as well as between the national government and the states. The powers and prerogatives of each institution of government are authoritatively adjudicated by the courts. The Supreme Court's momentous decision in *United States v. Nixon* is an excellent case in point. During the course of President Nixon's reelection campaign in 1972, a burglary was detected at the offices of the Democratic Party in Washington, D. C. Suspicions arose over possible White House involvement in that burglary. Claiming "executive privilege," Nixon refused to hand over documents to Congress, which was conducting investigations into the matter. When it became known that the president's White House conversations had been taped, the special prosecutor filed suit against Nixon to force him to release the tapes. The Supreme Court responded in this case by issuing an order to President Nixon requiring him to release the tapes. In its written opinion the Court ruled that executive privilege is not an absolute, unqualified presidential privilege. It did not extend to documents relevant to criminal prosecutions where a need was demonstrated for evidence in a pending criminal trial. The consequences for the Nixon

---

[5]Compare the decision of the Supreme Court in *Ex parte McCardle,* 7 Wall. 506 (1869) and *United States v. Klein,* 13 Wall. 128 (1872).

presidency were profound. Nixon released the tapes and resigned as president shortly thereafter.

Within the judiciary the concept of separation of powers has translated itself into the creation and perpetuation of a dual court structure (Ebenstein et al., 1980, pp. 366–371; Jacob, 1978, pp. 149–167; Wasby, 1978a, pp. 59–74). Our country not only has a federal court system but also possesses a separate court apparatus in each of the fifty states and the District of Columbia. This dual court structure reflects a compromise between the forces favoring states' rights and those advocating a strong national government. At the time the nation was founded, it was not clear whether a full complement of federal courts would be created. The Constitution established a Supreme Court but left to Congress the decision as to whether to set up lower federal courts as well. In the first Congress Federalists were successful in passing the Judiciary Act of 1789. This created a federal district court in each state. At the intermediate level there were no sitting judges. However, appeals could be heard by two Supreme Court justices and one judge from a United States district court, who served as circuit judges. Such "circuit-riding" responsibilities were finally eliminated in 1891, when a distinct group of circuit courts was established.

In both the federal and state court systems there are both trial and appellate courts. Trial courts are important because there are so many of them making decisions in so many legal disputes (Hays, 1978; Pound, 1937; Dolbeare, 1967a). State trial courts have traditionally been highly fragmented into a number of specialized units. However, this fragmented structure is increasingly being replaced by a more unified structure, in accordance with the reforms suggested by Roscoe Pound and the American Bar Association. In general, the decision of a trial court is the final word in a legal dispute. Not only may each decision have an important impact on the litigants to the case, but some may also have significant effects on community affairs.

If a trial court decision displeases one of the parties to the case, that party may file an appeal with a higher court (McLauchlan, 1977, Ch. 6; Howard, 1981; Meador, 1974; Wasby, 1978a, Ch. 3; Rubin, 1976; Shapiro, 1980; ABA, 1977 and 1974). A basic principle of American jurisprudence is that a party is entitled to one appeal. A court system may contain more than one level of appellate courts. Where there is an intermediate and highest court, as in the federal court system, the highest court generally can refuse to grant an additional appeal beyond that of the intermediate appellate court. In reaching decisions, appeals courts rely on the trial transcript as well as on written legal briefs and oral arguments from attorneys for both parties. A basic aim of appellate courts is to protect a losing party at the trial court level from an arbitrary, capricious, or mistaken decision by a trial court judge. Where intermediate appellate courts exist, their principal responsibility is to correct trial court "errors." Although few decisions are appealed and even fewer reversed, appellate courts also serve an important lawmaking function. Many of the key legal ground rules in our nation result from decisions of the Supreme Court and the highest courts in the fifty states and the District of Columbia.

The existing judicial structures in the United States are shown in Figure 1-1 (Ebenstein, 1980, pp. 366–371; Jacob, 1978, pp. 149–167; Wasby, 1978a pp. 59–74). As noted in the figure, the federal judiciary consists of a three-level hierarchy including United States district courts, circuit courts of appeals, and the Supreme Court. In addition, several functionally based, quasi-judicial structures (for example, Interstate Commerce Commission) are also present. District courts serve as the trial courts of the federal court system. There is at least one in every state, yielding a total of 94 district courts and 515 district court judges. The caseload of these courts includes over 100,000 civil cases annually, dealing with contracts, torts, antitrust actions, bankruptcy, commerce, labor, patents and copyrights, prisoner petitions, and disputes between citizens of different states ("diversity" suits). All federal criminal cases—about 40,000 per year—are heard in the federal courts. These involve narcotics, forgery, counterfeiting, larceny, fraud, and Selective Service cases, among others. Even so, not every type of case can enter the federal court system. Explicit limitations in the jurisdiction of the federal courts, concerning both subject matter and parties, are spelled out in Article III of the Constitution. Additional limits in jurisdiction have been established by Congress and the Supreme Court.

FIGURE 1-1

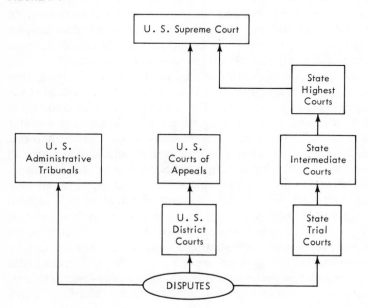

Most court cases are settled with finality at the trial level. However, a party that loses a decision in the federal district courts may enter an appeal to the circuit courts of appeals. These courts are also assigned the task of hearing appeals from administrative tribunals. Courts of appeals, like district courts, are organized along regional lines. There are a total of thirteen federal appeals courts and 132 appeals court judges. The Supreme Court is at the highest level of the federal judicial hierarchy. It serves primarily as an appellate court of last resort. Parenthetically, the Supreme Court also has original jurisdiction over a limited number of cases. While the Supreme Court receives over 4,000 appeals from losing parties in a given year, it does not render a decision in every case. Only a limited number of cases—fewer than 10 percent—are granted review. Where review is denied, the decision of the lower court is left standing as is, but with no national precedent established.

Existing alongside the federal courts are fifty independent state court systems. As with the federal court system, state judiciaries have trial courts and courts of last resort. In about one-half of the states there are also intermediate appellate courts. Most of the legal ground rules in the United States are enacted by state legislatures and can be adjudicated only in state courts. The highest court of each state fully controls the interpretation of state law. This permits considerable variation from state to state in what is legal and illegal. Normally, the United States Supreme Court will not modify the rulings of state courts. However, the decisions of state supreme courts which involve a substantial federal question may be appealed by the losing party to the High Court.

Even though state laws are normally the exclusive province of state judiciaries, many federal laws can be adjudicated in state courts. Because of the "concurrent jurisdiction" of state courts, there are only a few types of federal disputes—such as federal crimes and admiralty, patent, and bankruptcy cases—that can be brought solely to the federal courts. In other cases the choice of forum—state courts or federal courts—is made by the party bringing the legal claim. However, when a state court does consider a case involving federal ground rules, the judge is supposed to be bound by the supremacy clause contained in Article VI, section 2, of the Constitution. This provision declares that the Constitution, laws, and treaties of the United States are "the supreme law of the land." It requires obedience to federal ground rules by judges in every state, regardless of contrary state directives. Of course, state judges often have some discretion in determining whether federal or state law is applicable in the case at hand.

The existence of a legal system in which separated instutitions share power has some important consequences. Most notably, the laws of our nation do not reflect the values of any single individual or isolated elite. Instead, laws result from an extraordinarily complex process in which the attitudes of many individuals and institutions—both in and out of government—are taken into account. While the president is a powerful individual, that officeholder is no dictator. The president must share power with Congress, the courts, the bureaucracy, and state and local governments. Further, private institutions such as interest groups, political parties, and the mass media are forces to be reckoned with in the lawmaking process. Indeed, some people believe that the existing system is so complex that it is flabby and ineffective (Lowi, 1979). According to these observers, the legal system is paralyzed by the presence of multiple centers of power and is thus incapable of taking decisive action to deal with serious problems. Certainly, our legal system does contain some built-in biases against large changes in the law. The structure of our legal system helps to prevent the concentration of power in any one group's hands; however, this may be at the cost of failing to make changes in the law which some feel are needed.

DISPUTE PROCESSING

Nature of Disputes

A major role of law in society is to process disputes. Disputes, both large and small, are very much a part of daily life. Much human energy is devoted to avoiding disputes, engaging in disputes, feeling troubled by disputes, and trying to deal with disputes. Disputes are also important because they represent the raw stuff dealt with by our legal system. Courts do not on their own accord decide to confront a social issue. The judiciary waits for some aggrieved party to raise the issue in a genuine controversy.

A highly significant dispute in American legal history is that of *Gideon v. Wainwright*. Clarence Gideon had been charged in Florida State Court with a felony: breaking and entering into a poolroom. Lacking the funds for an attorney, he asked the the court to appoint counsel in his behalf. The judge refused, noting that state law permitted appointment of counsel for indigents only in capital cases. Gideon conducted his own defense and did so reasonably well. However, the jury returned a verdict of guilty. Gideon was sentenced to serve five years in state prison. Subsequently, Gideon filed a habeas corpus petition with the Florida Supreme Court.[6] The petition attacked his conviction and sentence. Gideon contended that he had been unjustly denied his constitutional right to an attorney. When denied relief by the Florida Supreme Court, Gideon entered an appeal to the United States Supreme Court. Overruling its earlier holding in *Betts v. Brady,* the Supreme Court ruled in favor of Gideon. Thus, the constitutional right to an attorney in state criminal trials was established. As to Clarence Gideon's own dispute with the state of Florida, Gideon

---

[6]A habeas corpus petition is an application made by a prisoner asking a judge for an order compelling that he or she be taken to court so that it can be determined if the imprisonment is unlawful.

was granted a new trial, this time defended by a competent attorney. The jury found Clarence Gideon not guilty of the charges against him (Lewis, 1964).

Disputes may vary greatly as regards both participants and objects of contention. There are two sides to every dispute (Howard and Summers, 1965, Ch 1). A dispute may involve two friends, two enemies, or two strangers. The participants might include two private citizens, a private citizen and a government, or two governments. Many disputes involve one or more private organizations such as insurance companies or collection agencies. The nature of the parties involved in a dispute may have an important effect on the course the dispute takes. For example, the closeness of a person's relationship with those with whom he or she is having a dispute affects the way that the dispute is handled. Disputes between those involved in a continuing relationship are generally processed in a less formal manner than disputes between strangers or acquaintances.

The disputes taking place in our society reveal a great deal of variety. They range from the banal to the bizarre. One *Chicago Tribune* reader, J. S., reported a rather unusual neighborhood dispute to the paper's "Action Line":[7]

> Q. I am 74 years old and reside on the city's northwest side. Recently I painted three sides of my building and took down the storm windows. When I started to paint the fourth side, my neighbor came over and ordered me off his property. My problem is I can't finish the job without putting my ladder on his property. The City Hall information office referred me to the clerk's office in the Civic Center and they sent me to the Chicago Bar Association, which charged me $10 and told me it would take a lot of money to fight it out in court. Can you help?
> —J. S., Northwest Side
>
> A. Your neighbor told this column that the dispute could have been resolved had you talked to him first. Instead, he contends, "he wanted to stick it to me" by filing numerous complaints with the building department, the Albany Park police station, and "he even took me to court." Your "sneaky" actions have cost him over $1,200, he said, adding, "I definitely do not want him on my property. He is painting these swastikas all over the place and putting up red and black crosses in his yard," he added. Perhaps seeing this in print might convince both parties that continued escalation won't end this feud. But then, our mediation didn't help either.
>
> —"Action Line," *Chicago Tribune*

If we can accept these facts as stated, it seems clear that both parties feel aggrieved. J. S. feels he has a right to paint the fourth side of his building, even if this means entering his neighbor's property. J. S.'s neighbor, meanwhile, is angered at the swastikas J. S. is painting "all over the place" and the apparent harassment that has been inflicted on him.

---

[7]"Action Line," *Chicago Tribune,* June 26, 1975. Copyrighted, 1975, Chicago Tribune. Used with permission.

It is always uncertain as to what course of action an aggrieved party will take in a dispute. Some disputes seem severe and require significant action of some kind. Other disputes appear more frivolous and readily resolved. Even so, it is important to realize that the perceptions of the disputants themselves are critical. In the neighborhood dispute noted above, those involved have already attempted to deal with the dispute through a variety of means. Yet, the matter has remained very much alive. There is no telling what will happen in this, or any other, dispute. It would be possible for the dispute to reach a quick conclusion if J. S. or his neighbor decided to back off or move away. Here the dispute would be terminated without any formalized settlement taking place. On the other hand, a dispute may also take strange, unpredictable, or even tragic twists. Perhaps the dispute in question will further escalate, leading to violence and the invocation of the criminal label on one of the parties.

Dealing with Disputes

Disputes can be processed in a variety of ways. Certainly, only a small portion of disputes ever enter the legal system. As a general rule, people engaging in a dispute never seriously consider submitting the matter to the courts for resolution. As Chief Justice Warren Burger has argued: "The notion that ordinary people want black-robed judges, well-dressed lawyers and fine-paneled courtrooms as the setting to resolve their disputes isn't correct. People with problems, like people with pains, want relief and they want it as quickly and inexpensively as possible."[8] Among the alternative ways of dealing with disputes, as discussed below, are (1) "lumping it," (2) avoidance, (3) persuasion, (4) coercion, (5) negotiation, (6) mediation, (7) arbitration, and (8) adjudication.[9] No method of dispute processing will invariably satisfy both parties or, for that matter, *either* of the parties to a dispute.

An important distinction in dispute processing can be made by looking at who becomes involved. The first five methods of dispute processing cited above involve only the two parties to a dispute. In the latter three methods (mediation, arbitration, adjudication) a third party becomes involved in dealing with the dispute. In any given dispute it is far from clear that a third party will become implicated. In fact, in our society there is a pyramidal structure to disputes. At the wide end of the pyramid there is a mass of perceived grievances. Only a small proportion of these are resolved by the complainants and their adversaries. An even smaller portion of unresolved disputes are appealed to a third party. Still fewer enter the judiciary. Disputants do not press their

[8]Address by Chief Justice Warren Burger at the ABA Conference on the Resolution of Minor Disputes (May 27, 1977), as quoted in *Wall Street Journal* (October 27, 1978), p. 48.

[9]Seven of these —all but persuasion—are discussed in Laura Nader and Harry F. Todd, Jr., eds., *The Disputing Process—Law in Ten Societies* (New York: Columbia University Press, 1978), pp. 8–11.

claims in the courts for a multitude of reasons. These include high court costs, a desire to compromise, a fear of endangering a disturbed social relationship, and the fact that some disputes simply do not have a legal remedy.

The eight methods of dispute processing have some distinctive characteristics. In no dispute will each method seem equally appropriate. "Lumping it" involves suffering the injustice. You understand that you have been wronged in some way. Even so, you decide not to press a claim or complaint. The decision to drop it may be the result of any number of factors—a lack of information about or access to a dispute-processing institution; a feeling that you would not win the dispute anyway; a belief that the gains would be too small; or a feeling that the costs would be too high. In lumping it, you ignore the issue in dispute and continue your relationship with the party who has wronged you. Obviously, the costs of lumping it may be very high in some disputes. In the neighborhood dispute reported earlier, neither party was content to simply take his lumps and let the other party have his way.

Avoidance consists of withdrawing from the situation or reducing or ending a relationship. You may or may not confront the other party with a complaint. What is crucial here is that you do react to the dispute. You do so by reducing or terminating social interaction with the offending party. For example, if cheated in a business transaction, you may decide simply to do your shopping elsewhere. Or, if you engage in a dispute with your landlord, you may opt to move to a new apartment. It has been suggested by William Felstiner (1974, pp. 76–85) that ours is such a mobile society that the costs of avoidance have diminished. According to this view, avoidance between generations within a family will usually not seriously threaten the disputants' economic security or general welfare. In other words, you can walk away from a vast number of disputes without suffering serious losses. This contrasts sharply with the situation in undeveloped, less mobile societies, where far more serious costs are associated with avoidance behavior. Even so, mobility is far from complete in our society. There are some people who find it very difficult to walk away from a dispute. In addition, the consequences of some disputes are so severe (for example, bad credit rating, arrest record) that it would be very difficult to escape from them. In the neighborhood squabble neither party seems willing to physically move away or psychologically withdraw in order to terminate the dispute.

Persuasion is an effort by one party to bring the dispute to an end by convincing the other of the merits of one's position. It involves no yielding of position by the persuader and a complete yielding of position by the person persuaded. Given the structure of our political system, Richard Neustadt (1960) has argued that the primary weapon of the president is the power to persuade. Where a disagreement occurs on a matter of policy, the president must convince other political leaders, such as those in Congressional subcommittees, that the most appropriate course of action has been proposed. As suggested in the works of various authors (Roloff and Miller, 1980; Rosnow and Robinson, 1967), persuasion is also important in everyday disputes. In *How to Win Friends and Influence People,* Dale Carnegie lists several rules for winning people to your way of thinking (1936, p. 171). For example, Carnegie advises that one avoid open argument, show respect for the other person's opinions, and never say that the other person is wrong. Carnegie also stresses the importance of a friendly demeanor, seeing things from the other person's point of view, and appealing to nobler motives. Carnegie suggests that friendly persuasion is the most successful method of resolving disputes favorably. However, it is probable that Carnegie underestimated the very real differences in opinion and interest among people in the course of everyday life. It is quite probable, for example, that neither J. S. nor his neighbor could use the power of persuasion to convince the other of the merits of his claim.

Coercion involves a unilateral resolution of the dispute. Both parties are aware that some dispute exists. The dispute is resolved when one of the parties imposes a solution on the other. In *Winning Through Intimidation* Robert Ringer argues: "The results a person obtains are inversely proportional to the degree to which he is intimidated." (1974, p. 123) In other words, while the meek may one day inherit the earth, they do not fare very well in everyday disputes. Ringer advises that we win disputes by intimidating our adversary. In the neighborhood dispute J. S.'s neighbor attempted to settle the dispute through coercion—that is, by ordering J. S. off his property and refusing to let him paint. Undoubtedly, he hoped that this would be the end of the matter. Unfortunately, in some cases the use of force—or even psychological arm twisting—may actually aggravate a conflict, making peaceful settlement of the dispute more difficult to achieve. Certainly, the attempted coercion did not resolve the dispute between J. S. and his neighbor.

Negotiation is an effort by two parties to find a mutually satisfactory resolution to a dispute (Druckman, 1977; Gulliver, 1973). It involves the use of debate and bargaining. The parties seek to work out the dispute by themselves, without turning to a third party for assistance. A prerequisite for successful negotiations may well be a desire by both parties to reach a settlement that will be mutually advantageous. In part negotiation involves a rhetorical contest aimed at moving an adversary closer to one's position. Each side attempts to steer the talks in a direction that will produce a favorable outcome for one's own side. Negotiation also involves a bargaining in which each side incrementally moves closer to the other in position. In the process of negotiation coercive tactics may also be used, such as warnings, ultimatums, and shows of force. In the neighborhood squabble J. S.'s neighbor resented his turning to third parties and told "Action Line" that the dispute could have been resolved had J. S. only talked to him first.

Mediation involves a third party who attempts to help the disputants reach a settlement. Both principals to the dispute must agree to the intervention of the mediator. The mediator may be an institutionalized neutral party or a person of acknowledged prestige. Significantly, the mediator is merely a facilitator, with absolutely no authority to impose a settlement on the disputants. A mediator may try to focus the discussion on the common interests of the parties to make their dispute seem less important. The mediator may also try to invent some solution and persuade the disputing parties that it is appropriate. Mediational services are often available for hire (Danzig and Lowy, 1975, p. 682). Lawyers help settle claims, counselors guide people through family tensions, and therapists work through the effects of disputes. Mediators are used particularly in organizational settings such as labor unions, businesses, and universities. Too often mediators are not available to deal with "everyday disputes" which have no organizational ties (Danzig and Lowy, 1975, p. 683). These include disputes between parent and child, husband and wife, landlord and tenant, consumer and businessperson, and one neighbor with another. Danzig and Lowy call for the creation of "community moots" in each neighborhood to hear disputes and try to resolve them. Presumably, this would significantly alter the number and types of disputes which would reach the courts. It might also decrease the extent of "lumping it" and avoidance as well as increase the number of disputants who are satisfied with the outcome of their dispute. Such a "community moot" might well have been helpful in the dispute between J. S. and his neighbor, although the mediation of "Action Line" did not meet with success.

Arbitration is another procedure making use of a third party to aid in resolving a dispute (MacKenzie, 1978; Coulson, 1978). In arbitration the two disputants agree to the intervention of a third party, who is believed to be neutral. They also agree beforehand that the judgment of the arbitrator must be accepted as binding on both parties. In recent decades arbitration has been increasingly used in areas such as labor relations and commercial contracts. In addition, arbitration is also taking hold in other areas of dispute. The nation's leading arbitrator is the American Arbitration Association (AAA), which has offices in most major cities in the United States. The AAA has long had a code of ethics specifying when an arbitrator should decline an appointment, the appropriate role of an arbitrator, the proper method of making decisions, and the kind of award that should be granted.[10] Arbitration has been praised as speedy and economical. In complex, highly technical cases the arbitrator selected is likely to have more expertise on the subject than a typical judge. Even so, it has been argued that there are real constraints on the continued spread of arbitration to new areas (Getman, 1979). In many kinds of disputes the two parties may find it impossible to agree voluntarily to allow a third party to dictate a binding solution. We must doubt whether J. S. and his neighbor could both agree to give some third party the power to hear the case and make an authoritative decision as to the outcome.

Adjudication is a dispute-processing technique in which there is a third

---

[10]For an early treatment of arbitration, see Frances Kellor, *American Arbitration* (New York: Harper and Brothers, 1948).

party who has the authority to intervene in a dispute without the permission of the complainant's adversary. Depending on state law, a disputant might opt to take a claim to a small claims court or regular trial court (Sarat, 1976; Yngvesson and Hennessey, 1975). J. S. did go so far as to investigate the possibilities of a court resolution of the dispute. In a case brought before a court, the judge can render a decision and then take steps to enforce compliance. Decisions are based on some principle or set of principles as applied to the facts of the case. The goal is not to reconcile the parties but to reach a decision as to which party is "right." The judge looks *back* at the events that have taken place and the rules of law that exist rather than looking *forward* at the consequences of the alternative decisions that can be made. Judicial decisions tend to emphasize the conflict between parties rather than facilitate compromise. Decisions are rendered only after an adversary proceeding in which each party has offered reasons why it is right and the other party wrong (Frank, 1949; Frankel, 1980). However, compromise may be inappropriate to some disputes, such as where one party wants to establish or confirm certain legal rights. Also, it is possible that courts are more likely to deal fairly with disputes between people of unequal income or power (Nader, 1979). Whatever their inadequacies, courts surely are useful as a last resort for dealing with the injustices embodied in disputes. They are an important mechanism for the peaceful resolution of disputes in our society.

Evaluating Disputing Methods

Ideally, we would want our dispute-processing methods to achieve certain goals. Julius Getman (1979, p. 916) has identified eight objective standards by which we can evaluate how well a dispute-processing mechanism is working. We can use these standards to evaluate the effectiveness of adjudication in processing disputes. *Finality* implies that once decided, the dispute is not likely to be reconsidered. We would want the dispute between J. S. and his neighbor to reach some sort of termination. Adjudication, for example, involves an authoritative decision with regard to a dispute. While the parties may not be satisfied with the outcome, the vast majority of court cases do not go beyond the trial level. *Obedience* suggests that the decisions which are made are likely to be carried out. We would want J. S. and his neighbor to obey the settlement. In the courts there is some degree of noncompliance both in routine cases (for instance, alimony and child support) and when courts engage in policymaking (for example, the school busing experience). *Guidance* means that the decisions made provide the needed direction to the parties in the dispute. We would want J. S. and his neighbor to understand the nature of the settlement that has been made. In a minority of cases court decisions may be rather ambiguous. A series of cases is sometimes required to fully clarify the direction of court policy on some issue, such as school busing. *Efficiency* indicates that the procedures used are adequate, economical, flexible, and suited to the particular case. For example, we would not want J. S. or his neighbor to suffer undue delay or expense while the dispute is being processed. Adjudication can be a slow, expensive, technical process.

A fifth standard for evaluating dispute-processing methods is *availabil-ity*. This implies that the disputants find the machinery routinely accessible without undue expense and with an equal opportunity to be heard. We would want J. S. and his neighbor to have a mechanism that is both economically and psychologically available to them. Using the judiciary is sometimes very costly. In addition, legal services for the poor are generally less effective than those available to the affluent. *Neutrality* suggests that decision makers avoid favoritism and bias toward one side or another. An appeal to "Action Line" would not have seemed very attractive to seventy-four-year-old J. S. if it almost always sided against the interests of elderly complainants. Since judges are human, they may sometimes have a more favorable attitude toward one party than toward the other. Even so, courts may be more neutral than other third-party mechanisms. *Conflict resolution* means that the entire process leads to more amicable relations and mutual respect between the disputants. Ideally, we would want J. S. and his neighbor to return to a less stressful relationship. The aim of the courts, however, is to achieve "justice" in a case rather than to bring about reconciliation. Finally, *fairness* indicates that disputes will be resolved in a way that appropriately recognizes the interests of those coming before the system. We would want due consideration to be given to the positions of both J. S. and his neighbor. The legal system has instituted an intricate system of due process that seeks to ensure fairness. There is some concern, however, that disadvantaged groups do not fare as well as the affluent in civil or criminal cases.

There appear to be inherent advantages and disadvantages associated with each method of dispute processing. Unfortunately, research on this question is only beginning. It is not clear in the dispute between J. S. and his neighbor that the "best resolution" (whatever that means) would come as a result of a court decision. Indeed, some critics have charged that the judiciary is unnecessarily technical, that it is disruptive of private relations, and that it unfairly favors the wealthy and powerful. What is needed in any society is a variety of dispute-processing institutions which are suitable for dealing with the whole gamut of disputes which arise. Congress in 1980 gave support to this notion by adopting the Dispute Resolution Act.[11] The aim of the act was "to assist the States and other interested parties in providing to all persons convenient access to dispute resolution mechanisms which are effective, fair, inexpensive, and expeditious." To this end federal grants were made available

[11]Dispute Resolution Act, Public Law 96–190 (S. 423); Feb. 12, 1980. United States Code, 96th Congress—Second Session, 1980, Vol. 1 (St. Paul, Minn.: West Publishing Co., 1981). On the emergence of new community dispute centers see Larry Ray, ed., *Dispute Resolution Program: 1981 Directory* (Washington, D. C.: American Bar Association, 1981). The directory reports that dispute centers have been established in 135 communities in 32 states.

for the purpose of establishing new dispute-processing centers and improving existing ones. Nevertheless, we can expect that the courts will still have a considerable amount of litigation to adjudicate.

LAW AND SOCIAL VALUES

Besides processing disputes, the other major role of law is to authoritatively allocate values in society.[12] By *values* we mean principles which are said to have some degree of merit.[13] The worth of a social value is the subject of much debate among public officials, scholars, and members of the general public. For example, liberals and conservatives are divided over the principle of equality. In making laws and taking action, the legal system necessarily promotes some values and impinges upon others. In the struggle between competing claims, government necessarily will be relevant to social values. Although countless values interplay with public policy, here we will focus on six: procedural justice, liberty, equality, social order, effectiveness, and democracy. Each is a worthy social goal. However, because these values often conflict with one another, it is not possible for government to fully realize each of these goals simultaneously. The result is a kind of "value relativism" in which conflicting values are balanced against one another by government. Of course, there is much disagreement both in and out of government as to which values ought to be given greater stress. No national consensus exists as to the proper hierarchy of values. It should be noted, however, that there are instances in which a value can be more completely fulfilled without substantially sacrificing other values. Thus, gains in equality do not always mean a commensurate loss of liberty.

Procedural Justice

When considering procedural justice, the central notion appears to be one of equal consideration (Benn, 1967, Vol. 4, p. 299): People should be treated alike unless there is some relevant difference which shows that disparate treatment is indicated. Constitutional protection of the right to an attorney is instructive in this regard. The Sixth Amendment, in part, reads: "In all criminal prosecutions, the accused shall enjoy the right . . . to have the assistance of counsel for his defense." This language could be taken to guarantee simply a right to *hire* an attorney in all criminal cases. However, in this instance the defendant who is indigent would be placed at a great disadvan-

[12]David Easton has defined politics in these terms. It is through politics, of course, that laws are enacted and implemented. See David Easton, "An Approach to the Analysis of Political Systems," *World Politics,* 1957, *9,* 383–400.

[13]See, for example, William K. Frankena, "Value and Valuation," Paul Edwards, ed., *The Encyclopedia of Philosophy* (New York: Macmillan, 1967), Vol. 8, pp. 229–32.

tage. Ultimately, the concern for equal consideration has led to a guarantee that an attorney be provided in criminal cases for those defendants unable to hire an attorney for themselves. Procedural justice is rightly a special concern in adjudication. In the adjudication process judges (and juries) take on the task of authoritatively determining the outcome of disputes. A defendant in the courtroom is in the unhappy position of being forced to participate in proceedings which he or she did not request. This suggests the necessity for developing protective standards of procedural justice for use in the courtroom.

Nine basic standards of procedural justice have been identified by Martin P. Golding (1975, pp. 122–123). Three of these relate to the issue of neutrality. Golding suggests that no person should be judged in his or her own cause, that the dispute settler should have no private interest in the outcome, and that the dispute settler should not be biased in favor of or against a party. Four other standards of procedural justice attempt to ensure persuasive conflict. Here Golding argues that each party should be given fair notice of the proceedings, that the dispute settler should hear the arguments and evidence of both sides, that the dispute settler should hear a party only in the presence of the other party, and that each adversary should be given a fair opportunity to respond to the arguments and evidence of the other party. Finally, Golding also suggests two standards of procedural justice relevant to the settlement of disputes. According to Golding, a judicial decision should take a specific form. To begin with, the terms of the settlement should be supportable by reasons. Additionally, the reasons should refer to the arguments and evidence presented. Such standards attempt to ensure that judicial decisions will not be arbitrary—or even *seem* to be arbitrary.

In the United States each of these standards of procedural justice has been important in directing the character of judicial activity. Even so, there have been some significant deviations from these principles. As to neutrality, corruption is not unknown in the legal system. There have been instances in which judges have accepted bribes and have only gone through the motions of dispensing justice (Borkin, 1962). Given the very nature of adjudication, detection of such wrongdoing by judges can be extremely difficult. Since judges are only human, biases may also creep into judicial decisions in particular cases. These biases may be deeply engrained in the experiences and attitudes of a judge (Goldman and Jahnige, 1976, Ch. 5). With regard to persuasive conflict, the parties to a dispute are not always given fair notice. There has often been a failure to notify defendants in debt proceedings of the action being taken against them (Carlin, Howard, and Messinger, 1967). Often in our courts cases are processed rapidly and routinely with no serious concern shown for the rights of defendants. This is true not only with debt cases on the civil side but also with misdemeanors such as drunkenness in the criminal courts (Feeley, 1979; Stern, 1967). Concerning the settlement of disputes, judicial decisions in lower state courts are rarely justified through written opinions. The jury and often the judge will simply announce the decision without stating supporting reasons. At the appellate level written opinions are far more common, but they are not universal.

Going a step beyond Golding, it is also important that the results of court decisions try to ensure procedural justice. It is a basic task of the courts to see that people have been treated fairly by government officials. The concern for fairness is reflected in Supreme Court decisions regarding police practices. In a series of decisions the Court has set down guidelines regulating the manner in which police officers may behave toward citizens. Judicial standards touch upon areas such as unreasonable searches and seizures, the exclusion of unconstitutionally seized evidence, self-incrimination, and the right to an attorney when under police investigation. (Relevant cases include *Boyd v. United States, Brown v. Texas, Miranda v. Arizona, Escobedo v. Illinois,* and *Mapp v. Ohio.*)

Liberty

Liberty involves freedom of choice unfettered by restraints (Partridge, 1967, pp. 221–225). As far as possible, in a state of liberty there is an absence of both direct coercion (for example, a law compelling or constraining certain conduct) and indirect coercion (for example, manipulation of people's lifelong choices through socialization). Actually, every organized society contains an intricate network of rules which constrain certain kinds of actions (Oppenheim, 1968, vol. 5, p. 557). In this regard it is noteworthy that John Stuart Mill, a leading advocate of widespread liberties, was well aware of the need for certain restraints. Mill argued: "All that makes existence valuable to any one, depends on the enforcement of restraints upon the actions of other people." (1912, p. 10) Mill suggests that what is important is the underlying nature of the existing restraints. According to Mill, restraints should be aimed at preventing the individual from harming someone else (1912, p. 15). Given the need for restraining the conduct of individuals to the extent that others are affected, it has been suggested that the sum total of liberty in a society cannot be increased (Oppenheim, 1968). In a sense societies differ only in the way that liberty has been distributed among the population. Thus, dictators have unlimited freedom over their subjects, while subjects are totally unfree with respect to their dictator. It might be suggested then that a free society is one in which liberties are evenly distributed.

When speaking of liberty, we are normally concerned with particular kinds of liberties. Among libertarians the deepest concern has long been the restraints imposed by government (Hayek, 1960). Mill suggests that the essential liberties include freedom of conscience, liberty of tastes and pursuits, and the freedom to unite with others (except in order to harm others) (1912, p. 18). The United States Constitution, as interpreted by judges, reveals a deep concern for protecting personal liberty. The First Amendment reads: "Congress shall make no law respecting an establishment of religion, or prohibiting the free exercise thereof; or abridging the freedom of speech, or of the press; or the right of the people peaceably to assemble and to petition the government for a redress of grievances.''[14] When a dispute regarding personal liberty arises, complainants may turn to the courts for an affirmation of their rights. Many of the key Supreme Court decisions concerning freedom of religion (*Zorach v. Clauson, Pierce v. Society of Sisters*), speech (*Whitney v. California*), press (*Near v. Minnesota*), and assembly (*Edwards v. South Carolina*) have been highly protective of personal liberty.

At the same time, it must be noted that violations of personal liberty are not unheard of in our nation. Surely, the grossest violation of personal liberty in our history was the enslavement of blacks in the seventeenth, eighteenth, and nineteenth centuries (Elkins, 1976; Stampp, 1967; Smith, 1966). Even after their emancipation from slavery, blacks were relegated to second-class status by "Jim Crow" laws, which legally enforced segregation and other restrictions on blacks. Other violations of liberty occurred with the establishment of war camps in the United States during World War II (Grodzins, 1949). Fearful that Americans of Japanese descent were disloyal and would behave in a subversive manner, the government forcibly excluded 112,000 of these citizens from their homes and detained them in war camps until the military hostilities came to an end. The only "crime" committed by those excluded was to be of Japanese ancestry. Yet, in *Korematsu v. United States* the Supreme Court declared that this exclusion was constitutionally permissible, given the war emergency.

Examples of the abridgment of personal liberty are also visible today. The extreme cases involve the forcible confinement of people. On the civil side involuntary commitment of people to mental institutions may be regarded as a serious abridgment of personal liberty (DuBose, 1976). Those committed are not guilty of any crime and yet have their liberty stripped from them. On the criminal side many of those facing trial are confined in jail, unable to pay bail (Wald, 1972). Their liberty has been abridged even though they have not been found guilty of the charges against them. Finally, many of those convicted of a crime are imprisoned for long periods of time (Sykes, 1958, pp. 65–78). The penalty of imprisonment has been justified on many grounds, such as retribution against offenders and deterrence against other potential offenders. Yet, for some a concern for liberty suggests the desirability of developing alternative forms of punishment (for example, probation) that, while appropriate to the crime committed, are not so disruptive of personal freedom for such a long period of time.

---

[14]Note that the original constitution, drafted in 1787, contained very few protections for personal freedom. Instead, the original constitution focused mainly on the structure of government. The Bill of Rights was adopted later, largely in response to criticisms of antifederalist opponents.

Equality

The presence of inequality in society has long been a fundamental concern. Montesquieu argued: "In the state of nature, indeed, all men are born equal, but they cannot continue in this equality. Society makes them lose it, and they can recover it only by the protection of the laws" (Lakoff, 1964, p. 90) If equality is the "state of nature," United States law has clearly been unable to restore it in full measure. Indeed, deep inequalities are found throughout American life—whether one looks at income, wealth, race, sex, status, geography, power, or other fundamental criteria (Rainwater, 1974). For example, over 40 percent of income in the United States is held by the top fifth of the income distribution. By contrast, the bottom fifth struggles with about 5 percent of national income (Greenberg, 1974, p. 131). This is not to say that our nation has been blind to the goal of equality. For example, since the founding of the nation, the right to vote has been broadened to include the nonpropertied as well as blacks, women, and young adults. Much equality-oriented activity occurs in the legislative arena rather than in the courts. Thus, our government dispenses free public education, welfare, food stamps, and a host of other social services. Still, the courts do not always sit on the sidelines in the matter of social equality. Significantly, the Supreme Court has utilized the equal protection clause of the Fourteenth Amendment to promote equality—particularly racial equality. Nonetheless, the extent of income gaps in the United States has remained relatively constant since World War II.

The application of equality to the judicial arena has been a special concern. As Justice Wiley Rutledge observed: "Equality before the law in a true democracy is a matter of right. It cannot be a matter of charity or of favor or of grace or of discretion."[15] Yet, the inequalities found in American society permeate the legal system as well. As Finley Peter Dunne's Mr. Dooley points out: "A poor man has a chanst in coort. . . . He has th' same chanst there that he has outside. He has a splendid poor man's chanst."[16] Serious inequalities can be found in the legal system whether one looks at legal participants, civil justice, criminal justice, or judicial activism. With regard to legal participants, the police are more likely to stop a poor person as a suspect than an affluent person (Wilson, 1968, pp. 38–41). Legal services to the poor are often inadequate to the task, partly because the most competent lawyers specialize in the property-related concerns of the affluent (Mayhew and Reiss, 1969; Stumpf, 1975). Judges, particularly at higher levels, come disproportionately from the

---

[15]Stated by Rutledge in a speech before the American Bar Association in Indianapolis in 1941 and cited in J. L. Allison and W. N. Seymour, "The Supreme Court and the Doctrine of the Right of Counsel," *Journal of the American Judicature Society,* 1963, *46,* p. 265.

[16]Mr. Dooley is a fictitious social commentator invented by Finley Peter Dunne. Cited in Joseph W. Bishop, "The Warren Court is Not Likely to be Overruled," Leonard W. Levy, ed., *The Supreme Court Under Earl Warren* (New York: Quadrangle, 1972), p. 101.

ranks of the affluent (Schmidhauser, 1961, p. 55). Juries are not a true cross-section of the population, since they contain fewer low-income people and blacks than are present in the country as a whole (Alker, Hosticka, and Mitchell, 1976).

In the area of civil justice poor people almost always appear as defendants trying to escape or minimize difficulties rather than as plaintiffs asserting some right (Galanter, 1974). In debt and housing cases—two common civil disputes—the poor almost always lose (Wanner, 1975). Many inequalities can also be identified in the criminal courts. To begin with, the crimes committed by the poor are punished more severely than the crimes of white-collar people (Wright, 1973, pp. 26–34). This occurs despite the fact that the economic costs to the nation resulting from white-collar crime are far greater than those attributable to street crime. The human costs of white-collar crime are also enormous (Swigert and Farrell, 1980–81). Further, in many communities bail is still used punitively rather than simply to ensure that the defendant appears at trial. The result is that many poor people, unable to afford bail, must spend time in jail while they await disposition of the charges. (Wald, 1972). Finally, over the course of United States history judicial decisions have generally favored the propertied rather than the poor (Schubert, 1974a, Ch. 6). Even today poor people in our nation have few economic rights. This is reflected in the Burger Court's 1977 decision in *Maher v. Roe*. Here the Court ruled that indigent women seeking an abortion did not have a constitutional right to have one provided at government expense.

Social Order

Social order is of fundamental importance in any nation (Buchanan, 1975; Huntington, 1968). People have a basic need for stability, consensus, regularity, and predictability in their lives. While conservatives place special emphasis on social order, it is also a matter of considerable importance to liberals. In the face of widespread racial disorder in the 1960s, President Lyndon Johnson assigned the Kerner Commission the task of assessing the ongoing unrest (Kerner Commission, 1968). In addition to calling for some basic social reforms, the Commission stressed the need for maintaining order. At one point the Commission observed: "Individuals cannot be permitted to endanger the public peace and safety, and public officials have a duty to make it clear that all just and necessary means to protect both will be used" (1968, p. 171).

When discussing social order, it is necessary to evaluate the character of the social order that is being maintained. Critics of the existing order point to unequal distribution of wealth, income, power, and status. Defenders note the presence of widespread civil liberties, a high standard of living, and a relatively open political process. Conservatives often oppose change—or, at least, change that is too swift. They are fearful that fundamental changes in society will prove to be disruptive. (It has been said that conservatives are people who do not want to do anything for the first time.) Liberals see a greater need for change, but they wish to work through the existing system, through "normal politics," to achieve these changes. On the other hand, there are those who subscribe to the aphorism "The squeaky wheel gets the grease." It is thus suggested that disadvantaged or dissident groups can stimulate social change only by using disruption to call attention to their problems. Yet, creating a climate of social disorder can be counterproductive to achieving group demands. Because people value social order, those who disturb that order may invite a backlash. As two leading analysts of civil disorder have concluded, "Reforms cannot be made if order is wholly lacking, and reforms will not be made if those who have the means to make them feel their security constantly in jeopardy." (Graham and Gurr, 1969, p. 814)

The legal system has a tremendous impact on social order in our nation (Hayek, 1973; Jenkins, 1980). Indeed, anarchy—the absence of an organized government—is often associated with disorder and disarray. Actually, the relationship between the legal system and social order is highly complex. To begin with, government plays an enormous role in spelling out the character of the existing order. The legal system promotes order in a very basic way by creating standard rules and procedures governing the resolution of certain kinds of disputes. Thus, even though a bank has a good deal more money than an individual, the law does not allow the individual to "redistribute" money from the bank through armed robbery. Written rules and a history of judicial rulings exist for a vast array of concerns, both in the civil and criminal areas. Given these preexisting rules, we may (aided by an attorney) have a reasonably good idea as to how the judiciary will deal with our legal problems.

Apart from its role in establishing the basic elements of the social order, the legal system acts to uphold or alter this order. In an effort to uphold order government may even make use of the police and prisons. Indeed, it was the fear of violence and disorder that led to the internment of Japanese Americans during World War II. It should be noted, however, that the use of coercion by government may be counterproductive. Coercion can contribute to disorder, particularly if it is carried out ineptly or in the face of intense public opposition.

It is also true that the legal system may attempt to change the social order. For example, the federal government in the 1950s and 1960s was instrumental in reducing overt racism against blacks. In *Brown v. Board of Education* the Supreme Court called for "all deliberate speed" in eliminating the segregated school system of Topeka, Kansas. Similar cases followed in which the Supreme Court called for desegregation of schools and other public facilities. Government in America does, however, appear to have a bias in favor of the status quo. Within the judiciary a basic norm is that of stare decisis. Adhering to this doctrine, judges rely on legal precedents when making decisions. If the decisions of the past are used to resolve current disputes before the courts, social changes are held to a minimum. A bias toward the status quo can be seen in other sectors of the legal system as well. Change is often constrained by the system of checks and balances operating among the institutions of government. Given the nature of the legal system, a policy change proposed by one institution of government may be blocked elsewhere.

Effectiveness

"Does it work?" is a question that is often asked by Americans (Pomper et al., 1972; Lowi, 1979; Ross, Campbell, and Glass, 1970; Friedman, 1975; Horowitz, 1977). Partly as a result of recent policy failures, the topic of effectiveness is increasingly discussed. Among these failures have been the shortcomings of the 1960s "War on Poverty," the aborted military effort in Vietnam, the inability of our criminal justice system to stem the mounting crime rate, and the increasing incapacity of our economic institutions to cope with foreign competition. Robert Kharasch has remarked that nothing in our society seems to work right (1973, p. 5). According to Kharasch, public and private institutions are highly ineffective, producing as their chief products bafflement, frustration, and rage. Of course, ineffectiveness is not a problem of recent vintage. Indeed, it was the ineffectiveness of the Articles of Confederation that led to the 1787 convention in Philadelphia which drafted the United States Constitution.

Evidence suggests that contemporary Americans are quite concerned about the effectiveness of key political and social institutions. In 1978 a sample of heads of households was asked to rate the ability of various American institutions to "get things done." (U.S. News and World Report, 1978, p. 12) Those surveyed rated the effectiveness of a series of institutions as *good, average,* or *poor.* In general, the ratings were quite low. Scores of *good* ranged from only 38 percent for science and technology to only 3 percent for politicians. Among government institutions the Supreme Court ranked highest, with 25 percent *good.* Other government institutions rated much lower concerning the ability to get things done. The White House rated 9 percent, the Senate 8 percent, the House of Representatives 7 percent, state and local government 7 percent, and the federal bureaucracy 4 percent. Only 16 percent rated the legal profession *good,* compared with 29 percent for the medical profession. In a major address to the American people President Carter attributed this disillusionment to a national "malaise"; others might characterize the ratings as a "realistic assessment."

Effectiveness is an issue with immediate relevance to law and the legal system. For example, when a law is passed, we would like to think that it will be effective in meeting its goals. Many doubt the effectiveness of government and its laws—hence the cynical adage "You can't legislate morality." Beyond that, we want the personnel of the legal system to carry out their roles effectively. It is important to us that the police be effective in preventing crime, in catching criminals, and in maintaining order. Many would even be willing to sacrifice some personal liberty in order to increase the effectiveness of the police. They would permit police officers to make greater use of wiretapping, stopping and searching, and entering homes in order to gather evidence. (Of course, few would relish these devices being used against them!) It is also important to us that private attorneys, prosecutors, judges, juries, and corrections officers be effective in their duties. Indeed, this concern for effectiveness is sometimes uppermost in our minds.

Democracy

"Let's take a vote" is a common expression among Americans (Mayo, 1960; Dahl, 1956; Rostow, 1952; Wasby, 1978a). A great deal of faith is placed in the principle of majority rule—the notion that decisions ought to be based on a head count. It might be asked why all public decisions are not based on democratic principles so that in every area of the law majority sentiment could prevail. As we have seen, the United States legal system does contain elements of democratic decision making. Most notably, many key government officials are elected by the public. At the same time, there are also some significant roadblocks which impede the operation of majority rule.

In constraining democracy, we prevent majority rule from impinging on other important values. For example, unencumbered majority rule might lead to sweeping abridgments of procedural safeguards such as the protections accorded suspects in the hands of the police. Equality might also suffer in a nation with unrestrained democracy. In a national referendum some legally enforced rights would be jeopardized, such as school busing, free speech, and legal counsel for those accused of a crime. If democracy became the sole criterion for determining policies, social order might suffer as well. Minority interests would undoubtedly receive less attention, thus laying the groundwork for unrest. Finally, the policies advocated by the majority are not necessarily the most effective. We would want a dispute over proper design of a bridge to be settled by experts rather than through a public referendum. Given the complexity of our national problems, expertise is often required to formulate and implement workable policies. In short, even though democracy is valuable, there are times when we want to sacrifice it in order to safeguard other values.

Democracy as a social value is of great relevance in discussions of the judiciary. In particular, a common charge is that the courts are an undemocratic institution.[17] Critics observe that federal judges are unelected and serve for life. This is in sharp contrast to the democratic selection of the president, Congress, governors, mayors, and state and local legislators. As a result, judges

---

[17] For such an argument applied to the issue of school busing, see Lino Graglia, *Disaster By Decree* (Ithaca, N. Y.: Cornell University Press, 1976).

may have fewer institutional incentives to be representative of the public. Also, the decision-making process used by judges is relatively undemocratic. While legislators often turn to public opinion polls and lobbyists for help in making decisions, the judicial process relies on previous court rulings, which were often made in a very different era. While departure from precedent sometimes occurs, decisions are "supposed to" result from an introspective process by individual judges rather than reflect a response to majority sentiment.

Given the seemingly undemocratic character of the judiciary, judges are commonly asked to exercise self-restraint and leave social change to legislators and executives. When judges fail to restrain themselves, the result may be a reversal of the Supreme Court's decision through corrective legislation or a constitutional amendment. Indeed, political attacks on the Court may occur. There may be an attempt to increase the number of justices on the High Court or an effort to reduce the scope of the Court's appellate jurisdiction.

Even so, it is hardly self-evident that all important matters of public policy ought to be left to executives and legislators (Krislov, 1968; Claude, 1970). There may be some concerns—such as freedom of speech and religion—which many wish to guarantee for all citizens, regardless of majority sentiment at a given time. Courts act to safeguard a number of personal rights. Ironically, among the rights protected by courts are the democratic rights of voting, assembly, and petitioning the government. The courts protect democracy from one of its great paradoxes. In a pure and unrestrained democracy citizens would be able to vote, by majority rule, to abolish majority rule. In the United States many democratic freedoms are protected and preserved by the Constitution, as interpreted by judges. Consequently, it would presumably require a constitutional amendment to withdraw voting rights from blacks, women, and eighteen-year-olds. Other democratic freedoms are also kept "out of bounds" as regards legislative or executive action.

Evaluating Values and the Law

We have analyzed the role of the law in allocating social values. By enacting and implementing laws, government necessarily has an effect on the distribution of values in society. Among the values which have been stressed by government are procedural justice, liberty, equality, social order, effectiveness, and democracy. This list, of course, does not exhaust the values of concern to the American people or their government. Because people differ in their beliefs, there will necessarily be disagreement as to which values should be stressed by government. Were you to survey the policies of government in the United States, you would no doubt be dissatisfied that one or another value is not being given greater stress. A related problem is one of ignorance: We sometimes do not know the effects of existing or proposed policies on the values we consider important. This is a problem faced not only by ordinary citizens but by academics and public officials as well (Rivlin, 1971). What should be clear, however, is that the laws of government inescapably affect the allocation of values in our society.

THE IMPACT OF LAW

Two Views

In the course of processing disputes and allocating values, the law sometimes attempts to introduce some fundamental changes in the social order. One highly unsuccessful effort of this kind was Prohibition in the 1920s and early 1930s. In some quarters there is little confidence in the ability of the law to bring about social change. This attitude is reflected in the position of President Dwight Eisenhower on civil rights policy. Eisenhower asserted: "You can't change men's hearts with laws." (Rodgers and Bullock, 1972, p. 203) This perspective would relegate the legal system to a rather limited role. At best, people will grudgingly comply with a law with which they do not agree. For example, we may be able to force white and black children to attend the same schools. However, according to this perspective, law can do little more than this. Surely, it is argued, the legal system cannot move people to change their values to reflect the intent of the law. In some cases—such as Prohibition—the legal system has been unable even to bring about compliance with the law.

Nevertheless, there is a contrary, more optimistic, view of the impact of law in society. Some argue that under some circumstances law can be a powerful weapon for changing the attitudes and behavior of people. For example, William Muir has studied the impact of the Supreme Court's school prayer decisions on the attitudes of a group of educators (1967). Muir assessed the attitudes of twenty-eight educators both before and after the Supreme Court's ruling in *Abington School District v. Schempp.* Here the Court ruled that openly exercised religion in the public schools was unconstitutional. Muir found that prior to *Schempp* most of the educators had a mixture of attitudes toward school prayer. For example, many professed to believe in the importance of inculcating religious beliefs in students. Yet, they also supported the school board's policy of permitting only a hurried recital of a forty-word prayer (Muir, 1967, p. 123).

Muir found that following *Schempp* a shift occurred in both the behavior and attitudes of school officials. He concluded that the law played a substantial role in motivating these changes. The *Schempp* decision forced the officials to integrate their equivocal attitudes into a consistent pattern. Of special importance in getting their indecision under control was the threat of a civil suit from opponents of school prayer. The direction of the educators' opinion change was heavily influenced by discussions within cliques to which they belonged (Muir, 1967, p. 125). Here the educators could air their various beliefs and resolve inconsistencies. Many managed to retain their old beliefs on the importance of religion while downgrading the significance of reciting a prayer.

The external protection provided by the legal system proved very helpful to the educators. Significantly, the legal system helped to reduce the hostility faced by an official who opted to support the *Schempp* ruling. School officials could count on the legal system for verbal support, an evenhanded application of the law, and the threat of punishment for those who considered violating the law. As Muir suggests, the law provided "a benign, post-operative environment where the individual needed only to flex his muscles, not depend on them for his very life." (1967, p. 131)

Three Factors

Three general factors have been identified which contribute to the ability of the law to produce social change (Friedman, 1975, Chaps. 3, 4, 5). First, the law must be adequately communicated to those for whom it is intended. Clearly, a law cannot influence someone's attitudes or behavior if that person is ignorant of the law. Thus, the legal system must make it known that a change in the law has occurred. Moreover, the content of that law must be communicated. This implies the adoption of unambiguous laws and a network of communication that links those who adopt a law to those who must carry it out. In fact, the imperfections of language, the heavy workload of public officials, and the need for compromise all contribute to ambiguity in law. Moreover, the fragmentation of authority in the legal system may contribute to a lack of understanding of the decisions that have been made elsewhere in government.

Second, it must be possible for people to obey the law. This capacity is not always present. Various psychological, sociological, and biological explanations of crime suggest that circumstances compel some people to break criminal laws (Vold, 1979). Certainly, there is some involuntary behavior among the many violators of drug laws, gambling restrictions, child abuse laws, and rape statutes. In the civil courts, some people are unable to avoid violations leading to civil commitment. Likewise, many people may be unable to avoid causing injury to others (that is, torts), as in certain automobile accidents.

Finally, a law will have impact only if people are willing to obey it. One element of this is the inner desire of people to obey the law (Friedman, 1975, Chaps. 3, 4, 5). This inner desire may exist for any number of reasons. These include self-interest, a sense of civic-mindedness, a feeling that it is immoral to violate the law, a belief that the law is fair because it is applied equally, a sense of trust in the effectiveness of government, and a feeling of support for the legitimacy of government. However, some external force is often needed to achieve social change (Bullock and Rodgers, 1976). As Al Capone, the Chicago gangster, once argued: "You can get more with a gun and a polite request than you can with only a polite request" (Bullock and Rodgers, 1976, p. 987). Typically, the legal system will threaten or carry out sanctions in order to achieve compliance with the law. To this end the legal system invests an enormous amount of resources to support the system of sanctions. Funds are expended for police officers, prosecutors, bailiffs, public defenders, jails, and prisons. Harrell Rodgers and Charles S. Bullock have applied utility theory to the study of legal compliance (Rodgers and Bullock, 1972, Ch. 8). This theory argues that people will maximize their utility by taking the action that entails the least personal costs and the greatest benefits. Thus, people will break the law only if they stand to suffer a greater loss from obedience than from disobedience.

Thus, there are certain circumstances under which the law can be an important source of social change (Muir, 1967, pp. 135–138). In recent decades the law has achieved significant successes in reshaping attitudes and behavior regarding race relations and many other problems. Still, it is essential that the law be used judiciously, lest it invite a backlash of opposition. In general, any effort to promote a social value should be made only after carefully considering its possible effects on other values. Extensive use of sanctions may be successful in securing compliance, but it may also bring about a loss of public support or even massive resistance. It must be realized as well that a law will be rather ineffective if it is opposed almost universally by the other institutions of society and by the general public. If the legal system pursues an unpopular policy, it risks losing some of its legitimacy and its capacity to act effectively in the future. In this regard, as will be seen in the final chapter, the courts have some special problems in trying to bring about social change.

AN ASSESSMENT

We have examined the nature of law and society. This has included a discussion of law and the legal system, the roles of law, and the impact of law on society. As we have seen, government in the United States has established a vast network of legal ground rules. These legal ground rules are enforceable in the courts and sometimes in administrative agencies. One role of the law is to process disputes. Many of the disputes occurring in our nation are relevant to one law or another. While most disputes are processed without direct reference to the legal system, the law is nevertheless a powerful force for dealing with disputes. The second role of the law is to authoritatively allocate values in our society. Legal ground rules will necessarily be relevant to significant social values such as liberty, equality, and social order. As people turn to the legal system for an authoritative resolution of their disputes, an emphasis on one value rather than on another will benefit some people and hurt others.

There can be no doubt that the legal system, including the courts, greatly affects "who gets what, when, how" in our society (Lasswell, 1958).

QUESTIONS FOR DISCUSSION

1. How does the legal system of the United States differ from a dictatorship? How does it differ from a direct democracy? If we wanted the laws of government to reflect public opinion perfectly, what kinds of changes would we consider making in the legal system? What place would courts have in a dictatorship? What place would they have in a direct democracy? What place do courts have in our own system of government?

2. Regarding court organization in the United States, are there really any benefits to having appellate courts as well as trial-level courts? How does the presence of state courts in addition to a federal court system affect public policy in the United States? Why are some disputes heard by administrative tribunals rather than by trial courts?

3. What was the most serious dispute you became involved in during the past year? Which "dispute-processing mechanisms" were used in the course of that dispute? Which methods seemed most helpful? Which were least helpful? Would adjudication have been an appropriate method? Were you satisfied with the outcome of the dispute? Was the other party satisfied? In retrospect, should you have dealt with the dispute through some other method of dispute processing?

4. Which of the social values discussed in this chapter are most important to you? How well are these values being achieved by the legal system? What changes might be made in the law to better achieve these values? Would these changes in the law really produce the intended effect of achieving these values more fully? Would these changes in the law seriously impinge on the achievement of other values by government?

FOR FURTHER READING

FRIEDMAN, LAWRENCE M.   *The Legal System.* New York: Russell Sage Foundation, 1975. A social science analysis of various legal topics, including the origins and impact of law.

LEWIS, ANTHONY.   *Gideon's Trumpet.* New York: Random House, 1964. The story of how Clarence Gideon's dispute with the state of Florida ultimately led to a Supreme Court ruling that defendants who cannot afford an attorney be provided one at government expense.

RODGERS, HARRELL R., JR., and BULLOCK, CHARLES S., III.   *Law and Social Change.* New York: McGraw-Hill, 1972. The difficulties of government in pursuing racial equality are analyzed.

United States Code: 1976 Edition.   Washington, D.C.: USGPO, 1977, with annual
supplements. Spend a few hours with the volumes of the U.S. Code and you will
appreciate the broad range of federal laws in the United States.

VAGO, STEVEN.   *Law and Society.* Englewood Cliffs, N. J.: Prentice-Hall, 1981. A nice
overview of the sociology of law.

SUPREME COURT RULINGS

Abington School District v. Schempp, 374, U.S. 203 (1963)
Betts v. Brady, 316 U.S. 455 (1942)
Boyd v. United States, 116 U.S. 616 (1886)
Brown v. Board of Education, 347 U.S. 483 (1954)
Brown v. Texas, 443 U.S. 47 (1979)
Edwards v. South Carolina, 372 U.S. 229 (1963)
Escobedo v. Illinois, 378 U.S. 478 (1964)
Gideon v. Wainwright, 372 U.S. 335 (1963)
Korematsu v. United States, 323 U.S. 214 (1944)
Maher v. Roe, 432 U.S. 464 (1977)
Mapp v. Ohio, 367 U.S. 643 (1961)
Miranda v. Arizona, 384 U.S. 436 (1966)
Near v. Minnesota, 283 U.S. 697 (1931)
Pierce v. Society of Sisters, 268 U.S. 510 (1925)
United States v. Nixon, 418 U.S. 683 (1974)
Whitney v. California, 274 U.S. 357 (1927)
Zorach v. Clauson, 343 U.S. 306 (1952)

2

THE POLICE

PREVIEW

Chapter Two focuses on the municipal police in America. It is the police who provide the caseload that is processed by our criminal courts. The chapter consists of five sections:

Members of the force
Roles
Discretion
Ethics
Community relations

First we look at various aspects of the members of the force. Our sketch will touch on the background, training, attitudes, and professionalism of police officers. We will see that the police are generally of working- or lower-class background; receive relatively little training; are conservative, suspicious, and secretive; and are low in occupational status. Next we focus on the three major roles of the police—law enforcement, order maintenance, and community service. Our discussion will include consideration of the argument that increased role specialization among police officers would enhance their effectiveness. In the third section we address the discretion inherent in police work. Some citizens are more likely than others to be stopped, questioned, and arrested. Efforts by courts, legislatures, and police administrators to constrain police discretion have met with only limited success. Police ethics is the subject of our fourth section. We will examine the three forms of unethical conduct by the police—lying, brutality, and material corruption. It will be seen that misconduct is not due to a few "rotten apples," but instead is relatively widespread. The final section deals with "PCR" (that is, police-community relations) programs. Special programs are regularly sponsored by the police to improve their public image. Unfortunately, there has been a failure to recognize that the strongest community relations effort would simply involve improving the on-duty behavior of police officers.

MEMBERS OF THE FORCE

While we clearly do not have a police officer on every doorstep, the number of police personnel in the United States is considerable. In 1977 a total of 685,881 persons were employed as police officers by some level of government in the United States (Flanagan, Hindelang, and Gottfredson, 1980, p. 39). Of these, 512,358 (or 74.7 percent) were employed at the local level. The average entrance salary in 1978 for police officers in cities with populations over 10,000 was $11,472 (International City Management Association, 1979, p. 176). After four years of experience a police officer will generally earn about $14,000. Apart from the general police departments of municipalities, police officers are also found at the federal, state, and county levels (Holten and Jones, 1978, p. 59). Federal-level police include those in the Federal Bureau of Investigation, Drug Enforcement Agency, Immigration and Naturalization Service, United States Marshals, and Secret Service. State police include highway patrol officers, fish and game wardens, as well as those serving in beverage or alcohol units, the bureau of narcotics, and intelligence or investigative units. At the county level police officers are present in sheriffs' departments. Total expenditures for police protection by federal, state, and local governments amounted to over $11.8 billion in fiscal year 1977 (Flanagan et al., 1980, p. 5). Nearly 70 percent was spent at the local level. In addition, there is a large and growing number of private police forces in our country (Rojek, 1979, p. 101; Scott and McPherson, 1971; Lodge, 1967).[1] Indeed, the size of our private police industry probably greatly exceeds that of the public police sector. Below we focus on the most important and most studied police personnel in America—the municipal police officer.

[1]See also Note, "Private Police Forces: Legal Powers and Limitations," *The University of Chicago Law Review,* 1971, *38,* 555–582.

Background

Demographically, the police do not represent a random cross-section of American society. For example, they tend to be white, high-school educated, and upwardly mobile from a working-class or lower-class background (Bent, 1974, pp. 92–98). The background characteristics of police officers reflect a process of self-selection as well as the official and unofficial qualifications set by departments. Recruitment qualifications are most stringent in the departments of large cities and of small but wealthy suburbs (Baker, 1971, p. 346). A call for increased selectivity in the recruitment process has come from the President's Commission on Law Enforcement and Administration of Justice. The Commission asserts: "Complexities inherent in the policing function dictate that officers possess a high degree of intelligence, education, tact, sound judgment, physical courage, emotional stability, impartiality, and honesty." (President's Commission on Law Enforcement and Administration of Justice, 1967a, p. 125) Clearly, if departments did adopt more stringent qualifications for entry, a larger number of potential applicants would be excluded from consideration. Thus, there are those who oppose the notion of adding such qualifications. James Q. Wilson notes, for example, that a case can be made against a more educated police force (1972, pp. 73–74). One effect of restrictive educational standards would be to limit a department's ability to recruit members of minority groups. In addition, college-educated police officers might be less able to identify and deal with the problems of disadvantaged people. Finally, police officers with a college background might find police work very dull, thus leading to an increased sense of dissatisfaction and cynicism. In short, it is necessary to think critically about each qualification set by police departments. While some standards perhaps ought to be tightened, others may be largely irrelevant.

Numerous qualifications are usually required by police departments (Baker, 1971, pp. 345–346; President's Commission, 1967a, pp. 125–132; Bent, 1974, pp. 15–17). One barrier to entry is age, as many departments accept only those between the ages of twenty-one and thirty or thirty-five. Obviously, any such restrictions can bring charges of age discrimination.[2] Physical requirements such as good health, perfect or near-perfect vision without glasses, weight and height limits, and good physical strength are also common. Some of these restrictions seem unduly prohibitive. For example, height as a criterion inherently poses some ethnic and gender biases. In addition, some departments attempt to recruit only those with a "high character." While the notion is valid, the practice is often simply to exclude those who have a criminal record. Such a practice has an indirect bias against those who grew up in an area with intensive police surveillance (for example, the ghetto).

Mental capacity is also tested by some departments. For example, an

---

[2]The Supreme Court has dealt with the issue of retirement ages for the police in *Massachusetts Board of Retirement v. Murgia*, 427 U.S. 307 (1976).

intelligence test and a high school diploma (or some college experience) may be required. The question of whether a police department can use a written exam as a criterion for recruitment was addressed by the Supreme Court in *Washington v. Davis.*[3] The exam, which tested verbal skills, was used by the District of Columbia Police Department. While the effect of this exam was to exclude a disproportionate number of black applicants, the Court's decision was to uphold the constitutionality of the written examination. Some departments also test for emotional fitness through some sort of psychiatric evaluation. A residency requirement is also present in some communities. Applicants to these departments must not only be citizens of the United States but also must be residents of the community whose department they wish to join. Some believe that police officers who live in the community they are policing will be more devoted to their job as compared with those who commute. Finally, it is not uncommon for departments to screen applicants for their ideological beliefs in oral interviews and written questionnaires. An individual with a liberal ideology may be denied admission to the police force because of "incompatible" views (Bent, 1974, pp. 15–17). Ideological exclusiveness becomes a self-fulfilling process, as many choose not to enter police work because departments are already composed of officers with a conservative viewpoint.

Training

Police officers, like members of many occupations, must generally submit to a period of formal training. Typically, police departments require only 200 to 300 hours of training (Flanagan et al., 1980, p. 210; ABA, 1972, pp. 202–210 and 1973 approved supplement). This is far less than the training undergone by police officers in many European countries. In Denmark, for example, a new police officer spends five years in a combined program of work experience and classroom preparation. Richard Harris examined the operation of a police academy in the United States which holds a twelve-week training course (1973). Admission requirements to the academy included satisfactory results in a civil service exam, physical endurance tests, a medical examination, and an in-depth background investigation. Four modest graduation requirements were set by the academy. These included a good attendance record, a satisfactory score in pistol testing, a typed notebook transcribed from class notes, and a 75 percent exam average on tests based on classroom lectures. These lectures focused on a variety of topics. Some 70 percent of instruction centered on patrol procedures, law and the courts, traffic, and police structure and functions. Other topics included self-defense, drill and inspections, departmental forms and regulations, first aid, and community relations.[4]

[3]426 U.S. 229 (1976).
[4]For state-by-state differences in basic training, see Flanagan et al. (1980), p. 211.

There is much dissatisfaction among both the police and outside experts with the training police officers receive. It is widely believed that training programs do not adequately prepare the police for the realities of police work. Harris reports that toward the end of training at the academy, recruits generally became bored (1973, pp. 86–87). Indeed, after the recruits spent their first week in the field, they concluded that their training at the academy was irrelevant to policing. Recruits feel they can learn far more about the realities of policing from contacts with older, experienced officers (ABA, 1972, p. 209). Further, some experts are concerned that training academies are failing to inculcate certain desirable values in recruits. The American Bar Association has recommended three basic changes in the content of police training programs (ABA, 1972, pp. 205–210). First, recruits should be equipped with a better understanding of the police role. This would include an acquaintance with the principles of the Constitution. The aim would be to enable police officers to better understand and accept the limits of police powers in our society. Whether such a program would really alter police behavior is, of course, unclear. Second, the personal skills of the police ought to be improved so that officers can carry out their responsibilities more effectively. For example, more attention should be paid to developing human relations skills. Finally, the ABA suggests that academies improve the decision-making skills of recruits. Given the infinite variety of complex situations they face, police officers must learn how to apply broad standards to varied situations in an effective manner.

Attitudes

Police possess a distinctive set of attitudes (Bent, 1974, pp. 15–17; Eisenstein, 1973, pp. 88–92; Lefkowitz, 1975; Skolnick, 1966, pp. 42–70; Bent and Rossum, 1976; Manning, 1971; Niederhoffer, 1967, Ch. 5). For some complex reasons these attitudes often take on a rather extreme tenor. From an ideological standpoint the police are almost universally conservative in their personal and political attitudes. Their morals are conventional. Generally, they have a low regard for minority groups. Many belong to right-wing political organizations. A major study of police conservatism was conducted by Alan Bent (1974, pp. 98–100). Bent surveyed samples of police officers and three other groupings of people (whites, blacks, students). He found that the police have the warmest feelings toward such groups as the American Legion, National Guard, John Birch Society, Ku Klux Klan, and the military. The police had the coldest feelings for the Black Panthers, Democrats, liberals, women's liberation groups, and blacks. Such attitudes clearly reflect a conservative orientation. In part these attitudes result from the working-class background of most police officers. Additionally, the police job itself encourages conservative attitudes, since policing involves maintaining the status quo. As Jerome Skolnick points out: "The fact that a man is engaged in enforcing a set of rules implies that he also becomes implicated in *affirming* them.'' (1966, p. 59) In addition, the negative nature of so many police-citizen contacts is bound to have an impact on the attitudes of members of the force.

Apart from this conservatism, researchers have identified a series of other attitudes which are characteristic of police officers. The police are generally convinced that they operate in a community which is unsympathetic, critical, and lacking in understanding. Members of the force believe that everyone hates a cop (Manning, 1971, p. 156). James Eisenstein notes: ''The feeling that the public does not appreciate them is particularly painful. Police . . . aspire to middle-class, professional status and the respect that goes with it. They do not feel they get it. Consequently, they crave and even demand respect.'' (1973, p. 90) The sense of citizen hostility also contributes to the development of other police attitudes. As Joel Lefkowitz points out, the police are ''a close-knit group of men'' with ''intense feelings of being misunderstood and misrepresented by outsiders, hence requiring absolute secrecy as well as suspicion towards all such outsiders.'' (1975, p. 9)

The perception among the police of citizen hostility is intertwined with other attitudes such as isolation, cynicism, suspiciousness, defensiveness, secrecy, and solidarity. To begin with, the police tend to isolate themselves from the rest of the community. As John Van Maanen observes: ''It is a lonely, largely friendless world the patrolman faces.'' (1974, p. 103) Isolation even extends to social lives, as police officers have few friends outside the force. In dealing with the public, the police are highly cynical. In past encounters with citizens police officers have heard all manner of excuses and explanations. As a result, the police come to believe nothing and distrust everything (Van Maanen, 1974, p. 104; Skolnick, 1966, p. 61). Given the nature of their work, the police must be constantly concerned about potential violence from others. Every police officer experiences dangerous situations and hears of the threatening experiences of fellow patrol officers. In fact, nearly 50,000 assaults on police officers occur every year (Flanagan et al., 1980, p. 439). Over 17,000 of these result in injury to the officer. Moreover, about 100 police officers are killed every year, nearly all while on duty (Flanagan et al., 1980, p. 434).

The police also tend to be defensive and secretive. The reasons for this are not mysterious. As John Van Maanen notes: ''No officer is free from the knowledge that in his past (and no doubt in his future) are certain acts which, if reported, could cost him his job and perhaps even his freedom.'' (1974, p. 103) In the course of police work, formal rules of the department are not infrequently violated. Such rule breaking leads to an informal code of silence among members of the force. A police officer feels obliged to protect co-workers when they break the rules. After all, the officer must also depend on fellow workers to remain silent about his or her violations. Finally, an attitude of solidarity is also characteristic of the police. William Westley found that three-quarters of police officers were willing to perjure themselves rather than testify against their partners (1956, p. 255). Given the public hostility they perceive, police officers believe they must stand together as a group to prevent damaging information from becoming public knowledge. In essence, the police seem to be a closed community which is fearful and distrusting of outsiders.

Professionalism

Police officers, like those in many occupational groups, are striving to attain professional status in our society. To date this effort has not been very successful. Harold Wilensky observes: "Many occupations engage in heroic struggles for professional identification; few make the grade." (1964, p. 137) Looking at the literature on professionalization, Arthur Niederhoffer cites nine criteria of professional status (1967, pp. 18–19):

1. High standards of admission
2. A special body of knowledge and theory
3. Altruism and dedication to the service ideal
4. A lengthy period of training for candidates
5. A code of ethics
6. Licensing of members
7. Autonomous control
8. Pride of the members in their profession
9. Publicly recognized status and prestige

On most of these criteria the police continue to fall significantly short of professional status.

With regard to the nine criteria the outlook for police professionalization looks gloomy. Niederhoffer notes: "If the law-enforcement occupation is successful in obtaining the status of a profession, it will be a Horatio Alger story." (1967, p. 20) On the one hand, like "true" professionals, police officers have engaged in an intense effort to increase their autonomy.[5] They have experienced some successes here, having unionized and fought back efforts at creating civilian review boards to handle complaints against them. It is also true that members of the force are generally proud of their work and wish to remain on the force (Bent, 1974, p. 98). At the same time, there are many roadblocks in the way of police professionalization. For example, admission standards to the police force are not particularly high in most communities.

---

[5]Increased police autonomy is not necessarily a positive development, however. Autonomy can insulate the police from civilian control. Also, unlike the clients of most professionals, the potential clients of the police (that is, suspects) have no choice in deciding whether the police should intervene in their lives.

Commonly, only a high-school diploma and various physical qualifications are required. In addition, the police do not really possess a special body of knowledge and theory in the same sense as academics or other professionals. Policing is more of an art than a science (Bent and Rossum, 1976, p. 362). Moreover, many police officers are not particularly service-oriented. Indeed, the movement for police professionalism has often stressed obtaining new equipment rather than meeting public demands. Also, the training period for police recruits is quite short. In fact, much discussion on professionalization has centered on increasing the period of training and perhaps even introducing some college requirements. Further, a number of observers believe that the police are not well socialized in key values relevant to their work, such as the importance of legality in a constitutional democracy (Skolnick and Gray, 1975, pp. xvii). A code of police ethics exists, but many officers are not even aware of it (Folley, 1976, pp. 112–114). Many police officers take a dim view of the constitutional protections available to suspects and defendants, which seem only to make the police's job more difficult. Finally, the general public emphatically does not regard the police as being high in occupational status. While members of the FBI may be regarded as professionals, the possibilities for police professionalization at the city level seem rather bleak.

ROLES

The police carry out a multiplicity of roles. Broadly, these roles include law enforcement, order maintenance, and community service. The police are not only our crime fighters but also our peacekeepers and 24-hour-a-day service providers. Some have argued that given the size of the police budget, we are asking too much of our police forces. Despite the billions annually expended on police work, David Stang suggests that present-day expenditures are "inadequate in light of current recruitment problems, resignations, early retirement difficulties, and widespread police 'moonlighting'. . . ." (1969, p. 287) While police spending has risen in recent decades, actual resources available to police departments have changed very little. David Bordua and Edward Haurek found that the increase in police expenditures which has occurred can be accounted for by urban population growth, inflation, urbanization, and increased police use of motor vehicles (1970). The authors conclude: "After the four components of increase are taken into account, it appears that local police departments have not made any gains since 1902 in terms of societal resources available to them." (1970, p. 670) Of course, one may question whether moderate increments in police funding would actually improve the effectiveness of the police in carrying out their various roles. We cannot fund police departments to the extent of placing a police officer on every doorstep or even on every street corner. Yet, a 10 percent increase in the number of police officers might not increase police effectiveness at all.

Law Enforcement

To most police officers law enforcement is the only "real" police work. As Alan Bent and Ralph Rossum note: "The 'good pinch' is the avenue for a policeman's career progression and the way the police are able to project a positive public image." (Bent and Rossum, 1976, p. 5) The emphasis on crime control is reflected in the administrative procedures of many departments (Greacen, 1980, p. 20). For example, deployment of officers is based largely on crime rates in various areas of the community. Even so, and notwithstanding "Dick Tracy" and "Kojak," only a minority of police time is spent enforcing the law. As part of a major study of police behavior, James Q. Wilson examined the radio calls to police cars made by the Syracuse Police Department for a one-week period (1968, p. 18). He found that only 10.3 percent of the calls were for law enforcement matters, such as burglary in progress. By contrast, 37.5 percent of calls dealt with the service role (for example, accidents), and 30.1 percent concerned order maintenance (for example, gang disturbance). Another 22.1 percent of calls were mainly clerical in nature (for example, asking routine questions and filling out forms). Despite the significance of the law enforcement role, police officers on patrol are faced with other significant demands upon their time. At the same time, there are some police personnel—detectives—who are specifically assigned the task of investigating crimes.

Law enforcement involves not only the arrest and processing of suspects but also the prevention and detection of crime. Two principal strategies aimed at holding down crime are preventive patrol and detective work. In preventive patrol police move by vehicle or foot in an assigned area, looking for something suspicious. The President's Commission on Law Enforcement and Administration of Justice has noted: "The object of patrol is to disperse policemen in a way that will eliminate or reduce the opportunity for misconduct and to increase the likelihood that a criminal will be apprehended while he is committing a crime or immediately thereafter." (President's Commission, 1967a, p. 1) The theory is that if police cars roam the city streets, the police presence will hold down the crime rate and detect offenses in progress. Likewise, a strong detective division in a city is intended to deter crime and apprehend those who have violated a criminal law.

The police seem to believe that they play an important role in influencing the level of urban crime. When crime rates go down, police departments attempt to take the credit; when crime rates rise, police departments almost always ask for more resources to wage their war against crime. Yet, the President's Commission on Law Enforcement and Administration of Justice has questioned the impact of the police on crime. The Commission concludes: "The fact is, of course, that even under the most favorable circumstances the ability of the police to act against crime is limited." (President's Commission, 1967a, p. 1) Three reasons for the relative ineffectiveness of the police as crime fighters have been suggested by Bent and Rossum (1976, pp. 6–10). First, while public resources are quite limited, there is a large geographic area in which crimes can take place. The eyes and ears of the police cannot be everywhere. Second, most crimes are not susceptible to prevention or control by the police. Homicide, for example, is usually committed before the police arrive, while white-collar and victimless crimes are carried out in private. Third, the public often refuses to "get involved." Eyewitnesses or those with information about a crime often fail to assist the police, thus impeding the crime-fighting effort.

Since so much police effort is devoted to preventive patrol, the impact of such patrol has critical implications for overall police effectiveness. An important test of the effectiveness of preventive patrol was conducted by the Kansas City, Missouri, Police Department in 1972–1973 (Kelling et al., 1974). One section of Kansas City was divided into three kinds of beats—reactive, proactive, and control. In reactive beats there were no routine patrol activities. In proactive beats neighborhoods were saturated with three to four times the normal number of patrol cars. Finally, in control beats patrol was carried on as it had been in the past. Remarkably, the results revealed few differences among the three neighborhoods in crime or victimization rates. These findings have led many to question the effectiveness of preventive patrol and urban police forces in general.

The effectiveness of detectives in enforcing the law has also been seriously questioned. Detectives are police officers who are assigned the task of investigating crimes (Folley, 1976, pp. 174–178; Kratcoski and Walker, 1978, pp. 80–81). Some of their key duties include searching the scene of a crime, gathering evidence, locating and interviewing witnesses, interrogating suspects, finding wanted criminals, maintaining surveillance of suspicious persons, preparing reports for use by prosecutors, and testifying in court. Most police officers would relish the opportunity to become a detective. Even so, there is persuasive evidence (from a two-year study by the Rand Corporation) that detectives are not a very significant factor in solving serious crimes (Greenwood, Chaiken, and Petersilia, 1977). The key factor determining whether a case will be solved is the information supplied by victims to the patrol officer who immediately responds. Unless the victim can identify the offender at that point, it is unlikely that the offender will subsequently be identified. Indeed, investigators give only superficial attention to most cases. Much of their time is consumed by administrative chores such as reviewing reports and documenting files. While some reforms may enhance the effectiveness of detectives (Greenwood et al., 1977, esp. Chaps. 14, 15), it is important to realize the enormous difficulties inherent in solving most crimes.

On the surface, at least, the results of the Kansas City experiment and Rand Corporation analysis seem to suggest that the police are irrelevant to the level of crime occurring in a community. Yet, such a conclusion is something of an overstatement. For example, James Q. Wilson is quick to note that the Kansas City experiment "does not show that the police make no difference, and it does not show that adding more police is useless in controlling crime." (1974, p. 98) The Kansas City experiment, after all, focused only on random preventive patrol in marked cars. Other methods of fighting crime may be more effective. For example, foot patrol may be of some value in areas of high street use (Kelling and Fogel, 1978, pp. 172–177). Such an approach, at a minimum, may serve to reassure the public of their safety and security (Bahn, 1974). The use of team policing (Gay, 1977), unmarked cars, and surveillance of frequently victimized homes and businesses may also be helpful in combating crime and catching criminals. More than anything else, the Kansas City and Rand Corporation studies suggest that police resources ought to be redirected to more productive methods of law enforcement. Further research is needed to learn precisely which law enforcement methods should be stressed.[6]

Order Maintenance

Order maintenance, which focuses primarily on social regulation, is also critical to the police function. Indeed, the original purpose of the police in our country was to maintain order. Only later did police functions broaden. The range of order-maintenance tasks executed by the police is quite wide. It includes settling violent family squabbles, dealing with disputes between strangers or neighbors, handling drunk and disorderly persons, intervening in fights, attending to charges such as trespassing and vagrancy, and controlling riots and protests (Bent and Rossum, 1976, p. 5). The police approach incidents such as these "not in terms of enforcing the law but in terms of 'handling the situation.'" (Wilson, 1968, p. 31)[7] The law does not supply patrol officers with a specific set of legal rules to be applied to each order-maintenance situation. As a result, the police possess enormous discretion in handling such incidents. While it is not an easy task to exercise this discretion effectively, relatively few police officers find the order-maintenance role personally satisfying. As Jesse Rubin observes: "After many such calls, the police are left with the feeling that they have accomplished little or nothing, and that they have wasted their time." (1972, p. 28) A patrol officer can expect few rewards for being an effective peacekeeper. It is almost impossible for a patrol officer to be promoted as a result of a good record in order maintenance (Stang, 1969, p. 302).

The effectiveness of the police in order-maintenance situations is questionable, given the ambiguity of such incidents and the lack of police training

---

[6]The Kansas City preventive patrol experiment should not be taken as demonstrating conclusively the ineffectiveness of preventive patrol. Notwithstanding the experiment's results, crime might substantially increase if preventive patrol was eliminated throughout a city for a long period of time and the new policy became widely publicized.

[7]The police are more likely to make an arrest under certain circumstances. For family disputes see Sarah Fenstermaker Berk and Donileen R. Loseke, "'Handling' Family Violence: Situational Determinants of Police Arrest in Domestic Disturbances," *Law and Society Review,* 1980–1981, *15,* 317–346.

and motivation to perform well. To begin with, incidents involving order maintenance are highly ambiguous. In any given situation it is not clear whether the peace has really been disturbed. Moreover, it may be difficult for police officers to know who was at fault in a fight or argument. Even if the source of the disorder can be isolated, the patrol officer may find it difficult to select an appropriate response. Statutes are vague, and in any case, the officer probably will not want to make an arrest. Often, the patrol officer will simply talk to those involved in the disorder and try to persuade them to act peaceably. This is a very different task from law enforcement, in which the arrest of a suspect is the proper form of police intervention. In general, police training to deal with order maintenance is inadequate. This is true of a variety of order-maintenance situations, ranging from everyday disputes to riots. James Auten notes that in dealing with family disputes, the police are often uncertain and apprehensive, in part because of inadequate training (1972). Further, David Stang suggests that in riots the police are often guilty of overresponse, inadequate crowd control, poor planning, and animosity toward protesters (Stang, 1969, p. 292).

In principle, it ought to be possible to identify and implement a set of appropriate procedures for dealing with various order-maintenance incidents. Research on this question is only beginning, largely because of a preoccupation with the law enforcement role of the police. One effort to compose guidelines for order-maintenance situations can be found in the work of Arnold Goldstein and associates (1977, Ch. 2). Goldstein identifies four basic stages of police intervention in a crisis. The first stage is observing and protecting against threats to officer safety. Even before arriving at the scene of the incident, police officers are advised to recall prior experiences on similar calls, anticipate that the unexpected might occur, and form a tentative plan of action. Upon arriving, the officer should remove and neutralize weapons or objects that can be used as weapons.

Second, police officers are advised to calm the crisis situation. This can best be achieved, according to Goldstein, by creating a first impression of a nonhostile authority. This means taking charge by instructing the person as to what is required in a firm, fair, even, and direct manner. Police can then calm emotional citizens by showing understanding, serving as a calm role model, reassuring the citizen (for example, saying that everything will be all right), encouraging talking, or using a distraction (for example, asking for a glass of water). In extreme cases it may be necessary to outshout the citizen, get assistance from trusted others, or make use of physical force.

The third stage in crisis intervention, as suggested by Goldstein, is gathering relevant information. The police officer is advised to first explain to the citizen what information is wanted and why. This will generally make citizens more cooperative. Different interviewing methods are suggested by Goldstein for different citizens. Open-ended questions (for example, asking in broad terms what took place) are generally preferred. Police officers are advised to be skilled listeners (for example, to maintain eye contact) to encourage openness and detailed responses. Hostile, resistive, or indifferent citizens are to be dealt with in a more demanding fashion, with information insisted upon rather than requested.

The fourth stage identified by Goldstein involves implementing some plan of action. This may be a different plan of action than the police officer might first have imagined. Generally, Goldstein favors mediation of the dispute by the police officer. Here the officer does not impose a solution but encourages the disputants themselves to suggest solutions (for example, to call some agency in the morning). If such an approach will not work, the officer may turn to more forceful methods of intervention, such as suggesting solutions, providing counseling, referring the parties to a specific agency, or even imposing a solution.

Clearly, the police generally do not adhere to guidelines as rigorous or as fully articulated as these when dealing with order-maintenance incidents. One result is that order-maintenance interventions are not nearly as effective as they might otherwise be. Another consequence is that police officers find this kind of work frustrating and of little real worth. Yet, the effective resolution of a human crisis can be a highly important task that is deeply valued by citizens. The police need to systematize their handling of such situations, consistent with our knowledge of what is most effective. Our knowledge of what works best must itself advance through further research by social scientists.

Community Service

The final role of the police in the United States is the performance of a variety of services for the community. These services include directing traffic, providing first aid, assisting people locked out of their homes, working with dependent and neglected children, locating missing persons, rendering medical and rescue services, and helping those who are inebriated (Bent and Rossum, 1976, p. 5; Wilson, 1968, p. 4). Unfortunately, many tend to ignore the police's service role and to evaluate police performance only in terms of law enforcement (and perhaps order maintenance). Yet, some very important services are provided by police departments. As Bernard Garmire notes, the police act "as a social agency of last resort—particularly after 5:00 P.M. and on weekends. . . ." (1972, p. 4) Across the globe a tremendous difference among police departments can be observed in the extent and variety of services performed. For example, the police in Denmark are responsible for performing a broad range of services (Bent and Rossum, 1976, p. 16). These include matters relating to fire brigades, health authority, trade, conscription, approval of divorces, child custody, alimony payments, paternity cases, adoptions, name changes, and motor vehicle registration and taxation. Surely, there is nothing inevitable about the functions assigned to a police department.

Given the current orientation of most officers toward crime fighting, police officers generally get little satisfaction out of their role as providers of community services. In fact, the President's Commission on Law Enforcement and Administration of Justice has suggested: "It might be desirable for agencies other than the police to provide community services that bear no relationship to crime or potential crime situations." (President's Commission, 1967a, p. 14) Some evidence suggests that the multitude of police roles contributes to fatigue and frustration on the part of the police (Rubin, 1972, pp. 13–16). According to this evidence, police effectiveness would improve markedly if the police specialized in certain functions.

One suggestion is that the police force be divided into peace officers (who would handle community service and order maintenance) and law enforcement officers (who would deal with crime fighting). This has been called the "split force" patrol concept (Tien, Simon, and Larson, 1978). Jesse Rubin notes: "If police roles can be clarified, simplified and specialized, men can be recruited and trained specifically for each role." (1972, p. 40) For example, peace officers might receive a heavy dose of training in personal counseling to help them deal with family disputes. Properly trained and motivated, the police might not leave a family dispute feeling they had wasted their time. A divided, specialized police force might produce the twin benefits of more effective services for the public and more job satisfaction for members of the force.[8] It must be kept in mind, however, that the job of policing is inherently difficult. Police officers must make some quick decisions in situations which are highly ambiguous. Research has discovered no magic potions which will dramatically increase the effectiveness of the police.

DISCRETION

Underenforcement and Overenforcement

The police exercise a great deal of discretion in the course of their work. In examining police discretion, we find the dual phenomena of police underenforcement and overenforcement of the law. Sometimes police officers will ignore violations of the law that they learn of or observe. At other times the police may falsely accuse someone of violating a law. While the former phenomenon is more common in the United States, both exist and raise some rather serious implications. When a police officer acts or fails to act against a citizen, there is a great deal at stake. As Erika Fairchild observes: "Nowhere in government is the use of discretion of more intense concern . . . than in

---

[8]An eighteen-month experiment was conducted by the Wilmington Bureau of Police to determine the efficacy of the split-force concept. The results of that experiment were generally positive—this is in spite of the failure in that experiment to provide specialized training for the separate divisions so that they could better perform their more narrowly defined duties. For a report of the findings see Tien et al. (1978).

the criminal justice system where the power of the state is aligned against the individual, who faces the possibility of loss of life, liberty, property, esteem, and future earning power. . . ." (Fairchild, 1978, p. 442) Those who are falsely accused of a crime may suffer serious losses, even if they are later vindicated. On the other hand, when the police fail to act against a lawbreaker, it is unlikely that the individual will ever be punished for committing the offense.

Theoretically, the police are supposed to arrest anyone who has violated the law (Wilson, 1968, p. 7; LaFave, 1965, pp. 75–82). Full enforcement is often heralded as a worthy goal. Yet, the police do not simply apply the law in a mechanical manner; underenforcement is common. Herbert Jacob suggests: "Even if all the preconditions are met—the victim complains, the police find the offender, and the crime falls within the category that the police actively pursue—policemen still enjoy considerable discretion in making the arrest." (1978, p. 170) The police underenforce the law when they release a drunk and disorderly person, fail to charge a juvenile, issue only a warning to speeding drivers, arrange for release of an addict in exchange for information, or ignore Sunday blue laws (Goldstein, 1963). Overenforcement of the law occurs when police officers "plant" evidence on a suspect, provoke disorderly conduct from a "wise guy" so that charges may be filed, or use illegal means to obtain evidence. Police discretion is important even after the decision to make or not make an arrest (Jacob, 1978, p. 171). It is, after all, the responsibility of the police to select the charges which will be made against the suspect. In making this decision, the police officer is doing no less than defining the seriousness of the incident which has occurred. From the broad range of alternatives, the choices made by the police will have critical implications for the character of the proceedings which follow.

Discretion in the criminal justice system is inevitable. Conceivably, police officers can make an arrest whenever they discover an apparent violation of the law. If such a police policy was adopted, far more people would be charged with crimes. However, unless we were willing at the same time to increase drastically the number of those labeled "criminal," it would be necessary for prosecutors or judges to exercise increased discretion by dismissing more cases. In our existing system of justice, enormous discretion is exercised by the police. Most commonly, police officers choose not to enforce the law even though they feel certain that technically the law has been violated. This underenforcement helps explain the animosity of the police toward prosecutors and judges when additional cases are subsequently dismissed. The police have had firsthand experience with the suspects and feel that further dismissals are almost always unwarranted.

Reasons for Police Discretion

Why is it that so much discretion is exercised by the police? Researchers have identified a number of reasons for the enormous amount of police discretion which prevails. To begin with, discretion is needed because there are a vast number of laws in our society. In fact, there are so many criminal laws that it would be unreasonable (as well as impossible) to enforce all of them all the time. Full enforcement of all laws would place an enormous strain on the criminal justice system. It would also drastically increase the numbers of people who have been charged and convicted of a criminal offense. In addition, criminal statutes in our country are often general, ambiguous, or obsolete. As a result, the police choose not to enforce the law under all circumstances. Sometimes laws are intentionally general and ambiguous so as to provide the police with greater flexibility (Goldstein, 1963, p. 141). At other times ambiguity of laws may be due to a lack of legislative foresight, the need for compromise in order to pass a law, or the limits of language.

Police discretion is also associated with the limited amount of personnel and resources of police departments. As Charles Breitel notes: "A society can only pay so much for protection. It cannot put a policeman on every street corner." (1960, p. 431) Given the presence of countless statutes but limited resources, the police must be selective as to which statutes will be enforced. Time spent enforcing Sunday blue laws is time that cannot be spent looking for thieves. The low visibility of the police also contributes to their discretion, since supervisors cannot put police officers under surveillance so as to monitor and direct their activities. As James Eisenstein concludes: "Given low visibility, it is impossible to force patrolmen to adhere strictly to specific standards of behavior. Much of what an officer on patrol does he does on his own with tremendous discretion." (1973, p. 93)

Another important factor contributing to police discretion is the ambiguity of the incidents encountered by the police. For example, police officers may be called upon to deal with a marital squabble which led to violence. Faced with such a situation, a police officer has the option of defining the incident either as a criminal violation necessitating an arrest or as a private family quarrel (Jacob, 1973, p. 27). The meaning the police attach to incidents is almost as significant as the very incidents themselves. A final factor associated with police discretion is that neither legislators nor the public would tolerate full enforcement of the laws at all times (Goldstein, 1963, p. 142). In many cases there is an expectation by the community that enforcement of the law will not be rigid. No one wants a nation of criminals. Often the main purpose of the legislation is to express community values rather than lead to police activity.

Because of the enormity of police discretion, there have been many efforts at imposing external controls. The aim of such controls is to prevent the police from exercising discretion. Examples of external control include court decisions, statutes, and rules set by police administrators. A number of possible police actions have been banned by the Supreme Court (Bent and Rossum, 1976, p. 97). Supreme Court activity in this area reflects the fact that thirteen of the twenty-three rights contained in the first eight amendments deal with criminal procedure. Still, police compliance with Supreme Court directives is far from complete.[9] Moreover, the Court has left an enormous range of police discretion untouched—not only in order-maintenance incidents but in law enforcement situations as well. In this regard legislative statutes are not entirely helpful, since they are often highly ambiguous. The police, in any case, do not fully enforce the law. Finally, police administrators also impose some limits on the discretion of their officers. Control is especially evident regarding the enforcement of traffic laws. Wide variation exists across communities in the number of traffic tickets issued. This variation can largely be explained by differences across cities in the orientation of police administrators. At the same time, there are countless situations where it would be exceedingly difficult for administrators to supply rules to patrol officers (Wilson, 1968, Ch. 3). Indeed, the formalization of certain rules—such as who does or does not look "suspicious"—would violate our basic tenets of equal treatment.

Exercising Discretion

Perhaps the most crucial question relating to police discretion concerns the criteria used by the police when exercising discretion. Of course, we expect the police to use some discretion when dealing with possible violations of the law. For example, if police officers concluded upon investigation that the evidence in a case was inadequate, we would expect them to decide to drop the matter. While few quarrel with the proper exercise of police discretion, the issue is not always uncontroversial. For example, the police are more likely to be suspicious of a disadvantaged individual. This suspicious attitude among police officers colors their exercise of discretion. More generally, research on police discretion has identified five factors which influence its exercise. These include external characteristics, police characteristics, the nature of the offense, the attributes of suspects, and the complainant's characteristics.

To begin with, certain external characteristics help explain police discretion. These include court rulings, statutes, departmental influences, and community pressures. For example, the court-imposed requirement that suspects be informed of their rights when arrested has surely had some influence on police behavior toward suspects. Of course, this does not mean that the police universally adhere to the *Miranda* rules (Medalie, Zeitz, and Alexander, 1968). Still, the courts clearly have some capacity to influence police discretion. It is also true that the norms of a police department regarding productivity affect the exercise of discretion by police (Wilson, 1968, Ch. 4). On occasion police are even guilty of "overenforcing" the law to meet the department's production standards, as by planting evidence on suspects police officers feel are really guilty (Bent and Rossum, 1976, p. 69). Another external characteristic influencing police activity is the nature of the community. For example, the

[9]For some case studies see Theodore L. Becker, ed., *The Impact of Supreme Court Decisions* (New York: Oxford University Press, 1969).

police departments of homogeneous middle-class communities generally emphasize providing services (Wilson, 1968, Ch. 7).

Second, certain police characteristics influence discretionary behavior. Indeed, the aim of police selection and training procedures is to influence the responses of the officers on the street. Suspiciousness on the part of the police is an important characteristic influencing their exercise of discretion. The police believe that suspicion is their most effective investigatory tool. For example, police officers are warned to be suspicious of persons wearing a coat on hot days, uniformed "deliverymen" with no merchandise on their truck, and "lovers" in an industrial area who may really be lookouts for a crime (Adams, 1963). Unfortunately, in exercising their discretion, the suspiciousness of the police often becomes intertwined with their negative attitudes toward minorities. James Q. Wilson observes: "The line between prejudging them [minorities] purely on the basis of police experience and prejudging them on the basis of personal opinion (showing 'prejudice') is often very thin." (1968, p. 38)

Third, the nature of the offense influences police discretion. In particular, the police will exercise more discretion in offenses that are less serious and less public (Jacob, 1973, p. 27). Officers who become aware of minor traffic violations, drunkenness, petty gambling, and minor fights will generally opt to ignore them. On the other hand, the police are more constrained in the exercise of discretion when a crime is serious or occurs in public. The concentration of police officers on highly visible crime works to the detriment of poor people, since the poor live a greater part of their lives in the open and on the street (Baker, 1971, p. 355). It is also true that the police, at times, will make a conscious decision to focus on certain types of offenses. For example, a rash of liquor store robberies may lead to increased surveillance of such stores in the affected areas (Baker, 1971, pp. 354–355).

Fourth, the suspect's characteristics have an effect on the discretion exercised by the police. Both the suspect's background characteristics and behavior toward the police are relevant. A disadvantaged person is more likely to be stopped, arrested, and treated harshly than a middle-class person. The police believe that they would be neglecting their duties if they did not treat teenagers, blacks, and low-income people with suspicion (Wilson, 1968, pp. 40–41). The police also take cues from the responses of suspects. A nervous, evasive, disrespectful response is more likely to lead to an arrest (Baker, 1971, pp. 355–356). "Wise guys" are treated by police with special harshness (Van Maanen, 1978, p. 224). Because of their deep-seated hostility toward police, the disadvantaged are more likely to respond to the police with negative cues.

Fifth, the complainant's characteristics influence discretionary behavior by the police (Black, 1970, p. 746; Jacob, 1973, p. 28). There is some evidence that the police discriminate in favor of white-collar complainants. In addition, the way that a complainant behaves when encountering police officers is also important. The police are more likely to make an arrest if the complainant insists that an arrest should be made. Moreover, a complainant who is deferential to the police will be more successful in bringing about an arrest. Finally, an arrest is also more likely if the suspect is not a close relative of the complainant.

ETHICS

Types of Police Malpractice

It is not unusual for workers to engage in wrongdoing while carrying out their jobs. Police are hardly immune from such malpractice. Moreover, unethical behavior by the police is no less important than malpractice by doctors, lawyers, judges, or other key occupational groups. Indeed, the President's Commission on Law Enforcement and Administration of Justice has noted: "Because the police are entrusted with the enforcement of the fundamental rules that guide society's conduct, a policeman's violation of the law or his corrupt failure to enforce it dishonors the law and the authority he represents." (President's Commission, 1967a, p. 208) Public confidence in the police, the criminal justice system, and government in general is undermined by unethical conduct among the police. Moreover, in many forms of police malpractice, there are individuals who are victimized, such as the citizen who is beaten or falsely accused of a crime. Not surprisingly, many forms of unethical behavior by the police have been declared illegal.

One form of police malpractice is lying in the course of enforcing the law. Paul Chevigny argues: "There can be no doubt that police lying is the most pervasive of all abuses." (1969, p. 141) In narcotics cases, for example, the police are sometimes guilty of illegally searching suspects, finding narcotics, and then later claiming that the narcotics were discovered when the suspect carelessly dropped them (Eisenstein, 1973, p. 229). The police officer who plants evidence on suspects, conducts an illegal search, or ignores violations of high-status citizens is guilty of unethical conduct. An informal experiment by F. K. Heussenstamm tested the willingness of police officers to press charges against political opponents (1971). Following a series of bloody encounters in Los Angeles between the police and members of the Black Panthers, Heussenstamm instructed fifteen student volunteers from California State College to place "Black Panther" bumper stickers on their cars. Clearly, the presence of a controversial bumper sticker on a car should not influence the exercise of police discretion. However, even though there was no prior record of traffic violations by any of the fifteen volunteers, they received thirty-three citations on the seventeen days the experiment was conducted. No participant escaped without a moving violation. The results of this experiment pose some serious implications, both for procedural justice and personal liberty.

Brutality, both verbal and physical, is another form of police malpractice. The use of force may be necessary in the course of police work. Yet, citizens may rightly feel abused if a police officer uses unnecessary force against them. Evidently, physical force is rare in ordinary encounters between police officers and suspects. Albert Reiss observed "undue force" in only 37 of 3,826 police-citizen encounters he witnessed (1968, pp. 15-16). Even so, beatings and clubbings sometimes do occur. One well-known incident occurred during the 1968 Democratic Convention, where the Chicago police engaged in unrestrained and indiscriminate violence against peaceful demonstrators, onlookers, and residents in the streets (Walker, 1968). Still, disrespect and verbal abuse are far more common forms of police brutality. Louis Radelet suggests that verbal abuses "are rampant in police-citizen encounters. . . . Frequently, 'communication' between police officer and citizen is in the rhetoric of racism or profanity." (1977, p. 300) Not surprisingly, evidence suggests that the victims of police brutality tend to be from low-income groups (Reiss, 1968, p. 16).

A third form of police malpractice is material corruption. This takes several forms (Barker and Roebuck, 1973, Ch. 4). Police officers sometimes accept gratuities from business persons or citizens, such as free meals, rooms, sex, and liquor. In addition, officers may receive kickbacks from towing companies, taxis, service stations, moving companies, and trucking firms. The police have also stolen unprotected or confiscated property. Further, the police may be paid for protecting illegal activities by both legitimate and illegitimate firms. Another example of police corruption is "the fix," in which a police officer accepts a bribe for helping to quash a criminal prosecution. Direct criminal activities—including organized burglary, extortion, or narcotics—also occur. Finally, internal payments within a department sometimes take place, in which a police officer purchases illegal favors from another officer. Investigating police corruption in New York City, the Knapp Commission found evidence of widespread corruption among both detectives and patrol officers (Knapp Commission, 1976). The Commission found that most police officers are "grass-eaters" who accept payoffs which come their way (Knapp Commission, 1976, pp. 4, 65-66). A few police officers are "meat-eaters" who aggressively misuse their police powers for personal gain. While most police officers do not deal in huge amounts of graft, it may well be that "grass-eaters" are the heart of the problem, since their large numbers tend to make corruption "respectable" on the force.

Explaining Police Malpractice

A prominent explanation for police malpractice (often promulgated by police chiefs) is "the rotten apple theory." (Knapp Commission, 1976, pp. 6-7, Ch. 18) The theory notes, metaphorically, that even the best barrel of apples contains a few rotten apples. Hence, the rotten apple theory of police malpractice suggest that most police officers are highly ethical, and that ethical standards are violated by only a few officers. If instances of police malpractice do indeed result from a few rotten apples, as the theory suggests, the solution would be to remove these unethical police officers from the force. Nevertheless, the Knapp Commission's investigation of the New York City police force found evidence of widespread unethical conduct throughout the force. This strongly suggests that the rotten apple theory is inaccurate. Indeed, the Knapp Commission asserts that even those who articulated the theory realize that it is a deception. For two reasons police chiefs believe that it is necessary to be dishonest about unethical conduct by the police. First, chiefs believe that even though most police officers are themselves aware of the problem, official recognition of widespread police malpractice would harm morale on the force. Second, official recognition would cause the public image and effectiveness of the police to suffer substantially. Despite these concerns, the Knapp Commission suggested that realistic self-criticism can reduce unethical conduct by the police without serious ill-effects.

Given the shortcomings of the rotten apple theory, we must seek alternative explanations for police malpractice. It is reasonable to believe that the underlying basis for such a theory rests on the nature of police attitudes and the situations that the police face on the job. Specifically, it is evident that police lying, corruption, and brutality would be impossible were it not for the police's code of secrecy and their low visibility when carrying out their job. Given this context, a common aim of lying by the police is to make a "good pinch" and make it stick. Corruption by police can readily be explained in terms of material self-interest.

Regarding police brutality, a useful explanation has been offered by John Van Maanen (1978). He suggests that suspicious people and ordinary citizens are rarely victims of police brutality. Rather, recipients of verbal or physical abuse are usually "wise guys" who behave in a stupid or insulting manner. Wise guys question the police officer's authority, control, and definition of the situation (for example, "Why the hell are you picking on me and not somewhere else looking for some real criminals?"). (Van Maanen, 1978, p. 228) Suspicious persons are rarely abused because they generally cooperate with police. They want to present a normal appearance and avoid further difficulties. In short, police brutality is usually a response to a threat to police authority. Like lying and material corruption, police brutality is made possible by the secrecy and low visibility of police officers.

Controlling Police Malpractice

Those seeking to deal with police malpractice have focused on both internal and external controls. To date these approaches have met with little success. It is the desire of most police officers that disciplinary actions be handled exclusively through internal controls. Among the forms of internal controls are complaint procedures, investigations, hearings, and disciplinary policies (ABA, 1972, pp. 144–170). Despite their preference for internal controls, the police generally hold a dim view of the officers assigned to the internal investigation division. In fact, it is common for these officers to be ostracized by the rest of the force. Perhaps the chief reason for the ineffectiveness of internal controls is the code of secrecy adhered to by the police. Obviously, investigations into malpractice can make little headway when faced with dead silence. A related difficulty is that citizens can file a complaint against a police officer only at their own risk. The individual who files a complaint against a police officer runs the risk of being charged with a misdemeanor such as filing a false report or resisting arrest (Bent, 1974, p. 76; Chevigny, 1969, Ch. 14). Paul Chevigny argues that only a frontal attack on police secrecy will be effective in dealing with police malpractice (1969, pp. 273–275). According to Chevigny, the police force needs leaders who will not cover up abuses as an expression of solidarity with the force. Chevigny suggests that rather than simply rising through the ranks, officers be required to receive specialized training.

A number of external controls also exist in practice and in theory. A free press can expose incidents of misconduct, thereby creating pressure for reform (Bent, 1974, p. 73). However, most police reporters are on permanent assignment. Since they rely on police officers for information, police reporters must ignore many damaging stories in order to maintain friendly relations. Second, it is possible for individual citizens to go to court and seek tort damages against the police (Chevigny, 1969, pp. 254–258). These efforts are generally unsuccessful, since judges and juries rarely show sympathy for a guilty, even if abused, plaintiff (President's Commission, 1967a, p. 31).

Another external control is the civilian review board. This is an independent committee of citizens empowered to review the way that police departments have processed citizen complaints (ABA, 1972, pp. 160–163; Bent, 1974, pp. 72–73; Hudson, 1972). Still, there are many problems with such review boards (Radelet, 1977, pp. 292–295). Experimental review boards in Philadelphia and elsewhere experienced problems of publicity, staffing, budget, and limited powers. In addition, civilian review boards can be criticized as symbolizing and assuming conflict between the public and the police. Moreover, police opposition to civilian review boards has been a significant roadblock in the way of their effectiveness and, in most communities, their very existence. Finally, some suggest appointing an ombudsman—a person or office that is empowered to deal with all kinds of administrative abuses, including those involving the police (Bent and Rossum, 1976, pp. 224–225). The ombudsman investigates complaints and can even launch personally initiated inquiries. The aim of this official is to reform through public criticism and to obtain compensation for those who have been harmed. There has been some success with the ombudsman system in Canada and various Scandinavian countries (Stacey, 1978, pp. 59–60; Gellhorn, 1966). While there are no easy answers to the problem of police malpractice, creating the office of ombudsman might be of some benefit.

COMMUNITY RELATIONS

PCR Programs

Police-community relations refers to "the reciprocal attitudes of police and civilians." (Radelet, 1977, p. 22) The aim of police-community relations efforts is to achieve mutual understanding and trust, with a view toward preventing lawlessness and disorder. It is essential for the police to maintain positive relations with the community. Citizen participation is crucial to effective performance by the police and the overall criminal justice system. As Alan Bent and Ralph Rossum note: "It is the citizens who are the major reporters of crime, witnesses of crime, and accusers of wrongdoers; they are the information sources that set in motion the criminal justice process." (1976, p. 25) Apart from that, citizens may be more likely to observe the law if they have positive attitudes toward the police and the legal system. Public relations efforts by the police may be helpful in this regard. Finally, many police-community relations efforts have been specifically directed toward the ghetto with a view toward preventing riots. Studies indicate that negative attitudes toward the police among black youths were a major factor in the disorders of the 1960s (Kerner Commission, 1968, Chaps. 2, 11). It is hoped that PCR programs can alleviate the stresses and strains between black civilians and members of the force.

When thinking about police-community relations, it is important to realize that most Americans have either neutral or positive attitudes toward police (Wilson, 1972, pp. 53–60). Most members of the force would be astonished to learn that relatively few Americans hold them in disregard. Police officers believe that they are confronted with a hostile, unappreciative public. To a large extent this perception results from the biased nature of police-citizen contacts. The police come into greatest contact with the very people who have the least favorable attitudes toward them. In particular, the police are held in low regard by young black men (Wilson, 1972, pp. 55–56). Overall, about 30 percent of the public have negative attitudes toward the police. Many of these citizens report that they personally experienced insulting police language, an unreasonable search, or a roughing up. Blacks are more likely to see the police as corrupt, unfair, excitable, harsh, tough, weak, lazy, less intelligent, less friendly, and more cruel (Jacob, 1971, p. 73). Another reason why blacks are critical of the police is that blacks feel that the police provide them with inadequate protection. Finally, blacks perceive the police as a symbol of a society that has treated minorities unjustly (Bent, 1974, p. 43). Whites, on the other hand, dismiss charges of police bigotry (Levy, 1968). The most positive attitudes toward police come from the white middle class (Jacob, 1971, p. 73).

Most departments have dealt with the problem of police-community relations by creating special units within the department. Three components which generally make up a city's police-community relations efforts have been identified by Bent and Rossum (1976, pp. 300–320; Radelet, 1977, pp. 26–27).

These programs are designed to enhance the police image, reduce tensions, and enable the police to improve their effectiveness. First, the public relations approach seeks to use the news media to create a favorable climate of opinion about the police. The main thrust of this effort is to maintain positive contacts with key media personnel and civic leaders. Examples of this approach in action include television appearances, public speakers' bureaus, guided tours of police facilities, cruiser tours (that is, citizens riding in patrol cars), and public relations programs (for example, "Lock Your Car"). Second, the community service approach focuses on providing needed services for various groups. Specific efforts include citizen crime prevention programs, coaching athletic teams, operation handshake (that is, police rookies visiting in high-crime areas), rumor control centers, and alcohol and narcotics education projects. Third, advocacy planning is also carried out as a means of improving police-community relations. Such programs attempt to coordinate police, citizen, and agency efforts to deal with community problems. This may involve police officers acting as advocates for various group needs vis-à-vis government bureaucracies. Examples include citywide advisory committees, meetings with neighborhood advisory committees, gatherings with committees of minority group leaders, and police-community workshops.

There is reason to believe, however, that police-community relations will not be appreciably affected by special programs such as "Officer Friendly," the "Police Athletic League," or "Operation Lone Women." As David Bordua and Larry Tifft argue: "No matter how good these programs are, the officers on the beat are the ones that count." (1971, p. 156; Scaglion and Condon, 1980) If daily contacts between the police and citizens are the key to good police-community relations, it is essential that we identify specific police actions that are upsetting to the public. For example, Bordua and Tifft found that the way the police approach citizens in patrol contacts strongly affects how citizens feel about the incident afterwards (1971). Smith and Hawkins suggest as well that general police on-duty behavior (for example, failure to obey traffic rules) is an important factor in public attitudes toward the police (1973).

The Kerner Commission called for sweeping limitations on police discretion, including recommendations on (1) when if ever a police officer should order the break-up of a street gathering, (2) how to deal with minor disputes, (3) whether to arrest in specific situations, (4) selection and use of investigative methods such as frisking, (5) how to handle demonstrations, (6) appropriate use of physical force, and (7) the proper way of addressing citizens (1968). Others have suggested that the key to better police-community relations lies in changing the recruitment policy and attitudes of members of the force. Indirectly, this would alter on-the-job responses of members of the force. Finally, James Q. Wilson argues that what may be needed is an increased number of police personnel (1972, p. 82). Where there is a large police force, crime might be so deterred that aggressive investigation by the police would be required less frequently.

Police Politicization

Another aspect of the relationship between the police and the larger community is police activity in the political process (Bent, 1974, pp. 76–87). A survey by Allan Hamann and Rebecca Becker documents the fact that many cities impose stringent restraints on political activity by police officers (Hamann and Becker, 1970). These include bans on running for political office, campaigning for candidates, and even contributing campaign funds. Yet, members of the force are increasingly frustrated, alienated, and angry. More and more, the police are not satisfied simply to act as enforcers of the law. Increasingly, the police are also trying to exercise political power to influence the content of these laws. The effort is being made largely through police unions, guilds, and social organizations. Nearly 60 percent of police officers are members of a police organization that is associated with a national organization such as the Fraternal Order of Police (Salerno, 1981, p. 37).

Like other trade unions, one objective of the police in the political arena is simply higher pay or other benefits. More militant unions have engaged in slowdowns, "blu flu," and strikes (Gentel and Handman, 1979; Halpern, 1974; Salerno, 1981; Stang, 1969). Following the famous Boston police strike in 1919, over fifty years elapsed before another police strike occurred in a major American city. In the next few years, however, a wave of strikes took place, touching New York, San Francisco, and numerous other cities. While strikers may win pay raises, a police strike may create serious antagonism between the police and both city officials and the community. Apart from trade union demands, police organizations have also sought to defeat civilian review board proposals (Halpern, 1974). Association leaders see review boards as a serious threat to police autonomy. Clearly, the police have had substantial success in blocking the adoption and retention of these external controls. The police have also been politically active in the sense of joining conservative organizations and engaging in electoral politics (Lipset, 1969). Members of the force have also engaged in "court-watching" and in efforts to limit the control of command officers. Some observers are disturbed at the prospect of a politically active, internally autonomous police force in a democratic society (Bent, 1974, pp. 76–87).

AN ASSESSMENT

The police have many problems. Many of their difficulties in enforcing the law stem from the inherent problems of policing a nation that has a large crime problem and yet is protective of personal liberty. Even under the best of social circumstances, policing is a difficult task. Police officers must make some quick decisions in highly ambiguous, sometimes dangerous, situations. At the same time, many problems faced by the police in our society are internal ones. The social backgrounds of police officers may lead to discriminatory behavior when the officers exercise discretion. Moreover, police training is both minimal and ineffective. The police do not yet possess a systematic body of knowledge on how best to enforce the law or maintain order. Nor do the police specialize as "peace officers" or "law enforcement officers" in order to take advantage of the knowledge about policing which does exist. Almost inherent in policing is enormous discretion. Police administrators cannot keep a watchful eye upon on-duty policemen. Unfortunately, some discretion is exercised unjustly (as shown by the greater tendency of the police to be suspicious of someone who is disadvantaged). The low visibility of the police also contributes to unethical behavior on their part. There is far too much lying, brutality, and material corruption on the police force. The common police response—PCR programs—is hardly adequate to the task. What the police need is to improve the quality of their performance on the job. This is a matter of some urgency. After all, the police are assigned the duty of enforcing our criminal laws and sending suspects to prosecutors and judges for further action through the criminal justice system. As we have seen, the police also have important responsibilities in maintaining social order and providing needed services. Unfortunately, research on the police and crime has not uncovered any simple solutions to these problems.

QUESTIONS FOR DISCUSSION

1. How might you change as a person if you became a police officer? Would you be more suspicious of blacks than of other citizens? Of teenagers? What if you got a B.A. in liberal arts before joining a police force?

2. If police are supposed to prevent crime, why do cities with more police officers have more crime? How effective are the police in preventing crime and catching criminals? What steps could be taken to increase the effectiveness of the police in law enforcement?

3. Do police officers exercise too much discretion when deciding whether or not to arrest a suspect? Are there times when police officers are unfair in the way they exercise discretion? Why don't police administrators reduce the discretion of police officers by exercising increased supervision?

4. What are the major forms of unethical conduct by the police? What factors contribute to the extent of police misconduct? Why isn't police misconduct punished more often and more harshly? If a police department could virtually eliminate unethical conduct by police officers, to what extent would police-community relations be affected?

FOR FURTHER READING

GOLDSTEIN, ARNOLD P. ET AL. *Police Crisis Intervention.* Kalamazoo, Mich.: Behaviordelia, 1977. Spells out some specific techniques that can enable the police to handle order maintenance situations more effectively.

KELLING, GEORGE ET AL. *The Kansas City Preventive Patrol Experiment: Summary Report.* Washington, D.C.: Police Foundation, 1974. Summarizes the much-discussed experiment on the effectiveness of preventive patrol in stopping crime.

PRESIDENT'S COMMISSION ON LAW ENFORCEMENT AND ADMINISTRATION OF JUSTICE. *Task Force Report: The Police.* Washington, D.C.: USGPO, 1967. An important and frequently cited analysis of the police and policing conducted by a presidential commission.

SKOLNICK, JEROME. *Justice Without Trial.* New York: John Wiley, 1966. An excellent study of police personality and behavior.

WILSON, JAMES Q. *Varieties of Police Behavior.* Cambridge, Mass.: Harvard University Press, 1968. A classic in the study of police discretion and how police roles vary among communities.

3
LAWYERS

PREVIEW

Chapter Three deals with lawyers. The legal profession plays a critical function in the processing of both civil and criminal cases. Our discussion contains five sections:

> Members of the bar
> Roles
> Service distribution
> Ethics
> Community relations

First, we examine several personal characteristics of members of the bar, including their backgrounds, training, attitudes, and professionalism. The high status and extensive training of attorneys will be emphasized. Second, we examine the varied roles of lawyers—counseling, negotiation, drafting, litigating, investigating, and researching. The effectiveness of private attorneys in carrying out these roles varies substantially. Many lawyers, of course, are not in private practice but instead are employed by government. Key judicial personnel such as judges, prosecutors, and public defenders come from the legal profession. Members of the bar also serve as legislators and bureaucrats. Third, we will discuss the distribution of legal services. Only a small portion of the disputes occurring in society come to the attention of attorneys. There are a variety of reasons why legal services are not used in certain cases. These include not only the low income of victims but also the orientation of the bar toward property concerns and the failure of some victims to discuss their problems with a third person, who might urge the use of a lawyer. Fourth, the chapter treats ethical misconduct by attorneys. Lawyers have an elaborate system of rules regarding ethics. Unfortunately, ethical violations are common—particularly among lawyers whose clients are low in status. Finally, we focus on community relations, including the issue of legal advertising.

MEMBERS OF THE BAR

Attorneys in America have certain identifiable personal characteristics. Here we will focus on their background, training, attitudes, and professionalism. From the outset it is important to realize that lawyers in the United States are found in many different settings (Jacob, 1978, pp. 71-76; Jacob, 1973, pp. 40-42). Lawyers are traditionally pictured as solo practitioners who deal with a wide variety of cases. Other attorneys belong to small firms, numbering about a dozen members. Like solo practitioners, these firms handle many different kinds of cases and clients. Another group of attorneys belong to large firms containing dozens, or even hundreds, of attorneys. Increased firm size permits individual lawyers to specialize in a small area of the law, gaining expertise and skill. Large firms perform complicated work for corporate clients and wealthy individuals. Finally, some attorneys are house counsel, or salaried employees of corporations, nonprofit institutions, and government agencies. Some large corporations contain huge legal departments that service their legal needs. While such lawyers are often highly competent, they do not have the prestige of attorneys who work in large private firms.

Background

It has been said that when asked the ages of her young grandchildren, the upwardly mobile grandmother will respond: "The doctor is four and the lawyer is two." Lawyers are part of the occupational elite of American society (Hodge, Siegel, and Rossi, 1964).[1] It is not surprising then that parents and grandparents would want their children to join those ranks. Attorneys' income, on the average, is considerably higher than that of the police. Like doctors, the nearly 535,000 members of the bar enjoy both high status and high income. The typical income of lawyers in the United States is well above

---

[1]In the survey ranking ninety occupations, lawyers were tied for tenth to twelfth place. U. S. Supreme Court justices ranked highest in occupational prestige and shoe shiners lowest.

the national median, though clearly not nearly as high as that of physicians. Attorneys' incomes tend to be highest among those who are partners in a firm, who have many years of experience, and who specialize in areas such as labor law, insurance law, and taxation (Weil and Bower, 1980).

Lawyers do not, in their social background, comprise a random cross-section of the American public. Social background helps to determine the likelihood of one's becoming a lawyer. For example, Jerome Carlin found that nearly all New York City lawyers are native-born white males (1966, pp. 18–19). A disproportionate number come from higher social backgrounds. Looking at a small city's bar, Joel Handler found the social characteristics of lawyers to be even more homogeneous (1967, p. 67). One critic of the lack of demographic representativeness in the bar, Robert Knauss, has called for stepped-up efforts along the lines of affirmative action (1976). He notes that nationally, only about one percent of lawyers are black. At the same time, an increasing number of women are now graduating from law school (ABA, 1979).[2] Knauss suggests that a more heterogeneous bar would contribute to a greater diversity of outlook, closer public identification with the bar and confidence in it, and the delivery of legal services to those now neglected. Other observers insist, however, that access to a professional career should be based solely on considerations of ability, without any special effort expended to make the bar more demographically representative.

A court case that bears upon the unrepresentative character of the professions is *University of California v. Bakke.* In this highly publicized case the Supreme Court dealt with the issue of admissions to professional school. Allan Bakke had been denied admission to the University of California at Davis because some of the openings had been specifically reserved for minorities. Bakke sued, claiming that because of this "reverse discrimination," his right to equal protection had been violated. The decision of the Court was to strike down the Davis program and order that Bakke be admitted. However, the Court did not rule that universities were forbidden to engage in affirmative action of any kind. Rather, the Court suggested that affirmative action, in forms other than quotas, is permissible. While the *Bakke* case dealt with admissions to medical school, it has obvious applications to law school, since minorities are highly underrepresented there as well. However, even though the Court has *permitted* affirmative action in professional school admissions programs, it has not taken the more substantial step of *requiring* colleges to make use of affirmative action.

Still, in many respects the bar in America is far from homogeneous. As John York and Rosemary Hale observe: "It has long been known that, as measured by dispersion of incomes, law is among the riskiest of professions." (1973, p. 16) The high income and high status of the bar as a whole masks a

---

[2]The number of women lawyers increased from 2.8 percent of all lawyers in 1970 to 7.5 percent in 1980. See *American Bar Association Journal,* 1981, *67,* 1098–1099.

substantial variation in economic and social standing. A lawyer might well attain an annual income of several times the national median. Yet, it is likewise quite possible that an attorney's income will be well below the national median. The degree of variation in attorney income itself varies according to city size. Large metropolitan areas—such as New York, Chicago, Washington, and Detroit—have far more stratification in their respective bars than do small cities (Carlin, 1966; Carlin, 1962; Green, 1975; Ladinsky, 1963; Handler, 1967). In large metropolitan areas stratification among lawyers is rigid, with large-firm lawyers at the apex and solo practitioners forming an underclass. There is little mobility from bottom to top and minimal contact between high- and low-status attorneys. In small cities stratification among lawyers is considerably less pronounced.

The stratification of the American bar is not solely due to differences in innate ability among lawyers. Success in the bar no doubt depends on several factors. Presumably, lawyers with more innate ability will be more successful. Yet, the bar is clearly not a rigid meritocracy—there is not a one-to-one relationship between competence and success. As Jerold Auerbach observes: "There are significant differences among lawyers which, the evidence suggests, are neither random nor necessarily meritocratic." (1976, p. 3) Similarly, Jack Ladinsky's study of the Detroit bar suggests that social background plays an important role in the career of an attorney (1963, pp. 52–53). Ladinsky found that social background has a strong influence both on educational attainment and access to the best clients. These factors, in turn, indirectly affect the success a lawyer will have. Professional differentiation within the bar is associated with race, ethnicity, religion, class, sex, and educational opportunity. At the upper end of the bar most of those in large firms have favorable social backgrounds, high incomes, and corporate or affluent clients (Carlin, 1966, pp. 22–24). Solo practitioners have less favorable social backgrounds and lower incomes, and they represent the lowest-status clients. Even in smaller communities lawyers from minority religious groups may be faced with a limited choice of clientele. In "Prairie City," a small city in Illinois, Handler found that no Catholic or Jewish attorneys represented the biggest business clients (1967, p. 67).

Training

Those wishing to enter the bar in the United States must undergo rigorous training in a law school and pass a formal examination (Jacob, 1978, pp. 48–54; Harno, 1960). Such strict entry requirements are a twentieth-century phenomenon. Throughout the nineteenth century lawyers generally learned legal skills through an apprenticeship in a law office. To be sure, some law schools could be found. The Litchfield School of Law, the first in America, was created in 1784. The Harvard Law School was established soon after in 1817. Yet, even after the Civil War only a small portion of prospective lawyers attended law school. Apprentices who felt adequately trained would ask a judge for admittance into practice and then set out on their own. Such a standard for entry into the legal profession was relatively lax, since the most lenient or charitable judge in a state could set the professional standards for the entire state.

The American Bar Association (ABA), organized in 1878, developed a major interest in the tightening of entrance requirements to the legal profession. Joined by state bars, the ABA was concerned both that unqualified attorneys were being admitted into practice and that easy entry to the profession increased competition among lawyers. Bar organization efforts focused on improving law school education and requiring applicants to pass a standardized bar examination. Elihu Root of the ABA's "Section of Legal Education and Admissions to the Bar" was instrumental in these efforts. As a result, admission requirements to law schools have been tightened, the period of training lengthened, and the curriculum redesigned. In addition, a bar exam is now held in every state—either for all applicants to the bar or for those who failed to attend a state-approved school. Finally, some states are now requiring that lawyers take continuing legal education courses throughout their careers.[3]

With the decline of the apprenticeship method of legal training, law schools have become an essential part of an attorney's education. There are now 169 law schools in the United States that have been approved by the American Bar Association (ABA, 1979). Legal education in the United States was strongly influenced by Christopher Langdell, whose career at Harvard started in 1870. The case method of studying law is a Langdell invention. With this method law students—particularly in their first year—study appellate court decisions in their classes. Classroom discussion is a dialogue, using the Socratic method. Students come to class prepared (in varying degrees) to field questions from their law professor on a group of appellate decisions assigned for the day.

Langdell saw the case method as introducing science to the study of law, with the library serving as the law student's laboratory. Through library study the student could analyze the past decisions upon which future judicial decisions would be grounded. A student who could "think like a lawyer" would be able to predict the future decisions of judges in a line of cases. In this way prospective lawyers would gain the skills needed to guide their clients toward most effectively dealing with legal problems. The Langdell method differs vastly from most college courses, where students are simply expected to absorb their professor's lectures and assigned readings. Certainly, it would be possible to redesign law school courses along the lines of undergraduate education. The Langdell method also differs enormously from its law school predecessor. Formerly, law schools offered lectures by practicing lawyers and judges on in-

[3]Commentary, "Once You're In: Maintaining Competence in the Bar," *Nebraska Law Review*, 1977, *56*, 676–691.

vented disputes between a mythical Flavius and Titus. Martin Mayer concludes that Langdell's method has made legal education more realistic and less abstract through the use of facts and decisions from actual cases rather than treatises and generalizations of book writers (1967, pp. 80–81).

Even so, the nature of legal education in the United States has come under sharp attack from some quarters. A provocative analysis of American law schools has been offered by John Bonsignore (1977). His remarks relate Erving Goffman's *Asylums* to the law school setting. Goffman's work examines the ways in which "total institutions"—such as prisons, the military, and mental institutions—exert control over participants and crowd out alternative values and identities (1961). In a total institution the "home world" of an individual comes to be replaced by the "institutional world." This occurs through a process of "identity stripping" in which entrants to an institution are intentionally mortified by those in charge through a series of abasements, degradations, and humiliations. According to Bonsignore, the law school can be seen as a "total institution." Law school can exert an enormous influence over the values and modes of thought of law students. Bonsignore suggests that the Socratic method is used by teachers to mortify law students.

The mortification process used in law schools literally serves to transform law students. They are forced to abandon their former selves and to be reborn, now thinking and acting like lawyers. Law students come "to accept the legal world view, the kinds of questions asked in law, and the way lawyers answer questions." (Bonsignore, 1977, p. 73) Consequently, law students learn that it is not a legal question to ask about the fairness of bargains; adequacy of consideration, they learn, is not significant in contract law. Jerold Auerbach, a historian and one-time law student, observes: "The more I learned how to think like a lawyer the less I wanted to become one. Legal education was designed to evade precisely those questions which, in my naiveté, I believed that lawyers should contemplate: Is it just? Is it fair? If not, how can law be utilized to make it so?" (1976, p. ix) One wonders whether law school must strip lawyers of the innate urge to give consideration to questions of justice and fairness in cases before them.[4] One must also wonder whether it is not possible to bring prospective lawyers into the legal world without identity-stripping through mortification.

Perhaps the most eloquent critique of law school is that by Jerome Frank (1947). In an article published in 1947 Frank asserted: "American legal education went badly wrong some seventy years ago when it was seduced by a brilliant neurotic." (p. 1303) In the article Frank refers to Langdell as "a cloistered, bookish man" who was unable to see the value of learning how to become a lawyer from lawyers. Law schools, according to Frank, ought

[4]On this see James C. Foster, "The 'Cooling Out' of Law Students," *Law and Policy Quarterly,* 1981, *3,* 243–256. Foster conducted interviews with first-year law students and detected some significant changes in their attitudes. One law school student remarked: "We talk about justice before we come here; we get here and we talk about jobs."

"unequivocally to repudiate Langdell's morbid repudiation of actual legal practice. . . ." (1947, p. 1313) Frank called for four basic reforms that would drastically overhaul the character of our law schools. First, Frank suggested that most law courses be taught by lawyers who have extensive experience in legal practice. Second, only a limited number of law school courses should review appellate decisions. As with the use of "case histories" in medical schools, other law school courses would include an elaborate treatment of a few cases. This would instruct students as to how cases are won or lost. Third, law students should visit trial and appellate courts on a regular basis, accompanied by their law teachers. Frank believed it essential that law students observe law in operation. Finally, Frank would want every law school to contain a legal clinic, staffed by the teachers and students of the law school. In this setting theory and practice would constantly interlace, providing law students with an excellent learning experience. In recent years law schools have, in fact, moved in some of the directions suggested by Frank—particularly regarding increased use of legal clinics and the exposure of second- and third-year students to the world outside the law library and the classroom.

Although progressive law schools have introduced some changes, many critics are concerned that when law students graduate from law school, they do not know how to practice law. A significant study along these lines is that by Frances Zemans and Victor G. Rosenblum (1980). First, the researchers attempted to learn which skills are most important for the practice of law. Through a random survey of Chicago attorneys, a large number of needed skills were identified. Among the most important skills were fact gathering, applying legal concepts to facts, winning the confidence of others, effective oral expression, ability to understand and interpret the law, knowledge of substantive law, legal research, negotiating, drafting legal documents, and understanding the viewpoints of other people. Assuming that these are the most important legal skills, we need to learn how well law school trains its graduates in each of these skill areas.

In their study Zemans and Rosenblum asked attorneys how well their law school education contributed to the development of these skills. The central finding of the study was that the skills that had been rated as most important to the practice of law were not learned in law school. Law schools were seen as especially deficient in teaching interpersonal skills. In addition, law schools were not very effective in training prospective lawyers in fact gathering. Law schools received high marks in only five areas—teaching knowledge of theory underlying law, imparting knowledge of substantive law, teaching ability to understand and interpret the law, teaching how to do legal research, and imparting ability to synthesize law. Many lawyers were critical of their law schools for failing even to make them aware of the importance of some of the other skills needed to be a good lawyer. In response to this kind of concern, the Counsel of the American Bar Association's "Section of Legal Education and Admissions to the Bar" has proposed that law schools be specifically required to teach courses in trial and appellate advocacy, counseling, negotiating, and drafting (ABA, 1981a, p. 142). However, this proposal has been "firmly" opposed by the Executive Committee of the Association of American Law Schools, which holds that each school should be free to set its own curriculum.

Of course, a lawyer's training does not end the day the attorney graduates from law school. Attorneys learn much of the law and the art of lawyering through experience with actual cases (Zemans and Rosenblum, 1980, pp. 26–28). This is true of all lawyers, whether they be solo practitioners, firm lawyers, or house counsel. Those who join a large firm as associates, however, can expect to receive extensive additional training (Leibowitz and Tollison, 1978). This added training pays dividends throughout their careers in the form of higher earnings. It should also be noted that some states are considering various mechanisms to ensure the continuing competence of those admitted to the bar.[5] At last count, two-thirds of the states had adopted voluntary continuing education programs. In some states these programs are mandatory. Some have argued for mandatory reexamination of all members of the bar on a periodic basis. Failure to pass such a reexamination would short-circuit the lawyer's career. Not surprisingly, members of the bar almost universally oppose this idea. Testing in conjunction with certified specialization has met with less resistance. Some have also called for a well-developed system of peer review in the legal profession to identify those lawyers in need of additional training of some kind.

Extreme

Attitudes

As a result of LawPoll surveys, which are regularly conducted by the *American Bar Association Journal,* the attitudes of attorneys in America are well documented. A question periodically asked of attorneys in the poll concerns issues being faced by the legal profession (ABA, 1982, p. 38). Specifically, the attorneys are asked to volunteer their impressions as to which issues facing the legal profession are most important. Table 3–1 reports the survey results from 1977, 1978, and 1981. Over the course of this period twenty-five different items have been identified by at least 1 percent of the attorneys. The various items can be grouped under four general headings—The Justice System, The Law and Society, The Practice of Law, and Conditions of the Bar. In the most recent poll the single item of greatest concern to the attorneys was their public image and credibility. Other leading concerns included legal fees, the clearing of court calendars, and criminal justice reform. In recent years the three other issues extensively mentioned have included advertising by lawyers, legal ethics, and more effective self-regulation by the legal profession. Interestingly, the only issue that has consistently remained high in degree of concern is lawyer image/public credibility. The concern with self-image may

[5]Commentary, "Once You're In: Maintaining Competence in the Bar," *Nebraska Law Review,* 1977, *56,* 676–691.

TABLE 3-1   Most Important Issues Facing the Legal Profession

	1981 %	1978 %	1977 %
THE JUSTICE SYSTEM (net)	55	19	21
Clearing of court calendars	19	3	3
Criminal justice reform	17	1	3
Streamlining of procedures	13	5	4
Judicial incompetency	7	2	*
Simplification of the system	5	1	2
Unequal justice	4	1	1
Government encroachment/regulation	3	4	2
Federal judiciary	1	3	3
LAW AND SOCIETY (net)	53	69	71
Lawyer image/public credibility	36	39	25
Legal services for the poor	7	8	8
Legal services for the middle class	6	9	14
Lawyer/community relations	4	7	4
Advertising	4	21	42
Prepaid legal services	1	2	5
THE PRACTICE OF LAW (net)	33	29	33
Fees	23	13	7
Ethics	7	12	18
Malpractice insurance	*	2	6
No-fault insurance	*	1	2
CONDITIONS OF THE BAR (net)	32	50	30
Lawyer incompetency	9	10	*
Self-regulation/disciplinary code	8	15	7
Mandatory continuing education	7	9	7
Too many lawyers	6	9	3
Raising bar qualifying standards	5	11	2
Specialization	4	8	8
Relicensing	*	1	4

*Less than $\frac{1}{2}$ of 1 percent
NOTE: Totals add to more than 100 percent because of multiple responses.
Adapted from LawPoll, "What's Important to Lawyers?" *American Bar Association Journal* (January 1982), p. 38.

seem paradoxical, given the high occupational prestige traditionally enjoyed by attorneys. Still, attorneys are well aware of the fact that the "shyster" image still haunts the legal profession.

In discussing the attitudes of attorneys, it is important to consider the possible role of law schools in shaping these attitudes. After all, as compared with police training, the professional training received by attorneys is far longer and more intensive. Consequently, the unique experience of law school may alter the attitudes of prospective lawyers on a range of political and social issues. Howard Erlanger and Douglas Klegon studied the effects of law school on the political orientation of law students (1978). The researchers conducted a panel study of the class of 1976 at the law school of the University of Wisconsin at Madison. Some 80 percent of entering law students with a political orientation identified themselves as "liberals," "left liberals," or "radicals." Erlanger and Klegon found that by the spring semester of their second year, almost all the change that occurred in law students' attitudes was in a conservative direction. However, two-thirds of the students continued to characterize themselves as left of center. Further, the law students became far more interested in focusing their legal careers on the needs of business and of wealthy individuals. There was also some loss of interest in pro bono (that is, public interest) work, although the law students continued to see an important role for the courts in helping lower-status clients. The students reported, however, that the biggest change they had experienced was in learning to "think like a lawyer"—that is, to distinguish legal from nonlegal issues, see all sides of a problem, reason analytically, and express themselves more clearly and less emotionally.

Professionalism

Lawyers in the United States are almost universally regarded as professionals. While the shyster image still haunts the legal profession, a career in law is widely seen as highly desirable. The bar fares quite well on the various criteria that have been cited as indicative of professional status. To begin with, standards of admission to the profession have become quite high. One simply cannot practice law without formal legal training or without passing a state bar examination. In addition, lawyers are professionals because they possess a special body of knowledge and theory. Unlike the study of medicine, this knowledge and theory are not scientific in nature (Rueschemeyer, 1964).[6] Still, few of those outside the legal profession have a firm grasp of the content or procedures of the law. Further, the profession aims to encourage altruism among lawyers and a dedication to the service ideal. Canon 8 of the ABA's Code of Professional Responsibility calls upon lawyers to assist in improving the legal system. Some lawyers have responded in the form of charitable and pro bono work as well as through government service. Lawyers are also professionals in that candidates to the bar must undergo a lengthy period of training. Law school is generally a three-year, full-time program. Most law schools now require an undergraduate degree for admission. In addition, lawyers have a code of ethics, licensing of members, and autonomous control—

[6]An abridged version appears in Vilhelm Aubert, ed., *Sociology of Law* (Baltimore: Penguin, 1969).

all signs of professionalism. Lawyers have pride in their profession and a great deal of publicly recognized status and prestige.

The professional ethic of lawyers has important implications for the character of lawyer-client relations (Rosenthal, 1974, Chaps. 1, 6). Traditionally, it has been suggested that lawyers should exercise predominant control over a case. According to this "traditional" view, clients ought to delegate responsibility to a lawyer and then passively follow the attorney's instructions. The traditional approach asserts that legal problems are routine, technical, and readily handled by a trained expert. It is also contended that effective, disinterested service is the norm. All paying clients, it is argued, have access to effective professional service. However, this perspective has been challenged by Douglas Rosenthal, who believes that responsibilities in a case ought to be shared between a lawyer and the client.

Rosenthal's "participatory" approach stresses the value of an active, skeptical effort by the client. Under this approach the client keeps informed and shares responsibility for making decisions in a case. According to Rosenthal, legal problems do not have a single, clear-cut solution. A suitable course of action can be found, however, if the client works with the attorney on the case. The participatory approach asserts that ineffective professional service by lawyers is common, and disinterested service is virtually impossible. It further suggests that paying clients often have difficulty in finding effective professional service. Rosenthal tested the effectiveness of the traditional and participatory models in personal injury cases. He found that active clients got better results than clients who passively allowed their attorney to handle their case. Although the professional status of attorneys often gives them substantial autonomy over cases, such autonomy evidently is not always in the best interests of clients. Rosenthal believes that as professionals, lawyers can offer considerable expertise to clients. However, Rosenthal is also convinced that clients ought to retain a highly active interest in the way their case is handled.

ROLES

Private Lawyers

Watching "Perry Mason" or other television programs about lawyers does not really teach someone what it is like to be a lawyer. Because a courtroom battle makes for exciting television programming, Perry Mason spent most of his time addressing witnesses, judges, and juries in a trial setting. It would not have been too entertaining to watch Perry Mason sitting at his desk for an entire episode putting the final touches on a will. Yet, many lawyers rarely enter a courtroom. Instead, they conduct most of their work inside their offices. Many attorneys feel they have failed their client if they have been unable to resolve the client's legal problem without a lengthy, costly trial.

Before discussing the roles of private attorneys, it will be instructive to consider, at a general level, the effectiveness of attorneys in America. There has been much concern over the effectiveness of attorneys in carrying out their roles.[7] Much of the information we have about lawyer effectiveness is only suggestive. It includes the academic ability of those in law school, the standards set in bar examinations, the number and nature of malpractice suits against attorneys, surveys on lack of public use of legal services, ratings of attorneys by the *Martindale-Hubbell Law Directory,* and remonstrances about attorney competence by knowledgeable people such as Chief Justice Warren Burger (Carlson, 1976, p. 296). Many of these indicators point to the presence of wide disparities in lawyer effectiveness. Indeed, even the most competent practitioners probably have off days when they make random blunders which jeopardize the rights of their clients. Rick Carlson concludes: "Simply put, clients are probably being injured today and, given the lack of measures of quality and the growing number of practitioners, there is a very real fear that more will be hurt in the future." (1976, p. 297) He adds: "There is probably a fairly high incidence of just plain screw-ups." (1976, p. 297)

The problem of gauging practitioner competence makes it difficult for someone with a legal problem to select an attorney (Freund, 1979; Gallagher, 1979, Ch. 1; Rosenthal, 1976; Rosenthal, 1974, Ch. 2). Perhaps the best hard evidence we have on lawyer effectiveness comes from Douglas Rosenthal's study of personal injury claims (Rosenthal, 1974).[8] In this research Rosenthal compared the actual results of fifty-seven negligence cases with the opinions of a panel of experts as to the worth of the claims. A "good result" was defined as one where the actual recovery was at least 70 percent of the panel's evaluation. The study found that client participation in a case was a key factor in the outcome. "Active clients" were those who engaged in a series of activities in the case, including expressing a special concern or making follow-up demands for attention. Rosenthal found that 75 percent of active clients got a good case result, compared to only 41 percent of the passive clients. He could detect no case in which a client fared worse as a direct result of active participation in the case.

Apart from client participation, there may be a number of other factors important in lawyer effectiveness (Freund, 1979; Zemans and Rosenblum, 1980). For example, Rosenthal found that lawyers in large firms and those who specialize in negligence law tend to do better in personal injury claims than lawyers in small firms (or solo practitioners) or those who are nonspecialists (1974, pp. 132–134). Only careful research can determine which additional factors are most important. It is noteworthy that continuing education courses for attorneys are becoming mandatory in some states in an effort to

[7]LawScope, "Enhancing Lawyer Competence," *American Bar Association Journal,* 1981, *67,* 265–267.

[8]For an earlier effort see Stuart S. Nagel and Felix V. Gagliano, "Attorney Characteristics and Courtroom Results," *Nebraska Law Review,* 1965, *44,* 599–613.

upgrade lawyer effectiveness. Research on the subject of lawyer effectiveness can be very instructive as to the proper focus of such courses. We may well learn that only some of the key factors contributing to lawyer effectiveness can be readily manipulated in these continuing education courses (Wolkin, 1975).[9]

Actually, the job of the lawyer in private practice is complex, involving a number of distinct roles. Quintin Johnstone and Dan Hopson have cited six significant roles primary in the work of lawyers (1967, pp. 77–130). One role of lawyers is that of counseling. Lawyers advise their clients to follow a certain course of action. Recommendations are based on the lawyer's view of relevant legal doctrine and the particular factual situation at hand. The advice that is offered tries to anticipate the reactions of courts, agencies, clients, and other parties. The average attorney spends nearly one-third of his or her time counseling clients; some devote as much as 80 percent of their professional time to that role (Shaffer, 1975; Freeman, 1967; Freeman, 1964). The usefulness of the information an attorney provides as a counselor will vary with the nature of the problem, the lawyer's ability, and the client's sophistication (Mayer, 1967, p. 55). Thomas Shaffer asserts that the self-identity and training of lawyers are not well-suited to the counseling role. As Shaffer suggests: "Most of the attitudes they bring to their professional training are poor attitudes for counselors, and most of their training in law school is useless training for counselors." (1975, p. 854) The ideal counselor is someone who is accepting, understanding, and agreeable. The ideal lawyer, on the other hand, is quite different—embodying sharpness, objectivity, a take-charge attitude, and a desire to win arguments.

Second, lawyers also engage in negotiating. In many situations they seek to represent their clients in bringing an accord with the other party to the dispute (Johnstone and Hopson, 1967, pp. 81–92). The negotiation process includes offering proposals, counterproposals, and reconsiderations, reaching compromises, advising clients, and taking instructions from the client. The lawyer plays the negotiator role both in criminal and civil cases. Nearly all criminal cases are terminated in negotiations in which the defendant, on the advice of an attorney, agrees to plead guilty in return for some consideration, such as a reduced charge or sentence. In general, civil cases are also resolved through negotiated settlements. Increasingly, courts use devices such as pretrial hearings and conferences in an effort to bring about a settlement and avoid a trial. Mayer questions the skill of most lawyers in handling the negotiator role. He observes: "The investment banker, the labor leader, the industrial psychologist, the sales manager, the dean of the faculty, are all more likely than the lawyer to be well equipped for negotiations." (1967, pp. 41–42)

[9]See also Commentary, "Once You're In: Maintaining Competence in the Bar," *Nebraska Law Review*, 1977, *56*, 676–691.

A third lawyer role is drafting. Drafting is the writing and revision of documents. Mayer refers to drafting as "the most legal" of a lawyer's skills (1967, p. 42). He observes: "Communal life in a modern society rests upon pieces of paper that tell people their rights, privileges, powers and immunities, duties, liabilities and disabilities. When challenged, these pieces of paper . . . must stand up. The lawyer assures that they will." (1967, p. 42) Legal-oriented drafting includes contracts, deeds, leases, mortgages, wills, and pleadings (Johnstone and Hopson, 1967, pp. 92–96). Because of their writing skills, lawyers may be asked to draft nonlegal documents as well, such as press releases, letters, speeches, staff memorandums, and advertisements. Sometimes drafting will involve the creation of an originally phrased document. Yet, the drafting function is so important that the skills of the attorney are rarely trusted entirely. To be certain that a document will stand up, it must be made identical with previous documents already declared valid. Consequently, standardized forms are printed by private publishers and official agencies for most kinds of legal problems. To a large extent the lawyer-draftsman is left with the job of filling in the blanks.

A fourth role of lawyers is litigating. Indeed, people generally associate lawyers with litigation. The litigator is "the man in court, questioning witnesses, objecting to another lawyer's questions, appealing to juries." (Mayer, 1967, p. 29) Mayer suggests that the job of litigating "is immensely demanding, both physically and psychologically." (1967, pp. 31–32) When conducting contested litigation, a lawyer must make repeated on-the-spot decisions of immense importance to the client's future. At the same time, only a small portion of attorneys regularly engage in trial work. Litigation has become a specialty; nonspecialists rarely participate in an actual trial. In addition, a distinction must be made between contested and uncontested litigation. Depending on whether the action is being contested, a lawyer's duties in litigation vary greatly. In the United States much litigation—such as debt cases, divorces, civil commitment, and criminal cases—generally goes uncontested. Contested litigation is much less significant to lawyers as a source of income than most people realize. As Johnstone and Hopson note: "A sizable minority of the bar never participates in contested litigation, and comparatively few lawyers are regularly engaged in it." (1967, p. 98)

A fifth role that lawyers carry out is that of investigating (Johnstone and Hopson, 1967, pp. 101–102). As an investigator, the lawyer seeks out data about events and develops theories of cause and effect. For example, a good defense attorney will often become actively involved in searching for the facts in a criminal case. Factual investigation is often a prelude to counseling, negotiating, and litigating. Thus, the nature of the defense attorney's investigation should strongly influence whether the lawyer advises the client to plead guilty or innocent and how the case is otherwise handled. There is reason to wonder, however, whether defense attorneys are really adequately adept at conducting investigations of this sort. Occasionally, an attorney will be asked by a client simply to collect data or to try to predict a future event, such as whether a bill is likely to be adopted as law by a legislature. Unfortunately, most lawyers lack the substantive knowledge of social science or the skills needed to evaluate the validity of scientific studies. The result is that an attorney's investigation may fail to take advantage of the full range of available social science knowledge.

Finally, lawyers engage in researching (Johnstone and Hopson, 1967, pp. 102–106). This role includes searching for authoritative statements of legal doctrine, adapting legal doctrine to specific factual situations, and predicting how courts and agencies will rule in particular cases. Research involves both plodding and creativity. The researcher must routinely locate relevant legal doctrine from the mass of existing information. At the same time, research is also a creative process of discovering new relationships, classifications, and rationales. A disproportionate amount of legal research is conducted by large-firm lawyers, appellate specialists, and lawyers working in an area of law that is new to them. Experienced members of the bar may do very little research, particularly if they are working in their specialty or for a small fee.

Because of the ambiguities inherent in many of the problems that come to their attention, lawyers may experience great difficulties in deciding which role is most appropriate to a given situation. As Johnstone and Hopson note: "In advising clients, the lawyer can often run into role conflict." (1967, p. 80) Samuel Brakel has investigated the role conflicts of lawyers working in mental institutions (1981). He suggests that the lawyer who is serving clients in a mental institution may face some very ambiguous situations and serious role conflicts. Thus, Brakel notes: "The lawyer's job in the mental hospital makes up in uncertainty and potential for conflict what it lacks in glamor." (1981, p. 25) Brakel is especially disturbed that some attorneys serving mental institutions automatically assume an adversarial posture. This, he believes, may be counterproductive, since it generates needless antagonisms between patients and staff. Brakel suggests that lawyering in mental institutions generally requires a focus on counseling, negotiating, and investigating. Some patient problems, however, may require litigation or the threat of litigation. The most important lesson from this study is simply that lawyers, like police officers, often experience role conflicts. It should be noted, though, that lawyers are probably in a more enviable position than police officers in dealing with these conflicts. While police officers on the street must often resolve their role conflicts and take some kind of action rapidly, lawyers can generally reflect on the nature of the problem and give their clients a response at some later date.

The problem of role conflict is intertwined with that of lawyer effectiveness. After all, if the most appropriate response of an attorney in a given case is to litigate, client welfare will not be maximized if the attorney opts for negotiating—not even if the attorney then attempts to do the best possible with that strategy. Of course, there are times when an attorney will err and adopt an inappropriate response to a legal problem. In some of these cases the attorney may have the opportunity to reverse gears and adopt a more useful strategy. A special concern, however, occurs when the interests of the attorney and the client are at odds. In such a situation an attorney may intentionally opt for a role that is not consistent with the client's best interests. Indeed, looking at criminal cases, Abraham Blumberg concludes that defense lawyers often neglect the interests of their clients and instead very effectively pursue their own interests and those of the court organization (1967a; 1967b). Blumberg believes that defense attorneys regularly make extravagant claims as to their influence and thereby dupe clients into pleading guilty. On the advice of their attorney defendants almost universally agree to plead guilty, fearful that otherwise they will upset the bargain that their defense attorney has made. Yet, contrary to popular belief, those who plead guilty do not, on the average, get a lighter sentence than those who go to trial (Eisenstein and Jacob, 1977, pp. 277, 283). The real beneficiary of plea bargaining is the criminal justice system, which saves the time and expense of conducting a trial. Public defenders and other defense attorneys often feel very much a part of this criminal justice system. This suggests that we must be concerned that attorneys sometimes effectively serve interests other than those of their clients. An effort to improve lawyer effectiveness must focus not only on the characteristics of attorneys but also on the relationship between attorney and client.

Public Lawyers

Woodrow Wilson once observed: "The profession I chose was politics; the profession I entered was the law. I entered one because I thought it would lead to the other." (Eulau and Sprague, 1964, p. 1) Not all attorneys are, or wish to be, in the private sector. The key positions of government in the United States, both elected and appointed, are dominated by attorneys. Indeed, Heinz Eulau and John Sprague have referred to lawyers as the "high priests of politics." (1964, p. 11) Clearly, a disproportionate number of Congress members belong to the bar (Congressional Quarterly Service, 1981, p. 199; 1979, p. 7). Even though only .1 percent of the members of the United States labor force are lawyers, 253 of the 535 members of the 97th Congress (1981–1982) held a law degree. By contrast, only 69 were educators, 28 were journalists, and 1 was a scientist. At the same time, the figure of 253 is down somewhat from the 96th Congress (1979–1980), in which 270 members were lawyers. A large number of Congress members who are not in the legal profession come from the business/banking community.

Lawyers are found throughout the government (Blaustein and Porter, 1954, Ch. IV). Apart from their presence in Congress, members of the bar are commonly found in state and local legislatures. A number serve on Congressional staffs. Supreme Court justices are always attorneys. The vast majority of other judges are also attorneys. Additionally, many bureaucrats at all levels of government have a legal background. In the bureaucracy lawyers are involved in drafting and interpreting documents, reviewing decisions, litigating, and policy advising (Brown, 1948, pp. 43–90). Civil service positions in the federal bureaucracy are graded by "GS" (government service) ratings which range upwards from GS–1. Higher-graded jobs, which carry larger salaries, are reserved for the most important positions. As a rule, a law school graduate who has recently been admitted to the bar will be offered a starting grade of GS–9 and may be promoted to GS–11 after one year of service (ABA, 1976, p. 2). More generally, the higher the status and importance of a government position, the more likely it is that it will be occupied by a lawyer. This is not to suggest that high-status members of the legal profession are commonly attracted to government service (Jacob, 1978, pp. 75–76). Indeed, large law firms discourage partners or associates from engaging in political activity. A career in politics is most attractive to solo practitioners and members of small firms. Still other lawyers may try to parlay short-term experience with a government agency into a move to a major law firm or a position as house counsel for a leading corporation (Spector, 1972). This career strategy may be especially inviting to those with a mediocre legal education or those who are stigmatized by their sex, religion, or ethnic background.

If lawyers are, in fact, the "high priests of politics," there are those who would like them to be excommunicated. A number of concerns have been expressed about the dominance of lawyers in American policymaking (Eulau and Sprague, 1964, pp. 17–30). The very fact that the bar is overrepresented in government has been a source of concern. Some argue that the background characteristics of government officials ought to be more representative of the general population. Yet, reducing the role of attorneys in government probably would not appreciably enhance the representativeness of government. Some have also voiced fears that lawyers in government conspire to produce policies beneficial to the bar. Studies of roll call votes in legislatures, however, do not reveal the presence of any "lawyer's bloc," even on matters of utmost concern to the profession (Eulau and Sprague, 1964, pp. 122–143). Another apprehension is that lawyers as individuals tend to be conservative. Thus, if lawyers dominate government, public policies will be biased in a conservative direction. There may be some basis for this concern. Still, there is a range of ideologies among attorneys; it would not make sense to restrict the entry of attorneys to government solely on the basis of this concern. Finally, some are fearful that legal training does not equip attorneys to solve the complex problems of our nation. Given their training, lawyers may be particularly ill-suited to the task of identifying the value choices which underlie alternative policies. At most, however, this merely suggests the need for more consultation between lawyers and nonlawyers in the process of formulating policies.

One of the key government positions invariably occupied by an attorney is that of prosecutor. Prosecutors are found at all levels of government in the United States (Holten and Jones, 1978, p. 60). At the federal level all prosecutors work under the Attorney General in the Justice Department. Prosecutors also play an important role at the state, county, and local levels. The job of prosecutor is crucial to the operation of justice in our nation. It has been observed: "The discretionary power exercised by the prosecuting attorney in initiation, accusation, and discontinuance of prosecution gives him more control over an individual's liberty and reputation than any other public official."[10] The destiny of many Americans has been greatly affected—even *controlled*—by decisions made by a prosecutor. Exercising discretion, a prosecutor may choose to drop charges, plea bargain, or vigorously pursue a conviction on the original charges.

The job of prosecutor includes a number of related tasks (Holten and Jones, 1978, pp. 152–161). Perhaps the most important is that of charging. It is the prosecutor who decides whether to prosecute a suspect or dismiss the charges. Further, prosecutors have the task of recommending bail levels, the charges to be brought, the number of counts entered on each charge, and what will be offered in return for a plea of guilty. Acting as trial advocates, prosecutors are also responsible for preparing cases, most of which they expect to win. Prosecutors also have a number of civil functions. They generally have the job of representing their level of government in any civil action. Other functions include providing legal advice to government agencies, training police officers in criminal law and procedure, preparing drafts of search warrants, and drafting wiretapping applications. Prosecutors also participate in decisions concerning court organization and engage in various public information and community relations programs.

In exercising their discretion, prosecutors can have an important impact on the direction of law enforcement (Eisenstein, 1973, pp. 103–104). They can launch investigations into areas previously ignored, such as white-collar offenses. Prosecutors can also discourage enforcement of certain statutes by declining to prosecute in specific matters, such as pornography. In making these decisions, prosecutors face few restrictions. No superiors dictate policy to them; their decisions generally have low visibility; and, as elected officials, they have an independent political base. Prosecutors do feel constrained in some cases, such as when a case has been heavily publicized. In addition, the prosecutor wishes to convey an image of effectiveness in routine cases by maintaining a high conviction rate. This may mean dismissing cases where the evidence is not solid or consenting to large reductions in the charges against defendants in exchange for a guilty plea.

Some defense counsel are also government lawyers. In a line of cases the Supreme Court has ruled that criminal defendants are entitled to the services of an attorney (see *Gideon v. Wainwright* and *Argersinger v. Hamlin*). When the defendant cannot afford an attorney, one must be provided by the govern-

---

[10]Note, "Prosecutor's Discretion," *University of Pennsylvania Law Review,* 1955, *103,* 1057.

ment. The method of providing an attorney varies from state to state. Many states, however, are now using the public defender system for this purpose. Here a government agency staffed by lawyers is entrusted to defend those accused of crimes who cannot afford their own attorneys. A key question is whether this system is more effective than others in providing assistance to defendants. Stuart Nagel assessed the impact of alternative types of counsel on how well the client fared (1973a; Oaks and Lehman, 1967). The results of this empirical investigation were complex and not entirely unidirectional. However, the findings do suggest that the best system, from the defendant's standpoint, would be a judicare plan. Under this arrangement an indigent could select a private attorney, using government subsidies for payment. The expense of such a system, however, raises questions of political feasibility. In the absence of a judicare system, Nagel concludes, an adequately financed public defender system is the best available alternative. He believes it is preferable to a system in which private counsel are simply assigned to indigent defendants by a judge (Casper, 1972a).[11]

All told, an enormous number of lawyers can be found in government, particularly in the highest positions. Several factors contribute to the predominance of lawyers in politics. To begin with, proximity to government is an important consideration. Heinz Eulau and John Sprague observe: "No occupational group stands in more regular and intimate relation to American politics than the legal profession" (1964, p. 11). In the course of their work lawyers come into regular contact with judges, prosecutors, and public attorneys. Once a part of the political subculture, an attorney may well pursue a government position. Second, availability is also critical to entering government service (Cohen, 1969). Lawyers have more control over their work arrangements than people in most other professions. This gives them more flexibility, making possible a greater involvement in government. Third, running for political office may help the career of a private attorney. As Joseph Schlesinger notes: "Political campaigning is generally regarded as an effective form of ethical advertising. In addition, political activity provides lawyers with the kinds of experience and contacts which can aid their private trade." (1957, p. 27) Members of few other occupations can benefit from a political campaign that does not end in victory at the ballot box. Finally, the presence of lawyers in key governmental positions may also be accounted for by the "ambition theory." This theory holds that lawyers are able to enter politics earlier in their working career than others and pursue more opportunities for advancement. The attorney who fails to advance can fall back on another public job or on temporary private practice. Many nonlawyers are reluctant to seek elective office because they might have nowhere to go in the event that they lose the electoral contest. Thus, it is likely that lawyers will continue to pop-

[11]Casper (1972a) found that defendants were far more likely to view privately retained counsel, rather than public defenders, as being on their side. In fact, when asked if he had a *lawyer* when he went to court, one defendant remarked (p. 101): "No. I had a public defender."

ulate the key positions of American government, particularly at the highest levels.

SERVICE DISTRIBUTION

Legal Problems

Most attorneys in America are in private practice. Thus, an important concern is the distribution of legal services in our country. An individual in the throes of a dispute does not automatically define the problem as "legal." Nor does that person automatically contact an attorney. A survey on this subject was conducted by the ABA Special Committee to Survey Legal Needs and the American Bar Foundation (Curran, 1978). The purpose of that study was to learn the nature and scope of the public's legal needs and determine how well these needs are being met by existing mechanisms. Some of the findings of this survey, as reported by Barbara Curran, are reported in Table 3-2. The table indicates the estimated probability that selected problems will be taken to an attorney in a given year. Also, the table reports the number of problems about which lawyers are consulted. It is clear that people are far more likely to turn to a lawyer for some kinds of problems than for others. Of those executing a will, 79 percent make contact with an attorney. Nearly 77 percent seek out a lawyer for obtaining a divorce. At the other extreme, only 1 percent of those experiencing job discrimination consult an attorney. Thus, the problems reaching attorneys in the United States are not representative of all problems experienced by the population.

Organization of the Bar

Three topics are especially relevant to the distribution of legal services. These include organizational style, specialization, and method of payment. As to organizational style, we have already seen that the existing bar includes solo practitioners; small firms; large firms; and house counsel in corporations, nonprofit institutions, and government (Jacob, 1978, pp. 71–76; Jacob, 1973, pp. 40–42). It seems reasonable to suppose that the organizational style of attorneys will have various effects. For example, there is reason to believe that lawyers in large firms generally operate more effectively than solo practitioners. This is largely due to their superior training and specialization. It is not surprising then that most affluent individuals take their legal problems to large firms. Likewise, corporations which do not have house counsel almost universally rely upon the expertise of large firms. Thus, it may make sense for government to attempt to manipulate the organizational structure of the bar. For example, they might make an effort to encourage the development of large private firms that serve the problems of disadvantaged people.

TABLE 3-2 Probability of Lawyer Use for Selected Problems and Total Number of Problems Taken to Lawyers Estimated from the Survey Results

PROBLEM	PROBABILITY THAT LAWYER WILL BE CONSULTED[a]	NUMBER OF PROBLEMS ABOUT WHICH LAWYERS ARE CONSULTED IN ANY YEAR
Executed will	79%	3.7 million
Obtained divorce[b]	77	1.5
Acquired real property for nonbusiness purposes	40	2.2
Serious personal injury tort caused by another	39	0.5
Spouse died	35	0.2
Serious difficulty with governmental agency (not business-related)	12	0.5
Consumer problem[c]	10	0.5
Violation of constitutional rights	10	0.2
Wage collection, excluding garnishment	8	0.1
Serious property damage tort or loss caused by another (not business-related)	5	0.4
Job discrimination	1	>0.1

[a] The estimate of current probability of lawyer use is based on lawyer use by "problem-havers" in the sample for the years 1971–1974 and for earlier years when no changes in utilization rates over time were detected.

[b] Based on the 1975 estimate.

[c] Covers serious disputes with landlords, including eviction; with retail sellers about major purchase; or with creditors, including repossession or wage garnishment.

Adapted from Barabara A. Curran, "Survey of the Public's Legal Needs," *American Bar Association Journal* (June 1978), p. 850.

Another aspect of the structure of legal services in the United States is the extent of existing specialization by subject matter. The recognized fields of law are those listed in Table 3-3. According to a recent survey, the leading fields of specialization include litigation, corporate law, real estate, taxation, labor, probate, negligence, and criminal cases (ABA, 1981b, p. 1451). Advocates of attorney specialization argue that it promotes competence, accessibility, and reduced costs. Traditionally, the legal profession has not recognized specialization to as great a degree as has the medical profession. Still, specialization among attorneys is a growing trend. In fact, by 1981 53 percent of attorneys indicated that they considered themselves to be specialists (ABA, 1981b, 1451). This was an increase from only 40 percent in a survey taken in 1977.

The subject of specialization has been under study by the ABA since 1952, when the Committee of Continuing Specialized Legal Education was established (Fromson, 1977). In 1961 the issue was reopened with the creation of the Special Committee on Recognition and Certification of Specialization in Law Practice. Its report, issued in August 1974, called for state pilot programs on specialization in those states lacking such a program. By 1977 four states were operating specialization plans—California, New Mexico, Florida, and Texas. The California model involves certification of specialists in particular fields. Applicants must pass a written (and sometimes oral) exam to receive a specialization certificate. Those who win certification may advertise this status in legal directories and in the classified pages of telephone books. Also eligible for specialist status, under a "grandfather clause," are those who have ten years of practice and can establish substantial work in a field.

The New Mexico model involves the self-identification of attorneys as specialists in a field. Rather than seeking to measure competence in written or oral tests, New Mexico demands only that a lawyer claim to devote 60 percent of his or her time to a particular field. The plan contains the designation of sixty-two fields of specialization, including general practice. Other specialization plans are adaptations of the California and New Mexico models. There is reason to believe that if lawyers would specialize and make their area of specialization widely known, both the quality and equality of legal services would be enhanced. Presently, specialized legal services are enjoyed primarily by the affluent, by corporations, and by other large organizations.

Another aspect of bar organization is the method of payment (Gallagher, 1979, pp. 43–48). Among those in private practice five primary methods are used in charging fees. The hourly fee involves compensation to the lawyer for services rendered, based on a dollar amount per hour. Some lawyers routinely keep careful time records of their work. They then base their billings on a fixed hourly rate for time spent. The contingent fee hinges compensation upon the successful outcome of a client's legal problem. The lawyer receives a fixed percentage of anything recovered for the client. This method is most frequently used for personal injury cases and debt collections. The flat fee is a set amount of money charged by lawyers for performing a service. It is used commonly for routine tasks such as drafting a simple will or contract. The bar publishes minimum fee schedules for many kinds of routine matters. With the percentage fee, lawyers are paid a proportion of the total assets for which they are responsible while performing the service. This is regularly used when a lawyer is probating an estate or acting as executor of an estate. Last, the retainer fee is a monthly or yearly charge by an attorney to a client. This ensures the lawyer's continued availability to deal with ongoing, routine legal tasks. For legal services not within the terms of the retainer agreement, additional fees are normally charged.

An interesting, underexplored question is the relationship between the method of payment and the effort expended by a lawyer in the client's behalf.

TABLE 3-3   Recognized Fields of Law

Accident and Health Insurance Law	Computer Law
Administrative Law	Condemnation Law
Admiralty Law	Condominium Law
Adoption Law	Constitutional Law
Advisor on Inter-American Law	Construction Law
Advisor on Laws of Africa	Consumer Law
Advisor on Laws of Austria	Contract Law
Advisor on Laws of Brazil	Cooperative Law
Advisor on Laws of British Common-	Copyright Law
wealth	Corporate Financing Law
Advisor on Laws of Canada	Corporate Reorganization & Insolvency
Advisor on Laws of China	Law
Advisor on Laws of Dominican	Corporation Law
Republic	Creditors Rights Law
Advisor on Laws of England and/or	Criminal Law
Wales	Criminal Tax Law
Advisor on Laws of Germany	Custody Law
Advisor on Laws of India	Customs Law
Advisor on Laws of Israel	Divorce Law
Advisor on Laws of Italy	Domestic Relations
Advisor on Laws of Japan	Drainage & Levee Law
Advisor on Laws of Latin America	Election Law
Advisor on Laws of Mexico	Eminent Domain Law
Advisor on Laws of Saudi Arabia	Employee Benefit Law
Advisor on Laws of Soviet Union	Employee Stock Ownership Plans
Advisor on Laws of Spain	& Financing
Advisor on Laws of Sweden	Employment Law
Agricultural Law	Energy Law
Aircraft Title Law	Entertainment Law
Antitrust Law	Environmental Law
Appellate Practice	Equal Opportunity Law
Arbitration Law	Equity Practice
Attorney-Adjuster, Claims, Investiga-	Estate Planning
tions & Adjusting	Family Law
Automobile Law	Federal Employers Liability Law
Aviation Law	Federal Excise Tax Law
Banking Law	Federal Gas Law
Bankruptcy Law	Federal Income, Estate & Gift
Business Law	Tax Law
Casualty Insurance Law	Federal Power Law
Cemetery Law	Federal Practice
Chancery Practice	Fidelity & Surety Law
Civil Practice	Fire Insurance Law
Civil Rights Law	Food, Drug & Cosmetic Law
Civil Service Law	Foreign Patent Law
Collection Law	Franchise Law
College Law	General Negligence Trials & Appeals
Commercial Law	Government (or Public) Contract Law
Commodities Law	Health Care & Hospital Law
Communications Law	Historic Preservation Law

Housing and Urban Development Law
Immigration & Nationality Law
Indian Affairs Law
Insolvency Law
Insurance Law
International Business Law
International Law
Interstate Commerce Law
Interstate Land Sales Law
Invasion of Privacy Law
Japanese Negotiations
Juvenile Law
Labor Law
Landlord & Tenant Law
Legal Ethics & Discipline Law
Legislative Practice
Libel & Slander Law
Licensing Law
Life Insurance Law
Liquor Control Law
Literary Property Law
Litigation
Livestock Law
Local Practice (Washington, D.C.)
Malpractice Law—Legal, Medical
Marine & Inland Insurance Law
Maritime Law
Maritime Negligence Law
Matrimonial Law
Medical Legal Law
Mental Health Law
Military Law
Mining Law
Mortgage Law
Motion Picture Law
Motor Carrier Law
Municipal Bond Law
Municipal Finance Law
Municipal Law
Natural Resources Law
Negligence Law
Nuclear (or Atomic) Law
Oil & Gas Law
Partnership Law
Patent Law
Patent, Trademark & Copyright Law
Pension & Profit Sharing Law
Personal Injury Law
Petroleum Law
Poverty Law

Probate Law
Products Liability Law
Project Finance Law
Public Authority Financing Law
Public Employment Relations Law
Public Housing Law
Public Improvement Law
Public Land Law
Publishing Law
Radio Law
Railroad Law
Real Estate Law
Reorganization Law
Retirement Plans—Qualified
Savings & Loan Law
School Law
Securities Law
Selective Service Law
Shopping Center Law
Social Security Disability Law
Space Law
Sports Law
State & Local Tax Law
Steamship Law
Subrogation Law
Surety Law
Taxation Law
Television Law
Theatre Law
Timber & Logging/Lumber Law
Tort Law
Trade Regulation Law
Trademark Law
Transportation Law
Trial Practice
Trust Law
Unfair Competition Law
Uninsured Motorist
University Law
Urban Affairs Law
Utility Law
Veterans Law
Wage & Hour Law
Water Rights Law
Worker's Compensation Law
Workmen's (or Worker's) Compensation
  Law
Workmen's Compensation Law
Zoning Law

Source: Jane Brazie (ed.), *Lawyer's Register By Specialties and Fields of Law, 1983* (Solon, Ohio: Lawyer's Register Publishing Company)

Some types of fees probably produce more mutuality of interest between the lawyer and client than do other types of fees. For example, Barry Gallagher suggests that the flat fee may lead to hurried work by an attorney who finds that full performance of a legal service requires more effort than originally estimated (1979, p. 46). The contingency fee has been heralded in some quarters as a method of payment which ensures mutuality of interest; after all, the lawyer's fee increases directly with that of the award won by the client. Yet, Douglas Rosenthal suggests that even though waiting out the insurer will often be of greatest benefit to the client, a quick settlement is often in the attorney's best interests (1974, pp. 95–116). A lawyer who is working for a contingency rather than for an hourly fee will often cut corners in preparing a case, build the fee by charging disbursements to the client, and persuade the client that a discounted early settlement is in the client's best interests. Another danger in using the contingency fee is that the best attorneys will take only those cases that are highly likely to be won or that involve very large sums of money (Leubsdorf, 1981). Further research is needed to determine which method of payment is most suitable to specific types of cases and circumstances.

Lawyers and Access to Justice

Equal justice is an important concern in studying the distribution of legal services. Ours is a society that recognizes the political principle of "one person, one vote" but does not recognize the economic equivalent of "one person, one dollar." (Okun, 1975) The mixture of a constitutional democracy with a capitalist economy has meant that dollars sometimes transgress on basic political rights. One important example is access to legal services (Auerbach, 1976). Because the bar in the United States is highly stratified, the quantity and quality of legal services available to the disadvantaged tend to be inferior. As Harry Stumpf notes: "The distributive system for legal services in the United States is clearly weighted in favor of individuals and interests representing wealth." (1975, p. 121) Similarly, Jerome Carlin concludes: "The best trained, most technically skilled, and ethically most responsible lawyers are reserved to the upper reaches of business and society. . . . As a result, the most helpless clients who most need protection are least likely to get it." (1966, p. 177) There is simply no question but that corporate clients and wealthy individuals purchase a better legal product than small businesses and disadvantaged individuals. Poor people cannot afford the legal fees charged by the best lawyers of the bar. Moreover, nearly all top-flight attorneys decide to specialize in lucrative, corporate-centered areas of law, which are far removed from the legal problems of the poor. Most lawyers see poor people as highly undesirable clients.

Certainly, the problem of unequal access to legal services has not gone unnoticed. A number of organizations have been established to provide legal assistance to disadvantaged people, particularly indigents. The legal aid movement in the United States is relatively recent. In 1900 only New York and Chicago had legal aid offices.[12] The number of such offices increased sharply after World War II. However, in 1948 there were still only fifty-five legal aid offices with paid staffs. Funding for legal aid has been rather meager, relying on community chests, bar associations, and the donations of private individuals (Stumpf, 1975, p. 124). Legal aid lawyers developed a well-deserved reputation for passiveness. Generally, they declined on moralistic grounds to take certain kinds of cases, such as bankruptcies. Rarely did they undertake social reform litigation.

An increasing role has been played by the federal government since the mid-1960s in providing legal services for the poor (ABA, 1981c, p. 414). Federal funding for poverty law programs had a modest beginning in 1965 under the Office of Economic Opportunity. By 1976, with the creation of the Legal Services Corporation, the level of funding had greatly increased. Funding for 1981 was set at $321.3 million, with more than 5,000 LSC lawyers dispersed across the nation. Lawyers in the Legal Services Corporation are quite different from those in the earlier legal aid offices (Erlanger, 1978). While legal aid lawyers received only marginal training, Legal Services Corporation lawyers have been among the best and the brightest. The Legal Services Corporation attempts to provide full legal representation to the poor. As a redistributive program, the LSC has been a natural target of conservatives. Despite broadly based support from the legal profession, the Reagan administration made repeated efforts to scrap the program. More deeply entrenched as a government service are the public defender offices established in most communities to assist indigent criminal defendants. The widespread existence of such offices reflects the constitutional guarantees enunciated by the Supreme Court that an attorney be provided to indigents in criminal cases.

Notwithstanding legal aid efforts, many who ought to have the assistance of an attorney fail to receive it. As Michael Zander notes: "There is no longer any room for doubt that a substantial unmet need for legal services does exist." (1978, p. 1676) The literature on access to an attorney generally stresses poverty as the key constraint. Actually, however, people from diverse economic backgrounds often fail to obtain an attorney when they need one. As a consequence, additional explanations are needed. Beyond the poverty explanation, a second factor in the failure to seek an attorney is the social organization of the bar (Mayhew, 1975; Mayhew and Reiss, 1969). The legal profession is organized around the property-related concerns of the affluent. This stimulates property-related claims. Meanwhile, there are many personal problems in society (for example, domestic relations, disputes with government) that are not being adequately treated.

A third factor explaining the failure to contact an attorney is the failure

---

[12]Note, "Neighborhood Law Offices: The New Wave in Legal Services for the Poor," *Harvard Law Review,* 1967, 80, 806.

to communicate with another person about a legal problem (Zander, 1978, p. 1678). The gap between lawyer and client is often bridged by intermediaries who encourage victims to see an attorney. Most individuals who contact a lawyer about a legal problem do so at the urging of some other person, such as a doctor, employer, relative, or friend. There may also be other factors contributing to the failure to contact an attorney. These include attitudes toward attorneys; the reactive nature of the bar; public knowledge about the law; and personal characteristics such as age, sex, and education. There is little reason to suppose that for the ordinary citizen, contacts with an attorney for a legal problem will soon become as habitual as contacts with a physician for a medical problem.

ETHICS

Sources of Ethics

Ethical misconduct is an important concern when evaluating the legal profession. As in the case of the police, a great deal of unethical conduct is present, but little of it gets punished. Over the decades various unwritten norms, customs, and practices have evolved regarding the ethics of lawyers: much of this has been put in writing (Carlin, 1966, p. 42). These sources include the canons of ethics of the American Bar Association and various state and local bars; the published opinions of committees on professional ethics; court rules and decisions; legislative provisions; and statements in various texts, treatises, and casebooks. Most significant, perhaps, is the ABA's code of professional responsibility. While only advisory in nature, it has become binding through adoption by state supreme courts and other disciplinary bodies.

The ABA code is divided into three parts—canons, ethical considerations, and disciplinary rules. The nine canons express the broadest and loftiest goals of ethical conduct. They call upon lawyers to assist in maintaining the integrity and competence of the bar, to help make legal counsel broadly available, to assist in preventing unauthorized practice, to preserve the confidences and secrets of clients, to provide disinterested service to clients, to represent a client competently, to provide zealous representation within the bounds of the law, to assist in improving the legal system, and to avoid even the appearance of impropriety. The ABA code also includes 139 ethical considerations, which are described as "aspirational in character and represent the objectives toward which every member of the profession should strive." (ABA, 1980, p. 1) They contain a more specific description of acceptable attorney conduct. Finally, there are forty disciplinary rules which expressly prohibit specific conduct. These rules are described as "mandatory in character" and "state the minimum level of conduct below which no lawyer can fall without being subject to disciplinary action." (ABA, 1980, p. 1) For example, specific rules focus on advertising, avoiding acquisition of interest in litigation, and trial conduct.

Existing guidelines for the conduct of lawyers imply three broad categories of possible malpractice (Carlin, 1966, p. 42; Jacob, 1978, pp. 54–55). The ethical standards include obligations to (1) clients, (2) colleagues, and (3) the administration of justice. Rules relating to clients focus on conversion of clients' funds, commingling (that is, the mixing together of clients' funds with those of the attorney), overcharging, conflicts of interest, abuse of confidential information, misinforming, and client neglect. Rules concerning colleagues prohibit solicitation of cases, breaking an agreement with another attorney, bypassing a colleague to deal with the colleague's client, or deceiving another attorney. Complex regulations in the ABA code distinguish ethical from unethical advertising. Other rules concern fee setting, dividing fees with other attorneys, and assisting nonprofessionals with unauthorized practice of the law. Finally, another set of rules concerns the administration of justice. Some of these rules prohibit payoffs, false representation, concealment of evidence, and pressing unfounded claims. Several rules in the ABA code govern the release of information by attorneys to the press. Another rule prohibits attorneys from degrading a court by failing to act in a dignified and courteous manner.

Variation and Stratification

Lawyers are not equally ethical. Jerome Carlin conducted a systematic study of adherence to ethics by members of the New York City bar (1966, esp. Chaps. 2, 7). Some thirteen "ethics items" were included in his questionnaire. These focused on a variety of concerns, such as referral fees, conflicts of interest, and advertising.[13] Carlin found considerable variation in ethical behavior among the New York lawyers. Some 25 percent had a low score (violators) of 0 to 6 on the 13-point scale, while 27 percent had a high score (conformers) of 10 to 13 (Carlin, 1966, p. 54). Joel Handler replicated the Carlin study in a small city in Illinois ("Prairie City"). He found much less violation of ethical standards. Evidently, lawyers in small communities are far less likely to violate bar norms than those in large metropolitan areas. On this Handler concludes: "The hierarchical nature of the metropolitan bar, the economic insecurities, the tensions between the actual practice and lawyers' professional expectations, the extreme competition for business, the corruption of courts and public officials—all these were absent in Prairie City." (1967, p. 154) Many of the New York City lawyers found themselves under

---

[13]The thirteen "ethics items" used by Carlin are too lengthy to list here. See Carlin (1966), pp. 248–54. As an example Carlin offers the following synopsis for the "referral fee" item (p. 45): "Lawyer A accepts one-third referral fee from Lawyer B. A's only connection with the case was to hear client and telephone B to say he was sending client to him." Carlin's findings demonstrate that lawyers do differ in their commitment to legal ethics and that low-status lawyers were particularly prone to commit ethical violations.

far more pressure to violate ethical norms than did members of the "Prairie City" bar.

Even more interesting than the mere fact of variation in adherence to ethics is the presence of stratification as well. Carlin found that adherence to ethical norms is strongly associated with an attorney's status in the bar (1966, p. 55). The large-firm lawyer is far more likely to adhere to lawyers' ethics. In the Carlin study 57 percent of those in large firms were high conformers, while only 5 percent were frequent violators of ethical norms. Only 20 percent of solo practitioners were high conformers, while 30 percent ranked low in ethical behavior. Carlin suggests that situational pressures operating on low-status lawyers play a powerful role in inducing unethical behavior. As Carlin notes, threats to the integrity of the low-status lawyer "may arise from the character of the market for legal services, from captivity to clients, and from the contaminating effects of certain courts and agencies." (1966, p. 7) To be sure, not every high-status lawyer is ethical; nor is every low-status lawyer unethical. A key mitigating factor is the lawyer's inner disposition to conform to ethical standards. Those with strong ethical concern are less likely to succumb to pressures to violate. Situational pressures in Prairie City to violate ethical norms are both less intense and less variant. Handler agrees that should "Prairie City," Illinois, increase in size and economic diversity, its bar would come to resemble that of New York City and a pattern of stratified malpractice would emerge (1967, p. 155).

Formal Discipline

Ethical rules are enforced in every state through the use of some procedure. In most states the state supreme court combines efforts with a state or local bar organization. (Steele and Nimmer, 1976). State supreme courts generally establish rules and impose formal sanctions. However, the primary responsibility for conducting preliminary investigations and hearings rests with the bar association. For example, in New York City virtually all complaints are initially referred to the bar's Grievance Committee (Carlin, 1966, p. 150). This committee decides whether to drop the charges, admonish the lawyer, or recommend prosecution. Prosecuted cases are heard in the Appellate Division of New York's supreme court. The Grievance Committee in New York deals with nearly all cases on an informal basis. From 1951 to 1962 a yearly average of only 60 to 1,450 cases were dealt with by a formal hearing before a panel of the Grievance Committee. Of these, only 19 cases per year brought a recommendation for court prosecution. Only about 10 of these, on the average, led to disbarment. Infrequent disciplining of attorneys was also found in a 1972 study (Garbus and Seligman, 1976). Thus, we find a pattern of (1) considerable breach of ethics; (2) little reporting of unethical behavior; (3) little disciplining of lawyers in the cases reported; and (4) lax punishment, in general, when punishment does occur.

If the rules governing misconduct by lawyers are rarely enforced, there must be some reasons for this failure. Three main factors have been cited for the underenforcement of ethical standards (Schnapper, 1978, pp. 203-204). First, lawyers themselves enforce ethical norms and wish to avoid creating broad precedents for attorney discipline. In this regard Michael Dorf has characterized existing disbarment proceedings as "a family affair" and has called for alternative means of disciplining attorneys (1975, p. 72). Second, the severity of the traditional sanctions of disbarment and suspension makes the regulators reluctant to impose them. Two sanctions now coming into use—the private reprimand and the public reprimand—may increase the total of lawyers disciplined in some way (Steele and Nimmer, 1976, p. 925). A third factor producing underenforcement of ethics is that grievance committees rely almost entirely on disgruntled clients for complaints. Much unethical conduct goes unreported because clients fail to detect it, choose not to complain, or are unaware of the existence of a grievance mechanism.

An alternative course of action for a client is a malpractice suit against the attorney (Mallen and Levit, 1977; Stern, 1979). Attorneys may be held liable in most jurisdictions for "a wrongful act or omission arising out of the rendition of professional services." (Mallen and Levit, 1977, p. 3) Beginning in the 1960s a dramatic increase occurred in legal malpractice litigation. Similar increases occurred in medical malpractice suits and other areas of litigation. Most reported cases of legal malpractice concern breaches of fiduciary trust or cases of outright fraud such as misappropriation of client funds. Carelessness and neglect of clients can also lead to serious problems for an attorney. Under the code of professional responsibility, attorneys have an ethical obligation to accept malpractice cases against other attorneys. Ethical consideration 2-28 states, in part: "The personal preference of a lawyer to avoid adversary alignment against . . . other lawyers . . . does not justify his rejection of tendered employment." (ABA, 1980, p. 9)

COMMUNITY RELATIONS

The organized bar associations provide a critical link between attorneys and the larger community. Apart from their guildlike activities (for example, restricting entry to the profession, seeking to control attorney conduct), bar associations "are also political interest groups, actively engaged in lobbying for proposals that the bar considers vital to its interests." (Jacob, 1978, p. 59) A major focus of bar associations is on court organization. Bar associations have developed and sponsored various schemes for reorganizing courts in the United States. In addition, the organized bar has been very active in trying to influence the selection of judges. On the state level bar associations have called for adoption of the Missouri Plan—a method of judicial selection which would greatly enhance bar influence. Elsewhere, bar associations conduct "bar primaries'' prior to judicial elections in the hope of influencing voters. At the federal level the ABA has sought to influence the president and attorney general before a judicial nomination is submitted to the Senate. Since the time of the Eisenhower administration, the ABA has been routinely consulted by the attorney general. Finally, the bar also promotes legislation which is in the interests of the legal profession. The ABA regularly takes a position on a full range of issues being considered by Congress.

Evidently, there are many lawyers who would like the organized bar to play a more active role in issues of a public nature.[14] In one installment of LawPoll, respondents were asked to evaluate whether bar activity is adequate for each of eleven issues and for public issues generally. As shown in Table 3-4, members of the bar generally believe that the organized bar is not involved adequately in public issues. Very few believe that the bar is too involved in public concerns. For public issues generally, 53 percent of attorneys believe that the bar is not involved enough, while only 6 percent believe the bar is too involved. Of the specific issues studied, the legal community is most supportive of greater involvement in welfare reform. The least support for increased bar involvement was in the areas of gay rights, electoral politics, and affirmative action. In general, the membership of the ABA believes that its leadership is playing too passive a role in public policy issues.

In the 1970s and 1980s the issue of advertising by attorneys has been one of the major concerns in lawyer-community relations.[15] Clearly, the nature and

TABLE 3-4 Perceived Degree of Involvement of Organized Bar in Public Issues

	NOT INVOLVED ENOUGH	INVOLVED TO JUST RIGHT DEGREE	TOO INVOLVED	NOT SURE
1. Public Issues Generally	53%	36%	6%	6%
2. Welfare reform	58	22	4	17
3. International human rights	36	36	7	21
4. Ecology	35	42	9	13
5. Prisoner's rights	33	45	10	12
6. Unemployment	32	42	5	21
7. Women's rights	32	44	5	19
8. Nuclear weapons	28	34	8	30
9. Electoral politics	28	41	15	16
10. Housing	27	45	7	21
11. Gay rights	24	40	11	25
12. Affirmative action	24	40	13	23

Adapted from LawPoll, ''Organized Bar and Public Issues: Majority Wants More Activism,'' *American Bar Association Journal* (January 1978), p. 43.

[14]LawPoll, ''Organized Bar and Public Issues: Majority Wants More Activism,'' *American Bar Association Journal,* 1978, *64,* 42–43.

[15]LawPoll, ''What's Important to Lawyers?'' *American Bar Association Journal,* 1982, *68,* 38–39.

extent of legally permitted advertising has important implications for the way lawyers relate to their community. Traditionally, stringent restrictions have been placed on lawyer advertising. This has been the case for numerous reasons (see *Bates v. State Bar of Arizona* at pp. 367–379). First, it has been said that advertising by attorneys would undermine the professionalism of the bar. Such advertising would harm the dignity and self-worth of lawyers and reduce public confidence in the profession. It has also been argued that advertising would be inherently misleading, that it would stir up litigation that might otherwise not occur, that advertising would increase the overhead of the profession and thus the costs to consumers, that it would adversely affect the quality of services, and that regulation to prevent misleading advertising would be extremely difficult.

Despite these objections, some observers have viewed the traditional restraints on advertising as highly excessive. Some have suggested that restrictions on advertising by bar associations constitute a restraint on trade. Others have seen these restrictions as a violation of free speech. In 1977 the Supreme Court dealt with the issue of lawyer advertising in *Bates v. State Bar of Arizona*. Here the Court focused on whether lawyers may constitutionally advertise the prices at which they perform certain routine services. On First Amendment grounds the Court struck down the disciplinary rule preventing lawyer advertising.

In its decision the Court asserted that advertising by attorneys would not diminish their professional standing, just as it does not undermine that of bankers or engineers. Indeed, the Court suggested that the failure of lawyers to advertise may create public disillusionment with the bar. In the absence of advertising, the public may feel that the legal profession is failing to reach out and serve the community. Moreover, the failure of attorneys to advertise might cause some people to suffer an injustice needlessly, feeling that the expense of an attorney would be too high or that finding a competent attorney would be too difficult. The Court suggested that deceptive advertising be dealt with through disciplinary proceedings rather than by a ban on all advertising. Both the bar and the public, said the Court, would benefit from an increased flow of information about legal services.

A survey taken following the *Bates* decision indicated that there was much dissatisfaction among attorneys with the Court's ruling.[16] Among the attorneys questioned, two-thirds believed that advertising would lower the professional status of lawyers. Fewer than one-third believed that advertising would either lower legal fees or help citizens in selecting an attorney. At the same time, 43 percent believed that advertising would bring legal services to the attention of those who need them but are unaware of that need. In subsequent decisions the Supreme Court has reaffirmed its commitment to the right of

[16]LawPoll, "Is Advertising Laying an Egg?" *American Bar Association Journal,* 1978, *64,* 673–674.

attorneys to advertise (see *Ohralik v. Ohio State Bar Association* and *In the Matter of R——M. J——*). While some state regulation is permissible, such regulation must be pursuant to avoiding possible false, deceptive, or misleading advertising. It also appears that most attorneys no longer regard advertising as an important issue facing the legal profession.[17] In 1977 42 percent of lawyers mentioned advertising as an important issue before the bar. However, by 1978 the number fell to 21 percent; by 1981 only 4 percent cited it. Further, an increased amount of advertising is apparent in both telephone directories and newspapers. Nevertheless, while advertising by attorneys has become more common, leading firms have generally resisted this trend.

AN ASSESSMENT

Lawyers occupy some key positions in American society. As private attorneys they play an essential role in identifying legal problems and dealing with these problems effectively. Lawyers also play important roles in public affairs, both in filling key governmental positions and in lobbying government on matters of interest to the bar. Notwithstanding the significant place of attorneys in our society, the bar today is faced with a number of serious problems. To begin with, many observers are critical of the lack of demographic representativeness in the bar. These critics would want the legal profession to open its ranks more fully to minorities. In addition, legal training has been criticized as narrow, tedious, irrelevant, and authoritarian. Certainly, there is much to be said for moving beyond the current preoccupation with analyzing appellate court decisions.

Other problems also permeate the bar. There is much room for improving the effectiveness of legal services and reducing the variation in such effectiveness. There must also be an increased effort to ensure that lawyers serve the interests of clients. Also critical is the presence of an unmet need for legal services. One element of this problem is the preoccupation of the bar with property-related concerns to the exclusion of other kinds of legal matters. Malpractice is also an important problem in the bar. We find both a violation of ethical norms and the failure of disciplinary agencies to enforce ethical rules. The fact that so many attorneys are concerned about public attitudes toward the legal profession may reflect the presence of so many unresolved problems in the bar. If the bar cannot put its own house in order, it may very well face increased governmental controls.

QUESTIONS FOR DISCUSSION

1. How do lawyers differ from police officers in their backgrounds and professionalism? In what respects are the concerns raised about law

[17]LawPoll, *American Bar Association Journal,* 1982, *68,* 38–39.

school education different from or similar to those raised about the training of the police? If you were to complete a three-year law school program, how might the experience change you as a person?

2. How does the popular image of the job of the lawyer differ from the reality? How effective are lawyers in carrying out their various roles? Do the most effective lawyers make the most money? To what extent can lawyers be made more effective? Would it be desirable to try to make lawyers equally effective?

3. To what extent are lawyers necessary in our society? In what respects could the use of lawyers be reduced? Are there any areas where increased use of attorneys would be desirable?

4. How concerned are attorneys about their image before the public? Is this degree of concern realistic? What changes in the nature of lawyers and the legal profession would enhance the public image of lawyers?

FOR FURTHER READING

AMERICAN BAR ASSOCIATION. *The American Bar Association Journal.* Chicago, Illinois. A monthly collection of diverse articles bearing on the legal profession.

CARLIN, JEROME E. *Lawyers' Ethics.* New York: Russell Sage Foundation, 1966. Analysis of ethical violations by New York City attorneys, particularly as they pertain to the stratification of the bar.

JOHNSTONE, QUINTIN, and HOPSON, DAN, JR. *Lawyers and Their Work.* Indianapolis: Bobbs-Merrill, 1967. Read this book if you want to know what it is like to be a lawyer.

ROSENTHAL, DOUGLAS E. *Lawyer and Client: Who's in Charge?* New York: Russell Sage Foundation, 1974. If you actively participate in the handling of your legal problem, you will get a better result.

ZEMANS, FRANCES KAHN, and ROSENBLUM, VICTOR G. "Preparation for the Practice of Law—the Views of the Practicing Bar." *American Bar Foundation Research Journal* (Winter 1980). Tells the qualities needed to be a successful attorney and how well law schools are training their students in these skills.

SUPREME COURT RULINGS

Argersinger v. Hamlin, 407 U.S. 25 (1972)
Bates v. State Bar of Arizona, 433 U.S. 350 (1977)
Gideon v. Wainwright, 372 U.S. 335 (1963)
In the Matter of R——M. J——, 50, LW 4185 (1982)
Ohralik v. Ohio State Bar Association, 436 U.S. 447 (1978)
University of California v. Bakke, 438 U.S. 265 (1978)

4
JUDGES

PREVIEW

Chapter Four examines judges in the United States. The chapter consists of five sections:

    Members of the bench
    Roles
    Decision-making process
    Ethics
    Community relations

First, we discuss members of the bench—their background characteristics, methods of selection, training, attitudes, and professionalism. Judges in the United States are recruited through a variety of means but receive little or no special training. Second, we turn to the roles of judges. Although judging in a trial court is quite unlike serving as a Supreme Court justice, judges at all levels may exercise four basic roles: norm enforcer, lawmaker, administrator, and politician. In exercising these roles, judges play an important part in our nation's political system. Third, we focus on the decision-making process engaged in by judges—a topic that has attracted an enormous amount of study.

This research has attempted to identify the way that judges make up their minds when deciding cases. Behavioralists have offered six basic explanations: fact pattern analysis, role theory, judicial backgrounds, attitudes, group dynamics, and environmental influences. Fourth, we examine judicial ethics, including the ABA's code of judicial conduct. Finally, we look at community relations. We will see that the public has little knowledge about the Supreme Court, but that Americans nevertheless are generally supportive of the judiciary.

MEMBERS OF THE BENCH

Judges are government officials who are supposed to provide a service (that is, justice) to the public. Although there are many private police officers and many attorneys in private practice, judges are found only in the courts of our government. Some judges are in the federal courts, and others are in state courts. As government officials, judges must be selected in some way. Mechanisms for judicial selection in the United States are varied and include election, appointment, and the "Missouri Plan." Particularly for prestigious judgeships, the recruitment process generally leads to the selection of high-status individuals. It is not clear which method of judicial selection works best, partly because we have not decided exactly what qualities we are looking for in judges. A notable feature of each selection process is the absence of formal training for judges. We ask much of our judges, and yet we believe they can "grow into" their job without classroom training or a period of apprenticeship. There is some evidence that judges in the United States tend to be moderate to conservative. Significantly, however, the political attitudes of judges are sometimes said to be irrelevant to their job. According to traditional theory, judges are professionals who are able to apply the Constitution, statutes, and precedents mechanically and in a uniform way. There are many who doubt whether judging is or can be like this.

Background

It should come as little surprise that the background characteristics of judges differ markedly from those of the American public as a whole. After all, we do not choose our judges through a lottery. Nor do judicial selectors try to achieve an equivalence in socioeconomic representation. This does not mean that there are stringent formal barriers to becoming a judge in the United States—even at the level of the Supreme Court. Constitutionally, Supreme Court justices need not even be attorneys. The only formal requirement is procedural—Supreme Court justices must be nominated by the president and confirmed by the Senate. Informally, however, the appointment process has imposed significant barriers in the way of those who would become Supreme

Court justices. The result is that one who possesses certain background characteristics has a greater likelihood than others of becoming a Supreme Court justice.

Judicial researchers have identified a set of background characteristics which are typical of Supreme Court justices (Schmidhauser, 1961, Ch. 3; Abraham, 1975, Ch. 3). Not surprisingly, Supreme Court justices have a superior educational background. A disproportionate number of Supreme Court justices have attended an Ivy League school either for their undergraduate work or to obtain a law degree.[1] Note, however, that there is no constitutional or statutory basis requiring that federal judges—even Supreme Court justices—be learned in the law. Paradoxically, nearly all the states do officially require that their judges be learned in the law (Council of State Governments, 1978, pp. 88–89). The official or unofficial requirement of superior education, including admission to the bar, is the one factor that excludes the largest number of Americans from possible service in the judiciary. Of course, much can be said in support of high educational standards. Still, the requirement of a law degree may exclude many qualified individuals, such as political scientists specializing in constitutional law or leading journalists who are well versed in the operations and decisions of the Supreme Court.

There are also some political requirements for becoming a Supreme Court justice. On a formal basis the Constitution requires that justices be nominated by the president and confirmed by a majority vote of the Senate. This process has given rise to the informal requirement of ideological compatibility. Supreme Court appointments—and appointments elsewhere in the federal judiciary—generally come from the same political party as the president. Not surprisingly, presidents normally select individuals who are politically and ideologically compatible with them. Indeed, some Supreme Court openings are used to reward political supporters and personal friends. Additionally, individuals from families with strong political roots are far more likely than individuals not so connected to be appointed to the Supreme Court. Many justices had a parent who served either as a judge or in some other political capacity. Also, nearly all those appointed have held some prior political post. A position in political life is virtually a prerequisite for becoming a Supreme Court appointee. However, this post need not be judicial. Indeed, only about one in five justices had ten or more years of experience on the bench prior to being selected to serve in the Supreme Court (Abraham, 1975, pp. 43–44).

[1]The justices of the 1981–1982 term received their law degree at the following institutions: Warren Burger (St. Paul College of Law, LLB), William Brennan (Harvard Law School, LLB), Byron White (Yale Law School, LLB), Thurgood Marshall (Howard University Law School, LLB), Harry Blackmun (Harvard Law School, LLB), Lewis Powell (Washington and Lee University Law School, LLB; Harvard Law School, LLM), William Rehnquist (Stanford University Law School, LLB), John Stevens (Northwestern University Law School, JD), Sandra O'Connor (Stanford University, LLB). For a brief biographical sketch of each justice in American history, see Congressional Quarterly, *Guide to the U. S. Supreme Court* (Washington, D. C.: Congressional Quarterly, Inc., 1979), pp. 793–866.

Many of the most highly regarded justices in American history had no prior judicial experience before reaching the Supreme Court, including eight of the fifteen Chief Justices.

Finally, a person's chances of appointment to the Supreme Court are also influenced by socioeconomic background. To begin with, very few justices have come from humble origins. More than 90 percent were raised in comfortable economic circumstances. Many of their families had considerable social prestige. In addition, throughout American history most judges were born in cities and towns. However, while most would-be judges have had an urban background, their high family income shielded them from the tensions of slum life. Moreover, justices have generally been Anglo-Saxon Protestants. Few could trace their ancestry to Eastern Europe. Members of the highest court have also, almost uniformly, been white males of a fairly advanced age. As to race and sex, the first black appointed to the Supreme Court was Thurgood Marshall, in 1967; the first woman appointed was Sandra O'Connor, in 1981. The advanced age of most justices at the time of their appointment can easily be understood as resulting from the difficulties of attaining recognition in the legal community early in life.

Because of a paucity of data, studies of the background characteristics of judges in lesser courts have necessarily been far less systematic (Goldman, 1974; Goldman, 1965). What evidence we do have seems to support the hypothesis of Donald Matthews concerning the relationship between political and social prestige (1954). As Matthews suggests, the higher the status of the political post, the greater the social status of the normal incumbent. Few federal judges come from humble origins. It is only in the lower-level positions of the judiciary, such as the state trial courts, that we begin to see large numbers of judges with lower social, economic, and professional prestige. Indeed, in the lower specialized tribunals still existing in some localities, many judges do not even possess a law degree.

The matter of judicial backgrounds is important for two reasons. To begin with, the background characteristics of judges may affect their decisions on the bench (Tate, 1981). A judge's background characteristics are likely to lead to certain experiences as well as a self-identification with various groups. This will inevitably have some effect on the judge's court rulings. Beyond that, judicial backgrounds may also have symbolic import. For example, the elevation of a Jew, black, or woman to the Supreme Court may be a source of great pride to citizens with the same background characteristic. Given the unrepresentative backgrounds of those who have served in the federal courts, Sheldon Goldman has suggested that there ought to be a policy of affirmative action for the judiciary (1979). Under such a policy special consideration would be given to women, blacks, and other minorities when filling judicial vacancies. A contrary argument holds that judges ought to be appointed solely on the basis of merit. Even so, it is clear that there are already many factors apart from merit that are considered in the appointment process. Clearly, we do not choose judicial candidates through a merit employment examination. Rather, judicial selection is a highly political process that results in the recruitment of judges with identifiable backgrounds. There are those who would wish to deal with some of the resulting biases in federal appointments by implementing judicial affirmative action.

Selection

The question of who shall be judge is answered in a variety of ways in the United States. Basically, three processes of judicial selection can be found— election, appointment, and the Missouri Plan. Presumably, the method of selection in use has some effect on what kinds of judges reach the bench. Part of our problem in choosing among these selection methods is that we do not fully understand their consequences (Volcansek, 1982). Further, there is no consensus as to the most important qualities for being a good judge. While some observers point to professional qualities such as superior craftsmanship skills, others note the relevance of representational skills—that is, being relatively responsive to public attitudes. Based on an in-depth examination of federal judicial selection procedures during three recent presidential administrations, Harold Chase concludes that "our present appointment system nets a good but not outstanding array of federal judges." (1972, p. 208) Chase's major proposal for reform of the federal selection process is rather novel. He suggests that the selection of federal district and appeals court judges be turned over to the Supreme Court. Chase asks: "Who could better make judgments about the professional credentials of prospects than the Court?" (1972, p. 206). Selection by the Supreme Court, according to Chase, would greatly increase the concern for "the purely professional capabilities and character of prospective judges" (1972, p. 206).

Elections are the principal means for electing the nearly 12,000 state and local judges in the United States. As James Eisenstein notes, the aim of elections in judicial races is to achieve democratic control (1973, pp. 15–16). In theory, an elected judiciary would be expected to be more representative of popular desires. The candidate or incumbent who is unrepresentative risks defeat in the upcoming election. According to democratic theory, candidates and incumbents will often modify their positions in anticipation of popular reactions. Once elected, a judge would be responsive to public opinion in order to remain in office. Elections may be either partisan or nonpartisan. Partisan elections for judicial races have their roots in the Jacksonian democracy of the mid-nineteenth century. For Jackson and his followers democracy meant short terms and long ballots—ballots which even included races for judicial positions. The nonpartisan election dates back to the Progressive movement of the early 1900s. In nonpartisan elections political party designations do not appear on the ballot. The purpose here is to reduce the influence of party leaders in selecting candidates for public office.

Social science evidence generally paints a dim picture of the effectiveness of judicial elections in achieving their democratic objectives (Eisenstein, 1973, pp. 26–34).[2] Several difficulties have been discerned. First, judicial elections are held very infrequently. Most judges serve even longer than the six-year term of United States senators. These long terms reduce the opportunity for popular control. In addition, judicial candidates commonly run unopposed— particularly incumbents and those running in electoral contests for lesser judgeships. Obviously, the aim of democratic control through elections is defeated if it is impossible for a judicial candidate to be defeated. Third, even when challenged, an incumbent is rarely defeated. Judicial elections are noncompetitive, largely due to their low intensity and salience. Fourth, voter turnout for judicial elections is quite low, especially when judicial elections are not being held concurrently with a major national election. Even in presidential election years many voters suffer from "ballot fatigue" and opt not to push any levers for the judicial races. Fifth, judicial elections are marked by low levels of voter information (McKnight, Schaefer, and Johnson, 1978). In one study only 15.4 percent of Texas voters could correctly name a candidate for the state's supreme court or court of criminal appeals. Presumably, even fewer were aware of policy differences among the judicial candidates. Sixth, judicial campaigns are generally issueless. In the course of campaigning, judicial candidates rarely take any significant stands on court issues. Indeed, they are constrained from running issue-oriented campaigns by the provisions of the code of judicial conduct. Finally, nonpartisan elections pose special difficulties for democratic control (Dubois, 1980, p. 244). When a party label is not on the ballot, voters lack a piece of information that can be quite useful. In short, judicial elections are not exactly a model of democracy in action.

Appointment is a second method of judicial selection (Abraham, 1980a, pp. 23–35; Abraham, 1975; pp. 15–23; Goldman, 1971, pp. 1–4; Chase, 1972; Danelski, 1964). This method is used both in the federal courts and in many state court systems. Federal judges are nominated by the president and confirmed by the Senate. This process is constitutionally mandated in the case of Supreme Court justices. A similar selection process is present in a number of states, with nomination of judges by the governor and confirmation by the legislature. In other states the nomination itself is made by the legislature. The appointment process is commonly used even in states that, formally, have an election method for choosing judges. Given the long term of judges, retirements often occur midway in a judge's term of office. When a vacancy occurs, it is normally filled by the governor through an interim appointment (Herndon, 1962). This process amounts to a de facto appointment method since few of those appointed are defeated in subsequent elections.

In practice, the process of selecting federal judges is considerably more

---

[2]For a more optimistic view see Philip L. Dubois, *From Ballot to Bench* (Austin, Tex.: University of Texas Press, 1980).

complex than simply nomination by the president and confirmation by the Senate. As Sheldon Goldman notes: "The appointment process is highly complex, with each appointment involving a different combination of participants, circumstances, and considerations." (1967, p. 212) One added dimension of the process is that the president often delegates responsibility for nominations to the Justice Department—particularly for circuit court and district court vacancies. Also very significant is the involvement of individual senators in the nomination and confirmation process. Especially for district court nominations, custom decrees that the president consult with any senators from the state with the vacancy who are members of the same party as the president. A nomination contrary to the expressed wishes of a same-party, same-state senator may be blocked at the confirmation stage through "senatorial courtesy." In general, the Senate will disapprove a district court nomination that is "personally obnoxious" to the senator involved—particularly if that senator has some good reasons and is willing to put up a fight. Also important to the federal judicial selection process is the American Bar Association's Committee on Federal Judiciary (Grossman, 1965), the White House staff, the FBI, state party leaders, interest groups, the contenders and their friends, and the Senate Judiciary Committee.

Selection by appointment has been justified as a means of recruiting highly competent, impartial judges to the bench. Even so, the method does have its critics. An extreme example is David Stein, who resents the enormous powers placed in the hands of appointed judges. Stein fears that too many of those appointed are "party hacks" or "expedient choices" rather than the most qualified people available (1974, p. 2). Still, most observers seem to believe that executive appointment of judges strikes a nice balance between the pursuit of democratic control and expertise. Presidents, governors, and mayors tend to appoint competent individuals, if only to avoid political embarrassment. The appointment method also has some traces of democracy, since those appointed to the bench will generally be similar in ideology to the elected officials who made the appointments. Of course, there are those who would want to tinker with the process. During the Carter administration the process of making nominations to the circuit courts was reformed through the creation of a nominating commission to help select candidates of superior professional expertise (Berkson, Carbon, and Neff, 1979). The stated aims were to select judges on the basis of professional merit, with a view toward nominating an increased number of women and members of minority groups. Critics have complained that the commission should have been nonpartisan but instead was loaded with partisan Democrats who almost always recommended Democrats. It might be countered, however, that judicial nominees ought to be of the same party as the president to promote a representative judiciary. In any event, our experience with the commission suggests that its composition greatly influences the impact of this reform.

The Missouri Plan, now in use in a number of states, is a third method of judicial selection (Abraham, 1975, p. 14; Goldman, 1971; Volcansek, 1982).[3] Referred to as "merit selection" by its proponents, it is a complex method which involves both the appointive and elective methods. Developed early in the twentieth century, it has long been advocated by the American Bar Association, the American Judicature Society, and other key elements in the bar. A basic premise of the Missouri Plan was that "judges were not in the same category as other officeholders, but were a special type of public official for which the Bar had a unique responsibility." (Watson and Downing, 1969, p. 330) The stated aim of the method is to somehow remove politics from judicial nominations and thus increase the competence and independence of those selected.

Under the Missouri Plan, when a judicial vacancy arises, candidates are considered by a commission composed of lawyers, judges, and laypeople. For each vacant judgeship commission members nominate three candidates. The governor is then obliged to select one of these three to serve a term of one year. After this brief term the appointee faces the electorate in a "retention election," running unopposed. Voters are simply asked: "Shall Judge _____ of the _____ Court be retained in Office?" If retention is favored by a majority of voters, the judge may serve a full term. In Missouri this term is twelve years for appellate judges and six years for judges at the trial court level. A number of other states have since adopted the Missouri Plan, although sometimes altering certain elements of it, such as the judges' term of office.

While the organized bar continues to support the Missouri Plan, critics of this selection method have raised a number of important objections (Volcansek, 1982, pp. 86–87). One basic criticism is that members of nominating commissions are generally unrepresentative of the public. For the most part, commissions are comprised of a fairly homogeneous group of high-status people (Ashman and Alfini, 1974). It is argued that such commission members are not likely to appoint women or members of minority groups and perhaps no more likely to choose qualified judges than other selection methods. It is also argued that the Missouri Plan gives undue influence to the bar in the selection of judges. State bar association officials have themselves stated that the Missouri Plan is their most effective means of influencing the selection of judges (Sheldon, 1977). Finally, many fear that the Missouri Plan seriously insulates the judiciary from democratic control. While the method includes a retention election, such elections are marked by even lower rates of voter interest, knowledge, and turnout than other judicial elections. Indeed, fewer than 1 percent of judges standing for retention elections have been removed through this process (Carbon, 1980, p. 213).

Research on judicial selection suggests that the type of selection process in use has at least some impact on the kinds of people selected (Jacob, 1964;

---

[3]See also "Judicial Selection and Tenure in Indiana: A Critical Analysis and Suggested Reform," *Indiana Law Journal,* 1964, *39,* 364–386.

Canon, 1972; Watson and Downing, 1969; Volcansek, 1982; Nagel, 1973b). As Jacob notes, the "formal selection procedures are more than a facade." (1964, p. 104) Formal procedures establish certain informal qualifications, giving greater access to some groups than others. Existing research suggests that the selection process may have an impact on the kinds of people recruited to judgeships—their partisan affiliation, religion, educational attainments, and previous offices. Additional research might uncover further differences in the impact of judicial recruitment on who gets selected.[4] Before we can fully evaluate which selection method is most desirable, we must decide what qualities are most desirable in a judge. This may vary considerably from the state trial judge to the Supreme Court justice. No doubt, we would want a selection method which is not heavily biased against any class, race, sex, or ethnic group. Among the other considerations are expertise and accountability. Having established criteria, it is then necessary to evaluate in what respects various selection methods will produce different kinds of judges. The most appropriate selection methods are those which have built-in biases toward selecting judges with the desired attributes.

Training

Judges in the United States receive little specialized training for their position. This is quite unlike the situation in other nations. Extensive judicial training of one sort or another is taken for granted in many countries (Institute of Judicial Administration, 1965, pp. 14–21). For example, a schooling approach predominates in France. Potential French judges are trained through an educational institution with a planned curriculum. After completing law school, the graduate decides between law practice and a career on the bench. Graduates desiring a judicial career must pass a competitive exam for admission to the National Center for Judicial Studies. Those admitted receive intensive training over a four-year period, consisting of classroom work as well as apprenticeship experience. After completing the course, the applicants must take another exam. Those who are successful are chosen to fill vacancies as they occur on the magistrate level. Vacancies on higher courts are filled by promotions within the judiciary. In short, France has a career judiciary requiring specialized training as a prerequisite to becoming a judge.

An apprenticeship approach is used in other nations, such as Denmark. After completing a general university law course, those graduates wishing to enter the judiciary seek positions as assistants to lower court judges. At first, the judges perform duties similar to those of American bailiffs, notaries public, and sheriffs. After acquiring some experience, assistants are delegated duties relating to administering wills and estates. The apprenticeship is supplemented by course work conducted by the Danish Judges' Assistants As-

---

[4]An example of the research needed in this area is Nagel (1973b).

sociation and the Ministry of Justice. Assistants remain in this capacity for a long time—until they reach their forties or fifties—when they finally get appointed to the bench. However, given their long apprenticeship, experienced assistants are assigned increasing responsibilities, even to the extent of assuming the judge's full duties when the latter is ill or on vacation. When finally appointed to the bench, the new judge becomes responsible for duties with which he or she is completely familiar.[5]

In contrast, the training of American judges is highly unsystematic. Apart from the customary law degree, no special educational course or period of apprenticeship is required to become a judge in the United States. There is an assumption that those appointed or elected will somehow "grow into" their judgeship and serve with competence. Parenthetically, a few judges have made use of voluntary educational programs (Ford Foundation, 1974, pp. 23–24; Institute of Judicial Administration, 1965; Leflar, 1960; Leflar, 1956). There are several national organizations involved in providing short-term training to judges, such as the Institute of Judicial Administration. Training programs serving about one-half of the states also exist. There are four basic types of judicial education activities (Reaves, 1981, p. 525). Orientation training aims at facilitating the transition of appointees and new judges to the bench. Basic training provides a survey of typical skills required to be an effective judge. Continuing programming focuses on an in-depth treatment of narrowly defined judicial skills or areas of substantive knowledge. Finally, specialty courses cover topics that are infrequently encountered by most judges. While there has been a considerable increase in the availability of judicial education courses, it must be noted that these courses are generally of only short duration. Clearly, little training can occur in a program of about two weeks.

It is not apparent whether federal and state judges should be required to submit to a more systematic training period. Certainly, newly appointed judges in the United States have far less formal training than judges in many other countries. We have no extensive course work or period of apprenticeship for judges in our country. Indeed, it has been said that American judges are simply lawyers who have the right connections. At the same time, it is not apparent that extensive training is a prerequisite to becoming a good judge. Many believe, for example, that Earl Warren was very effective as Chief Justice of the Supreme Court. Yet, prior to his appointment to the apex of the judiciary, Warren had never even served as a judge. The best judges are said to have attributes such as common sense, knowledge of the law, courtesy, open-mindedness, and strong work habits (Goldman, 1971, p. 8; Watson and Downing, 1969, pp. 296–297). They must also have skills in case management, impartial decision making, and court administration (Reaves, 1981). We do not know to what extent course work or an apprenticeship enhances these

---

[5]In Denmark some judicial appointments are also made from the personnel of the Prosecutor's Office and the Ministry of Justice.

qualities—or other important qualities—in potential judges. Nor has it been shown that requiring systematic training would encourage a pattern of self-selection leading to the presence of more competent judges. Certainly, there does exist an informal process in which judges become trained for their position (Carp and Wheeler, 1972). Then too, for critics who look only at "the bottom line" of a judicial decision, the most important characteristic of a judge may simply be that judge's ideology.

Attitudes

As informed individuals, most judges presumably have some rather well-defined political attitudes. Even so, we lack conclusive evidence of attitudes typical to judges or the extent to which they vary. What evidence we do have suggests that judges are generally moderate to conservative in political outlook. For example, a study of federal circuit court judges conducted by J. Woodford Howard indicates that most of the judges considered themselves to be political moderates before entering the judiciary (1981, pp. 115–116). Few of those interviewed saw themselves as highly ideological. A study of judicial attitudes by Stuart Nagel found that American judges tend to be conservative (1963). The study indicated that judges, in fact, tend to be more conservative than the general public as well as more conservative than legislators and administrators. Nagel attributed these conservative attitudes to factors such as class and family background, previous occupations, training, age, and ethnic characteristics. As noted earlier, judges tend to be relatively homogeneous with respect to these criteria (Schmidhauser, 1961, Ch. 3; Abraham, 1975, Ch. 3). Most of them are white males of advanced years with high socioeconomic status and training in the law. They also tend to be Anglo-Saxon Protestants. These characteristics would seem to bias the attitudes of the judiciary in a conservative direction.

At the same time, in considering the attitudes of judges, we must also be attentive to the process of judicial selection. At the federal level, and in many of the states, judges are chosen through a political process of appointment. Federal judges are nominated by the president and may serve for life. A president may try to use this appointment power to influence the ideological make-up of the federal judiciary. It is likely that the pool of individuals available for judgeships is more conservative than the general population. However, it is also likely that there is enough variation within that judicial pool to permit a liberal Democratic president to nominate liberals to the judiciary. In fact, recent presidents have almost uniformly filled judicial vacancies from within their own political party (Goldman, 1981). For example, 92.2 percent of Richard Nixon's appointments to United States district courts and 93.3 percent of appeals courts appointees were Republicans.

The above suggests that the attitudes of those appointed will usually parallel the attitudes of the appointing president (Tate, 1981). The nature of the selection process also suggests that if a party can retain power for a long period of time, the ideological viewpoint of that party will ultimately come to dominate the judiciary.[6] A more heterogeneous judiciary is likely where there has been frequent turnover in party fortunes in recent presidential elections. The judiciary will also tend to be heterogeneous in periods of transition, when leadership has passed from one party to another. However, heterogeneity in judicial attitudes is probably constrained somewhat by the common backgrounds and training of judges (Grossman, 1966, p. 144). To some extent attitudinal heterogeneity is also mitigated by the processes of socialization present in the federal judiciary (Carp and Wheeler, 1972).

A fascinating feature of judicial attitudes is that they are supposed to be irrelevant to the decisions made by judges. Traditional thought about judging portrays judges as professionals with the unique capacity to apply preexisting legal guidelines to the cases before them (Ball, 1978; Cardozo, 1921; Hart, 1961; Wechsler, 1961). From a normative standpoint the notion of stare decisis suggests that judges have a professional obligation to abide by existing precedents (Ball, 1978, pp. 8–17). To the extent that judges adhere to stare decisis, their latitude in decision making is sharply curtailed, since decisions made in the past serve as binding guidelines in current cases. It appears that much judicial decision making is, in fact, consistent with the principle of stare decisis. Relatively few trial court decisions are subsequently reversed at the appellate level. In collegial courts, moreover, judges decide the vast majority of cases unanimously. These facts lend some credence to the belief that judges often are able to set aside their personal attitudes and base their decisions on the nature of existing legal guidelines.

At the same time, there are many cases in which the attitudes of judges become expressed in their decisions. Clear-cut legal precedents are not present in every case. In other cases judges enjoy discretion with regard to which precedent to select in a case. In still other cases a judge may opt to exercise lawmaking powers by reversing precedent and establishing a new jurisprudence. Evidence suggests, in fact, that there are many civil and criminal cases in which judges disagree with one another. A fine body of scholarship suggests that the attitudes of judges play an important role in the kinds of decisions made (Schubert, 1974b). In the Nagel study noted earlier, for example, a liberalism score was assigned to each judge. This score was correlated with decisions made in criminal, business regulation, and workmen's compensation cases. On the basis of these findings, Nagel concludes: "Off-the-bench judicial attitudes thus do seem to correlate in a meaningful way with on-the-bench judicial decisions." (1963, p. 40) We can expect, moreover, that judicial attitudes will be especially important in shaping the decisions of Supreme Court justices

---

[6]Historically, a single party has dominated the presidency for very long periods of time. In time a new "majority coalition" has then emerged which similarly dominated national politics. See Walter Dean Burnham, *Critical Elections and the Mainsprings of American Politics* (New York: W. W. Norton and Co., 1970).

and judges in other appellate courts. After all, in the cases heard by these courts, precedents will be less conclusive and far more opportunities will be present for engaging in lawmaking.

Professionalism

In discussing police officers and lawyers, we did not find it especially difficult to conclude whether each occupation was a profession. It seemed evident that the police were not professional in status, while lawyers clearly met the standards we set for professionals. It is rather more complicated to assess whether the occupation of judge should be regarded as a unique profession. Of course, virtually all judges are professionals in the sense that they are also attorneys. The issue we wish to consider here is whether we ought to regard the occupation of judge as a profession in its own right. Our analysis will be framed in terms of the nine criteria of professionalism cited earlier (Niederhoffer, 1967, pp. 18–19). The discussion will also be informed by existing evidence as to how judges rate on these criteria.

Five of the nine criteria for professional status are licensing of members, altruism and the service ideal, occupational pride, a code of ethics, and public prestige. On each of these five criteria judges fare quite well. Judging, of course, is a restricted occupation—a person cannot simply rent a building and open up shop as a judge. While no licensing exists as such, the system of formal selection and the swearing-in process are somewhat akin to a licensing system. Regarding the second criterion, a good deal of altruism and service orientation seems to exist among judges. Indeed, one of the major motivations for becoming a judge is to improve the working of the judicial system (Volcansek-Clark, 1978, pp. 173–174). In addition, judges generally wish to remain in their work despite a number of job-related burdens, such as lost income, loss of personal freedom, limits on business activities, and removal from law practice. Occupational pride is also very common among judges. Federal circuit judges see "their jobs as terminal positions, filled with professional gratification. . . ." (Howard, 1981, p. 118) Similarly, Florida judges regard as among the major benefits of their position a feeling of professional accomplishment, prestige of office, and a sense of personal accomplishment (Volcansek-Clark, 1978, p. 173). Also indicative of judicial professionalism is the judicial code of ethics, as set forth by the American Bar Association and state bar associations (ABA, 1980). It is likely that judges are not ignorant of the contents of that code. Moreover, the existence of the code may influence the attitudes of judges regarding appropriate conduct (Volcansek, 1980, p. 493). Finally, the occupation of judge enjoys enormous public prestige. A poll rating the prestige of ninety occupations placed Supreme Court justices at the very top (Hodge, Siegel, and Rossi, 1964). The position of county judge also ranks quite high, tied for thirteenth, fourteenth, and fifteenth in occupational prestige. These rankings compare quite favorably with lawyers, who were tied with chemists and foreign diplomats for tenth, eleventh, and twelfth place.

Still, there are some reasons for wondering whether judges should be regarded as professionals. Our doubts center on four criteria of professional status—high admissions standards, a lengthy training period for candidates, autonomous control, and the existence of a special body of knowledge and theory. To begin with, it is true that lengthy legal training is informally required for appointment to the federal judiciary. Such training is formally required in many states. Moreover, federal judges—especially at the upper levels—generally receive their legal training in prestigious law schools. Yet, these admissions standards may be more relevant to being a good lawyer than a good judge. While effective judges presumably need to have an excellent knowledge of the law, there are probably other qualities (for example, good judgment, common sense, fairness) that are also of great importance. Existing admissions standards for becoming a judge, as reflected in current selection processes, fail to consider whether an individual possesses these desirable qualities. Nor do judicial candidates go through a period of formal training designed to improve judging skills. This is quite unlike the procedure in a number of European countries (Institute of Judicial Administration, 1965). Indeed, few opportunites for specialized training exist for those selected as judge (Carp and Wheeler, 1972, pp. 381–383). To a very large extent judges must simply try to develop judging abilities on their own, especially during their early years on the bench.

How judges rate on the criterion of autonomy is rather murky. It is true that judges enjoy a lengthy tenure. Federal judges may even serve for life. Also, external controls upon judicial misconduct generally have been ineffectual, although some states have recently approved independent disciplinary commissions. Yet, judges occupy only one branch of a broader political system in which separated institutions share power. Clearly, judicial autonomy is limited by the operation of constitutional checks and balances. For example, judges do not control their own salary levels. Rather, salary decisions are made by legislators and executives. Further, the staffing of the judiciary is externally controlled. New judges in the United States are selected through the political processes of appointment and election. Indeed, the justices of the Supreme Court do not even have the discretion to choose their own Chief Justice. Additionally, the judiciary is highly dependent upon the executive branch to carry out its decisions. While the judiciary enjoys considerable independence in some respects, it also operates in an environment of constraints and shared power.

The greatest doubts about judicial professionalism relate to whether judges possess a special body of knowledge and theory. Certainly, the law school training of judges helps to make judges well versed in the law. This legal knowledge is one of the reasons we regard lawyers as professionals. More relevant here is the question of whether judges have any special knowledge of *judging*. The traditional view of judicial decision making suggests that judges have exceptional judging skills (Rumble, 1968, pp. 49–51). According to this view, judges arrive at their decisions in a rather mechanical manner by applying preexisting rules to the facts of particular cases. Neutral principles are relied upon (Wechsler, 1961). As Howard Ball suggests: "The justices' fidelity is to the law, not to partisan interests." (1978, p. xiii) In adjudging cases, the professional judge observes the rules of stare decisis (Ball, 1978, pp. 8–17). This means that judges are obliged to make clear what the law is, apply the law consistently, and avoid creating legal uncertainties by departing from stare decisis. It may be asking a great deal to expect a judge to adjudicate a caseload in a professional manner. It may be asking the impossible—given the inherent difficulties in making judgments, the lack of intensive training for judges, the ambiguity of preexisting rules, the uncertainty over the facts in a case, the presence of so many courts which are not specialized by subject matter, and simple human nature.

Regarding the nature of judging, a major challenge to thinking of judges as professionals was made by the legal realist movement of the 1930s and 1940s.[7] Legal realists pointed to a number of factors which suggest that judges do not have the capacity to mechanically apply preexisting rules in cases before them. First, legal realists suggested that judges usually have a diverse set of precedents which can justify a multitude of decisions. The presence of these diverse precedents means that judges must necessarily exercise discretion in a case before them. Second, judges can manipulate precedents in any number of ways. For example, precedents can be interpreted in a wide or in a restrictive fashion. Thus, a judge can capitalize on or evade the implications of previous court cases. Third, specific decisions in prior cases do not necessarily imply any particular rule. Almost every decision or set of decisions can be subsumed under several general rules. Fourth, legal language (for example, "due process") is quite ambiguous in character. This ambiguity permits a wide range of discretion in particular cases.

Several additional arguments suggest that judges do not have any special "professional" skills at judging. A fifth argument of legal realists is that judges must sometimes create new rules. They must do this because the old rules in some cases are unable to provide clear guidance in new situations. Sixth, the factual situations involved in each case are quite unique. Judges can, indeed must, "force" a case to fit under one general principle or another. Seventh, legal realists pointed to psychological theories which suggested that people really begin with a decision and only later rationalize it with reasons. This is contrary to traditional theory, which argues that judges apply preexisting rules deductively to individual cases. Eighth, legal realists believed that some judges were using the notion of enduring rules only as a rationale for refusing to adapt law to new social circumstances.

[7]For an excellent summary and critique of legal realism, see Rumble (1968).

Finally, another argument holds that the "facts" in a case are simply guessed at by a judge. Moreover, the way the judge will react to these "facts" is unpredictable. As a result, it is impossible to predict how a judge will apply rules in a particular case. Given the discretion of judges in fact-finding, a judge may very well "fudge" the facts in order to achieve the favored result. In short, powerful factors may constrain a judge from behaving in a professional manner. Even for those judges who attempt to apply the law in cases before them without introducing personal biases, the task may be very difficult and sometimes impossible.

ROLES

From the trial court judge to the Supreme Court justice, there is a great deal of variety in the work of judges. At one end of the process, trial court judges are largely involved in the quick processing of routine cases. At the other end, the nine Supreme Court justices are immersed in drafting written opinions for unusual cases which often have dramatic policy implications. However, despite the variety in job descriptions, it is also true that judges at all levels can carry out four basic roles. These include acting as norm enforcer, lawmaker, administrator, and politician. Their overall effectiveness in carrying out each of these roles has been debated. In addition, we lack conclusive evidence as to what qualities are most likely to make a judge effective.[8]

Norm Enforcement

Norm enforcement by judges involves the application of established legal standards to particular cases (Ball, 1980, pp. 23–44; Jacob, 1978, p. 23–31). In a very real sense, it may be considered a form of policymaking.[9] While norm enforcement does not involve the creation of new norms, it unmistakably does involve upholding existing norms. Essentially, then, a judge engaging in norm enforcement affirms the existing distribution of values in society as they are reflected in the case before the bench. This clearly involves maintaining the existing social order, but it may bear upon other values as well. All judges, but particularly trial court judges, engage in norm enforcement. In cases before them they try to apply a set of precedents and other preexisting rules in arriving at a decision. Appellate judges also engage in norm enforcement when they reaffirm existing legal standards rather than setting out on some new course. The Constitution is the most fundamental source of legal

---

[8]For one effort see Howard (1981), p. 230.

[9]Thomas R. Dye defines public policy as "whatever governments choose to do or not to do." Thus, if a government chooses not to change the status quo, that in itself is rightly regarded as a policy. See Thomas R. Dye, *Understanding Public Policy* (Englewood Cliffs, N. J.: Prentice-Hall, 1981), p. 1.

norms. As Howard Ball notes, the "document established the nature of the governmental structure, the powers of the agencies of the government, and the basic limitations of the central and state governments." (1980, p. 23) Other sources of judicial norms include statutes, prior court decisions, and the traditions of the community.

Clearly, norm enforcement is closely related to the notion of judicial professionalism. The difficulties inherent in applying preexisting rules to cases before them have led some observers to wonder whether judges may even be considered to engage in norm enforcement. For example, studies by political scientists of appellate decision making suggest that judges arrive at decisions in accordance with factors such as their personal backgrounds and attitudes. An implication of such studies is that judicial decisions can best be explained, not by the nature of existing legal norms, but by the exercise of policymaking discretion. Yet, it is important to note that most studies of this kind focus only on the subset of cases where the justices disagree (Becker, 1964). It may well be that in the numerous cases where Supreme Court justices unanimously agree, their agreement may be explained by the presence of a very clear precedent. In this regard Benjamin Cardozo has observed: "In countless litigations, the law is so clear that judges have no discretion. They have the right to legislate within gaps, but often there are no gaps." (1921, p. 129) To say that judges engage in norm enforcement is not to suggest that preexisting guidelines provide perfect guidance to judges in enforcing norms. Still, even if preexisting guidelines are not self-executing, they clearly are not irrelevant to the decisions rendered by judges (Neubauer, 1974, esp. pp. 11–12). After all, judges are well versed in the law and have a great deal of respect for it. Studying criminal justice in America, David Neubauer observed that "law and discretion interact. The law provides a context for decision making, sets forth certain criteria, and the law appliers must adapt the law to the situations as they find it." (1974, p. 12) Thus, it may be argued that much judicial activity consists of norm enforcement.

There are important social consequences to the enforcement of norms by judges. In broad terms norm enforcement helps to reaffirm in people's minds the validity of certain behavior and the impropriety of other behavior. At a general level much Supreme Court activity involves norm enforcement. The Court has established various rights relating to personal liberty, due process of law, and equal protection. In its decisions the Supreme Court generally reaffirms these principles and the extent to which they are constitutionally protected. At the same time, many Supreme Court decisions involve creating new legal norms, although generally at the margins of public policy. Trial courts more clearly engage in norm enforcement. For example, convictions and sentences are made on the basis of rather detailed legal guidelines which spell out what is a crime and what kinds of sentences may be imposed. As a result of court decisions, over 300,000 persons were in prison at the end of 1980 (U. S. Bureau of the Census, 1981, p. 189). Sentencing decisions were made by judges, albeit often in close consultation with prosecutors as well as defense attorneys. Considerable norm enforcement by judges also occurs in civil law. There is much at stake in these cases. Civil courts grant divorces, arrange for custody of children, garnishee wages, grant bankruptcies, commit people to mental institutions, and award damages for personal injuries. Acting as norm enforcers, judges apply existing standards of the civil law to the facts of these cases.

In some quarters the importance of trial judges in enforcing norms has been questioned. One sympathetic analyst, Norval Morris, has noted: "Over the past half century there has been a steady decline in the significance of the trial judge's role in the criminal justice process." (1972, p. 373) Factors in the decline of the trial judge's power include increased discretion by the police and by prosecutors and correctional officers. A study of criminal defendants by Jonathan Casper lends support to the view that trial judges have become "a figurehead" or "a rubber stamp" to the decisions made by prosecutors (1972a, p. 135). Asked "Who runs the show?" a typical response by a defendant was that the prosecutor is the key decision maker. Asked "What's the judge's job?" one defendant answered that the role of the judge is to just sit there "and do what the prosecutor tells him to do." (Casper, 1972a, pp. 135–136) While this is something of an overstatement, it is certainly true that most criminal trial court judges have delegated considerable responsibility to prosecutors. Legislative action to create fixed sentences for specific crimes would further erode the discretion of judges in norm enforcement (Alschuler, 1978).

The effectiveness of judges in norm enforcement has also been questioned. Presumably, judges should try to apply norms in an evenhanded manner. As Howard Ball notes: "We expect that a trial judge will fit the legal norms, as best he or she can, to the particular factual circumstances in the case before the court." (1980, p. 21) One line of inquiry has attempted to learn the consistency of trial judges in sentencing decisions. For example, William Austin and Thomas Williams assembled a group of state district court judges (1977). The judges were asked to render decisions in five hypothetical legal cases. Each case description provided the basic facts of a case as well as nonevidentiary information. The Austin-Williams simulation eliminated the problem of trying to equate different legal cases held before different judges.

On verdict, sentencing mode, and penalty, Austin and Williams found substantial disparities among judges. For example, in a marijuana possession case eighteen voted guilty while twenty-nine ruled not guilty (even though each judge was presented with an identical set of facts!). Of those deciding guilty, eight recommended probation, four called for a fine, three would impose both probation and a fine, while three favored a jail term. Clearly, this case evoked considerable disagreement among the judges. This strongly suggests that sentencing disparities is a basic problem in norm enforcement. In response to this problem, Eric Edmunds and others would require written explanations by judges of their sentencing decisions. Currently, written opinions are generally found in the appellate courts and in federal district courts. According to Edmunds: "A required explanation will tend to force the decision-maker to reflect and articulate. . . . Ultimately an explanation in each case will encourage the sentencer to be consistent." (1977, p. 363)

Lawmaking

Lawmaking by judges involves the creation of new norms through court decisions (Ball, 1980, pp. 44–52; Jacob, 1978, pp. 32–42). It involves changing the existing social order in some way, such as by placing a greater or lesser stress on personal liberty, social equality, or procedural justice. When judges engage in lawmaking, they are changing the nature of an existing legal ground rule. Judges can engage in lawmaking when some existing norm is challenged in a live legal controversy. Through a series of court rulings, judges can alter the public policies of the United States in very fundamental ways. Note, however, that the traditional theory of judging bars judges from the lawmaking role. In *United States v. Butler* Justice Owen J. Roberts noted: "When an act of Congress is appropriately challenged in the courts as not conforming to the constitutional mandate the judicial branch has only one duty,—to lay the article of the Constitution which is involved beside the statute which is challenged and to decide whether the latter squares with the former." (at 62) Such a narrow conception of the judicial role would seem to limit judges merely to the enforcement of existing norms.

Because lawmaking is normally associated with legislatures, much controversy may ensue when a judge departs from norm enforcement and declares that new legal norms exist. Nevertheless, judges are members of a coequal branch of government in our nation. Consequently, it should not be surprising that some important decisions are made by the American judiciary. Many of these decisions may quite rightfully be characterized as lawmaking. As Frank Coffin has observed: "Although the skills of the craft determine the outcome of most cases, the public and the press sense that in some of the most important cases there is more at work than professional judgment alone." (1980, p. 199). Similarly, Herbert Jacob notes that the power of judicial review "constantly involves American courts in conscious policy-making." (1978, p. 35) When deciding upon the constitutionality of a law or action, a judge may have great latitude in deciding what meaning to give the Constitution and for what purposes (Moore, 1981). Judges who stress the lawmaking role believe it is proper for them to consider their personal attitudes when making decisions. Rather than applying existing norms when rendering their decisions, judges may create new—sometimes controversial—norms.

Lawmaking may take place when courts interpret the Constitution, statutes, or even judicial precedents. To begin with, the constitutionality of controversial statutes and executive actions is often tested in the courts. The ambiguity of the Constitution makes it possible—even necessary—for judges to place their own interpretation on its provisions. As Walter Murphy points out: "Since the Constitution is written in broad terms of such convenient vagueness as "due process," "equal protection," "unreasonable searches and seizures," "commerce among the several states," saying what this law is allows, perhaps even requires, the Justices to apply their own value preferences." (1964, p. 13) Courts may also make new law when interpreting statutes. Theodore Roosevelt once observed: "The President and Congress are all very well in their way. They can say what they think they think, but it rests with the Supreme Court to decide what they really thought." (Pringle, 1931, p. 259) Because legislative intent is sometimes ambiguous, when a litigant makes a claim, it becomes necessary for justices to engage in lawmaking. When judges overrule existing precedents or limit their scope, they are also acting as lawmakers. In a series of cases beginning with *Brown v. Board of Education,* the Supreme Court rejected its prior ruling in *Plessy v. Ferguson,* which asserted that maintenance by the states of separate facilities for blacks and whites is not inherently unequal. The desegregation of schools and other public facilities which followed was among the most dramatic policy changes in American history.

Judicial policies seem to differ in certain fundamental ways from the policies of other government institutions (Jacob, 1978, pp. 39–41). First, judicial policies have tended to be narrower in scope. Judges sometimes refuse to issue a ruling in cases concerning "political" rather than constitutional questions. Most notably, cases involving foreign affairs are rarely ruled upon by judges. Second, judicial policies are often directed at government agencies as opposed to the public at large. In making their decisions, judges are involved in interpreting constitutional provisions. In so doing, they often permit or prohibit the actions of government agencies. Finally, the intended impact of judicial decisions is often ambiguous. The reason for this ambiguity is that judges make policy in response to the particular fact situations of cases before them. The intent of courts is usually made clear only after a series of cases has been adjudicated.

Court-made policy has come under much criticism in recent years (Berger, 1977; Graglia, 1976). The basic instruments used by judges are the legal weapons of the judiciary—the authority to decide cases, to issue orders, and to publish opinions which justify their rulings (Murphy and Tanenhaus, 1972, p. 87). Yet, the mere possession of such weapons hardly means that judges will use them to pursue policy goals effectively. A leading critic of the courts has been Donald Horowitz (1977). A centerpiece of his critique of court effectiveness is the argument that judges are generalists and as such lack detailed information on complex social issues. Horowitz asserts: "That judges are generalists means, above all, that they lack information and may also lack the experience and skill to interpret such information as they may receive." (1977, p. 31)

It is possible that courts are in the poorest position to make effective new policies. To begin with, Congress is specialized by subject matter into an elaborate committee system (Clapp, 1963, esp. pp. 110–124). This specialization allows individual Congressmembers, aided by their large staffs, to develop expertise on specific issues. In reaching decisions, Congress as a whole relies heavily on the expertise of committee members. Similarly, the president has access to considerable expertise from the White House staff, the Executive Office, and other bureaucracies (Johnson, 1977). Conversely, the judiciary is thinly staffed. Even the justices of the Supreme Court have only a handful of law clerks to gather information. Moreover, judges often refuse to consider nonlegalistic evidence and arguments. The primary focus of judges is on upholding legal rights. Far in the background—some say too far—are concerns such as avoiding government waste or selecting policies that will have minimal unintended effects. Still, if we want to protect some matters as "rights," keeping them beyond legislative or executive discretion, some reliance on judicial lawmaking seems to be required.

Administration

Judges are responsible for a number of administrative tasks. As Herbert Jacob notes: "A judge resembles a high-level administrator in many of his duties. In most parts of the United States judges are responsible for administering their own courts." (1978, p. 94) Trial-level judges must appoint clerical assistants, draw up the budget, and ensure that the court's physical facilities are adequate. Often this involves presenting the legislature with a budget request. Judges must also keep track of thousands of documents in court files (Jacob, 1973, p. 67). These documents must be held safely (so they will not be lost) and yet kept accessible (so that attorneys may examine them).

At the Supreme Court level each justice must supervise a staff which includes a secretary and three or more law clerks (Schubert, 1974a, p. 48). The principal administrative officer is the Clerk of the Supreme Court. Other staff members of the High Court include a librarian, a marshal, a reporter, messengers, bailiffs, and custodial employees. For each justice there are about twenty-five persons in the supporting administrative structure. Meanwhile, the Administrative Office performs a wide range of housekeeping duties for the courts of appeals and district courts. The director and deputy director of the Administrative Office are appointed by the Supreme Court. In a sense, the entire Department of Justice also provides administrative support to the federal courts.

Also administrative in character is the gatekeeping function of judges (Baum, 1978). In exercising this function, judges determine which disputes they will address and the kind of consideration that will be provided. Most notable is the exercise of discretionary jurisdiction by the Supreme Court and many state supreme courts. Through the certiorari process the Supreme Court decides whether it will consider a case. Unless four of the nine justices agree to hear the case on its merits, a case is not granted Supreme Court review. If the Supreme Court declines to grant certiorari, the decision from below is unaltered, but no national precedent is established. Important policy consequences flow from the certiorari process, since the justices refuse to grant review in nine out of ten cases. Thus, to a large extent it is through the certiorari process that the justices determine which issues they will address and which will not be addressed.

Judges at the appellate level exercise gatekeeping functions in other ways. In some cases they give only abbreviated consideration to a case through summary dismissal of appeals or summary affirmance of lower court decisions. Some cases are dealt with through a truncated procedure, such as a per curiam opinion for the court. Judges can also act as gatekeepers by manipulating the financial costs of litigation. If these costs are excessive, some litigants will be discouraged from using the courts. Acting as administrators over the docket, judges can also manipulate the rules of jurisdiction.

Further, judges administer the rules of criminal and civil procedure (Eisenstein, 1973, pp. 108–110). This is an important function. As Austin Sarat points out: "When judges discuss what they do inside the courtroom it is most often in terms of insuring that trials are conducted fairly." (1977a, p. 371) Judges must maintain order in the courtroom, set bail levels, accept or reject motions by prosecutors and defense attorneys, decide on the admissibility of evidence, and provide instructions and comments to juries. A highly controversial administrative process in the trial courts is plea bargaining. This is the procedure in which defendants forego a trial and plead guilty, often to reduced charges. Here the traditional adversary system of the courts is replaced by an essentially bureaucratic process. It has been suggested that in plea bargaining, trial court judges resemble administrators, since their primary orientation is toward the quick processing of cases rather than the dispensing of justice (Blumberg, 1967b). Others note that trial judges have little choice in the matter, given the heavy criminal caseloads they encounter.

The aphorism "Justice delayed is justice denied" finds support from many court analysts. Court delay is a significant administrative problem in the judiciary. As H. Ted Rubin observes: "Far too many courts operate essentially in the same fashion as fifty years ago. . . . Too many judges have failed to effectively administer control of their own court calendar." (1976, p. 185) A number of problems associated with court delay have been noted by Hans Zeisel and associates (1959, pp. xxii–xxiii). For example, delay in the courtroom jeopardizes justice because evidence may deteriorate over time. It also causes severe hardship to some parties, even depriving some of a basic public service. Finally, court delay also produces an unhealthy emphasis on the desirability of settling out of court. As a result of problems such as these, trial judges are increasingly taking vigorous measures to speed the flow of civil cases (Jacob, 1978, pp. 95–97). They may do this through a variety of means, such as systematically calling their calendars, being restrictive in granting delays and continuances, and limiting the cases that a single attorney or firm can bring to any one court.[10] In addition, a pretrial conference may be used to promote the settlement of cases. Here lawyers for both parties in a civil dispute meet with the trial judge to frame the issues involved. Some judges will go so far as to suggest a settlement to the case. However, some regard the pretrial conference as an ineffective device. Others suggest that it undermines the adversary system and the neutrality of the presiding judge (Ramsey, 1973).

Much attention has been focused on the mounting caseload of the federal courts. For example, in 1960 there were 2,296 cases on the Supreme Court docket. By 1970 this increased to 4,212 and by 1980 there were 4,781 cases on its docket. Similar increases—though involving far more cases—could be observed in the district courts and circuit courts of appeals. To a large extent this increased caseload reflects Supreme Court decisions regarding constitutional and criminal procedures as well as Congressional legislation creating new rights (Ball, 1980, pp. 222–224). Congress has responded to the problems of district and circuit courts by increasing the number of federal judges. In addition, the Judicial Council of the United States has introduced new machine technology and organizational and management techniques. Regarding the mounting caseload of the Supreme Court, two national commissions have called for the creation of a new National Court of Appeals, which would sit in between the Supreme Court and the Circuit Courts of Appeals. The Freund Commission suggested that the new appeals court be assigned the certiorari powers of the Supreme Court (Federal Judicial Center, 1972). However, Arthur Goldberg, a former Supreme Court justice, has argued that the certiorari process actually consumes little of the Supreme Court's time (1973). The main effect of the proposal, according to Goldberg, would be to take from the Supreme Court the important power to decide what cases it wishes to act upon. Clearly, the loss of this power would significantly limit the discretion of the Supreme Court. Three years later the Hruska Commission also supported the creation of a National Court of Appeals (Commission on Revision of the Federal Court Appellate System, 1975, pp. 5–39). This commission suggested that the function of the court be to decide cases of lesser importance which were assigned to it by the Supreme Court.

Finally, judges increasingly act as administrators through their involvement in mandating social services such as schools, mental institutions, and prisons (Glazer, 1978). Here judges are not only establishing rights but also handling the administrative details of institutions in order to implement these rights. Judicial administration of social services may involve elaborate provisions for supervision, contain detailed statements of how government agencies should operate, and provide for continued oversight by the court for an in-

---

[10]There is also increasing use of special trial court administrators. See Rubin (1976), Ch. 9.

definite period. For example, a school desegregation order may include a detailed plan for school assignment; require school closings, construction, and repair; mandate the hiring of additional employees; and require the purchase or rental of buses and other equipment. Nathan Glazer has expressed doubts about the propriety of judicial administration of social services.[11] He notes, for example, that the focus of a judge is on the immediate case before the bench. The judge may not consider other significant concerns such as the effect of the decision on other services, taxpayer resistance, or the ultimate impact of the services provided.

Judges as Politicans

In some sense judges are also politicians. Because this statement is antithetical to the common view of judges, further clarification is required. Few find it difficult to attach the "politician" label to legislators (or presidents or governors). This can be readily understood by referring to some of the activities that these officials engage in. Legislators are selected in a highly political process and base many of their lawmaking decisions on political considerations. In addition, David Mayhew points to three other activities which Congressmembers engage in as politicians—advertising, credit claiming, and position taking (1974, pp. 49–77). Through advertising, members of Congress constantly try to place their names before constituents to create a favorable image. Through credit claiming Congressmembers try to generate a belief that they are personally responsible for some positive government program, project, or action. Finally, members of Congress also engage in position taking. This involves public enunciations of a judgmental character designed to enhance a member's political career. The direct aim of these three activities is to promote the career of the Congressmember rather than improve the chances of passing any proposed legislation.

It is likely that we hesitate to call judges politicians because they generally shun activities such as advertising, credit claiming, and position taking. Still, there may be some other very good reasons for characterizing American judges as politicians. Certainly, the recruitment process of judges in the United States is quite political in character. Unlike the typical bureaucrat, for example, judges do not obtain their position by passing a civil service exam. Supreme Court justices and other federal judges are appointed by the president with the advice and consent of the Senate. Further, nearly all Supreme Court justices were primarily politicians before entering the High Court. Virtually every Supreme Court justice in United States history previously held a public office (Jacob, 1978, p. 110). Moreover, nearly all federal court appointees

---

[11]It should be noted that judges generally enter into administration of social services only very reluctantly, after repeated failures by agencies to comply voluntarily with court orders. See Abram Chayes et al., *An Imperial Judiciary: Fact or Myth?* (Washington, D. C.: American Enterprise Institute, 1979), pp. 38–41.

come from the same political party as the president. Recent presidents have appointed nearly 90 percent of judges from their own political party. Political considerations are important as well at the state and local levels. Governors and mayors generally make appointments from their own political party. In addition, as we have seen, many state and local judges are elected to office like other politicians.

Beyond that, we may regard judges as politicians because of the patronage powers they possess. At the state level patronage positions are commonly controlled by judges (Jacob, 1978, p. 101; Sayre and Kaufman, 1960, pp. 530–531). For example, judges in Connecticut appoint district attorneys. Elsewhere, judges appoint minor officials such as court clerks. Also, when judges probate wills, they sometimes have the authority to select assessors. The patronage power of judges gives them the opportunity to reward people who are loyal to their political party as well as to influence government policy.

Finally, the policy decisions of judges may be influenced by political motivations. Given the ambiguity of the Constitution, judges have enormous discretion when deciding cases of constitutional law. Most statutes also permit a good deal of discretion. The discretion of judges is often used to exercise political leadership or to be responsive to public desires. As Justice Robert Jackson observed: "The ultimate function of the Supreme Court is nothing less than the arbitration between fundamental and ever-present rival forces or trends in our organized society." (1941, p. vii) Here Jackson is expressing a highly political view of the role of the Supreme Court, not unlike our image of presidential and legislative decision making. A study by Stuart Nagel suggests, in fact, that the party affiliation of judges is significantly associated with the outcome of many types of cases (1961). Nagel found that Democratic judges are more likely to favor the defense in criminal cases, the administrative agency in business regulation cases, and the claimant in unemployment compensation cases. Some judges are more responsive to the public than others. Nagel suggests that judges elected on a partisan ballot would be particularly responsive. The notion here is that if we elect our judges, they will behave more like politicians.

DECISION-MAKING PROCESS

Perhaps the question most frequently raised by political scientists is "How do policymakers arrive at their decisions?" This interest in understanding the process of decision making has been paramount for students of the judiciary. It has also been an especially difficult question to answer satisfactorily. The relative isolation of judges as they decide cases has placed judicial researchers in a rather precarious position. Indeed, judges themselves may not fully comprehend the way in which they arrive at decisions. As Benjamin Cardozo observed: "The work of deciding cases goes on every day in hundreds of courts throughout the land. Any judge, one might suppose, would find it easy to describe the process which he had followed a thousand times and more. Nothing could be farther from the truth." (1921, p. 9) If judicial decision making is something of a mystery to judges, it is also a riddle to judicial researchers.

In trying to describe judicial decision making, legal analysts have gone through three phases. These phases include traditionalism, realism, and behavioralism. Dorothy James has used the tale of the emperor's new clothes as a metaphor to depict the three approaches (1968, p. 160). According to James, the traditionalist firmly claims that the emperor is majestically appareled. (In other words, judges truly base their decisions on preexisting rules in a highly mechanical manner.) The realist, meanwhile, indignantly asserts that the emperor is stark naked. (Judicial decisions are based on unpredictable "hunches.") Finally, the behavioralist seeks to establish empirically why the emperor is not clothed. (Behavioral studies focus on sets of variables that may be factors which explain judicial decisions.) Having earlier addressed traditionalism and realism, our main focus now is on the behavioral explanations of judicial decision making (Goldman and Jahnige, 1976, Ch. 5; Rohde and Spaeth, 1976). These include fact patterns in cases, judicial roles, background characteristics, attitudes, group dynamics, and the external environment.

Fact Patterns

Fact pattern analysis is an outgrowth of traditionalism. Both approaches assert that judicial decisions are based on the facts present in a case. Jerome Frank has characterized traditional theory by the simple equation: R × F = D—or, decisions are the product of the rules and the facts in a case (1949, Ch. 3). According to traditionalism, if you know the facts of the case and the legal guidelines which apply, you can easily predict the outcome of a case. Frank, a legal realist, is critical of this approach, suggesting that the facts as determined in court are really only guesses at the truth. Fact pattern analysis, on the other hand, deviates from traditionalism in a quite different way. Basically, it broadens the range of facts that might be considered relevant to a case.

Like traditionalism, fact pattern analysis considers "legally relevant" facts to be critical to the outcome of cases. Thus, in a sentencing decision fact pattern analysis examines such factors as the severity of the law violated and the offender's prior record. However, unlike traditionalism fact pattern analysis also investigates the role of "legally irrelevant" criteria. These include the race, class, sex, and age of the defendant. Practitioners of fact pattern analysis have asserted that legally irrelevant factors may play an important role in the outcome of cases. Essentially, fact pattern analysis seeks to uncover "by systematic examination of a set of decisions, the patterns of facts that are related to decisional results." (Goldman and Jahnige, 1976, p. 193) This is quite unlike legal realism, which suggests that judicial decisions are so erratic that they cannot be reduced to regular patterns. According to Fred Kort, a leading fact pattern analyst, the purpose of the approach is "to obtain a precise and exhaustive distinction between combinations of facts that lead to decisions in favor of one party and combinations of facts that lead to decisions in favor of the opposing party." (Goldman and Jahnige, 1976, p. 193) Fact pattern analysis requires a content analysis of the facts of a set of cases. In its most sophisticated form simultaneous equations or Boolean algebra is then used. Less sophisticated analyses use cross-tabulations or correlations with particular case facts and decisional outcomes.

Of special interest is the assertion of some fact pattern analysts that legally irrelevant factors are important in judicial decision making. The evidence on the subject is somewhat mixed. Some analysts are convinced that the personal characteristics of defendants are critical in judicial decisions. For example, Richard Quinney argues: "Obviously, judicial decisions are not made uniformly. Decisions are made according to a host of extralegal factors, including the age of the offender, his race, and social class." (1970, pp. 141–142) This view has been challenged by Edward Green, who examined official court and police records in Philadelphia (1961). Green's data did reveal some differences in sentences according to sex (favoring women), age (favoring youths), and race (favoring whites). However, careful analysis indicated that these variations in sentencing severity could be attributed to the seriousness of the crime committed and the defendant's prior record. A more recent analysis by Cassia Spohn and associates suggests that even though race has no direct effect on the severity of sentences, blacks are somewhat (20 percent) more likely than whites to be sent to prison (1981–82). Apparently, in borderline cases whites are more likely to receive probation, while blacks are sentenced to a short term (one or two years) in prison. More generally, while fact pattern analysis cannot provide a complete explanation of judicial outcomes, it can account for some of the differences in judicial decisions.

Roles

Role theory begins with the notion that an individual in a specific position (for example, a judge) has certain expectations as to how to behave. Likewise, those around the individual have a set of expectations about that person as well. For example, people think of a federal judge as "a late middle-aged or elderly black-robed gentleman who is dignified and learned." (Goldman and Jahnige, 1976, p. 201) In addition, people expect a judge to be impartial when processing litigation. Decisions are to be based on relevant precedents and the intent of the law. A judge is also expected to render justice in the cases before the bench. The judge who fails to adhere to widely accepted norms may be subject to various sanctions (Sheldon, 1974, p. 77). Judges may not be reelected or promoted; they may be overruled by a higher court; they may fall into disgrace within the profession; they may be removed from office; and they may be ostracized by peers. That such sanctions are rarely invoked partly reflects the fairly widespread adherence to judicial norms by those on the bench.

The notion of role divergence is critical to the application of role theory to judicial decision making. Judges differ in their ideas about the nature of their proper role. Our thinking about judicial role has advanced through the work of James Gibson (1981; 1978). According to Gibson, the role orientation adopted by a judge will identify "the criteria that are legitimate for proper decision-making. Some judges may believe it proper to be influenced by a particular stimulus while others regard it as improper." (1981, p. 302) Judges in California and Iowa were asked by Gibson whether they believed it was proper for various criteria to enter into judicial decisions. According to his findings, only some judges want to rely almost exclusively on precedents. Other judges thought it proper to consider other factors as well, such as fair results, common sense, public needs, public demands, personal values, and social consequences. In related research on judicial roles, Gibson found that, overall, there was little relationship between judicial attitudes and the severity of sentencing decisions (1978). Gibson also found, however, that the role orientation of judges was an important intervening variable. According to his findings, attitudes are a good predictor of judicial decisions only among judges with broad role orientations. Thus, if a judge believed that it was legitimate to take personal attitudes into account when making decisions, that judge's attitudes were in fact likely to be associated with the kinds of decisions actually made.

Another line of role theory research has focused on the role orientation of judges toward activism on the bench (Howard, 1977). For example, J. Woodford Howard conducted thirty-five interviews with judges from the second, fifth, and D. C. circuits of the United States courts of appeals. His key finding was that some of the judges were more favorable to the idea of judicial policymaking than were others. Five of the judges interviewed were "Innovators"—that is, they felt that the best part of their job was "launching new ideas." At the opposite pole were nine "Interpreters." They argued that judicial lawmaking should be held to a minimum. In fact, two of the judges bitterly denounced judges who "seize power for themselves" rather than "wait for the people's representatives" to act. A middling position was taken by two-thirds of the judges. Looking at judicial rulings in the mid-1960s, Howard found that Innovators generally were more libertarian in civil rights and criminal justice. Although the ideological orientation of Innovators may vary from one era to another, the evidence does suggest that role orientation makes a difference in judicial decisions.

Backgrounds

Investigators have also examined the extent to which the background of judges affects their behavior on the bench (Goldman and Sarat, 1978, pp. 372-374; Goldman and Jahnige, 1976, pp. 174-178). These studies seek to learn whether there is a relationship between the socioeconomic, political, and professional background of judges and the decisions they make on the bench. Judges are seen as the product of the sum total of their experiences. Some of these experiences will result from or be influenced by their background characteristics. In addition, judges will have a self-identification with the groups to which they belong and may vote in behalf of the interests of these groups. Thus, we can expect that specific types of background characteristics will be associated with judicial decisions.

Most of the research relating judicial background to decisions has produced insubstantial results (Goldman, 1975). Nevertheless, a recent study by C. Neal Tate suggests that Supreme Court decisions are closely tied to certain background characteristics of the justices (1981). Tate studied the twenty-five justices who served on the Supreme Court from the 1946–1947 term to the end of the 1977–1978 term. The cases analyzed involved civil rights/liberties and economics. In this study Tate wished to learn whether justices with certain background characteristics were more likely to vote in either a liberal or conservative direction. Several kinds of personal attributes were examined, including birth, upbringing, education, career characteristics, age, tenure, and partisanship. Overall, Tate found a strong relationship between judicial backgrounds and decisions. Among the most important variables explaining judicial decisions were party identification, extent of judicial experience, type of prosecutorial experience, and the president who made the appointment. Thus, the background characteristics of the justices—and particularly their political backgrounds—were significantly related to their decisions on the bench.

A basic problem with the backgrounds approach is that any given attribute (for example, ethnicity) masks a multitude of different life experiences (Goldman and Sarat, 1978, pp. 372–374). As a result, background studies using crudely drawn classifications have generally failed to explain a substantial portion of the variance in judicial behavior. Even so, the individual judge certainly is strongly affected by life experiences, which in turn have some basis in background characteristics. It should also be noted that to date, researchers have focused only on part of the picture. They have viewed differences in judges' backgrounds as a cause of disparate judicial decisions. Yet, judges in the United States have essentially similar backgrounds, particularly within a given level of the judicial hierarchy. This homogeneity on the bench must be seen as a force promoting unity and consensus (Grossman, 1966, pp. 1563–1564).

Attitudes

Judicial decisions can seemingly also be traced to the attitudes of judges (Schubert, 1974b). Nearly one-quarter of Supreme Court rulings are decided by a split vote. Attitudinal researchers argue that we can attribute much of the disagreement in voting to differences in judicial attitudes. The predominant technique employed is Guttman scaling. Here researchers examine the votes of justices on a preselected group of cases which relate to some dimension (for example, civil liberties). It is theorized that when the law is unsettled (and hence some disagreement among justices is likely), liberal justices will be aligned in opposition to conservative justices.

A persuasive study of judicial attitudes and decision making is that by Sheldon Goldman (1966). The analysis focused on the nonunanimous decisions and unanimous reversals of district court decisions by the United States courts of appeals. In part, Goldman sought to learn the extent to which voting on one type of issue was related to voting on all other issues or categories of cases. If Goldman could find a significant amount of consistency in attitudes, there would be a strong basis for believing that underlying attitudes affected decisions. Goldman's results indicated a positive relationship among seven categories of cases: criminal, civil liberties, labor, private economic, personal injury, court activism, and liberalism. In many cases the degree of association was quite high, reaching .72 for cases involving civil liberties and liberalism. Thus, the same judges who oppose each other on one issue are likely to oppose each other on other issues as well. These findings suggest that attitudes do play a part in the decisions made by judges.

Still, there are critics of the attitudinal approach to explaining judicial decision making. For example, Wallace Mendelson steadfastly maintains that the traditional approach, emphasizing the reliance on precedents, best explains the decision making process of most judges (1963). According to Mendelson, researchers have been led astray by the behavior of a handful of activist judges. It is only these activist judges who are imposing their personal view of justice on the realities of the law. Mendelson also argues that from a methodological standpoint, attitudinal researchers are being quite presumptuous. When researchers use the Guttman technique, they must assign cases to certain categories (for example, civil liberties, business). However, Mendelson suggests that each case actually represents a variety of conflicting issues that cannot be viewed in isolation for the convenience of a Guttman scale. In Mendelson's view attitudinal researchers cannot possibly know how a judge has defined a given case. Despite Mendelson, there is little doubt that judicial attitudes play an important role in rulings by judges. As Goldman and Jahnige suggest: "It is beyond serious question today that the judges of the Supreme Court have their own conceptions of public policy and that their attitudes and values affect the thrust of their decision making." (1976, p. 164)

Group Dynamics

Group dynamics may also play an important role in judicial decision making. After all, appellate judges are members of collegial courts. The Supreme Court, for example, is now composed of nine members. While the Court offers plenty of room for individual thought, judges also interact with one another in many stages of the decision making process. This interaction often produces decisions which differ from the simple sum of nine individual preferences.

As J. Woodford Howard notes, there may be considerable "fluidity" of judicial choice (1968). As a result of their interaction with other judges, some judges may switch their vote before publication of the written opinion. In the flow of ideas and arguments that transpires among the judges, positions on cases often alter—even in cases with highly ideological overtones. In particular, pressures may be exerted on dissenters to conform with the majority opinion. Howard observes: "Clearly, judges of all ideological persuasions pondered, bargained, and argued in the course of reaching their decisions, and they compromised their ideologies, too." (1968, p. 55) Howard based these conclusions on impressionistic evidence. Subsequently, Saul Brenner tested Howard's notion of the fluidity of judicial choice by studying the papers of Justice Harold Burton (1980). Brenner compared the way that the judges voted in conference with their final vote in the case. He found that some change of vote occurred in 61 percent of the cases studied. In some of these cases a vote shift even converted a minority on the Court into a majority. Thus, a complete explanation of judicial decision making requires that we understand the interpersonal interaction among the judges on a collegial court.[12]

A classic in the group dynamics literature is Walter Murphy's *Elements of Judicial Strategy* (1964, esp. Chaps. 3, 8). In an analysis with Machiavellian overtones, Murphy outlines how a policy-oriented justice could behave to maximize personal influence on the Court. The main problem faced by a policy-oriented justice is one of group dynamics. Given that the justice has only one vote in nine, the policy-oriented justice must use various interpersonal activities to gain the support of (at least four) colleagues in a given case. Because of the heavy workload, the justice would ideally win this support using as little time or effort as possible.

Murphy identifies several strategies which the policy-oriented justice might employ. These include persuasion, bargaining, friendship, and social amenities. A look at the memoirs and personal papers of former justices indicates ample examples of each of these strategies. Through persuasion the justice would use logical argument to influence colleagues. Such efforts might occur in the course of the weekly conference, subsequent meetings, and circulation of memorandums and drafts of opinions. Through bargaining a justice may offer his or her vote or concurrence with an opinion in exchange for concessions. There is evidence that a good deal of such negotiation has gone on in the courts. Clearly, the bargaining power of a judge is enhanced when that judge's support is needed (for example, when the division of votes is close). Finally, friendship and social amenities may be influential in some cases. With

[12]Trial court judges are also part of a small group of sorts. This group is comprised of the judge, prosecutor, defense attorney, and other "regulars." See James Eisenstein and Herbert Jacob, *Felony Justice* (Boston: Little, Brown, 1977), esp. Chaps. 2, 3.

this in mind, some justices have become embroiled in appointment politicking to promote a particular candidate to the judiciary. A new justice to the Supreme Court is commonly wooed by colleagues for support. This may include notes of praise for the justice's written opinions. Obviously, the hope is to win over that judge—a possibility not altogether remote in cases where the judge lacks an intense preference.

Another important analysis of group dynamics in the appellate courts is David Danelski's investigation into the role of the Chief Justice (1978). By virtue of this position on the Supreme Court, the Chief Justice has a unique opportunity to exercise leadership. Among the Chief Justice's goals may be a majority vote for the position favored by the Chief Justice, written opinions satisfactory to him (or her), social cohesion in the Court, and unanimous decisions. The Chief Justice has several points of intervention, including the certiorari process, oral argument, conference, assignment of the majority opinion, and opinion writing. For example, since the days of the Hughes Court, the Chief Justice has had the authority to decide which certiorari petitions are frivolous and which are worthy of discussion by the justices. While this is not an absolute power, it is rare for an associate justice to demand discussion of a case that the Chief Justice has excluded (Baum, 1981, p. 83). Apart from that, the Chief Justice serves as the presiding officer during oral argument, speaks first during conference, assigns the majority opinion when voting with the majority (often retaining key opinions for personal attention), and stands at the center of intracourt communication during the opinion-writing stage. While the Chief Justice is not necessarily the most influential member of the Supreme Court, the position does offer the opportunity to lead. Chief Justices such as Marshall and Warren took good advantage of this opportunity.

External Environment

On the subject of judicial decision making, Mr. Dooley has observed: "Th' supreme coort follows th' iliction returns." (Dunne, 1906, p. 26) This statement—likely an overstatement—suggests that the external environment has a significant impact on judicial decisions. Certainly, there are some mechanisms which help to insulate judges from public pressures. These include the dissemination of legalistic norms for judicial decision making, certain methods of judicial selection, and secure tenure. Also, judicial identification with the national "community of jurists" (and the legal profession as a whole) tends to safeguard judicial independence. Nonetheless, external pressures on judges can be quite strong. These pressures are likely to be strongest at lower levels of the judicial hierarchy. The fact that federal district courts are organized along state boundaries has several consequences (Goldman and Sarat, 1978, pp. 335–336). To begin with, the judges in these courts are usually long-term residents of the area they serve. In addition, they process disputes involving at least one resident from the area in cases coming before them. Finally, in some cases judges may feel pressure from the community as to the decision that is expected of them. As a result of these factors, judges—especially at the trial level—may sometimes feel obliged to be responsive to their "constituents." (Richardson and Vines, 1970; Vines, 1963)

A highly regarded examination of environmental influences on the federal courts is that by Jack Peltason (1961). The study focused on federal district court judges in Southern states following the Supreme Court's 1954 school desegration decision. It was these "fifty-eight lonely men" who were responsible for implementing school desegregation in an area highly resistant to such change. As Peltason makes clear, the district court judges could not divorce themselves from the Southern milieu: "The district judge is very much a part of the life of the South. He must eventually leave his chambers and when he does he attends a Rotary lunch or stops off at the club to drink with men outraged by what they consider 'judicial tyranny.' " (1961, p. 9) Judges who ordered desegregation risked their prestige and acceptance in the community. Meanwhile, judges who circumvented desegregation became local heroes. The fact that federal judges were judicial officers of the national government provided only partial insulation from the often intense community demands.

It may be possible either to increase or reduce the extent of environmental influences on the judiciary. In the case of school desegregation Peltason suggests that the Supreme Court's order in *Brown v. Board of Education* (that is, "all deliberate speed") served to increase the pressures on Southern district court judges needlessly. He suggests that the Supreme Court, given its national constituency, was in a far better position to "take the heat" for school desegregation (1961, p. 246). In addition, a study of sentencing decisions by James Gibson suggests that judges with certain attributes are more likely to be influenced by the external environment (1980). Pressured most by external factors are judges who have greater contact with their constituencies, who have experienced electoral defeat at some time, and who believe that they ought to reflect popular sentiment. Thus, there is evidence indicating that certain strategies may be adopted—both in court orders and judicial selection—that will alter the effects of environmental influences.

The overall literature on judicial decision making, while sometimes obscured by scales and matrices, has some very practical political applications. In fact, the literature provides some very direct guidance to a president faced with an opening on the Supreme Court. Clearly, the literature would advise presidents to select a nominee whose political attitudes are similar to their own. Ample studies indicate that the nature of judicial decisions is strongly influenced by the attitudes of individual justices. Beyond that, the president should also look to other qualities in potential justices. For example, the group dynamics literature suggests the importance of a persuasive personality in swaying colleagues to a particular decision. Thus, if there is a vacuum of leadership on the High Court as regards the president's position on some key issues, the president may be well advised to look for a judicial candidate with strong leadership skills as well as a set of similar attitudes.

ETHICS

Judicial Misconduct

In Nepal a statute was once enacted which provided that if a judge's decision was reversed, the judge would be imprisoned and either flogged or beheaded (Stein, 1974, p. 104). The rationale was that since judges are presumed to know the law, any error by a judge must be due to dishonesty. While this seems a bit rash, the concern for genuine judicial misconduct is quite understandable. As Joseph Borkin observes: "At a stroke, the corrupt judge substitutes the rule of force and fraud for the rule of law. A bribed judge not only sacrifices his own morality but poisons the well of justice itself. . . ." (1962, p. 17) Of course, not all misconduct by judges is due to bribery. Unethical behavior may result not only from dishonesty but also from senility, sickness, incompetence, or capriciousness. Misconduct on the bench includes the failure to render decisions in an impartial, diligent, and ethical manner. By some definitions judicial misconduct might also include extreme rudeness, habitual tardiness, short hours, and long vacations (Braithwaite, 1971, p. 5). There are also those who wish to punish off-the-bench misconduct by judges, for example, the commission of a felony.

The conduct of judges is rightfully a concern of considerable importance. Misconduct off the bench by a judge, such as commission of a felony, may reflect adversely on the entire judiciary. Meanwhile, the actions of a judge on the bench can have a very negative effect on the life of those who have appeared before that judge as litigants. As a case in point, one judge was charged with committing a man to a mental institution illegally "and without reasonable or probable cause and solely motivated by malice and caprice."[13] The man in question was placed in a mental institution but released by the institution shortly thereafter. Naturally, the man felt quite victimized by this experience. His response was to sue the judge for money damages. Nevertheless, this civil suit was not successful. The reason for this is that judges in America have granted themselves broad-ranging immunity from tort damage actions (See *Randall v. Brigham* and *Bradley v. Fisher*). Dismissing the suit without trial, the court explained: "Judges are exempt from liability in a civil action for acts performed in the exercise of their judicial functions." Thus, if error or misconduct by a judge harms a person in some way, it is nevertheless quite unlikely that the person will be able to recover damages through court

[13] *Whitehead v. De Andrea,* 60 N. Y. S. (2d) 44, as discussed in Stein (1974), p. 99.

action (*Stump v. Sparkman*).[14] Of course, there may be merit in providing judges with such immunity from civil suits. Still, the presence of this judicial immunity makes it even more important that we have some effective mechanism for dealing with judicial impropriety.

The Canons

Judges are expected to abide by a code of judicial conduct that was formulated and adopted by the American Bar Association in 1972 (ABA, 1980, pp. 59–68). The code consists of seven canons that seek to regulate the behavior of jurists. Canon 1 calls upon judges to "uphold the integrity and independence of the judiciary." This involves maintaining high standards of ethical conduct so as to prevent outside intrusions into judicial authority. Canon 2 states: "A judge should avoid impropriety and the appearance of impropriety in all his activities." This includes conducting oneself in a manner that promotes public confidence in the judiciary. For example, judges must never even convey the impression that others are in a special position to influence them.

Canon 3 reads: "A judge should perform the duties of his office impartially and diligently." This requires faithfulness to the law as well as professional competence. A judge must maintain decorum, be patient and courteous, avoid excessive delay, and abstain from public comment on a case. The canon also requires prohibiting distracting media coverage, handling administrative responsibilities diligently, and disqualifying oneself from proceedings in which one's impartiality might be questioned. Canon 4 calls upon judges to "engage in activities to improve the law, the legal system, and the administration of justice." Judges are permitted to speak, write, lecture, teach, and participate in other activities regarding the law. They may also appear at a public hearing or serve on a commission aimed at improving the judiciary.

Canon 5 states: "A judge should regulate his extrajudicial activities to minimize the risk of conflict with his judicial duties." For example, a judge may not practice law, serve on commissions unrelated to the judiciary, act as an arbitrator, serve as a fiduciary, or engage in financial and business dealings that reflect adversely on the judge's impartiality. Canon 6 requires that judges "regularly file reports of compensation received for quasi-judicial and extrajudicial activities." Compensation should not be excessive and must be publicly reported. Finally, Canon 7 reads: "A judge should refrain from political activity inappropriate to his judicial office." For example, a judge or judicial candidate should not be an officer of a political organization, speak for or

---

[14]In *Stump v. Sparkman,* the court ruled that judges enjoy absolute immunity from suits for damages unless they act clearly outside their subject matter jurisdiction. See J. Randolph Block, "*Stump v. Sparkman* and the History of Judicial Immunity," *Duke Law Journal,* 1980, pp. 879–925 and Stephen Craig Voris, "A Judge Can Do No Wrong: Immunity Is Extended for Lack of Specific Jurisdiction—*Stump v. Sparkman,*" *Depaul Law Review,* 1978, *27,* 1219–1239.

endorse a political organization or candidate, or solicit funds. In addition, judges and judicial candidates are barred from making "pledges or promises of conduct in office" excepting "the faithful and impartial performance of the duties of the office. . . ." They must avoid making statements on disputed legal and political issues.

Clearly, the promulgation of canons of ethics has not eliminated judicial misconduct. However, this does not mean that the attitudes and behavior of judges are unaffected by ethical canons. Mary Volcansek examined the impact of a change in the Texas Canons upon the attitudes of judges (Volcansek, 1980). In 1974 a stringent ethical code replaced one that was more lax. For example, Canon 7 of the 1974 code specifically prohibits judges from holding an office in a political organization, making speeches in behalf of a political organization or candidate, endorsing a candidate for office, and soliciting funds for a political organization. Through a questionnaire administered among Texas district judges in 1973 and 1975, Volcansek was able to observe any changes in attitudes among judges that may have occurred following the adoption of the new canons. In fact, dramatic changes were observed in attitudes with respect to political activities appropriate for judges. For example, in 1973 only 30.6 percent of the judges believed it was improper for judges to make campaign contributions. By 1975 the figure had grown to 82.5 percent. It is quite possible that changes occurred not only in the attitudes of judges but also in their behavior.

Formal Discipline

Of course, the judicial canons are not adhered to universally. When an ethical violation occurs, disciplinary sanctions may be invoked. A rich variety of disciplinary devices is available at the state level (Jacob, 1978, pp. 116–118; Davis, 1967). Apart from impeachment, there are up to five removal devices present in the states. These include elections, recall, legislative address, abolishing a court, and the judicial commission. In states with judicial elections an obvious way of removing an unethical judge is by defeating that judge in the voting booth. Given the infrequency of elections and their low salience, however, the effectiveness of elections in removing an unethical judge is questionable. Through recall voters may remove an official from the bench before the judge's term expires. If enough voters sign a petition, the judge must submit to a referendum. The recall was used by labor leaders early in the twentieth century against so-called "injunction judges." A few states permit a procedure known as legislative address, which involves a vote by the legislature to remove a judge. It has rarely been invoked. Another method of dealing with misconduct is abolishing the court on which a judge sits. In this way such judges may no longer exercise judicial powers, although it may be necessary to pay their salaries for the remainder of their tenure.

The judicial commission is another method of removing judges from office. It has been one of the most widely adopted court reforms during the past two decades (Tesitor, 1978; Roelke, 1973; Davis, 1967). Existing commissions are of two forms. Unitary commissions—such as California's pioneering Commission on Judicial Performance—consist of a single permanent agency. They are authorized to receive and review complaints, conduct investigations, convene formal hearings, and make appropriate recommendations for action to the state supreme court. The two-tier procedure separates the investigation and adjudication roles into two distinct bodies. In general, judicial commissions are comprised of a mixture of judges, lawyers, and members of the public. A unique advantage of judicial commissions is their variety of sanctions, which include removal, retirement, public censure, and private reprimand. Such disciplinary diversity may be desirable, since all forms of misconduct do not merit removal. At the same time, some analysts fear that judicial commissions will seriously jeopardize the independence of individual judges.

At the federal level judicial misconduct traditionally could be dealt with only through the tortuous process of impeachment (Abraham, 1980a, pp. 44–50). Under Article III of the Constitution federal judges hold their position during "good behavior." Since the precise meaning of this phrase remains unsettled, it is unclear what constitutes an impeachable offense for federal judges. For decades Congress considered instituting alternative disciplinary mechanisms. However, the constitutionality of such alternatives was doubted. Impeachment (that is, the accusation) occurs by a simple majority vote of the House of Representatives. A vote of two-thirds of the Senate is required for conviction and removal from office. The House has launched impeachment proceedings against only nine federal judges. Another nine resigned before formal charges were made against them. Of the nine judges who were impeached, only four were convicted and removed from office. Presumably, through the entire course of American history a far larger number of federal judges have been guilty of serious ethical violations. Many argue, therefore, that the impeachment-conviction route is not a very effective device for dealing with judicial misconduct (Barkin, 1962, pp. 189–204). Its cumbersome character helps to insulate the federal judiciary, but only at the cost of failing to deal with most instances of ethical violations.

Given the inadequacy of impeachment-conviction as a means of dealing with misconduct among federal judges, there has been a call for supplementary mechanisms (Culver and Cruikshanks, 1982). In 1939 judicial councils were created in each of the federal circuits. However, while these councils had some authority over the misconduct of judges, their main function was administrative. Finally, Congress passed the Judicial Councils Reform and Judicial Conduct and Disability Act of 1980 (PL 96–458). The act established a procedure for processing complaints against federal judges. Specifically, it created a Court on Judicial Conduct and Disability, which is staffed by five judges in each circuit. These judges are appointed by the chief judge within each appellate district. Sanctions may be imposed for any mental or physical disability that interferes with judicial duties. In addition, sanctions may also be imposed for conduct "inconsistent with the effective and expeditious administration of the courts. . . ." Among the available sanctions are a request for voluntary retirement, temporary or permanent suspension of cases, private or public censure, reprimand, or even a recommendation to the House for impeachment. An increased number of errant federal judges may be disciplined as a result of this mechanism. However, there is the danger that the device will be used as a political weapon against independent-minded judges.

COMMUNITY RELATIONS

Judicial Activity

Relatively little community relations activity is carried out by members of the bench. In particular, while legislators and chief executives often debate issues in the public forum, the decision-making process employed by judges occurs outside the public eye. Although trials in many states are now being opened to television coverage, the rulings made by judges are generally expected to stand on their own, without public discussion. Rarely will a judge justify decisions in speeches or interviews. At the appellate level the only justification offered is a written decision that few members of the public ever see or become familiar with. At the trial level such written opinions are generally not even offered. Similarly, there is little judicial involvement in bar association matters or community relations work (Ryan et al., 1980, pp. 41–42). Ninety percent of trial judges spend the equivalent of four hours or less per month on bar-related matters. Nearly 70 percent of trial judges spend four hours or less per month on speeches, interviews, civic meetings, performing weddings, and other community relations activities.

Public Knowledge

"Ignorance" is the byword when discussing public knowledge of the judiciary—even the Supreme Court. In part, this may reflect the relative aloofness of judicial personnel in dealing with the public. If Americans are ill-informed about their government in general, they are especially ignorant of the courts. For example, there are probably few Americans who are aware of the fact that the Supreme Court will hear a case only if one in four agree to grant review. This is known as the certiorari process. (Some Americans, I fear, may even believe that "certiorari" is a skin disease.) As Austin Sarat notes, the studies of public knowledge about the judiciary demonstrate "that courts are not particularly visible or salient to the American people. The level of public awareness and knowledge of courts, court personnel, and court decisions is quite low." (1977b, p. 438)

A convincing study on public knowledge about the judiciary was conducted by Kenneth Dolbeare (1967b). In the study respondents were presented with a list of eight subject areas. Four of these had been the focus of recent Supreme Court action—rights of defendants, state legislature redistricting, school prayer, and school segregation. The other four areas had not received attention by the High Court—aid to education, medical care for the aged, urban renewal, and the John Birch Society. Respondents were asked simply to indicate whether the Supreme Court had recently made a decision in each area. The results revealed remarkably little knowledge of Supreme Court decisions by the public. For example, only 10 percent knew that no decision had been made on federal aid to education. Further, despite the heavy focus of the Warren Court on rights of defendants, only 26 percent knew that the Supreme Court had addressed this issue. No more than 2 percent of the respondents correctly answered all eight items. Knowledge was particularly low where the issue did not directly affect the individual. Thus, respondents had more knowledge of Supreme Court decisions in school prayer and school busing than they did in defendants' rights or legislative redistricting.

That the public has such little knowledge of the courts can best be explained by the insulation of the judiciary from the public (Jacob, 1966). To be sure, the public does have some contact with the courts. Americans serve directly as litigants, witnesses, and jurors. In some states people may elect their judges. Indirectly, some keep informed of court developments through the media—particularly with respect to ongoing criminal prosecutions. Still, the operating characteristics of the courts make judges relatively remote. For example, judicial recruitment is low-key compared to either presidential or Congressional elections. Even where judges are elected, highly salient campaigns do not occur because of restrictions in the code of judicial conduct. In the decision-making process Supreme Court justices make no effort to arouse public opinion about an upcoming case as a means of persuading their colleagues. The public is removed from the decision-making process, except in the limited form of amicus curiae briefs by interest groups. Finally, Supreme Court justices do not "go public" to rally public sentiment behind a decision that has been made. Judges, at most, simply issue a written opinion—a formal document not normally read by the public. Given these factors, it is difficult to fault the public for knowing so little about the judiciary.

Public Support

Americans may support their courts even if they know little about them (Engstrom and Giles, 1972). Here a useful distinction can be made between specific and diffuse support. Specific support refers to approval of a court's decisions (or personnel, or other features). Most people neither support nor oppose the specific decisions of the Supreme Court. Rather, they are simply ignorant of those decisions. Of course, it seems likely that most Americans *would* support most decisions of the Supreme Court *if* they became aware of them. It is likely that in a given year only a small minority of court decisions would be strongly opposed by a majority of Americans. At the same time, there seems to be considerable diffuse support for the Supreme Court. That is, most people do not hold the judiciary in disregard even if they are ignorant of much of its work and perhaps even disagree with some of its policies. Most Americans accept the legitimacy of the judiciary. Few would want to abolish the courts or radically alter the character of the judicial process.

This diffuse support among Americans for the judiciary may have several sources. Most notably, many accept political myths which tend to "deify" the Supreme Court. As Austin Sarat notes: "Those who believe in a mythic or highly idealized version of what the Court does and how it operates are more likely to support the Court than those whose perception is more realistic." (Sarat, 1977b, p. 440) Gregory Casey has examined the extent to which Americans attach legitimating myths to the Supreme Court (1974). A sample of Missouri residents was asked: "What would you say the Supreme Court's main job in government is? That is, what is it supposed to do?" Casey found that many of those responding saw the Court in the glow of its myths. To most Americans judges are something apart from politicians. They do not make deals or balance interests. Rather, judges "enforce the Constitution," "uphold the laws of the land," make "wise and fair judgment of cases that are brought before them," and protect the "rights" of individuals. Thus, there is a reservoir of diffuse support for the judiciary based on the mythology of the courts. Other sources of diffuse support for the courts may include a perception that judges try to be "fair," that judges have considerable expertise and therefore will make wise decisions, and that the judiciary is a part of the nation's "governing coalition" along with the president and Congress. Many observers believe that as long as judges handle themselves in a professional manner, they will not risk losing the support of the public.

Still unanswered is the nature of the relationship between specific knowledge about the judiciary and support for it. Some fear that familiarity with the judiciary—particularly a controversial Supreme Court decision—will undermine public support. Here various studies have produced differing results. For example, Gregory Casey attempted to learn whether people with more knowledge about Supreme Court decisions have a deeper belief in judicial myths (1974, pp. 398–403). He found a direct relationship between knowledge about Supreme Court decisions and belief in the mythology surrounding the Court. This suggests that the more you know about the judiciary, the more you support it. However, this view is contradicted by a study done by Walter Murphy and associates (1973). They conclude: "A belief that increased public knowledge of what a constitutional court is doing will bring increased support has a slim evidentiary basis." (1973, p. 53) According to Murphy, increased familiarity with the courts is about as likely to create dissatisfaction as support. The key is the kinds of issues addressed by the courts and whether they decide these issues in a manner that is popular or unpopular. Murphy believes that if the public becomes aware of court decisions which it strongly opposes on ideological grounds, public support for the court will decline appreciably.

Although we do not yet know the relationship between specific knowledge about the judiciary and support for it, the search for an answer is essential if we are to better understand the problem of community relations and the judiciary. If it is the case that knowledge about the Supreme Court diminishes public support, it may be important for the Court to maintain a low profile and avoid controversy lest it lose its legitimacy. It is possible that a Court that drifted too far from the opinions of mainstream America would arouse the public, causing the loss not only of specific support but of diffuse support as well. However, it is also possible that the judiciary has considerable leeway in specific cases. One study suggests that people *want* to support the Court and will selectively perceive the nature of court rulings in order to maintain this support (Casey, 1976). At the same time, the study also suggests that the Court might lose public support if it drifted too far from the mainstream ideologies.[15] Finally, Murphy and associates make the point that courts may be able to continue functioning even without the presence of popular support (1973, p. 58).

AN ASSESSMENT

There is a basic tension throughout the literature on judges. On the one hand, we would like to believe that judges are professionals who are able to apply preexisting rules mechanically to cases before them. It is on this basis that much of the support for judges (among legal scholars as well as among laypeople), is grounded. On the other hand, there is much to suggest that judging is not really like this. Even if mechanical jurisprudence was possible, judges in the United States do not receive the kind of training that might be necessary to carry it out. American judges have political backgrounds and are appointed in a political process. At times they even behave as lawmakers and politicians. Empirical research has also discovered that when judges differ on a decision, this disagreement can be accounted for by factors such as the attitudes and backgrounds of judges. The significance of such factors runs counter to the traditional view of judicial decision making.

Given that judges do not act like robots—mechanically applying rules to cases—we must reconsider their methods of selection and removal. For example, it is important that we decide what qualities we want in judges at various levels of the judicial hierarchy. With such information in hand it may be possible for social scientists to establish empirically the selection methods that are most

[15]However, see Richard Lehne and John Reynolds, "The Impact of Judicial Activisim on Public Opinion," *American Journal of Political Science,* 1978, *22,* 896–904.

appropriate for obtaining such judges. If much public support for the judiciary is now based on myth, perhaps a more realistic basis for public support can be established. One approach would try to make mechanical jurisprudence a more feasible process. This would require spelling out more precisely the kinds of policies the judiciary is expected to enforce. More detailed legislation and constitutional amendments would be required. The aim would be to reduce judicial discretion in decision making as far as possible, leaving lawmaking more completely the responsibility of Congress and the president. Courts would still be responsible for upholding rights, but the character of these rights would be more completely spelled out by others, particularly through the amendment process. While a judge must necessarily have some discretion in applying preexisting rules to individual cases, the range of this discretion would be reduced if the rules were clearly explicated. What is not clear is whether constraining the judiciary by spelling out the rules more fully would make the governing of America more equitable, libertarian, effective, accountable, stable, or just.

QUESTIONS FOR DISCUSSION

1. What requirements are imposed by the Constitution for becoming a Supreme Court justice? What accounts for the nature of the background characteristics of the justices? Should all justices be attorneys? If you were president, what qualities would you look for when making a Supreme Court appointment?

2. Under what circumstances can we consider a judge to be effective? Which method of judicial selection is most likely to yield effective judges? To what extent would it be possible to improve the performance of judges through a program of training?

3. Are judges politicians? Why do people look upon judges differently than they look upon legislators or executives?

4. To what extent should judges base their decisions on legal precedents? Is it always possible for us to know whether a judge has faithfully tried to follow precedents? What factors other than legal precedents are important in determining judicial decisions? If you were a judge, under what circumstances would you want to break with precedent and establish a new judicial interpretation?

FOR FURTHER READING

CHASE, HAROLD W.   *Federal Judges: The Appointing Process.* Minneapolis Minn.: University of Minnesota Press, 1972. Describes how federal judges get selected.
HOROWITZ, DONALD.   *The Courts and Social Policy.* Washington, D. C.: Brookings Institution, 1977. According to this analyst, courts lack the institutional capacity to make social policy.

MURPHY, WALTER F.   *Elements of Judicial Strategy.* Chicago: University of Chicago Press, 1964. A true classic on group dynamics within the Supreme Court.

RUMBLE, WILFRID E., JR.   *American Legal Realism.* Ithaca, N. Y.: Cornell University Press, 1968. Concludes that judges cannot mechanically apply preexisting rules when making judicial decisions.

WOODWARD, BOB, and ARMSTRONG, SCOTT.   *The Brethren.* New York: Simon and Schuster, 1979. Two journalists present an inside look at the Burger Court.

SUPREME COURT RULINGS

Bradley v. Fisher, 80 U.S. 335 (1871)
Brown v. Board of Education, 347 U.S. 483 (1954)
Plessy v. Ferguson, 163 U.S. 537 (1896)
Randall v. Brigham, 74 U.S. 523 (1868)
Stump v. Sparkman, 435 U.S. 349 (1978)
United States v. Butler, 297 U.S. 1 (1936)

5
THE PUBLIC

PREVIEW

Chapter Five explores the impact of the public on the judicial process. While lawyers occupy many of the key positions in the courtroom, ordinary citizens also play some indispensable roles. Our discussion considers the involvement of six major courtroom participants:

Litigants
Witnesses
Juries
Interest groups
News media
Scientists

Litigants are obviously essential to the courts. Given the reactive nature of the American judiciary, the courtroom would be very quiet if initiators failed to file suit. As we will see, certain classes of litigants are more likely to be successful than others. Next, the role of witnesses is analyzed. We will take a look at the rules of evidence and examine some social science evidence suggesting the fallibility of eyewitness testimony. Third, we will analyze juries in terms of their backgrounds, attitudes, roles, decision-making function, and public relations. Fourth, we note the influence of interest groups on the judiciary. While pressure group activity is normally associated with legislatures, we will see that interest groups use a variety of methods to make their influence felt in the courts. Fifth, the role of the news media is investigated. We will discuss media coverage of both the appellate and trial courts. In particular, we will be concerned with the "free press, fair trial" controversy. Finally, the chapter analyzes the impact of scientists on the judiciary. We will see that science already plays an important role in the courts and that this role is likely to expand in the future.

LITIGANTS

Initiator v. Defendant

Court cases involve disputes between two parties—an initiator and a defendant. In civil cases the initiator is a "plaintiff," while in criminal cases the government acts as "prosecutor." Under our system of justice courts are reactive in nature. This means that judges do not seek out cases to adjudicate. Rather, they wait for an initiator to file a lawsuit. As a consequence, courts are not the guardians of victims in the throes of a dispute. A victim must assert his or her rights to obtain justice in the courts. Also necessary for litigation is a combative adversary. If the "harmdoer" is willing to yield to the demands of the victim, there will be no lawsuit or, at most, perfunctory litigation. It is not uncommon for harmdoers to acquiesce when asked to make reparation or to offer voluntary reparation if they realize they are at fault (Macaulay and Walster, 1971). Such behavior on the part of harmdoers may result from a sense of guilt, empathy, or fear of retaliation. The result is that the disputes which enter the courtroom are not a representative cross-section of all disputes occurring in our society. Moreover, the litigants in a case are not representative of all victims and harmdoers in America. In particular, disadvantaged people are more likely to appear as defendants than as plaintiffs asserting some legal right.

These days it seems as if everybody is suing everybody else. Jethro Lieberman has characterized our nation as "the litigious society." (1981) As Lieberman suggests, we are far less willing than our forerunners to characterize injuries as acts of God or the result of blind fate (1981, p. 188). Instead, we increasingly identify someone as being blameworthy and thus are more likely to seek legal redress. In 1980 there were as many as twelve million civil and criminal cases filed in state courts and in the local courts of the District of Columbia and Puerto Rico. Also, some 170,000 suits were filed in the federal courts. Some of these cases appear to be insignificant and unworthy of court proceedings. In one case a group of Washington Redskins fans went to federal court, arguing that in a game with St. Louis, the referees had mistakenly called a pass a touchdown. The fans claimed that the receiver had dropped the ball in the end zone; they wanted the federal court to overturn the disputed call. However, while some cases may seem uncalled for, in other instances a genuine harm may have occurred for which a court remedy actually exists. In such cases if victims cannot otherwise find satisfaction, it is understandable if the victims choose to pursue justice in the courts (McLauchlan, 1977; Sarat and Grossman, 1975).

OS v. RP

Given the great variety of cases that come to the courts, it would require a great leap of the imagination to generalize as to who usually wins and who loses. One noteworthy effort is that by Marc Galanter (1974). His theory of victory in the courtroom is grounded on a fundamental distinction between the various parties in court disputes. Galanter observes that there are two basic types of parties—one shotters and repeat players. One shotters (OSs) are those who have only occasional recourse to the courts. They include spouses in divorce cases, family members in civil commitment proceedings, and auto injury claimants in accident suits. Repeat players (RPs) are parties who are engaged in many similar litigations over time. Examples include insurance companies, finance companies, and landlords. RPs are usually larger, richer, and more powerful than OSs, but this is not always the case.

Repeat players in general play the litigation game more effectively than one shotters. Many advantages are enjoyed by RPs. To begin with, because RPs are experienced, they have advance knowledge that may be helpful in future transactions. It is the RP who writes the form contract, requires the security deposit, and so on. In addition, RPs develop expertise, have ready access to lawyers and expert witnesses, and have low start-up costs for any case. RPs also have the opportunity to develop favorable informal relations with those in public office. Moreover, RPs have more credibility in bargaining situations, since they have a reputation for bargaining to establish and maintain. Beyond that, RPs can play the odds and think strategically about a series of cases. They can play for rules as well as immediate gains. It pays for them to hire lobbyists and otherwise expend resources to influence legal rules. RPs can also play for rules in litigation itself, whereas an OS is unlikely to do so. While the OS is concerned only with the outcome of the immediate case, the RP is concerned about likely outcomes of future similar cases. As a result, when RPs expect to get an unfavorable rule outcome, they will settle cases out of court. In addition, RPs can concentrate their resources on rule changes that are likely to make a real difference, rather than those that are merely symbolic. Finally, RPs invest more resources in information gathering, attentiveness, and expertise. For all these reasons, RPs are in a distinctly advantaged position in most litigation.

We can think of litigation as typically involving various combinations of one shotters and repeat players as initiators and defendants. As Galanter notes, there are four possible combinations of OSs and RPs acting as initiators and defendants. Some typical cases are represented in Figure 5-1.

OS v. OS: The most numerous examples of OS (initiator) v. OS (defendant) are divorces and insanity hearings. Many of the OS v. OS cases are pseudolitigation in which a settlement was worked out in advance and only ratified in the courts. When real OS v. OS litigation does occur, it is generally between intimates fighting over some unshareable good. Neither party is likely to have much interest in the long-term state of the law. There are few appeals or test cases and little expenditure on the development of rules.

RP v. OS: Repeat players often act as initiators against one shotters. Indeed, this confrontation comprises the great bulk of court litigation, including debt cases, criminal prosecutions, and landlord-tenant disputes. The law is used for routine processing of claims by parties who make these claims as a regular business activity. Cases are often mass-processed rather than given individualized attention and full-dress adjudication. The state of the law is of more interest to the RP than the OS. RPs are able to shape transactions to fit the rules.

OS v. RP: It is rare for a one shotter to act as a plaintiff against a repeat player. The major exception is in personal injury cases. This type of case is regularly litigated by OSs largely because the contingent fee which is used permits free entry. (Under the contingent fee the attorney receives a fixed per-

FIGURE 5-1   A taxonomy of litigation by strategic configuration of parties

INITIATOR, CLAIMANT

	One-Shotter	Repeat Player
One-Shotter	**I** OS vs OS Parent v. Parent (Custody) Spouse v. Spouse (Divorce) Family v. Family Member (Insanity Commitment) Family v. Family (Inheritance) Neighbor v. Neighbor Partner v. Partner	**II** RP vs OS Prosecutor v. Accused Finance Co. v. Debtor Landlord v. Tenant I.R.S. v. Taxpayer Condemnor v. Property Owner
Repeat Player	**III** OS vs RP Welfare Client v. Agency Auto Dealer v. Manufacturer Injury Victim v. Insurance Company Tenant v. Landlord Bankrupt Consumer v. Creditors Defamed v. Publisher	**IV** RP vs RP Union v. Company Movie Distributor v. Censorship Board Developer v. Suburban Municipality Purchaser v. Supplier Regulatory Agency v. Firms of Regulated Industry

(left margin label: DEFENDANT)

Adapted from Marc Galanter, "Why the 'Haves' Come Out Ahead: Speculations on the Limits of Legal Change," *Law and Society Review* (Fall 1974), p. 107.

centage of what is recovered for the client through the litigation.) In auto injury claims litigation is routinized and the settlement is closely geared to the likely outcome of a trial. Other OS v. RP litigation is not routine. Usually, it represents the effort of some dissatisfied OS to invoke outside leverage on an organization that is causing personal problems. The OS claimant generally has little interest in the state of the law, while the RP defendant is greatly interested.

RP v. RP: In general, repeat players avoid court fights with other repeat players, preferring to work out the problem privately through negotiation, mediation, or arbitration. Special exceptions do exist. For example, there may be a genuine fight over differences in values. In addition, government frequently acts as an RP against other RPs. Finally, a pair of RPs that generally litigate against OSs may find themselves squaring off between themselves over some dispute. In RP v. RP situations we find a great deal of expenditure on rule development, a large number of appeals, and rapid and elaborate development of the doctrinal law.

Thus, it can be seen that in certain types of cases one party will have a distinct advantage over its adversary. Repeat players, usually consisting of "haves," are frequently in the favored position. Galanter suggests that four types of reforms would be helpful in "breaking the interlocked advantages of the 'haves'. . . ." (1974, p. 150) One type of reform is rule changes in the way litigation is conducted. Unfortunately, OSs rarely seek rule changes, since their interest is in the immediate case only. When a rule change is won by an OS, the effect is often merely symbolic. Frequently, RPs can absorb rule changes and avoid any alteration in the distribution of power. Another reform would be increasing the institutional facilities of courts to create an activist judiciary. A judicial establishment like this would seek out litigation, conduct investigations, and have greater flexibility in devising outcomes and monitoring compliance. Obviously, however, such a sweeping reform of the judiciary would face enormous resistance. Third, legal services to the poor and other OSs could be increased in both quality and quantity. A reform of this nature would have many effects. It would tend to reduce costs, remove the advantage of legal expertise, produce increased litigation by OSs with more favorable outcomes, and create new rules benefiting OSs.

According to Galanter, however, the single most effective reform would be reorganizing parties. By this Galanter means the creation of repeat players out of some of those that are now one shotters. Organized into coherent groups, OSs could act in a coordinated manner, play long-run strategies, and benefit from high-grade legal services. An organized group is better able to secure favorable rulings and ensure that these rules are implemented. Unfortunately, have-nots are rarely organized as RPs. A major exception is the NAACP Legal Defense Fund, which sponsors many test cases on behalf of the disadvantaged. Also, the federal government's Legal Services Corporation sometimes has acted in behalf of disadvantaged groups in test cases. If Galanter is correct, reformers ought to seek changes in the rules in order to improve the strategic position of OS parties. These rule changes could help to facilitate the organization of OSs, increase the supply of legal services, and raise the costs which must by paid by opponents.

Winners and Losers

The losing party in a civil or criminal case, of course, is not always a disadvantaged person. Indeed, the disadvantaged have benefited from several changes in the law. For example, bankruptcy has evolved into a mechanism that debtors can use to get a fresh start. In addition, the federal government has placed restrictions on the maximum percentage of income which can be garnisheed. Also, there have been favorable changes in the law with regard to landlord-tenant relations. Many other disputes in the civil courts are related only secondarily to class-based concerns (for example, divorce law, auto accident cases, malpractice, civil commitment). Even so, it is true that the poor (and other OSs) generally do lose in the civil courts and are almost always the people convicted in the criminal courts. In debt actions, the most numerous type of civil case, the poor routinely lose. Moreover, nearly all landlord-tenant cases involve evictions. Here tenants are almost always defeated. Poor people and other OSs rarely use the civil courts as plaintiffs asserting some right. The poor have serious problems which could be adjudicated in the civil courts— landlord disputes, problems with public authority, and disputes about purchases and repairs. Yet, the legal profession is not organized to deal with such problems (Mayhew and Reiss, 1969). Craig Wanner suggests that the usual winners of civil cases are organizations acting as plaintiffs against individuals. As Wanner argues: "On the whole, courts are vehicles by which organizational plaintiffs gain goods and opportunities at the expense of individual defendants." (1975, p. 306)

WITNESSES

Role and Procedure

Witnesses are utilized by parties to provide evidence in the parties' behalf. The parties presume that the evidence provided will persuade the judge or jury to render a favorable ruling. Under our system of justice it is the task of both parties to seek out witnesses who will bolster their case. A witness who is called to testify is "sworn in" by the bailiff. Each witness must "solemnly swear to tell the truth, the whole truth, and nothing but the truth." It is noteworthy that witnesses are not wired to a polygraph machine so as to help the judge and jury detect deceit. The trial proceeding presumes that most witnesses will tell the truth and that dishonest or inaccurate information will be detected by the judge and jury. The witness gives initial testimony in response to questions from the party who called the witness to the stand. The party has asked (or demanded) that the witness take the stand in expectation that favorable testimony will be forthcoming. These expectations are not always met. For example, a witness may be nervous and botch testimony or else somehow evoke an image of unreliability. Moreover, after the witness' initial testimony, the opposing attorney may cross-examine. Given the adversarial character of the proceedings, the aim of the cross-examination is to denigrate the reliability and significance of both the witness and the testimony. Sometimes this effort is successful.

Rules of Evidence

Witnesses are not permitted to say anything they would like. In everyday life we often listen to rumor and gossip and then assign it some degree of reliability. The rules of evidence in the courtroom are far more stringent (Cleary and Strong, 1975).[1] This stringency is quite understandable, as "it is only within the law that a person's life, liberty, property, and all else he holds dear may be forfeited." (Forkosch, 1971, pp. 1380–1381) It was due to the establishment of the jury system that the law of evidence developed (Forkosch, 1971, p. 1360). Legal professionals feared that ordinary citizens serving as jurors would not be sophisticated enough to evaluate the quality of the evidence they were hearing. The result was a determination that some forms of evidence would not be permitted at all. It is the task of the party introducing the evidence to demonstrate to the judge that it is both relevant and admissible.

Legal rules of evidence begin with the evidence accepted in everyday life and then proceed to whittle it down (Forkosch, 1971, p. 1378). The "whittling-down process" occurs in a threefold manner. First, the rules prescribe how the evidence is to be presented. For example, evidence must generally be presented personally, in open court, with personal knowledge, and followed by cross-examination. Second, the rules of evidence fix the qualifications and privileges of witnesses as well as the mode of examination. Third, the rules determine what classes of evidence will be excluded. The law of evidence is chiefly concerned with the exclusion of otherwise probative evidence. Thus, there are some facts which are relevant in a dispute but nevertheless are not admissible in a court of law because of the rules of evidence. However, even where an exclusionary rule is applicable, an exception may be created permitting the otherwise inadmissible to be admissible. There are those who believe that the existing law of evidence is too stringent, given the increasing sophistication of the American people (Forkosch, 1971, p. 1381).

---

[1]Some of the concerns in the law of evidence include the burden of proof, direct v. circumstantial evidence, relevancy, the competency of witnesses, hearsay, and privileged communications.

Witness Fallibility

Witnesses are not infallible. Simply because a witness insists "I saw it with my own eyes" does not mean that he or she remembers the events correctly. In fact, the reliability of eyewitness testimony is open to serious question (Woocher, 1977; Yarmey, 1979; Gardner, 1933; Kubie, 1959; Loftus, 1974; Nahstoll, 1962). While there is much that the human memory recalls, there is also a great deal that it forgets or incorrectly recalls. Initially, it was thought that the human brain functions like a videotape recorder. Early analysts argued that information is stored by people on "memory tape" and can be recounted on demand. However, this conception of human memory is no longer accepted as valid. No doubt, dishonesty accounts for some of the misinformation offered on the witness stand. However, most erroneous testimony is unintentional and based upon faulty recollection by witnesses.

The fallibility of the testimony voiced on the witness stand is suggested by three general problems with human memory (Woocher, 1977; Yarmey, 1979; Kubie, 1959). To begin with, perception of an event by a witness is not a passive recording. Rather, it involves an active process of selective construction. Both consciously and unconsciously, the witness focuses upon and stores a limited set of stimuli. During the course of the experience certain significant details such as the height, weight, and age of participants may be ignored. Personal biases may readily distort perceptions. A witness may remember an offender as having certain physical features simply because the witness has always associated these features with criminality. A particular problem is that witnesses find it difficult to accurately identify offenders of a different race. In some cases the result is an incorrect identification rather than a failure to make any identification. Witnesses may genuinely believe that they are correctly identifying an offender when, in fact, they are mistaken. Problems of perception are often compounded by poor observation conditions (for example, lighting, fast-moving events, great distances, stressful situation).

A second problem characteristic of human memory is that our representation of an event alters over time. Memory is affected by various sources of bias, distortion, and loss of recall. Some of these sources of memory change include police questioning, newspaper accounts, discussions with friends and acquaintances, and the experiences of daily life. Evidence suggests that a person's memory of an event declines over time. This is particularly disturbing for the legal process, where substantial time may separate the event from the trial. Interestingly, over time witnesses become increasingly confident that they are accurately recalling the events, even as the validity of their recollections deteriorates.

Finally, the process of retrieval and communication also diminish the accuracy of eyewitness testimony. The recollections of witnesses are altered by subtle, imperceptible suggestions that they receive. Under questioning by a police officer, the memory of a witness may be altered by changes in the officer's voice intonation; the hint of a smile; obvious gestures such as nodding; or a request that the witness "take another, more careful, look" at a photo. Evidence suggests that testimony will be least accurate when a witness is asked highly structured questions. Many witnesses feel compelled to respond in a complete manner in spite of their incomplete knowledge. Then, having verbalized this information, the witness's mental representation of the event becomes altered. The police lineup poses special problems for human memory. An implicit suggestion in such a lineup is that it includes the criminal. Thus, witnesses may treat their task as one of identifying the best match to their recollection, when in fact the genuine culprit is not even present. Also, the communication process may distort the testimony of witnesses. Few can use language so precisely as to convey exactly what is intended. A witness in court may recollect accurately but convey the recollections in a way that misleads the judge and jury.

People may suffer serious personal losses as a result of mistaken eye-witness testimony. One such alleged incident is the 1921 case of Nicola Sacco and Bartolomeo Vanzetti in South Braintree, Massachusetts (Frankfurter, 1927). The two men, both Italian anarchists, were tried for murder and robbery at the height of our nation's hysteria over radicalism. The only issue at the trial was the identity of the murderers. Sacco testified that he was in Boston on the day of the crime, seeing about a passport to Italy, which he was planning to visit soon. This claim was confirmed at the trial by an official of the Italian consulate. Vanzetti, a fish peddler, said he was working at his trade on the day of the crime. This was confirmed by a number of witnesses who said they had been his customer on that day. There was, however, a mass of conflicting evidence at the trial. Some fifty-nine witnesses testified for the prosecution, while ninety-nine spoke for the defendants.

An important prosecution witness testifying against Sacco was Mary Splaine. At the trial Splaine described the man she saw at the scene of the crime (Frankfurter, 1927, pp. 11–12):

> He weighed possibly from 140 to 145 pounds. He was muscular, an active look-ing man. His left hand was a good sized hand, a hand that denoted strength. . . . The forehead was high. The hair was brushed back and it was between, I should think, two inches and two and one-half inches in length and had dark eyebrows, but the complexion was a white, peculiar white that looked greenish.

Although all of us have some vivid recollections, one is struck by the great detail in Splaine's account of the person she remembers seeing at the scene of the crime. This detail is remarkable—and, from what we know of memory, it is surely impossible. The history of Splaine's eyewitness account casts serious doubt on its reliability. Most important, Splaine's initial view of the offender was very incomplete. Splaine had been at work in a nearby factory and went to a second-floor window after hearing a gunshot. She looked upon the scene of the crime from a distance of sixty to eighty feet. The offender she observed (allegedly Sacco) was in an escaping car, traveling from fifteen to eighteen miles per hour. Her glimpse at the offender was for only a few seconds. Indeed, Splaine testified at the preliminary hearing that she was unable to identify Sacco as the offender. Some thirteen months later, at the trial, Splaine offered the comprehensive description of Sacco noted above.

The Splaine testimony in the courtroom was probably neither an accurate recollection nor a deliberate distortion. There is evidence in the Sacco-Vanzetti case of improper police conduct in dealing with witnesses. For example, between the time of Sacco's arrest and trial the police showed him to Splaine on several occasions. It is likely that over time Splaine simply developed a false memory of what she saw. The reliability of the other eyewitness testimony against Sacco, as well as Vanzetti, can also be seriously questioned. For example, one witness claimed to recognize Vanzetti as a man he saw sitting in the front seat of the car used in the crime. However, the prosecution was claiming that Vanzetti was seated in the rear of the car. There is always doubt about the reliability of eyewitness testimony. A witness may not be telling the truth or may be failing to accurately recollect the events that actually occurred. The stakes in the civil and criminal courtroom are enormous. Largely on the basis of eyewitness testimony, Sacco and Vanzetti were convicted by the jury, sentenced to death, and ultimately executed. Some believe that justice was done in this case; others view the Sacco-Vanzetti trial as a persecution of radicals; still others remember it as a case of mistaken identity.

Policy Action

The problem of eyewitness identification was first addressed by the Supreme Court in a landmark trilogy of decisions: *United States v. Wade, Gilbert v. California,* and *Stovall v. Denno* (Woocher, 1977, pp. 989–1000). These cases focused on the possibility that mental suggestions might develop when a suspect is presented to witnesses for pretrial identification. The Supreme Court established a series of constitutional safeguards to reduce the chances of erroneous identifications due to such suggestive influences. In *Wade* and *Gilbert* the Court ruled that under the Sixth and Fourteenth Amendments, an accused is entitled to counsel at a lineup. Identifications made at illegal lineups were to be excluded as evidence. Also excluded were any courtroom identifications found to have been prejudiced by an illegal lineup.[2]

In *Stovall v. Denno* exclusionary rules were extended by the Court. Here the Court acknowledged that a witness-suspect confrontation may be preju-

---

[2]Subsequently, the Supreme Court placed limits on the scope of these cases. In *Kirby v. Illinois,* 406 U.S. 682 (1972), the Court held that identifications were permissible without an attorney's presence in the period after arrest but prior to initiation of an adversarial criminal proceeding. However, in *Moore v. Illinois,* 434 U.S. 220 (1977), the Court held that an identification could not be made at a preliminary hearing if the accused did not have legal counsel. Thus, *Wade* and *Gilbert* seem to apply from the point of the preliminary hearing to the final disposition of the case.

dicial even if it occurs in the presence of an attorney. To protect due process rights, courts are obliged to consider the fairness of the confrontation, as indicated by the composition of any lineup, the conduct of the police at the confrontation, and the lapse of time between crime and confrontation. If these factors are conducive to mistaken identification in a given case, under *Stovall* all evidence from the pretrial identification must be suppressed.

Of course, these Supreme Court decisions only skim the surface of the problems in eyewitness identification. The decisions are intended to prevent government officials from inducing false memories in witnesses. Beyond that, there remains a complex set of factors that may influence the observation, memory, and recall of witnesses. It would require an enormous effort to reduce the eyewitness identification problem. A full-scale effort would involve training all potential witnesses (that is, 220 million Americans) to improve their observation, memory, and recall skills. While the effect would be to create a more attentive, knowledgeable public, the feasibility of such a proposal is clearly questionable. A more practical suggestion is that expert testimony be regularly admitted into evidence as to the factors influencing the reliability of eyewitness testimony (Woocher, 1977, p. 1029). The purpose of such testimony would be to warn jurors of the pitfalls of relying on the testimony of even the most sincere, persuasive eyewitness.

JURIES

Citizens may also become involved in the judiciary through participation in both grand and petit juries.[3] As David Kairys and associates argue: "The jury provides a vehicle for direct citizen participation in an arena otherwise dominated by professional advocates and government officials." (1977, p. 782) The following discussion focuses on several features of juries in the United States—their backgrounds, attitudes, roles, decision-making function, and relations with the general public. This analysis will raise several intriguing questions about the American jury. For example: Should juries consist of a cross-section of the general public? How effective are grand juries and petit juries in carrying out their functions? Are the background characteristics of jurors influential in their behavior? How important is the size of juries to the decisions they reach? Should juries have the right to disregard the law if they do not wish to convict a defendant? On such questions there is an extensive amount of existing literature. We can only touch upon this body of theory and research in our discussion.

[3]The grand jury is a group of citizens who decides whether an accused will be indicted for a crime, based on evidence presented by the prosecutor. A petit jury is a group of citizens who hears civil and criminal trials and renders a collective decision.

Backgrounds

Much controversy has been attached to the matter of the background characteristics of jurors. Alexis de Tocqueville noted: "The institution of the jury may be aristocratic or democratic, according to the class from which the jurors are selected. . . ." (1875, p. 286) In contrast to the aristocratic juries of England, de Tocqueville characterized American juries as highly representative. More accurately, the history of American juries has been one of unrepresentativeness, but with increasing efforts to ensure that juries be a representative cross-section of the public. Among those routinely excluded from jury duty are the transient and illiterate as well as those convicted of a felony. However, these are not the only groups underrepresented on juries. More broadly, there is a "middle-American" bias in jury composition, with underrepresentation of blacks, women, urbanites, the young and the elderly, and the poorly as well as highly educated (Alker, Hosticka, and Mitchell, 1976).

A series of court cases has addressed the issue of jury representativeness. Since the ratification of the Fourteenth Amendment there has been a piecemeal effort by the Supreme Court to ensure more representative juries. In 1880, in the case of *Strauder v. West Virginia,* the Supreme Court invalidated a state statute prohibiting blacks from serving on grand or petit juries. Subsequent rulings outlawed de facto efforts aimed at totally excluding or underrepresenting black participation on juries. A key decision was *Smith v. Texas* in 1940. Here the Court ruled that it was not necessary for a party to prove intentional and systematic exclusion. A probability standard was set for assessing the representativeness of juries. Later rulings mandated jury representativeness as to sex and class (*Glasser v. United States, Thiel v. Southern Pacific Co., Ballard v. United States*).

Notwithstanding these court decisions, the problem of jury representation has persisted. There are two possible sources of bias in the composition of juries. First, there may be biases in the source list(s) from which jury venires (that is, panel of potential jurors) are selected. It is the representativeness of the source lists which has been the focus of the Supreme Court. Also relevant is the passage by Congress of the Jury Selection and Services Act of 1968 (PL 90–274) (Alker et al., 1976). The act demands that juror lists provide a "fair cross-section of the community." While the act sanctions use of multiple lists to create venires, it has been implemented primarily through use of voter registration lists. David Kairys and associates have called for the use of multiple source lists as a means of improving the representativeness of juries (1977, pp. 776–777). Apart from voter registration, other source lists include records of licensed drivers, income taxpayers, property taxpayers, utility customers, and welfare recipients. The city directory and state census might also be used.

The excuse process is the other fundamental source of jury unrepresentativeness (Abraham, 1980a, pp. 120–125). Through this process certain classes of people are required or permitted to be excused from jury duty. Those excluded generally include professionals such as lawyers, physicians, military personnel, government officials, police officers, firefighters, clergy, and teachers. Indispensable workers, nursing mothers, and busy housewives can also be excused. In addition, it is possible for irresponsible citizens to evade jury duty by professing a bias in a case. Jury composition may also be affected by various challenges granted to the defense and prosecution. In the United States two types of challenges exist—peremptory and for cause. Under a peremptory challenge either party is entitled to request the removal of a potential juror. The attorney need not offer any reason for making this request. The number of such challenges is limited, often varying with the seriousness of the charges. In a challenge for cause an attorney must advance a bona fide reason for a demand for disqualification. Any number of challenges for cause may be made, but they must be related to the substantive and procedural aspects of the case. Sometimes attorneys will make use of their challenges quite intentionally to manipulate the background characteristics of the jury that is selected (Simon, 1980, pp. 29–47). A common belief among attorneys is that certain background characteristics are closely associated with the predilections of jurors.

Attitudes

What are the attitudes of jurors toward jury service? While this is a largely unexplored question, it was the subject of a 1972 study conducted in New York City (Simon, 1975). Surely, the most important question is whether attitudes toward the jury system altered as a result of jury duty. Here the results were somewhat positive. The study revealed that 32.2 percent of jurors became more favorable in their attitudes toward jury duty. However, 47.8 percent of jurors maintained the same attitudes, while 20 percent became less favorable. Least positive were the attitudes of those jurors who served in the criminal courts.

Some specific complaints about jury duty were registered by the respondents. One complaint is that much of jury duty consists of sitting around in the waiting room and doing nothing. Those responding spent an average of 61.8 percent of their time in the waiting room. Some 6 percent of the jurors remained in the waiting room during their entire tenure as jurors. Those who were in the waiting room a great deal were more likely to develop negative attitudes toward jury service. Another complaint regarded the physical comfort of court facilities. Objections were expressed concerning inadequate ventilation, uncomfortable seats, and overcrowded waiting rooms. A minority of jurors were concerned about their physical safety within the courthouse (3.7 percent) or outside the courthouse (4.3 percent). Finally, about half the jurors felt that the fee they received for jury service ($12.00 per day plus $.70 travel expenses) was inadequate.

Roles

Given the pervasiveness of plea bargaining and out-of-court civil settlements, the use of juries is clearly the exception rather than the rule. Even in the rare cases which go to trial, the right to a jury trial may be waived. Despite this, juries may play some significant roles in the courts. Actually, up to three types of juries exist in many states (Jacob, 1978, p. 126). The grand jury, usually composed of twenty-three citizens, hears allegations about crimes which may have taken place. The role of the grand jury is to vote indictments where the evidence suggests that a particular individual has committed a crime. If the grand jury indicts, further court action may occur. Many states also have a coroner's jury. The role of this type of jury is to hear evidence about mysterious deaths and to rule whether they were natural, accidental, or caused by another party.

Most important, and most common, is the petit jury. This is a body of six to twelve citizens who hear civil and criminal trials and decide their outcome. The decisions made by petit (trial) juries culminate the judicial process in most cases and are rarely overturned. In fact, in most states a finding of innocence in a criminal case cannot be subsequently overturned on appeal. Noting that most cases are disposed of before trial through plea bargaining, W. Boyd Littrell nevertheless suggests that the jury system has three key roles (1979, pp. 178–185). According to Littrell, one role is to induce defendants to plead guilty. The specter of a jury trial is used by prosecutors as a subtle means of coercion. Second, juries are used to decide cases which pose difficulties from a legal or organizational standpoint. Finally, Littrell suggests that criminal justice personnel make use of "imaginary juries" to assess the quality of evidence and strength of witnesses. The nature of the plea bargain agreed upon will depend on what a jury *would do* if the case were brought before it.

The effectiveness of juries in carrying out their roles has been debated. For example, detractors of the grand jury have characterized it as "an unsupervised strong arm of the prosecution." (Gerstein and Robinson, 1978, p. 338; Carp; 1975) Grand juries have been termed the "rubber stamp" of prosecutors, since they rarely refuse to obey a prosecutor's request to indict. Typically, a grand jury spends five minutes on a case and almost always acts unanimously (Carp, 1975, pp. 856–861). Critics also suggest that grand juries are inadequately trained and that they are shielded from public scrutiny, unregulated by courts, virtually unlimited in subpoena powers, able to question witnesses behind closed doors, and capable of jailing a recalcitrant witness without trial.

In view of problems such as these, the American Bar Association has endorsed a comprehensive series of grand jury reforms (Gerstein and Robinson, 1978, pp. 337–338). Under these reforms counsel would be permitted to accompany a witness into the grand jury room; prosecutors would be forbidden from using the grand jury to investigate someone already indicted; and witnesses would be protected against harassment, unreasonable delays, and repeated appearances. Opponents of these reforms fear that they will make the job of law enforcement more difficult. At issue is whether the primary goal of the grand jury should be ensuring procedural justice or the efficient return of indictments. At the extremes, the grand jury can either serve as part of a due process "obstacle course" or as an appendage of the prosecution.

The effectiveness of petit juries has also been the source of much discussion. Skepticism about their effectiveness has been voiced by Finley Peter Dunne's Mr. Dooley: "Whin th' case is all over, the jury'll pitch th' testimony out iv th' window, an' consider three questions: 'Did Lootgert look as though he'd kill his wife? Did his wife look as though she ought to be kilt? Isn't it time we wint to supper?'" (1898, pp. 141–145) Critics of the petit jury allege that it is expensive, causes delay, and will produce amateurish decisions. Many critics would replace jury verdicts with verdicts by judges. A particular concern of Jerome Frank is that juries do not seem to follow legal rules, as embodied in the judge's instructions, when making decisions (Frank, 1949, pp. 108–145). Rather, a jury will simply issue a verdict it believes is "fair." As Frank suggests: "They determine that they want Jones to collect $5,000 from the railroad company, or that they don't want pretty Nellie Brown to go to jail for killing her husband; and they bring on their general verdict accordingly." (1949, p. 111) In Frank's view juries lack adequate training, are ineffective fact-finders, do not understand the instructions they are given,[4] and may be easily swayed by a sharp attorney.

Nevertheless, some evidence suggests a far more optimistic portrait of the American jury (Kalven and Zeisel, 1966, esp. pp. 55–57). Harry Kalven and Hans Zeisel sought to learn what difference it would make if judges, rather than juries, rendered verdicts in cases. They examined the verdicts of juries in 3,576 criminal cases. For each case the actual jury verdict was compared with the judge's hypothetical verdict, which was privately reported to the researchers. Critics of juries would point to substantial judge-jury disagreement as indicative of the jury's fallibility and incompetence. However, the results of the Kalven-Zeisel study indicate that judge and jury disagree in only 19.1 percent of all cases. Also significant is that where disagreements do occur, juries are far less likely than judges to convict a defendant. The researchers also report that in civil cases jury-judge agreement is quite high (1966, p. 63). Here, however, the jury does not lean toward any particular ruling. While interpretation of the data is difficult, the findings do suggest an enormous amount of agreement between judges and juries. On the criminal side the results suggest that juries sometimes serve to protect defendants from convictions where judges would be less protective. These findings tend to bolster one's faith in the efficacy of the jury.

[4]A study reported in *The New York Times* confirms the failure of jurors to understand the judge's instructions. In one experiment thirty-four volunteer jurors were read the instructions of a Nevada judge for a trial for attempted murder. Only one juror was able to tell the difference between the highest and lowest charges. See *The New York Times,* "Study Urges Plain Language for Jury Instructions" (June 7, 1981), p. 25.

Decision Making

Before there was trial by jury, there was trial by ordeal (Tewksbury, 1967; Bonsignore et al., 1979a).[5] The ordeal was a primitive form of trial used to determine the guilt or innocence of the accused. It involved the use of some "test" and assumed that the outcome of that test would be determined by divine intervention. The ordeal came into prominence in medieval England and was used particularly where the evidence of a case was in doubt. We have long since abandoned the ordeal in favor of the right to a jury trial. This right is guaranteed to Americans in Article III, section 2 of the Constitution and by the Sixth and Seventh Amendments. Regarding serious crimes, the guarantee of the Sixth Amendment was applied to the states in 1968 in *Duncan v. Louisiana.* What is striking is the immense amount of faith placed in the jury trial today. It is a faith not unlike that associated with the ordeal of ages past. While the ordeal turned to God for justice, the jury trial looks to the rationality of jury decision making (Simon, 1980). The inherent assumption is that justice will result when an impartial group of people is presented with the facts of a case and allowed to deliberate on a verdict.

The jury process is governed by an intricate set of rules. The first phase is known as voir dire—literally, "to see, to tell." (Fried, Kaplan, and Klein, 1975) It is in this phase that prospective jurors are questioned and selected to serve as jurors (Schatz, 1977). The prospective jury panel is randomly chosen from a large group of assembled citizens. Typically, the judge asks them general questions on their fitness to serve. This is followed by further questioning from the prosecution or defense. Either party may challenge the array if it believes that the entire panel has been irregularly selected. Peremptory challenges and challenges for cause are also permitted.

The voir dire procedure fulfills three major purposes (Fried et al., 1975, p. 50). First, it is used by the initiator and defense to gather information to help select jurors. Many attorneys believe that the composition of a jury will determine who wins and who loses. A second purpose of voir dire is to enable the two attorneys to develop a rapport with prospective jurors. Finally, both sides use the voir dire procedure to try to change the attitudes, values, and perspectives of jurors. The literature on voir dire generally focuses on the first of these three purposes—voir dire and jury selection. In voir dire lawyers play "amateur psychologist," using their intuition as to which jurors would be most helpful and which most troublesome (Simon, 1980, p. 32). Often lawyers look beyond the attitudes of jurors to their sociological and psychological characteristics. Most attorneys seem to feel that the jurors who will be most receptive to defendants include women, Democrats, members of middle and lower economic groups, social scientists, and minorities. However, even though

---

[5]For a case study of one contemporary juror's experiences see Edwin Kennebeck, *Juror Number Four* (New York: W. W. Norton and Co., 1973).

many lawyers are preoccupied with the demographics of jury selection, the evidence suggests that only weak relationships exist. Rita Simon concludes: "Attorneys may be spending time and money elaborating on a process that has only slight empirical support and that can provide little practical help." (Simon, 1980, p. 46)

Sitting *en banc,* the jury hears a case collectively from beginning to end (Abraham, 1980a, pp. 128–135; Jacob, 1978, pp. 129–137). Jurors are excused only when attorneys are arguing about the admissibility of evidence. However, the jury acts as a passive observer. Jurors may not directly question witnesses or discuss the ongoing case, either among themselves or with outsiders. To ensure their impartiality, jurors are also expected to avoid any media discussion of the trial. In general, jurors may not take notes of the proceedings but must simply be attentive and try to remember what has taken place. After the closing arguments of the two sides, the judge gives a charge to the jury. In many states the instructions have been standardized to avoid mistakes and possible mistrials. In these states the task of the judge is simply to read the proper paragraphs from a handbook of instructions. The judge's instructions include an explanation of alternative decisions and the evidence required for each verdict. In some states the judge is permitted to comment on the quality of the evidence presented. Unfortunately, the judge's instructions are often quite complex and beyond the grasp of many jurors.

Before reaching a verdict, the jury deliberates in complete privacy in a special room with locked doors. Jurors select a foreman—usually, according to available evidence, someone of high social status (Strodtbeck, James, and Hawkins, 1957). The most influential jurors in the deliberations also tend to be of high status. When deliberating, much of the time is spent simply discussing personal experiences related to the trial. The jury may ask the judge to clarify the legal questions involved. Also, the jury may examine some of the items of evidence. One or more ballots may take place. If the deliberations are lengthy, the jury may be sequestered in a nearby hotel for one or more evenings.

Usually, the jury is required to return a general verdict in favor of one party or another. It is presumed that juries will base their decision on the facts of the case, consistent with the law as explained by the judge. In practice, the general verdict permits great leeway to juries to do as they please. There is no mechanism in a general verdict to prevent juries from returning a decision they think is "fair" even if contrary to the demands of the law. Some have called for a fact verdict, in which the jury would simply resolve a series of factual questions in the case. It would then be the job of the judge to apply the law to the factual determinations made by the jury. The fact verdict is, in fact, used in several states and was authorized in 1938 for federal civil suits. If the jury is unable to reach a verdict, the judge will declare a hung jury, dismiss it, and return the case to the docket for a new trial.

When we think of a jury verdict, we usually think of the unanimous verdict of twelve jurors (Zeisel, 1972). However, in an effort to save time and money, and perhaps secure more convictions, there has been some movement for decreasing jury size and eliminating the unanimity rule. Jury size was the focus of *Williams v. Florida* in 1970. In its decision the Court characterized twelve as an arbitrary size for juries and sanctioned the use of smaller juries in noncapital criminal cases. The Court cited "empirical evidence" suggesting that jury size did not have a significant impact on case outcomes. Actually, the "empirical evidence" cited by the Court amounted to "a series of informal observations and assertions" rather than any hard evidence (Vollrath and Davis, 1980, p. 74). However, it is likely that the Court did make a lucky guess, as subsequent research has detected few differences in the outcomes of trials with juries of differing sizes (Roper, 1979). The decision rule of juries became the focus of the Supreme Court in 1972 in *Johnson v. Louisiana*. Here the Court held that unanimous decisions are not required in criminal cases as a requisite to due process of law. A verdict of guilty (or innocent) could be returned by a vote of 9 to 3. This decision has come under sharp criticism, since recent evidence suggests that the decision rule does in fact influence jury outcomes. As one might expect, a hung jury is considerably less likely when a unanimous decision is not required (Vollrath and Davis, 1980, pp. 77, 102). The effect of permitting less-than-unanimous convictions appears to be to encourage more verdicts of guilty.

Debate has also centered on what limits ought to be placed on the discretion of juries in arriving at decisions. Jury nullification involves the power of a jury to render a general verdict of acquittal in the face of the law and of evidence to the contrary (Christie, 1974, p. 1297). Juries are generally unaware of this power. In California the judge informs jurors: "It is your duty as jurors to follow the law as I shall state it to you." (Van Dyke, 1970, p. 225) As a consequence of such instructions, according to Jon Van Dyke: "American jurors have become a docile and well regimented group." (1970, p. 225) Proponents of jury nullification contend that the judge's instructions should specifically inform jurors about jury nullification. These instructions should tell jurors that they need not apply the law to the action of the defendant if they believe this would produce an unjust result. Critics of jury nullification argue that the biases of individual jurors should not stand in the way of the application of the law to the facts of a case (Christie, 1974, pp. 1303–1304). According to this view, jurors will act irresponsibly if they are told they may choose to disregard the law. The famous "free press" trial of John Peter Zenger exemplifies the issue of jury nullification (Scheflin, 1972, pp. 173–174). In this 1735 case a New York jury refused to convict Zenger even though he clearly did violate a law forbidding the printing of material not authorized by the British. Subsequently, however, the Supreme Court ruled in *Sparf and Hansen v. United States* that while juries clearly have the power to exercise jury nullification, they do not have the constitutional right.

Public Relations

Whatever its problems and controversies, the American jury does not seem to be suffering from a problem of public relations. It is probable that most Americans would agree with the statement that "the representative, popular character of the jury lends legitimacy, integrity, and impartiality to the judicial process." (Kairys et al., 1977, p. 782) Most Americans prefer a jury trial to trial by a judge (Flynn, 1960; Jacob, 1966, p. 814). Those who favor a jury trial are distrustful of judges who act alone. Some fear that judges are corrupt, prejudiced, or too harsh. Others simply believe that "twelve heads are better than one." Beyond that, people who have been jurors are generally pleased with the experience and are willing to serve again. Evidently, some of the best public relations for the American jury comes from former jurors.

It is also important to know the views of judges toward juries. After all, it is the judge who "is the daily observer of the jury system in action, its daily partner in the administration of justice, and the one who would be most affected if the civil jury were abolished." (Kalven, 1964, p. 1073) Even though juries subtract from the power of judges, few judges wish to abolish the jury system (Kalven, 1964). A survey of trial judges indicates that few of them consider juries to be unsatisfactory—only 3 percent hold this view for criminal cases, and 9 percent for civil cases. While some judges support certain reforms of the jury system, on balance most judges regard the system as "thoroughly satisfactory."

INTEREST GROUPS

Interest groups have captured the interest of many political analysts. A leading theory of power—pluralism—observes that large numbers of competing groups are present in our society (Truman, 1951; Dahl, 1967). Pluralist theory asserts that these groups play a central role in lawmaking. According to pluralists, government officials are responsive to interest groups in rough approximation to the strength of their resources. These resources may include wealth, numbers, organizational skill, knowledge, and effort. Interest groups are most closely associated with Congress, where large numbers of lobbyists are in regular contact with legislators. Pluralists take delight in these legislator-lobbyist contacts, believing that the laws which result are relatively democratic in substance.

The judiciary might seem to be rather foreign turf for interest group activity. After all, the traditional view of legal jurisprudence suggests that judicial decisions are based on preexisting rules, such as those contained in the Constitution. If preexisting rules determine judicial decisions, this would appear to leave little leeway for the pressure politics of interest groups. Even so, the footprints of interest groups are scattered throughout the judicial landscape. Various groups make their views known in judicial recruitment, litigation, amicus curiae briefs, and legal periodicals. At the same time, it has not been demonstrated that these techniques are truly effective in influencing judicial decisions. Indeed, from a normative standpoint it is not clear whether we would want the courts to be responsive to interest group demands.

Recruitment

The recruitment of personnel to the judiciary provides one point of access for interest groups (Ziegler, 1964, pp. 308–314). This activity reflects the involvement of interest groups in the recruitment process throughout government in America. Interest groups participate in the selection of both elected and appointed officials. For elected officials interest groups may provide a source of campaign funding, endorsements, volunteers, and political savvy. For appointed officials interest groups attempt to exert influence on those who do the appointing. As noted earlier, federal judges in the United States are chosen exclusively by appointment, while on the state level there is a mixture of selection methods. The aim of this interest group activity is to promote judicial candidates favorable to the group's interests and block the selection of candidates who would be detrimental.

A variety of groups may become involved in the recruitment of judges. Recently the confirmation of Sandra O'Connor to the Supreme Court drew stiff opposition from conservative groups concerned about her views on abortion. Without doubt, however, the American Bar Association is the most important interest group in the realm of judicial recruitment. The ABA's Committee on the Federal Judiciary has had special access to the Justice Department ever since the Eisenhower years. The Committee has been permitted to offer evaluations of possible choices for federal judgeships. On the state level the ABA has sought to promote the Missouri Plan as a means of judicial selection. In short, interest groups—and especially the ABA—play some role in judicial recruitment. At the same time, interest group activity is probably not among the most decisive factors in the appointment process.

Litigation

While interest groups are normally associated with Congressional lobbying, courtroom litigation is also an important interest group technique. As Clement Vose observes: "Organizations—identifiable by letterhead—often link broad interests in society to individual parties of interest in Supreme Court cases." (1958, p. 21) Groups enter the courtroom to press for rulings favorable to their interests. Although an individual is the formal litigant, interest groups may provide financial backing, legal skills, and psychological support. They can also offer continuity to a process that may take several years to run its full course through the judiciary.

Because so many legal rules impinge upon the goals of most interest groups, there will be no shortage of relevant rules to litigate. In some cases an interest group will lend its support to individuals already involved in litigation. The American Civil Liberties Union is well known for its use of this approach. A more aggressive strategy, as employed by the NAACP Legal Defense Fund, has been to actually develop a dispute for litigation to serve as a "test case" on some point of law (Ziegler, 1964, pp. 317–320; Vose, 1959). After its successful litigation of *Brown v. Board of Education* and some follow-up efforts, Southern states retaliated against the NAACP to inhibit its litigation campaign. These states accused the NAACP of soliciting cases in violation of state laws regulating the ethical conduct of attorneys. However, in *NAACP v. Button* the Supreme Court upheld the NAACP litigation methods as protected by provisions of the First and Fourteenth Amendments. Recognizing litigation as a proper interest group activity, the Supreme Court noted that "under the conditions of modern government, litigation may well be the sole practicable avenue open to a minority to petition for redress of grievances." (at 430)

It should not be surprising that certain interest groups have made greater use of litigation than others. Among the most frequent litigators have been racial, consumer, and environmental groups. The courts will be a particularly attractive arena for those interest groups who lack the economic resources or numbers to be successful in the halls of Congress. Theoretically, the court requirements regarding legal standing could block much potential litigation by interest groups. In order to initiate a case, a litigant must be able to demonstrate that it is an aggrieved party in a live dispute. It is significant, however, that the courts have recently liberalized the requirements of standing substantially (Orren, 1976). This liberalization has increased the litigiousness of interest groups. Also significant is the development of public interest law firms for groups too poor to hire their own attorneys (Hall, 1977). Legislation adopted by Congress in 1976 enabled these firms to collect fees from defendants where the firms have successfully litigated certain kinds of cases. This may produce significant changes in legal rules, since the orientation of public interest law firms is toward the litigation of "big cases."

Amicus Curiae Briefs

An amicus curiae brief enables nonlitigants to express their views to the Supreme Court regarding specific litigation (Ziegler, 1964, pp. 321–326; Vose, 1958; Krislov, 1963). In general, a court case in our country is a duel between two opposing parties. The amicus curiae—or "friend of the court"—brief is an exception to this generality. It permits participation of third parties who have some interest in the outcome of a case. Such briefs may be filed with the consent of one of the parties or by special permission from the Supreme Court. Most state courts also permit amicus briefs. Some of the groups which frequently file amicus briefs include the American Civil Liberties Union, American Jewish Congress, AFL–CIO, and the National Lawyers Guild. A brief may develop legal arguments or cite precedents that the parties to the litigation have overlooked.

There is some dispute as to the impact of amicus curiae briefs on Supreme Court decisions. Clement Vose suggests: "Many *amici curiae* briefs are workmanlike and provide the Court with helpful legal argument and material." (1958, p. 27) Yet, Harper and Etherington argue that "for the most part, briefs amici are repetitious at best and emotional explosions at worst." (1953, p. 1172) In the 1960s and 1970s the number of amicus curiae briefs filed by interest groups increased dramatically.[6] Moreover, on occasion a written opinion of the Supreme Court will make use of material presented in an amicus brief. No doubt, one effect of the amicus brief is to give groups a feeling of participation in the decisional process of the judiciary. Yet, in most cases amicus briefs probably play little or no role in the decision of the justices.

Legal Periodicals

Legal periodicals are publications largely comprised of scholarly articles written by professors of law. They are generally published by law schools and read by the legal community. Many of these articles advocate certain types of court decisions and legal reasoning. In 1931 Justice Benjamin Cardozo noted the increased respectability of law reviews as sources of legal authority. Cardozo argued that "the sobering truth is that leadership in the march of legal thought has been passing in our day from the benches of the courts to the chairs of the universities." (1931, p. ix) Ten years later Chief Justice Hughes characterized law reviews as the "fourth estate" of the law. According to Hughes: "It is not too much to say that, in confronting any serious problem, a wide-awake and careful judge will at once look to see if the subject has been discussed, or the authorities collated and analyzed, in a good law periodical." (1941, p. 737) An analysis by Chester Newland disclosed a great increase between 1924 and 1956 in the citing of legal periodicals in court decisions (1959, p. 64). The most frequently cited law journals were the *Harvard Law Review* (cited 399 times), *Yale Law Journal* (176), and *Michigan Law Review* (65).

Normally, a law review article simply presents the opinions of a particular legal scholar. However, it is interesting to note that groups sometimes encourage like-minded legal scholars to write articles supporting a particular viewpoint (Ziegler, 1964, p. 321; Vose, 1959, p. 161). This is especially useful where the existing body of legal precedents runs counter to the group's goal.

---

[6]Compare Nathan Hakman, "Lobbying the Supreme Court: An Appraisal of 'Political Science Folklore,'" *Fordham Law Review,* 1966, *35,* 15–50 with Karen O'Connor and Lee Epstein, "Amicus Curiae Participation in U.S. Supreme Court Litigation: An Appraisal of Hakman's 'Folklore,'" *Law and Society Review,* 1981–1982, *16,* 311–320.

By getting favorable scholarly articles published, the group's arguments are given a measure of learned status. This technique was used by the NAACP Legal Defense Fund to secure a court decision against restrictive covenants. Partly because of the NAACP drive, more than thirty books and law review articles were published between 1946 and 1948 urging the Supreme Court to reverse itself on restrictive covenants (Peltason, 1955, p. 52). By 1948 the Supreme Court did, in fact, outlaw restrictive covenants in *Shelley v. Kraemer.* Clement Vose concludes that the Court's decision in this case "was an outgrowth of the complex group activity which preceded it." (Vose, 1959, p. 252) Still, it is probable that legal periodicals do not play a decisive role in very many Supreme Court decisions. Moreover, it is doubtful whether a very large share of law journal articles are written at the urging of an interest group. Even regarding restrictive covenants, many law review articles were written quite independently of NAACP Legal Defense Fund efforts (Vose, 1959, p. 161).

NEWS MEDIA

Court Watching

Court watching is a favorite avocation of the news media in America. Media attentiveness to the courts should not be surprising, given the enormous impact of the civil and criminal courts. Not only are the parties to a legal dispute affected by court decisions, but in many cases the American public is affected as well. However, it is important to note the selective character of court watching by the media. A common criticism of the news media, both print and electronic, is that they are "fascinated with glitter and glamor at the expense of significance." (Radelet, 1977, p. 412)

Certainly, a disproportionate amount of court coverage is devoted to sensational crimes and criminal prosecutions. By comparison, media reporting of Supreme Court decisions is microscopic. Without doubt, the job of the journalist is a difficult one. From among the millions of events that take place every day, the media must select for coverage only a few. Still, even if the sum total of court-related coverage is appropriate, there seems to be a serious misallocation of print space and air time. Public understanding of the courts would be enhanced if the media were less preoccupied with "soap opera coverage" of a few sensational crimes. The space and time thereby liberated could well be utilized to provide coverage of significant Supreme Court decisions and present investigations of critical issues in civil and criminal justice. At the same time, a concern for liberty suggests that no one—certainly not a government official—ought to be in a position to tell the media what they can or cannot report.

Supreme Court Coverage

If press coverage of Supreme Court decisions is inadequate, the reasons are not obscure (Grey, 1968). In essence, even as journalists find it painstaking work to report an appellate case in a provocative manner, Supreme Court practices make the job even more difficult. Journalists are highly dependent on government officials to provide them with newsworthy information. A presidential or Congressional decision will make "good press" if some sort of public debate transpires—complete with "trial balloons," attacks and counterattacks, and news leaks from "informed sources." Press coverage of the Supreme Court is constrained by the secrecy of the Court's decision-making process and by the justices' distaste for acting as advocates in behalf of Court decisions. As David Grey observes: "In contrast to Congressmen, who may think in terms of headlines, the justices seem to ignore much of what will be written about their opinions." (Grey, 1968, p. 20) Court members seem content to quietly issue written opinions and let these opinions speak for themselves. As a result, for any case of potential importance the thoroughly conscientious reporter will need to uncover relevant background and human interest material; read the legal briefs of attorneys (and *understand* them); attend oral arguments; and, on decision day, read the actual full opinion of the Court, complete with technical legal jargon. Even if the reporter were to do all of this, which is unlikely, the process of converting these informational sources into an interesting series of stories is truly a Herculean task.

One result of the above is the underreporting of many important Supreme Court decisions. When we consider the enormous policy implications of various Court rulings, the coverage provided seems quite inadequate. Beyond that, the misreporting of Court decisions is also a problem. At times the news media misrepresent the thrust of Court rulings. A well-known example of media misreporting was that of *Engel v. Vitale*, where the Court banned recitation in public schools of a prayer composed by the New York Board of Regents. In its written opinion the Court carefully pointed out that other government practices which related to religion—such as the "In God We Trust" motto on coins—were unaffected by the decision. Yet, media reports at the time indicated that all public symbols having a religious connotation might now be unconstitutional. Clearly, when the news media misinform the public, they are badly failing to fulfill their basic function.

The Supreme Court justices have evidently not lost much sleep over the difficulties the media encounter in reporting their activities. However, they have not entirely ignored the problems either. Traditionally, the Supreme Court announced its decisions only on Mondays. The result was a glut of decisions emanating once a week while the Court was in session, with little to report during the remainder of the week. For reporters this practice only added to the difficulties of preparing accurate, in-depth analyses of Court decisions. Finally, on April 5, 1965, the Supreme Court eliminated the "Decision Monday" tradition and began scattering the issuing of opinions. More recently the

Court has also begun to release its opinions with headnotes that summarize the major points of decisions.

Still, there is much more that might be done, by both the Court and the media, to improve the quality of coverage of Supreme Court decisions (Grey, 1968, pp. 137–150). One suggestion is that the Supreme Court hire a skilled interpreter to explain its decisions to news reporters. In addition, it might be made a matter of Court policy to include within each opinion a summary statement of the specific legal rule being issued. Beyond that, there is much the media themselves can do to improve their Supreme Court coverage. Perhaps, more reporters assigned to the Court should possess a law degree. The media might also make regular use of legal experts to help prepare interpretive features, news analyses, and editorials.

Trial Court Coverage

Because of the media's preoccupation with sensational crimes, the constitutional right of a defendant to a fair trial may be jeopardized. On July 4, 1954, a twenty-nine-year-old pregnant woman, Marilyn Sheppard, was found murdered.[7] She had been stripped and beaten to death with a blunt instrument. Her husband, Dr. Samuel Sheppard, was a socially prominent and wealthy osteopath in Bay Village, Ohio—a suburb of Cleveland. Dr. Sheppard told the police that he and his wife had been entertaining friends that evening. When their guests left, Mrs. Sheppard went up to bed, but he remained downstairs and fell asleep on the couch. Before dawn, according to Dr. Sheppard, he was awakened by his wife's screams and raced upstairs. He fought with one or two people in the bedroom and was struck on the back of his neck. He examined his wife and realized she was dead. According to Sheppard, he then went downstairs, chased an intruder outside, wrestled with a man on his private beach, and fell unconscious there. Sheppard said that when he came to, he went back to his house, reexamined his wife, wandered about in a daze, and finally called his friend, the mayor of Bay Village.

The murder of Marilyn Sheppard caught the attention of the Cleveland media, including the *Cleveland Press* and *Plain Dealer*. Much of the media seemed to reach the conclusion that Dr. Sheppard had killed his wife and that law enforcement officials were intent on covering up the crime. When no indictments were made, a series of highly prejudicial headlines appeared in the Cleveland newspapers. From the time of the crime to the arrest of Dr. Sheppard, the *Cleveland Press* used the case as its page-one lead story on each of the twenty-three days it published. Media coverage of the Sheppard case con-

---

[7]See the extensive account of the case in *Sheppard v. Maxwell* and the discussion in Alfred Friendly and Ronald L. Goldfarb, *Crime and Publicity: The Impact of News on the Administration of Justice* (New York: Twentieth Century Fund, 1967). See also Alan Barth, "Background Paper," The Twentieth Century Fund Task Force on Justice, Publicity, and the First Amendment, *Rights in Conflict* (New York: McGraw-Hill, 1967).

tinued at full force after his arrest. In the fifty-three days of publication between Sheppard's arrest and trial, the *Press* gave the story a banner headline
twenty-three times and front-page coverage thirty-one times. Prejudicial stories were printed, many of them apparently leaked by law enforcement officials. The media appraised these leaks as damning to Sheppard. Ten days
before the trial the paper actually printed a public opinion poll on page one,
indicating that the vast majority of Cleveland residents favored a verdict of
guilty. The paper also predicted that there would be testimony at the trial
showing that Sheppard had a personality much like Dr. Jekyll and Mr. Hyde.
This testimony never actually materialized. Still, such media coverage clearly
did contribute to creating a presumption of Sheppard's guilt among the residents of the Cleveland area.

The trial proceedings themselves were quite imperfect in the Sheppard
case. Twenty-five days before the case was set, seventy-five veniremen were
chosen as possible jurors. Their names and addresses were published in Cleveland newspapers. Consequently, prospective jurors were subjected to anonymous letters and phone calls. The trial took place in a tiny courtroom which
was literally jammed with members of the press, telegraphic and broadcast
equipment, spectators, and witnesses. There was massive coverage of the trial,
which continued for a period of nine weeks. Coverage included the photo-
graphing and televising of witnesses, counsel, and jurors whenever they entered or left the courtroom. Movement of media representatives in and out of
the courtroom during the trial caused so much confusion, it was often difficult
for the witnesses and counsel to be heard. The jurors themselves were constantly exposed to the media. At voir dire every juror but one claimed to have
read or heard about the case in the media. Pictures of the jury appeared more
than forty times in Cleveland papers during the course of the trial. The jury
took five days and four nights to deliberate on the verdict. Although the jury
was sequestered, jurors were permitted to make unmonitored phone calls to
their homes every night. Finally, the jury's verdict was announced: Sheppard
had been convicted of murder.

Sheppard spent nearly a decade in jails and in appellate courts. Finally,
he secured from the Supreme Court a reversal on the grounds that pretrial
publicity had deprived him of due process of law. Justice Tom Clark, writing
for the Court in *Sheppard v. Maxwell,* argued that the trial judge had permitted a prejudicial "carnival atmosphere" to prevail. In failing to adequately
supervise the press, the judge had denied Sheppard the "judicial serenity and
calm to which he was entitled." Clark noted that the deluge of publicity clearly
had reached some of the jurors. Beyond that, the Clark opinion also outlined
a variety of specific measures that the trial judge should have followed. These
included limiting the access and movement of reporters at the trial; insulating
witnesses; and controlling the release of information to the press by the police,
witnesses, and counsel. Ultimately, Dr. Sheppard received a new trial and was
declared to be innocent.

A variety of judicial procedures have long been available to safeguard the impartiality of juries (Friendly and Goldfarb, 1967, pp. 96–140). Prior to trial the defense can make a motion for a change of venue (new trial location) or a continuance (later trial date). If the trial is relocated to some other community, potential jurors will be less likely to have been exposed to prejudicial press coverage. Similarly, a continuance may help the memories of potential jurors to fade, so that they no longer recall any media accounts of the crime that they may have heard. In addition, careful use of voir dire can screen biased jurors and socialize those selected to base their verdict only on courtroom evidence. After their selection, jurors may also be sequestered to prevent them from hearing media accounts of the ongoing trial. Moreover, the judge's instructions to the jury may emphasize the importance of ignoring outside information about the crime. Poorly issued instructions may subsequently be challenged by the defense attorney.

Since the Sheppard case, however, judges have gone beyond these traditional procedures in order to ensure that the defendant receives a fair trial. Fearing as well the possibility of a mistrial, some judges have issued gag orders, which are enforced through the court's contempt powers. A gag order is a restraint issued by a judge preventing the dissemination of information about criminal proceedings. In England there are strict restraints on what the press may publish about criminal trials. In the United States, on the other hand, the doctrine of no prior restraint has generally protected freedom of the press (see *Near v. Minnesota*). Despite the presumption against the validity of prior restraint, gag orders have recently been issued preventing those participating in a case—lawyers, witnesses, jurors, bailiffs, marshals, clerks, police, court employees—from leaking information to the press. In isolated instances judges have gone so far as to hear a secret witness, seal off an entire criminal trial, and even forbid the disclosure that a gag order has been issued (Landau, 1976, p. 56). The press has almost uniformly considered these gag orders to be a serious abridgement of its First Amendment rights.

In two recent cases the Supreme Court has addressed the issue of trial secrecy. In *Nebraska Press Association v. Stuart* the Supreme Court addressed the constitutionality of a gag order forbidding reporters to mention a confession for eleven weeks. While accepting the principle of prior restraint by judges under extreme circumstances, the Court said there was a strong presumption against its use. The Court suggested that pretrial publicity may indeed have an adverse impact on the views of potential jurors. Yet, the Court noted that all that is needed for a jury trial is to find twelve jurors "who would, under proper instructions, fulfill their sworn duty to render a just verdict exclusively on the evidence presented in open court (at 569). In the case at hand the Court ruled in favor of press rights, arguing: "We cannot say on this record that alternatives to a prior restraint on petitioners would not have sufficiently mitigated the adverse effects of pretrial publicity so as to make prior restraint unnecessary." (at 569)

More recently, in *Richmond Newspapers v. Virginia* the Supreme Court focused on the right of the public and the press to attend criminal trials. The Court ruled that the First Amendment guarantees the public and the press this right. As Chief Justice Burger wrote: "We hold that the right to attend criminal trials is implicit in the guarantees of the First Amendment; without the freedom to attend such trials, which people have exercised for centuries, important aspects of freedom of speech and of the press could be eviscerated'" (at 580).[8]

Clearly, the traditional methods of ensuring an impartial trial are not infallible. Special problems are posed in those select cases that receive sensational press coverage. Surely, however, there could be an increased reliance on some of the traditional techniques, such as change of venue. Moreover, when defendants feel they have been denied procedural justice, they may seek habeas corpus relief or request that a mistrial be declared. In contrast to the use of gag orders, these alternative methods do, at least, show a healthy regard for the right of the press to report about a crime and the right of the public to know about the operations of government. As a task force for the Twentieth Century Fund observed: "It is not enough that trials be fair; they must be known to be fair. Except in the most compelling circumstances, judges must not interfere with journalists in reporting on the process of justice." (1976, p. 7)

Another media-trial court concern is whether the electronic media ought to be permitted to telecast trials (Graham, 1978; Whisenand, 1978; Jacob, 1978, pp. 143–144). The issues involved are somewhat different than pretrial publicity, since here jurors would already have been selected. Yet, the subject of cameras in the courtroom does raise concerns as to procedural justice. It is feared "that the presence of the electronic paraphernalia in the courtroom, plus the possible psychological effects on the trial's participants of being on the air, could deny the defendant his constitutional right to a fair trial." (Graham, 1978, p. 546) Of relevance here is Canon 35, adopted in 1937 by the American Bar Association as part of its Canons of Judicial Ethics. The canon banned the use of still photography and radio from the courtroom. In 1952 television was added to this ban. However, a few states—including Texas, Oklahoma, and Colorado—did permit television coverage to continue. While this generally created few problems, it did lead the Supreme Court to overturn the conviction of Billie Sol Estes in 1964 (*Estes v. Texas*). The Court ruled in this case that Estes had been denied a fair trial because of the presence of television cameras over his objection. However, the Court's opinion conceded that changes in technology and in people's attitudes toward being televised might one day minimize this problem.

In July 1977, prompted by a petition from the Post-Newsweek Stations of Florida, the Florida Supreme Court began a one-year pilot study of cameras in the courtroom. The experiment permitted entry of the electronic media and

---

[8]Inner cite is from *Branzburg v. Hayes,* 408 U.S. 665 at 681.

still photographers without first obtaining the consent of the participants or the presiding judge. Strict standards were adopted governing the equipment which could be used, their location and movement, and the personnel that would be permitted at the trial. For the most part the cameras were employed for purposes of spot coverage of trials on the evening news. However, two murder cases did receive extensive coverage. When the pilot program ended, the Florida Supreme Court reviewed evidence of its effectiveness. It concluded that with some revisions in the guidelines, cameras would continue to be permitted to cover ongoing trials. The new guidelines gave the judge in each case the discretionary power to forbid coverage whenever the judge was satisfied that it would be detrimental to the defendant's right to a fair trial.

Shortly thereafter the constitutionality of cameras in the courtroom was challenged in *Chandler v. Florida*. The defendant had been convicted on various counts of burglary. During the trial a television camera had been present and had provided some coverage. Here the defendant charged that he had been denied a fair trial because of the electronic coverage of his case. Chandler had made several unsuccessful efforts to prevent his trial from being televised or broadcast. Because of the television coverage, defense also made a motion to sequester the jury. This motion was denied, but the judge did instruct the jury to avoid contact with any reporting of the case from print or electronic sources. In *Chandler v. Florida* the Supreme Court upheld the right of Florida's Supreme Court to permit electronic coverage of trials, notwithstanding defense objections. The decision does not mean that the media are considered to have a constitutional right to have testimony recorded and broadcast (see *Nixon v. Warner Communications, Inc.*). The effect of *Chandler* is simply to permit a state supreme court to allow cameras in the courtroom if it so desires. Of course, it is possible for televised trial proceedings to create an unfair trial. Yet, on this the Court argued in *Chandler*: "The risk of juror prejudice in some cases does not justify an absolute ban. . . ." (at 575) Rather, in such cases the remedy is the right to appeal and to demonstrate that in this particular case media coverage had an adverse impact sufficient to constitute a denial of due process.

SCIENTISTS

The reach of science is becoming all-encompassing, even embracing public policy (Finsterbusch and Motz, 1980; Lindblom and Cohen, 1979). The scientist tries to tell us the decisions we should make for ourselves and our society—from how to raise our children to how to redesign our political institutions. According to science, there is a technical solution to most empirical questions which can be discovered through the scientific method. What is involved here is the development of hypotheses about a problem and the rigorous testing of these hypotheses through experiments, surveys, and other techniques. Many scientists promise us that if we will only follow their advice, the result will be a more effective society in which to live.

Critics of science, on the other hand, have voiced a number of concerns. For example, some believe that science has not adequately developed to the point of providing valid, reliable information. If scientific knowledge cannot be counted on as accurate, the courts would be remiss in relying upon such knowledge. Paradoxically, other observers fear that scientific knowledge may be too accurate, leading ultimately to the sacrifice of other important values. Along these lines, it is feared that a police state might one day emerge which relies on hypnosis, polygraphs, and other devices to detect criminal wrongdoing. Such a society would sacrifice liberty and procedural justice in the name of social order through scientific effectiveness.

For the judiciary, the range of questions relevant to social science is truly enormous. Just to skim the surface, the social scientist may be able to tell us how the police should go about fighting crime (Kelling et al., 1974; David and Knowles, 1975; Larson, 1975), why some lawyers are more effective than others (Rosenthal, 1974), which factors should be considered when selecting judges (Murphy, 1964), the effect of jury size on case outcomes (Roper, 1979; Vollrath and Davis, 1980), and whether school busing is really beneficial to the disadvantaged (Armor, 1972; Pettigrew et al., 1973; St. John, 1975). The scientist is unable to tell us in what values we ought to believe. However, scientific research can inform us as to whether a given policy really impinges upon a value that is important to us. For example, easy access to bail seems to embody a value conflict between personal liberty and social order. On the one hand, a concern for liberty suggests that defendants should not be jailed for crimes they have not been found guilty of committing. On the other hand, a concern for social order suggests that we should have some assurance that if set free, the defendant will actually appear at subsequent criminal proceedings. Scientific research can inform us as to whether freed defendants normally do return for trial (Ares, Rankin, and Sturz; 1963). Scientists and their supporters suggest that systematic research can make possible more intelligent policy choices. In the following discussion we focus on the role of science in two areas of the judiciary—as a source of evidence and in the selection of jurors.

Evidence

Within the courtroom surely the most important use of social science is as a source of evidence. For example, criminal courts make use of a wide range of scientific devices. These include fingerprints; blood and hair identification; ballistics; microscopic and chemical analysis; radar; techniques which test blood, breath, and urine alcohol; and psychiatric testimony as to responsibility (Loevinger, 1974, p. 14). When statutory or judicial standards call for empirical verification, attorneys make regular use of social science evidence

(Lochner, 1973, pp. 823–824). This is true, for example, in the area of antitrust litigation. Section 7 of the Clayton Act states that economic analysis is proper for determining the effects on competition of a proposed merger. Beyond that, in complex cases such as those involving medical malpractice, the contest may essentially be reduced to a battle over expert testimony (Bonsignore et al., 1979b). In short, expert testimony is already highly valued in many kinds of courtroom situations. Indeed, some expert witnesses receive $250 to $1,000 per day for their testimony.

It is possible that one day new scientific techniques will be introduced, transforming the very nature of presenting evidence (Botein and Gordon, 1963). We are speaking here of methods of getting at the truth such as hypnosis, the polygraph, and drugs such as sodium pentothal and sodium anytal. Currently the judiciary is skeptical of such evidence. It should be noted, however, that the judiciary was also reluctant in the past to permit the use of fingerprints and other forms of scientifically obtained evidence. Further, science has greatly deflated our notions about the infallibility of eyewitness testimony. We have learned that there are limits to the capacity of conscious memory. Moreover, some witnesses have self-interested motivations that distort their testimony. By now our reliance on cross-examination to overcome these inevitable problems seems rather naive. Historically, we have lacked a more suitable alternative to cross-examination for obtaining the truth. Yet, science may one day be in a position to offer agreed-upon methods for reliably reproducing the truth. Some would say that this day has already arrived.

However, there are some genuine problems in using the new methods available from science (Botein and Gordon, 1963). To begin with, these methods are not entirely reliable. Drug treatments may induce confessions from neurotic people for crimes they never committed. Meanwhile, others may be able to withhold information or lie while under the influence of the drugs. Hypnosis and the polygraph may also produce inconclusive results. Given the stakes that are involved, it is not clear that the well-being of an individual should be entrusted to such imperfect devices.

Moreover, the use of these methods raises serious questions of due process. In particular, the new methods may collide with the right of the individual to avoid self-incrimination as well as the presumption of the individual's innocence. There may come a day when we will presume defendants to be guilty if they refuse to undergo the indignity of a polygraph test or sodium pentothal interrogation. If such methods gain scientific acceptance, we may well become highly skeptical of existing methods of presenting evidence in the courtroom. It is even possible to envision a day when crime is prevented by forcing all Americans to undergo an annual polygraph examination to uncover any criminal acts that were committed during the previous year. Clearly, this application of science to criminal justice would be greatly at odds with our notions of personal liberty.

Also of some interest is the increasing use of research studies by the

Supreme Court as evidence to guide its opinions (Rosen, 1972). Traditionally, the Supreme Court has made use of common sense in place of scientific study. It could hardly be otherwise, since the social sciences have matured only recently into a body of systematic knowledge. In *Gibbons v. Ogden* in 1824 the Court was called upon to determine whether navigation was included within the meaning of the commerce clause. In his decision Chief Justice Marshall asserted: "All America understands, and has uniformly understood, the word 'commerce' to comprehend navigation." (at 190) Clearly, Marshall was simply asserting a fact; he did not have a public opinion poll at hand to support his contention. As the social sciences developed, the knowledge they produced came into increasing use in American society. For the Supreme Court a leading advocate of "sociological jurisprudence" was Benjamin Cardozo. According to Cardozo, statutes should not be viewed "in isolation or *in vacuo,* as pronouncements of abstract principles for the guidance of an ideal community, but in the setting and the framework of present-day conditions, as revealed by the labors of economists and students of the social sciences in our country and abroad." (1921, p. 81)

There has been some resistance to the use of social science data in Supreme Court decisions. The introduction of such data in *Brown v. Board of Education* became the focal point of controversy in the *Congressional Record,* scholarly journals, law books, classrooms, and at public lectures (Rosen, 1972; Davis, 1973). The object of this controversy was footnote eleven in the Court's decision. The Court had made a finding of fact that segregation induces a feeling of inferiority in children from the disadvantaged group. In support of this factual claim the Court made reference to seven social science studies. Opponents of the Court's decision argued that the decision was grounded only on social science data and lacked any legal basis whatsoever. For example, Senator James Eastland of Mississippi argued: "I think it was an incredible thing that the Court in rendering its school-segregation decision, should cite as authorities books on psychology and sociology written by certain persons in this country. Of course, these persons are not legal authorities. They have nothing to do with the law." (Davis, 1973, pp. 9–10) To be sure, much of the dissatisfaction that was expressed after *Brown* simply reflected a distaste for court-ordered desegregation. Yet, there was also a feeling that constitutionalism had given way to science. With the Court ordering busing because of social science data, it was feared that social scientists would now be in a position to dictate court policy.

Yet, this concern was based on a misunderstanding of how social science data were being used by the Supreme Court (Rosen, 1972). The role of social science in *Brown* was not to supply a constitutional principle, but to provide empirical evidence on the nature of social behavior. The *Brown* decision was based on the equal protection clause of the Fourteenth Amendment. The Court argued that segregated school facilities are inherently unequal, in violation of the Fourteenth Amendment. Supporters of that decision noted that in order for the Fourteenth Amendment to be applied to school desegregation, factual evidence on the effects of segregation had to be considered. Social science may be used to resolve differences over fact, such as the impact of school segregation on disadvantaged children. Social science cannot, however, be used to authoritatively determine which social values ought to be pursued. This is a question that courts, and other institutions of government, must resolve.

Even today the Supreme Court continues to show some reluctance to make use of social science as a supplier of facts. In part this reflects a lack of confidence in the validity of social science data. The fear here is that the methods of social science are so imperfect that the use of social science data may lead to ineffective or counterproductive policies. Yet, if the facts used in Court decisions do not come from social science, the sources used are likely to be far less reliable (Rosen, 1972, p. 201). There is a large and growing body of scientific knowledge about the attitudes and behavior of people. Some of this knowledge is relevant to the factual questions in various Supreme Court cases. Given this, we should rightly expect judges to avoid making empirical assertions without citing appropriate research. As Victor Rosenblum observes: "It is not for judges to posit subjective or naive armchair notions of social science in the course of decisions conditioned on attitudes or behavior of people." (1971, p. 479) Unfortunately, judges rarely seek out social science data that litigants have failed to supply in their briefs.[9] To some extent this is due to the lack of training among judges in the social sciences. One suggestion is that a public agency be created to act as a depository for social and technological data (Rosenberg, 1976). The agency would receive and catalog social impact studies whose design and methods meet accepted scientific standards. Relevant studies would be made available by the agency to members of the Court on a case-by-case basis.

Juror Selection

Another application of science to the judiciary is in the selection of jurors (Etzioni, 1974). In recent years defense lawyers have made increasing use of scientists to assist them in voir dire. For example, in the Angela Davis, Harrisburg Seven, and Mitchell-Stans cases, psychologists played an important role in juror selection. In each case defense attorneys hired psychologists to help select jurors who would be likely to acquit their clients. There is some question as to the appropriateness of this use of the scientific method. The danger here is that science might be too effective, leading to the acquittal of people who would have been found guilty by a more representative jury. Indeed, the motivation of defense lawyers in using science in juror selection is to gain an advantage over the prosecution. This is a questionable practice, all the more so since affluent clients are better able than others to afford an expert

---

[9]However, on information flow, see Charles M. Lamb, "Judicial Policy-Making and Information Flow to the Supreme Court," *Vanderbilt Law Review,* 1976, *29,* 45–124.

on jury selection demographics. Another danger is that prosecutors may begin making use of such experts if they lose large numbers of cases, seemingly as a result of jury selection. Ultimately, the entire system of peremptory challenges for defense and prosecution may come under attack. If there is a science to jury selection, in the future only judges might be permitted to question and remove prospective jurors. Interestingly, there is some evidence that the background characteristics of jurors do not really play a substantial role in jury decision making (Simon, 1980, pp. 29–47). If this evidence is correct, then science may not, after all, have an important role to play in the selection of jurors.

AN ASSESSMENT

By now it should be apparent that public involvement within the judiciary is often of considerable significance. Certainly, it is the legal profession that holds top billing in the courtroom. Nevertheless, members of the public also play some very important roles. Public participation in the judiciary is evident from the activities of litigants, witnesses, jurors, interest groups, the news media, and scientists. In one respect or another, some of these roles may even be seen as indispensable.

A useful way of evaluating public involvement in the judiciary is in terms of its effectiveness. Among litigants, effectiveness is variable. We have seen, for example, that "repeat players" (usually the haves rather than the have-nots) are more successful in the courtroom than "one-shotters." This may, in some areas of the law, raise questions about equal justice under the law. As to witnesses, grave doubts have been voiced about their effectiveness in providing reliable testimony. There is convincing evidence indicating that witnesses are far from infallible. At stake here is nothing less than justice, for incorrect testimony may well lead to incorrect verdicts. Unfortunately, we lack adequate remedies for dealing with the problem of fallible witnesses. The evidence is more favorable regarding the effectiveness of juries. While the jury trial is an imperfect system, we surely have come a long way from trial by ordeal. One major study indicates that jury verdicts are typically not at odds with those privately favored by judges. Also significant is the fact that judges, who are the closest observers of juries, give the jury system some very high marks.

Public involvement in the judiciary also extends to the activities of interest groups. Such activity is aimed at influencing the policy choices of judges. Interest groups are somewhat successful in these efforts, particularly when serving as litigants. The news media also play an important role in the judiciary. Through the media the general public learns about court cases at the trial and appellate levels. Our discussion has been critical of the news media for their preoccupation with a few sensational crimes and inadequate coverage of Supreme Court decisions. However, even if these criticisms are valid, the problems they pose are not insurmountable. With some institutional reforms and a redirection of media personnel, a noticeable improvement in news media coverage would be observed. Finally, scientists also serve some important functions in the judiciary. Most notable is the role of science in producing evidence. As the body of scientific knowledge grows in scope and accuracy, we can expect its impact to become ever deeper.

QUESTIONS FOR DISCUSSION

1. What kinds of experiences have you had in the courtroom as a member of each of the following groups? As litigants? Witnesses? Juries? Interest groups? News media? Scientists? How effective are each of these courtroom participants in their activities?

2. How influential are interest groups in their courtroom activity? Why do some interest groups—particularly racial, environmental, and consumer groups—take to the courts more often than other kinds of interest groups?

3. Do you find yourself paying a great deal of attention to the way in which sensational trials unfold? Does the news media provide too much coverage of criminal trials? What limits have been imposed by the courts on news media coverage of criminal trials? Given the constitutional provision regarding freedom of the press, should there be any restrictions placed on trial court coverage by the news media?

4. Would trial by polygraph examination produce more valid verdicts than trial by judge or jury? Will we ever have trial by polygraph in this country? What is the proper place of science in the courtroom?

FOR FURTHER READING

KALVEN, HARRY, JR., and ZEISEL, HANS. *The American Jury*. Boston: Little, Brown, 1966. The efficacy of juries is systematically studied.

LIEBERMAN, JETHRO K. *The Litigious Society*. New York: Basic Books, 1981. According to this book, disputants are increasingly fighting it out in court.

ROSEN, PAUL L. *The Supreme Court and Social Science*. Urbana, Ill.: University of Illinois Press, 1972. Describes how the Supreme Court is and ought to be using social science data.

The Twentieth Century Fund Task Force on Justice, Publicity, and the First Amendment. *Rights in Conflict*. New York: McGraw-Hill, 1976. The free press versus fair trial controversy is analyzed here.

WOOCHER, FREDRIC D. "Did Your Eyes Deceive You?: Expert Psychological Testimony on the Unreliability of Eyewitness Identification." *Stanford Law Review*, 1977, *29,* 969–1030. An excellent analysis of the inadequacies of eyewitness identification.

SUPREME COURT RULINGS

Ballard v. United States, 329 U.S. 187 (1946)
Brown v. Board of Education, 347 U.S. 483 (1954)
Chandler v. Florida, 449 U.S. 560 (1981)
Duncan v. Louisiana, 391 U.S. 145 (1968)
Engel v. Vitale, 370 U.S. 421 (1962)
Estes v. Texas, 381 U.S. 532 (1964)
Gibbons v. Ogden, 22 U.S. 1 (1824)
Gilbert v. California, 388 U.S. 263 (1967)
Glasser v. United States, 315 U.S. 60 (1942)
Johnson v. Louisiana, 406 U.S. 356 (1972)
NAACP v. Button, 371 U.S. 415 (1963)
Near v. Minnesota, 283 U.S. 697 (1931)
Nebraska Press Association v. Stuart, 427 U.S. 539 (1976)
Nixon v. Warner Communications, Inc., 435 U.S. 589 (1978)
Richmond Newspapers v. Virgina, 448 U.S. 555 (1980)
Shelley v. Kraemer, 334 U.S. 1 (1948)
Sheppard v. Maxwell, 384 U.S. 333 (1966)
Smith v. Texas, 311 U.S. 128 (1940)
Sparf and Hansen v. United States, 156 U.S. 51 (1895)
Stovall v. Denno, 388 U.S. 293 (1967)
Strauder v. West Virginia, 100 U.S. 303 (1880)
Thiel v. Southern Pacific Co., 328 U.S. 217 (1946)
United States v. Wade, 388 U.S. 218 (1967)
Williams v. Florida, 399 U.S. 78 (1970)

6
CIVIL LAW

PREVIEW

Chapter Six explores civil law in the United States. The chapter focuses on both the civil court process and the substance of civil law and includes the following six sections:

Caseload
Process
Property
Contracts
Torts
Domestic relations

We look first at the caseload of civil courts. Although many types of civil cases are litigated, only a few are dealt with frequently. The most commonly raised cases are debt actions. The process used is complex, involving choices of forum, preliminary motions, extrajudicial negotiations, pretrial conferences, and—occasionally—a trial. We turn next to a discussion of four basic types of civil law. Property law focuses on the relationships between people about things. The section includes a discussion of economic due process and zoning restrictions. Contracts involve agreements between two or more parties. When a contract is broken, the victim may seek legal redress in the courts. This unit contains an analysis of debtor default, including judgments, garnishment, and bankruptcy. Torts are civil wrongs other than breach of contract. Tort law is designed to protect individuals from wrongdoing by others. The torts section includes consideration of automobile accidents and medical malpractice. Finally, various domestic relations are dealt with by civil courts. Our section on domestic relations treats divorce cases and civil commitment.

CASELOAD

The civil courts have an enormous impact on American society—an impact whose magnitude we often fail to appreciate. The stakes are enormous, covering the full range of our social values. The jurisdiction of civil courts is quite broad. As Herbert Jacob observes: "Every broken agreement, every sale that leaves a dissatisfied customer, every debt that is uncollected, every dispute with a government agency, every libel and slander, every accidental injury, every marital breakup, and every death may give rise to a civil proceeding." (Jacob, 1978, p. 194) In the state courts well over four million civil cases are disposed of annually (National Center for State Courts, 1979, Table 17). In the federal district courts nearly 92,000 private civil cases and 47,000 civil cases involving the federal government are also filed annually (Administrative Office of the United States Courts, 1978, p. 77). From the litigant's perspective civil courts provide three basic services (Jacob, 1969, pp. 16–17). First, the civil courts provide a forum for negotiating settlements of private disputes. Generally, the mere threat of taking a dispute to court will promote private negotiations and settlement. Second, the civil courts act to legitimize private settlements. Civil courts are invoked not only to deal with ongoing disputes but also to formally process disputes that have been privately settled. This often occurs in cases involving family members—divorces, wills, and adoptions. Finally, the courts also authorize parties to borrow the power of government for their private purposes. This power is wielded for many purposes, including debt collection, ousting tenants, and prohibiting some harmful activity.

Some kinds of cases occur more frequently than others. Examining the civil court caseload of Baltimore, Cleveland, and Milwaukee, Craig Wanner identified a total of thirty-one different subject areas which were treated in urban trial courts (1974).[1] Yet, Wanner also found that some types of cases

[1]Note that the caseload of civil courts differs from place to place and varies over time. For two longitudinal studies of civil caseload see Richard Lempert, "More Tales of Two Courts: Exploring Changes in the 'Dispute Settlement Function' of Trial Courts," *Law and Society Review,* 1978, *13,* 91–138 and Lawrence M. Friedman and Robert V. Percival, "A Tale of Two Courts: Litigation in Alameda and San Benito Counties," *Law and Society Review,* 1976, *10,* 267–301.

were litigated far more frequently than others. Indeed, the five most common types of cases accounted for over 81 percent of the civil court docket. As noted in Table 6–1, such cases include debt actions, money damage contracts, liens, divorce-related actions, and torts for personal injuries and property damage. Ranking sixth through tenth, with less than 5 percent of all cases, are foreclosures, evictions, administrative agency appeals, habeas corpus petitions, and injunctions. Wanner found that many kinds of cases are litigated rarely or not at all. Accounting for less than 1 percent of the cases in the sample are those involving inflicting emotional distress, inadequate drug warnings, fraud, libel,

TABLE 6–1   A Frequency Distribution of the Ten Most Common Types of Civil Cases

TYPE OF CASE	FREQUENCY RANKING	NUMBER OF CASES	PERCENTAGE OF ALL CASES
Debt Actions[a]	1	1935	25.03
Money Damage Contracts[b]	2	1503	19.44
Liens[c]	3	1202	15.55
Divorce-Related Actions[d]	4	869	11.24
Personal Injury and Property Damage Torts[e]	5	762	9.86
Foreclosures[f]	6	319	4.12
Evictions[g]	7	210	2.71
Administrative Agency Appeals[h]	8	194	2.51
Habeas Corpus Petitions[i]	9	139	1.79
Injunctions[j]	10	121	1.56
N		7254	93.81*

[a] Debt Actions include all cognovit notes, consent judgments, *scirie facias,* replevin, garnishment and *fi-fa* (aids to execution).

[b] Money Damage Contracts include all suits to collect money damages for breach of an agreement.

[c] Liens include all hospital, tax, and mechanic's liens.

[d] Divorce-Related Actions include all annulments, divorce *a mensa et thoro* (separation), divorce *a vinculo,* alimony, visitation privileges, custody *capias* to compel support, reciprocal support proceedings and petitions for permission to remarry.

[e] Personal Injury and Property Damage Torts exclude all other torts.

[f] Foreclosures include all tax, mortgage, land contract and chattels foreclosures.

[g] Evictions include all evictions, ejectments, actions for unlawful detainer and for tenant holding over.

[h] Administrative Agency Appeals include all appeals from local workmen's compensation commissions, from zoning boards, from condemnation boards, from tax court and from liquor license boards.

[i] Habeas Corpus Petitions include all petitions for bail, post-conviction review, for sanity hearing and child custody.

[j] Injunctions include all injunctions and writs of mandamus.

* N for all cases is 7732.

Adapted from Craig Wanner, "The Public Ordering of Private Relations; Part One: Initiating Civil Cases in Urban Trial Courts," *Law and Society Review* (Spring 1974), p. 422.

false imprisonment, malicious prosecution, civil rights claims, product liability, and medical malpractice.

Much of the civil court caseload falls into five broad categories of cases. These include property law, contracts, torts, human relationships, and various constitutional law cases (discussed in Chapter Eight). Property law is often associated with issues such as economic regulations, zoning, foreclosures, wills, estates, easements, adverse possession, bailment, and conveyances of land. Contract law may include cases such as wage garnishment, liens, bankruptcy, and breach of contract. Tort litigation includes automobile accidents, medical malpractice, slander, libel, battery, assault, and false imprisonment. Cases involving domestic relations include divorce, separation, annulment, custody, alimony, illegitimate children, and civil commitment. Finally, constitutional law focuses on questions such as separation of powers, freedom of expression, due process of law, and equal protection.

PROCESS

Civil court proceedings are quite complex, involving a number of different steps (Cound, Friedenthal, Miller, 1980; Louisell and Hazard, 1979; McCoid, 1974; Jacob, 1978, pp. 197–202). The origins of civil court cases are found in the conflicts between people. Cases in the civil courts are disputes. As we have seen, a broad range of disputes may be taken to the civil courts. Normally, a victim in a dispute will not initially turn to the courts. A variety of alternatives may be pursued, such as negotiation, persuasion, and coercion. If these efforts fail, the victim may turn to the courts for justice. In part, justice means the close adherence to procedural rules that are regarded as just. The federal courts are governed by the Federal Rules of Civil Procedure (FRCP), as set forth by the Supreme Court in 1938 (Holland, 1981). These rules have also been adopted or emulated by nearly all the states. The objectives of the rules are "to secure the just, speedy, and inexpensive determination of every action." The major effects of the FRCP were to simplify procedures and make it easier to learn the opposing party's case prior to trial.

A party who wishes to sue someone else will seek out the assistance of an attorney. The lawyer will begin by determining the facts of the dispute. A thorough investigation will allow the attorney to determine if a law has been violated. Litigation is an inappropriate response if the courts do not offer relief for the kind of dispute involved; if the evidence needed to win the lawsuit cannot be gathered; and if litigation is impractical given considerations of time, effort, expense, and anguish. A major consideration of the attorney in deciding whether to accept a case is prospects for obtaining an adequate fee.

A plaintiff who wishes to litigate may have a choice as to the court in which the case may be brought. The court must have jurisdiction over both the subject matter and the person being sued. Also, venue requirements must be met. Various state and federal tribunals are available to plaintiffs. However, only in some kinds of cases will there be a real choice as to where the suit may be filed. Most notably, the jurisdiction of the federal courts is sharply limited by Article III of the Constitution. As a result, the federal courts are not open to a large number of court cases (Summers, 1962). In most state court systems two sets of trial courts may be found. One type—courts of limited jurisdiction—handle only cases involving lesser claims. Other state courts are courts of general jurisdiction, which hear cases involving more substantial stakes. State courts have jurisdiction over any person presently living in the state. Depending on state law, the state courts may also have jurisdiction over out-of-state residents in certain kinds of cases. In selecting a court, venue requirements must also be met. (Venue refers to the location at which the trial will be held.) Typically, this means bringing the case to a court whose district includes the county where either the plaintiff or defendant resides. A defendant who so desires may waive the rules of jurisdiction over person and venue. However, the rules of jurisdiction over subject matter are zealously guarded and may not be waived.

After selecting the court, the plaintiff must draw up a complaint and serve notice on the defendant. The complaint is a written statement containing the plaintiff's claim against the defendant. It contains a series of allegations which specify why the plaintiff feels entitled to recover a judgment. The plaintiff takes the complaint to the courthouse and files it with the court clerk. Through this filing the suit is generally considered to have officially commenced. The plaintiff must also serve notice on the defendent that a suit has been filed.[2] When filing a complaint, the plaintiff hands the clerk a summons. The clerk places the court's seal upon it, thus making it an official notice. The plaintiff then hires a process-server, who normally must physically deliver the summons to the defendant. A defendant is thus put on notice that failure to appear in court in one's own defense means losing the case by default.

The complaint is only the first of several pleadings that may take place. A pleading is a formal, written statement of a party informing an opponent and the court of the pleader's position on the case. The complaint is a statement of the claim the plaintiff wishes to make. The defendant may respond to this claim with some preliminary objections to the suit. For example, the defendant may argue that the complaint was incomplete in some way, that the complaint is too general or confused, or that the court lacks jurisdiction over the defendant. If the preliminary motion to dismiss is denied, or no such motion is made, the defendant must file an answer. Here the defendant must admit or deny the allegations made by the plaintiff in the complaint. The answer must also contain any affirmative defenses that the defendant wishes to

---

[2] But see David Caplovitz, *Consumers in Trouble* (New York: Free Press, 1974).

use to contest the litigation. There may also be further pleadings, such as a reply by the plaintiff. Moreover, the defendant may wish to file some counterclaim as part of the answer. If so, the plaintiff must respond to it.

Following the completion of pleadings, the litigants may also be involved in a process known as discovery. Here the two sides use various devices to probe the merits of each other's case. This is accomplished by bringing the facts of the case into the open. Through discovery each party may learn in detail what the litigation is all about. As a result of discovery, some issues that had been raised in the pleadings may no longer be contested. The strengths and weaknesses of both parties' case may be ascertained through discovery. The deposition is the most useful and most commonly used method of discovery. Here one party may require the other party (or the latter's witnesses) to appear before a court reporter and answer questions posed by the opposing attorney. Another important discovery technique is the use of written interrogatories. Generally, these can be addressed only to a party in the suit. Because they may be answered with the aid of an attorney, the answers will be less spontaneous than those in a deposition. However, they are also expected to be far more complete. Other discovery devices include orders for producing documents, a physical or mental examination, and requests for admissions to certain facts. As a result of discovery, surprise is no longer a major feature of civil cases and many cases are settled before a trial is conducted (Holland, 1981, p. 212). Sometimes a pretrial conference is also held. Here the issue at dispute may be clarified. In addition, the judge will determine whether any amendments to the pleadings are required. Often a judge may even suggest a particular settlement to the case. In the federal courts and in many states a summary judgment may be requested. If some fact crucial to the lawsuit can be established beyond real dispute, the judge may make a ruling without conducting a trial.

Actually, few cases go to trial. Pending trial, a case may remain dormant for several months or even years. By requesting a continuance, either party may delay the case if the attorney is busy or is not yet ready to proceed. Some have suggested that pretrial delays be reduced by having judges, rather than attorneys, control the progress of cases (Church et al., 1978). Negotiations generally occur during this delay before the start of the trial. Indeed, plaintiffs often file cases only to demonstrate their willingness to use the courts as a last resort. Generally, out-of-court settlements are preferred. More than three-quarters of civil cases do not get beyond the preliminary stages. Some kinds of cases are settled by well-established rules of thumb, which take into account the nature of the injustice and any extenuating circumstances. Only a small portion of cases go to trial, and only a minority of these make use of a jury.

If there is no settlement, the next stage is the trial. Typically, either party may request that the case be placed on the trial calendar. In most cases the parties have a right to a jury trial. If such a right exists, either party may assert it. If a jury has been demanded, the jurors must be selected. Potential jurors may be rejected by the plaintiff and defendant through peremptory challenges or challenges for cause. Once the jurors are impaneled, the lawyers for the plaintiff and defendant make opening statements. Following this, the plaintiff's witnesses are called upon to testify. Each witness offers testimony in response to questions from the lawyer who called that witness to the witness stand. Cross-examination by the opposing attorney follows. Re-direct and re-cross may also take place. It is the responsibility of each lawyer to introduce evidence and object to evidence that may be inadmissible under the rules of evidence. After all plaintiff's witnesses are called, the plaintiff rests.

When plaintiff rests, the defendant's lawyer may request a dismissal or a directed verdict for the defendant. Here the defense lawyer asserts that the plaintiff has not established an adequate case. If the judge denies the motion, defendants will generally present witnesses of their own. These witnesses are subjected to the same process of examination. When the defense has rested, the plaintiff may introduce additional evidence to meet any new matter raised by defense witnesses. The defense lawyer may counter with new evidence as well. This procedure continues until both parties rest.

When both have rested, either or both may make a motion for a directed verdict. Defendants may also move for dismissal. If these motions are denied, the case must be submitted to the jury. The plaintiff, and then defendant, give their closing argument, stressing the most favorable evidence. It is then the task of the judge to instruct the jury regarding the facts and issues, applicable substantive law, credibility of witnesses, and required burden of proof.[3] The jury deliberates in closed session. When it reaches a verdict, this verdict is accepted by the court and the jury is discharged. The clerk then enters the judgment—the formal order disposing of the case. The judgment may be in the form of an award of money, a declaration of rights, recovery of property, or an order requiring or prohibiting some future activity.

Following the trial a number of posttrial motions are possible. The purpose here is to question the legal sufficiency of the opposing party's claim. Either side may call for a judgment notwithstanding the verdict. Alternatively, a party may assert that errors occurred in the conduct of the trial itself and call for a new trial. After a final trial court judgment the losing party may appeal to an appellate court. Generally, any judgment may be appealed to at least one higher court. An appellate court is supposed to limit itself to correcting errors on questions of law. When all appeals and proceedings are concluded, the judgment is *res judicata*—a thing decided. This means that the legal case, and the legal issue underlying it, have been decided with finality through the civil court process.

It should be noted that some civil justice in the United States is carried

---

[3] In most civil cases the burden of proof required is "by a preponderance of the evidence." The precise meaning of this term is unsettled but clearly requires less proof than that required in criminal cases, where the government is obliged to prove the guilt of the defendant "beyond a reasonable doubt."

out by administrative agencies rather than by the courts (Lorch, 1980; Vago, 1981, pp. 94–105). An increasing variety of disputes are dealt with by agencies such as the Interstate Commerce Commission, Federal Trade Commission, and Federal Communications Commission. While these agencies carry out an "adjudication" of sorts, the process they employ does differ from that of courts. For example, courts are reactive, while agencies may seek out violations of the law to process. In a sense, an administrative agency is a union of police officer, prosecutor, legislator, and judge in a single body. Also, most administrative adjudication is less formal than that of courts. Many disputes are disposed of quickly and inexpensively at lower levels of an agency. Moreover, regulatory agencies specialize in a narrow subject area and are staffed by individuals who are experts in the field. Finally, administrative agencies are not theoretically bound to rule according to precedent. Sanctions of such agencies include cease-and-desist orders and civil fines. The rise of the regulatory agency has not been universally applauded. In particular, many are critical of the procedural shortcuts such agencies commonly employ when hearing disputes. However, the growth of administrative agencies has not meant the wholesale displacement of courts. In most instances, those adversely affected by administrative agencies may ultimately take the matter to the civil courts for further redress.

PROPERTY

Private Property

Property law concerns the relationships between people about things (Browder, Cunningham, and Julin, 1966, pp. 3–6). The "things" involved may be chattels (that is, movable physical objects), parcels of land, or intangible property (for example, shares of corporate stock, bonds, patents, copyrights). When we say that someone possesses property, we are suggesting that the person has an interest in something that is protected against invasion by others. In any society only certain things may be held as private property. However, the nature of these things varies considerably from place to place and over time. As R. H. Tawney notes: "In the past, human beings, roads, bridges and ferries, civil, judicial and clerical offices, and commissions in the army have all been private property." (1920, p. 73)

Property is an important value. Charles Beard suggests that the right to property was uppermost in the minds of the framers of the United States Constitution (1913). Also, Immanuel Kant began his discussion of law with an analysis and justification of the right to property (1965). In the Bible "Thou shalt not steal" appears as one of the ten commandments. While property has been attacked in some quarters (Proudhon, 1966), surely one does gain a sense of pride, self-esteem, and even self-identity through having property (Pennock, 1980, p. 178). How would Linus of the "Peanuts" comic strip feel without his prize possession, a security blanket? Although adults shed their childhood blanket in a very real sense they replace it with other "security blankets" such as autos, stereos, and jewelry. A fundamental feature of American property law is that it permits individuals to own interests in the means of production of society—this being the key distinction between capitalism and socialism (Bauman, 1976, esp. Ch. 4). Americans can possess not only pastry, soda pop, and pornography but also shares of stock in Pillsbury, Pepsi Cola, and Playboy.

While private property is taken for granted in our society, it has been the subject of some controversy. "Property is robbery," according to Pierre Joseph Proudhon (1966, p. 12). When one American holds property, the more than 200 million nonowners may be denied access to that asset (Okun, 1975). Moreover, we live in a society with a highly unequal distribution of economic resources. The wealthiest one-fifth of American households possesses over three-quarters of privately owned wealth (Greenberg, 1974, Ch. 4). Over 90 percent of all private wealth is owned by the wealthiest two-fifths of American households. The poorest 40 percent of the nation possesses only 2.3 percent of the nation's wealth. Property law in the United States serves to support this unequal distribution. It provides legal force to the claims of people to their property. Property law also permits wealthy individuals to transfer their property to whomever they choose.

People commonly assume that property involves ownership of a thing. However, the notion of property is actually far more complex. It consists of a bundle of rights, including the right to possess, to use, to manage, to derive economic benefits from, to consume or destroy, to modify, to transfer or bequeath to another, to have immunity from expropriation, and to have an indeterminate period of ownership (Becker, 1980; Honoré, 1961; Grey, 1980). Another common assumption, as implied above, is that property involves full dominion over a thing. However, it is important to realize that legal restrictions on property are widespread. Indeed, a complex web of legal guidelines both protects and restricts the use of property. For example, a will allows an individual to bequeath property to another. However, estate taxes place limits on an individual's ability to transfer property to another through a will.

For a long time in American history property owners had an enormous amount of autonomy as to how they used and disposed of their property (Schwartz, B., 1974, Ch. 9; Dietze, 1963). During the course of the twentieth century, however, the power of property rights diminished substantially. As Gottfried Dietze observes: "Not only was static property attacked, but also, the free use of property was restricted. To make things complete, even the freedom to acquire property was curtailed." (Dietze, 1963, p. 94) The legal system has placed a number of restrictions on private property. With regard to static property, zoning regulations increasingly limit the uses to which a parcel of land may be put. As a result of zoning laws, land owners may not be permitted to use their property as they wish. Similarly, a complex body of environmental regulations has been put into law. The result is that property owners—particularly in industry—are limited in their rights to emit pollution into the earth, air, or water. A web of governmental regulations also limits the freedom of property owners with regard to physical conditions at the work place and in the home.

While some believe that the existing distribution of wealth is unfair, a provocative defense of property rights has been made by Robert Nozick (1974).[4] Most theories of distributive justice suggest that economic resources ought to be redistributed according to some principle, such as merit, needs, or work effort (Nozick, 1974, p. 156). Yet, Nozick asserts that people are entitled to what they earn and that no government has the right to redistribute. As Nozick suggests: "There is no *central* distribution, no person or group entitled to control all the resources, jointly deciding how they are to be doled out." (1974, p. 149) Nozick makes an appeal for the "minimal state," in which the functions of government are narrowly limited to protection against force, theft, fraud, enforcement of contracts, and the like. To Nozick among the most important rights of people is the right to property. This suggests to him that government must not force people to help others (for example, redistribution). It also means that government ought not restrict the individual through economic regulations in the interests of public safety. From Nozick's standpoint people have a right to their property, to use as they see fit.

Economic Due Process

Historically, the right to private property has had a substantial basis in American constitutional law (Chase and Ducat, 1979; Abraham, 1980b; Mason and Beaney, 1972; Gunther, 1980; Funston, 1978). It might even be said that the Supreme Court was preoccupied with this issue for much of its history. As Henry Abraham notes: "Even a cursory glance at the Court's history proves that the economic-proprietarian sphere *was* very much the focus of the Court's work *prior* to the arrival of the New Deal. . . ." (1980b, p. 54) It was under Chief Justice Marshall's stewardship (1801–1835) that the Court's concern for property rights was set in motion. The object of the Marshall Court's attention was Article I, section 10, known as the contract clause. This clause of the Constitution reads: "No state shall . . . pass any . . . Law impairing the obligation of Contracts. . . ."

The Marshall Court made use of the contract clause in many of its property-oriented decisions. For example, in *Sturges v. Crowninshield* the Court invalidated the bankruptcy act that had recently been passed in New York. The law had made it easy for debtors to be relieved of their preexisting financial obligations. The Marshall Court also took a broad view of the mean-

---

[4]For a defense of equality see John Rawls, *A Theory of Justice* (Cambridge, Mass.: Belknap Press, 1971).

ing of the term "contract." It expanded this meaning beyond its application to individuals to cover arrangements made with government or with a corporation (*Fletcher v. Peck; Dartmouth College v. Woodward*). However, as the Marshall years faded into history, successive Courts gave less force to the contract clause (*Charles River Bridge Co. v. Warren Bridge Co.*). The contract clause was no longer a device for subordinating the interests of government to those of business.

With the decline of the contract clause those concerned with property rights looked to the Fourteenth Amendment for relief. The amendment commands that no state shall "deprive any person of life, liberty or property, without due process of law. . . ." During the tenure of Chief Justices Fuller, White, Taft, and Hughes, from 1888 to 1937, the Fourteenth Amendment was frequently used to strike down economic regulation of business. The due process clause was given substantive content, as liberty was associated with the "liberty to contract." As Chase and Ducat note: "Legislation which limited this absolute freedom was almost invariably adjudged a denial of due process and, hence, unconstitutional." (1979, p. 672) In addition, the Supreme Court applied the doctrine of dual federalism to invalidate regulatory legislation which was passed by Congress. In a classic example of "Catch-22"[5] the Supreme Court invalidated national economic regulation, holding that it infringed on states' rights, and then invalidated state economic regulation, holding that it violated the Fourteenth Amendment's due process clause. The upshot of these decisions was that relatively few restrictions were permitted on those with property.

Perhaps the prototypical case of the economic due process era was *Lochner v. New York*. Indeed, this period in the nation's history is often called "the Lochner Era." The case concerned a New York labor law which prohibited the employment of bakery workers for more than ten hours per day or sixty hours per week. The feeling of the New York legislature was that conditions in the baking industry demanded that the state make use of its "police powers" (that is, regulations) in behalf of workers. Lochner was convicted and fined under the labor law for permitting an employee to work more than sixty hours in one week. On appeal the Supreme Court ruled that the law had no direct, substantial relation to employee health and thus went beyond the regulatory powers of state govenments. The statute was invalidated as an unconstitutional interference with the right of an employer and employee to contract. By holding a restrictive interpretation of state regulatory powers, the Supreme Court during the Lochner Era prevented government from seriously interfering with property rights. Not until 1937, under threat from Franklin Roosevelt to "pack" the Court, did the Supreme Court finally retreat from this position. This occurred in *West Coast Hotel Co. v. Parrish,* where the

[5]As in, "There's always a catch"—see Joseph Heller, *Catch-22* (New York: Simon and Schuster, 1961).

Court upheld the constitutionality of a minimum wage law in the state of Washington. This decision, and those that followed, are widely seen as representing a triumph of New Deal liberalism over the principle of laissez faire. As the Supreme Court retreated from its posture as protector of property rights, it began to focus increasingly on the protection of civil liberties.[6]

Of late some have questioned the retreat of the Supreme Court in its defense of property rights (Funston, 1975; Reich, 1964). The dichotomy of personal rights and property rights has been criticized as a false double standard. Among those on the right of the political spectrum, there is a desire to again interpret the Constitution as imposing strict limitations on governmental regulatory powers (Dietze, 1963). Among those on the left, Charles Reich has called upon the Supreme Court to reaffirm the principle of economic due process and to then use the principle to grant substantial property rights to the disadvantaged, including guarantees of unemployment compensation, public assistance, and retirement insurance (1964, pp. 785–786). Advocates of property rights have long recognized the value of personal property to the well-being of the individual. Reich would couple this with a concern that broad numbers of people, including the disadvantaged, should be able to share in the pleasure of owning property. Essentially, Reich would place the welfare state on a solid constitutional footing.

Zoning

Zoning is the principal technique used by government to exercise control over private property (Browder et al., 1966).[7] Zoning authority is generally exercised by localities pursuant to an express delegation of the "police power" of states. Through zoning a municipality is divided into districts, with land use restrictions imposed within each of these districts. Zoning is one form of the police powers constitutionally reserved to the states. The extent to which zoning may be employed is limited by the Fifth and Fourteenth Amendments to the Constitution as well as by provisions in nearly all state constitutions.

The right to private property is constitutionally protected by the Fifth Amendment, which is made applicable to the states by the Fourteenth Amendment. The "takings" clause of the Fifth Amendment reads: "Nor shall private property be taken for public use without just compensation." Clearly, zoning does, in some sense, "take" from land owners the ability to use their property as they see fit. However, when adjudged to be constitutional, zoning laws are not regarded as a "taking" as such and require no compensation to land owners. Although not every zoning ordinance is declared constitutional in the

---

[6] See footnote four in *United States v. Carolene Products Co.,* 304 U. S. 144 (1938) at 152. Here Justice Harlan Fiske Stone postulated a dichotomy between "personal" rights and "property" rights, with only the former to receive strict judicial scrutiny.

[7] See also "Developments in the Law—Zoning," *Harvard Law Review,* 1978, *91*, 1427–1708.

courts, judges generally permit zoning in order to protect the public health, safety, or welfare.

Zoning spread rapidly in America early in the twentieth century. In 1915 only five cities had zoning laws; by 1925 nearly 500 had such ordinances. By 1926 all but five states had enacted enabling legislation which permitted local governments to adopt zoning laws. This was encouraged, in part, by the Standard State Zoning Enabling Act, promulgated by a national advisory committee. Even so, at this point judicial acceptance of zoning was not universal. While many state courts had adjudged zoning to be constitutional, adverse decisions had been made by the highest courts in Delaware, Georgia, Maryland, Missouri, and New Jersey.

In October 1926 the constitutionality of zoning reached the Supreme Court in the case of *Village of Euclid v. Ambler Realty Co.* Ambler Realty owned a tract of sixty-eight acres in Euclid, a municipality just outside of Cleveland. On November 13, 1922, the Village Council created a comprehensive zoning plan that regulated and restricted the location of types of uses, the lot area to be built upon, and the size and height of buildings. Ambler Realty argued that the ordinance was depriving it of liberty and property without due process, denying it equal protection, and was contrary to certain provisions of the Ohio constitution. Ambler Realty pointed to the serious financial losses it would suffer because industrial uses were prohibited by the zoning law. The company argued that by restricting and controlling the lawful uses of the land, the Village of Euclid was confiscating and destroying a great part of its value. However, the Supreme Court upheld the constitutionality of the zoning law in question. The Court ruled that zoning authorities do have the right to separate industrial from residential development, as the Village of Euclid had done.

The Supreme Court's decision in *Euclid* did not mean that zoning authorities have unlimited powers. The limits to zoning were suggested in *Euclid* and reaffirmed two years later by the Court's decision in *Nectow v. City of Cambridge.* In *Nectow* the Court ruled in support of the property rights of the land owner. The Court suggested that while the zoning power of government "is not unlimited," regulations may be imposed if they "bear a substantial relation to the public health, safety, morals, or general welfare." (at 188) The *Nectow* decision left intact the Cambridge zoning ordinance. However, the ruling prohibited the municipality from applying its otherwise constitutional zoning ordinance to a particular tract of land (that is, Nectow's). It was the finding of the Court that the health, safety, convenience, and welfare of Cambridge citizens would not be adversely affected by a ruling for Nectow. In general, however, the courts have ruled that zoning authorities do· have rather broad powers. The near universality of zoning in America today is indicated by the fact that among cities with a population of 250,000 or more, only Houston, Texas, has not enacted a zoning ordinance.

Perhaps the most controversial aspect of zoning is its use by affluent suburbs to exclude low-cost housing. By restricting low-cost housing, affluent suburbs are able to keep out low-income people and thereby create an atmosphere of concentrated affluence (Downs, 1973). At the same time, because poor people must live somewhere, slum conditions are created elsewhere in the metropolis. Poor people in poor places live in a deteriorating environment and are denied access to employment, decent housing, and adequate education. There are a number of methods of exclusionary zoning, such as minimum lot sizes, minimum floor space, restrictions on multiple-family dwellings, and strict building codes. Obviously, poor people cannot afford to live in a community which permits the construction of only large, single-family houses built on large lots. It has been suggested, therefore, that exclusionary zoning denies the disadvantaged equal protection of the law under the Fourteenth Amendment.[8] Even so, the Supreme Court has upheld the constitutionality of exclusionary zoning (*Village of Belle Terre v. Boraas; Arlington Heights v. Metropolitan Housing Corp.*).

CONTRACTS

Contracts and Markets

Contract law has been characterized as the legal reflection of the free market. A contract is defined as "an agreement between two or more parties, usually for the exchange of what the parties consider equivalents." (Friedman, 1965, p. 15) It is a promise between parties, including an offer and an acceptance, which creates a legal obligation (U.S. News and World Report, 1973, p. 61). Contracts may be written or oral; express (that is, clearly written) or implied; and valid, void, or voidable. In the contract the parties promise to do or not do a certain activity. After the contract is created, both parties are obliged to carry out what they have promised to do. If one of the parties fails to adhere to the contract, the other has a legal right to turn to the courts. In court the party can ask for monetary damages equivalent to the injury suffered. Alternatively, the party can ask the court for specific performance—a direct court order to the other party to carry out the promise. Parties to a contract may include any combination of individuals, private organizations (Macaulay, 1966), and government (McBride, Wachtel, and Touhey, 1976).

Entering into contracts is a fundamental part of daily life. Most contracts are very basic transactions which are soon forgotten (U.S. News and World Report, 1973, p. 61). When you order a newspaper, you are creating a contract. When you agree to purchase an automobile, you are bound to a contract with the purchaser. In credit accounts a basic premise is that a contract is in existence. Indeed, even when you use a telephone or turn on a radio,

---

[8] Note, "Exclusionary Zoning and Equal Protection," *Harvard Law Review,* 1971, *84,* pp. 1645–1646; pp. 1649–1650.

you are implicitly accepting a legal oblication to pay the telephone and electric utilities for the services provided. There are an enormous number of contracts in society, very few of which ever enter the courtroom. Lawrence Friedman tabulated the contract cases in Wisconsin courts over time (1965, Chaps. 1, 2). He found that the three major fact categories of contract cases were labor, land, and sales. Historically, the content and reach of contract law have been affected through various kinds of legislation. Relevant legislation has included antitrust law, labor law, insurance law, business regulation, public utility regulation, and social welfare legislation. For example, a contract between two competing industries to merge may violate the Sherman Antitrust Law or other such legislation. Thus, the merger may not be permitted even if it does not offend the law of contracts. The proposed merger must also meet the standards of the antitrust legislation.

Sellers have traditionally been in a favored position in contracts. Caveat emptor—"Let the buyer beware"—has been a fundamental maxim of consumer transactions. This remains true to a large extent even today. However, in recent years there has been some erosion of this principle (Robinson, 1978, p. 279). Many victories were won by the consumer movement in legislatures, courts, and administrative agencies. For example, nearly every state has consumer laws dealing with deceptive trade practices such as false and misleading advertising, not clearly expressing guarantee terms, steering customers from advertised specials, and falsely labeling goods. There has also been some change in laws regarding landlords and tenants (Robinson, 1978, p. 184). Traditionally, the law placed landlords in a favored position. Landlords had few obligations other than furnishing the dwelling place. In general, dissatisfied tenants had only one recourse: moving elsewhere. Recently, however, courts have held that landlords are obliged to make the premises habitable for their tenants. Under some circumstances tenants may even withhold their rent until the condition of the dwelling has been improved. Usually, this right is limited to situations where the tenant's health is adversely affected—insufficient heat or water, rat infestation, and improper garbage disposal. Some states have also required landlords to install proper locks on doors and repair broken windows in hallways.

Debtor Default

Debtor default is an ever-present phenomenon in our nation, largely because credit has become so widespread (Caplovitz, 1974; Jacob, 1978). To be sure, credit sales are normally paid for more-or-less expeditiously. Even when debtors are delinquent in their payments, creditors do not immediately resort to court action. Instead, they attempt to pressure debtors to resume payment. Collection techniques range from letters and phone calls to more questionable activities such as contacting friends, relatives, and employers. Some people are more likely to go into default than others. Ironically, the very poor rarely go bankrupt. This is mainly due to the enormous difficulties they experience in obtaining credit to begin with. A disproportionate number of those who default are blue-collar workers, generally in young families, and often from racial minorities. David Caplovitz interviewed debtors in an effort to learn why they defaulted (1974, Chaps. 4-9). In nearly four out of five cases the primary cause of default could be traced to the debtor. Prime factors were loss of income and overextended credit. Meanwhile, creditors were implicated in one-fifth of the interviews. Specifically, debtors cited creditor fraud or payment misunderstandings. Another study stresses the importance of involuntary incursion of a debt due to catastrophic events such as medical expenses, marital difficulties, or personal liability suits (Mathews, 1969).

When a debtor fails to adhere to a contract, the creditor may bring suit in civil court (Eisenstein, 1973, p. 259). The purpose of such a suit is to establish the legality of the debt. It is state law which determines the procedures used in obtaining judgments. Historically, there has been much violation of due process in this area. In many cases defendants failed to appear because they did not receive a summons informing them that they were being sued. The 1974 Caplovitz study showed that in New York City only 54 percent of debtors who were acted upon received notice (1974, pp. 192-195).[9] Failure to provide notice was less common—but still substantial—elsewhere. Evidently, the rules governing the issuance of summary judgments without notifying a defendant vary considerably from one state to another.

Having obtained a judgment, the creditor may make use of a variety of tools such as garnishment, liens, and forced sale of a debtor's property. The most important method is wage garnishment. In this procedure a court requires that an individual's wages be withheld by the employer and diverted for payment of a debt (Yearout, 1979, p. 1000). In 1969 the Supreme Court sought to protect the debtor's right to be notified with its decision in *Sniadach v. Family Finance Corporation*. This decision barred the deprivation of wages unless the debtor had an opportunity to be heard. Historically, broad responsibility for determining the scope of permissible wage garnishment has been held by state legislatures. States could choose a maximum level of garnishment or forbid it entirely

The contours of wage garnishment are now regulated nationally. This is as a result of the Consumer Credit Protection Act (PL 90-321), passed in 1968 (Yearout, 1979; Robinson, 1978). The act focuses on four primary concerns. First, it tried to bring about the orderly payment of consumer debts. To achieve this goal, the act sanctioned wage garnishment as a legitimate tool for debt collection. Second, the act sought to protect consumers from being driven into bankruptcy by excessive garnishment of wages. Toward this end the maximum

___

[9] But see also David Hittner, "Summary Judgments in Texas," *Texas Bar Journal*, 1980, *43*, 11-23.

amount of employee's wages subject to garnishment was limited to 25 percent of weekly disposable earnings. Clearly, this limitation makes garnishment less attractive to creditors as a means of collecting debts. Third, the act dealt with the tendency of some employers to discharge workers whose wages have been garnisheed. It expressly forbade discharging an employee for this reason, subject to a fine of $1,000 and/or a prison sentence of up to one year. Finally, the act attempted to give priority status to family support obligations. To achieve this goal, garnishment for child support and alimony was exempted from the 25 percent ceiling on garnishment levels. The act did not apply at the time to federal employees, who were totally exempt from wage garnishment. This exemption was lifted in 1974 with the passage of the Social Services Amendments. Additional amendments were passed by Congress in 1977.

Bankruptcy is another important legal remedy for dealing with indebtedness. At one time bankruptcies could be initiated only by creditors (Stanley and Girth, 1971). The purpose of bankruptcy was to force the liquidation of debtors' assets and apply the proceeds to pay the claims against the debtors. When debtors were unable to pay their debts, creditors' claims were ranked into classes to determine who would be repaid first. If proceeds from the sale of a debtor's property failed to meet creditors' claims, the bankrupt individual remained in debt for the unpaid balance. At the end of the nineteenth century the character of bankruptcy began to change. At this time bankruptcy took on the additional function of granting relief to honest but unfortunate debtors. Now debtors were permitted to file for bankruptcy, thus wiping out their debts. In fact, voluntary bankruptcies today outnumber involuntary ones by more than 100 to 1. Not surprisingly, most of those who have gone through bankruptcy feel that their financial position improved as a result.

There has been a substantial increase in the extent of bankruptcy during the past quarter century. David Stanley and Marjorie Girth note: "Each year nearly one American in a thousand files a petition in bankruptcy, and nearly $2 billion in debts are canceled in the bankruptcy courts." (1971, p. 1) Although business bankruptcies have also increased, they now represent fewer than one in twelve bankruptcies. American bankruptcy laws were revised by the Bankruptcy Reform Act of 1978 (PL 95–598), also known as the Edwards Act (Klee, 1978). This repealed the Bankruptcy Act of 1898 (PL 55–541). Depending on the needs of the individual debtor, the Edwards Act permits debtors to alter their obligations toward secured or unsecured creditors or stockholders. Involuntary bankruptcies may be initiated by creditors, who also have the right to file a plan of reorganization. Creditors are also permitted to ask the court to appoint an examiner or trustee if the management of the debtor is inadequate. The new Title 11 also contains a number of substantive provisions concerning the fresh start of debtors. Under the optional federal plan reaffirmation of a debt is prohibited unless the bankruptcy court approves the reaffirmation as in the best interests of the debtor. In addition, the debtor has the right to invalidate liens against exempt household goods and to redeem property from a lien.

Surprisingly, bankruptcy does not appear to seriously affect the bankrupt's ability to obtain credit in the future (Stanley and Girth, 1971, pp. 62–65). Evidently, creditors are willing to risk losses on bad debts in order to conduct business. At the same time, there does remain some social stigma attached to those who declare bankruptcy. Still, there are some who fear that the Edwards Act makes it too easy for debtors to enrich themselves by purchasing merchandise and then canceling their debts through bankruptcy.

TORTS

The purpose of the law of torts is to protect the individual from wrongdoing by others. Torts are based on the idea of individual responsibility—that is, individuals should be held liable if they injure other persons or the reputation or property of other persons. William Prosser defines tort as "a civil wrong, other than breach of contract, for which the court will provide a remedy in the form of an action for damages." (1964, p. 2) Most often, the redress provided is in the form of money. Torts are said to differ from crimes in two respects—the interest affected and the legal remedy provided (Prosser, 1964, pp. 7–14). As to the first, a crime is regarded as an offense against the public. Consequently, it is government that prosecutes the offender. Such proceedings are designed to punish the offender so as to protect and vindicate the interests of the public. On the other hand, a tort action is conducted by the injured parties themselves. Regarding legal remedy, the purpose of a tort action is to compensate the victim at the expense of the wrongdoer for the damages that have been incurred. Unlike a crime, there is no effort per se to punish the guilty party in tort actions. Many wrongful acts can be adjudicated both as a crime against the state and as a tort against an individual.

The fundamental issue addressed by the law of torts is: Under what circumstances should people be required to pay damages for injuries they cause to someone else? (Law and Polan, 1978, p. 1–8) One policy response would be to require all those who injure someone else to compensate the victim. However, such a policy might lead to excessive caution in the way that people deal with one another, such as a refusal to come to the aid of someone else. During the second half of the twentieth century the notion of fault became central to the law of torts. Under tort law there is a presumption that the victim alone will bear the costs of any injuries caused by someone else. In order to recover damages, the victim must be able to prove that the other party was at fault. Here the notion of fault means that the other party was unreasonably reckless or failed to pay proper attention to a situation to which a reasonable person would be attentive.

There are several doctrines of culpability which underlie the notion of torts (Shapo, 1977, esp. pp. xi–xxi). These doctrines range from intentional torts and types of reckless conduct through negligence and into the broad category of strict liability. The law of torts implies a positive duty to take action to avoid injuring others. These doctrines translate into a number of specific torts, both intentional and unintentional (Cohen, 1979, p. 41). Intentional torts include battery, assault, false imprisonment, trespass to land, trespass to chattels, conversion of chattels, deceit, intentional causing of emotional distress, intentional invasion of privacy, malicious prosecution, and abuse of due process of law. Unintentional torts include breach of duty of due care, negligent misrepresentation, negligent causing of emotional distress, and negligent invasion of privacy. Although there is a long list of torts, not all wrongs can be taken to court as a tort. As Prosser notes: "The basest ingratitude is not a tort, nor is a cruel refusal of kindness or courtesy, or a denial of aid." (1964, p. 18)

Some argue that torts are far from ideal for dealing with various types of injuries (O'Connell, 1975). One problem associated with torts is that few of those injured actually receive compensation. Victims who do seek compensation are faced with burdensome and expensive litigation. In response to the shortcomings of the traditional tort system, some have suggested other schemes, such as comparative negligence, no-fault coverage, or social welfare programs. Defenders of the tort system suggest, however, that torts are superior since they indirectly deter individuals from injuring others. According to this view, the threat of tort action will encourage adults to drive more carefully, encourage manufacturers to design safer products, and encourage professionals to avoid malpractice. Consequently, torts are seen as deterring harmdoing, thereby benefiting society as a whole. Nevertheless, available evidence indicates that torts are not very effective as deterrents (O'Connell, 1975, pp. 22–23). Tort cases apparently have little impact on product design or warning decisions. Moreover, insurance companies do not make the effort to encourage manufacturers to show a more general concern for safety.

One major response to the defects of the traditional tort system has been the adoption of "comparative negligence." (Schwartz, V., 1974) The underlying aim is "preserving the basic principles" of torts "while making the system more responsive. . . ." (Schwartz, V., 1974, pp. 1–2). Comparative negligence has been favored by the American Bar Association, the American Trial Lawyers' Association, and the Defense Research Institute. Under comparative negligence the cost of an accident is apportioned according to the relative fault of the responsible parties. Thus, a party who has been injured may recover some damages even if partly at fault. The amount recovered, however, will be reduced in proportion to the extent of that party's own degree of negligence. Many states have adopted comparative negligence, replacing the traditional doctrine of "contributory negligence." Under contributory negligence, if an injured plaintiff's negligence contributed to the happening of an accident, the plaintiff could recover nothing in damages from a defendant who negligently caused the injury. By limiting or moving away from contributory negligence, government makes it easier for victims to recover for injuries which were not entirely of their own making. Tinkering with the tort system, therefore, is one means of dealing with the defects of torts.

A leading student of the subject, Jeffrey O'Connell, has suggested that mere reform of the tort process is not an adequate response. Instead, he calls for a wholesale abandonment of torts. O'Connell argues: "It is time we turned to ambitious legislation for reform instead of relying so much on the tortured, tortuous, even torturing tort system with its case-by-case common law crawl— a system from which law professors derive so much fascination, law practitioners so much income, and the general public so few benefits." (1975, p. 67) A social welfare alternative to torts would involve reliance on social security. Under this scheme those injured in accidents would be compensated through social security for wage losses and medical expenses. At the same time, the costs of such a plan raise serious questions of political feasibility. As a result, most efforts at reform focus on specific remedies for individual types of torts. Several states have shifted various injuries from torts to some sort of no-fault coverage. Under no-fault auto insurance all injured parties are compensated for direct losses by their own insurance company. The issue of fault need never arise and the huge sums allocated for legal fees under the tort system is saved. With widespread adoption of no-fault, torts would be used only where one party has intentionally inflicted an injury on another party. As we will see, however, the no-fault system is not without faults of its own.

Automobile Accidents

Traditionally, automobile accidents in the United States have been dealt with through the use of torts. Under the tort system for auto accidents the victim makes a claim against the person at fault—or, in reality, against the insurance company of the wrongdoer (Schmid and MacMillan, 1976). In modern tort law liability for personal injury is defined in terms of negligence. Four general categories of problems may receive compensation: (1) physical injury, (2) economic loss, (3) death, and (4) pain and suffering. Few auto cases actually come to trial. In New York City 98 percent of bodily injury negligence claims were terminated without adjudication (Ross, 1970). Most cases were settled out of court by insurance companies or between an insurance company and the claimant's lawyer. Even so, the threat of a costly, lengthy court struggle is helpful in assuring a reasonable settlement for the claimant. A key figure in the settlement process is the insurance adjuster. Adjusters attempt to negotiate a settlement consistent with formal law while avoiding expensive courtroom procedures. The ideal settlement, in their view, is paying no more or less than the tangible losses involved. However, the greatest organizational pressure they face is not to keep payments low but rather to close files quickly.

The validity of using tort law for compensating auto-related injuries aroused much debate. Finally, on January 1, 1971, the nation's first no-fault auto insurance law became operative in Massachusetts (Gillespie and Klipper, 1972). The aim of the state's Personal Injury Protection is to provide compensation on a no-fault basis to all those injured in any automobile accident. A payment of up to $2,000 is guaranteed, regardless of fault. This $2,000 maximum can be reached through any combination of three types of losses: (1) full payment of reasonable medical expenses, (2) payment of 75 percent of actual wages lost, and (3) full payment for the cost of hiring substitute help. No economic losses in excess of $2,000 are compensated by the Massachusetts no-fault program. Should the combination of expenses exceed $2,000, the victim must sue the individual at fault to recover the economic loss. Only under limited circumstances can there be a tort suit for pain and suffering, disfigurement, emotional distress, or loss of profits. Moreover, certain persons are excluded from coverage: (1) those eligible for workmen's compensation, (2) persons who intentionally injure themselves, (3) those driving under the influence of drugs or alcohol, (4) persons who were committing a felony at the time of their injury, and (5) a driver who was attempting to injure other people at the time of injury. A survey of Massachusetts claimants indicated that the vast majority have positive attitudes toward the Massachusetts system (Widiss, 1975).

Some form of no-fault compensation for automobile accidents is now found in more than half of the American states. The plans vary in many respects, such as the limits on no-fault payments, whether no-fault coverage is optional or mandatory, and the accessibility of the tort system where costs exceed the no-fault maximum. Apparently, no-fault has met the limited goals sought by reformers (Schmid and MacMillan, 1976, p. 61). The plan has removed small claims from the courts, reduced delays in payments, assured more equitable payments for small injuries, and kept premium costs low. However, critics have expressed reservations about no-fault automobile coverage. They wonder whether it is really equitable to exclude payments for pain and suffering. Moreover, no-fault has given a great deal of power to the insurance industry. As Paul Gillespie and Miriam Klipper observe: "The law of negligence is displaced by the law of the insurance industry, and we find the wolf left to guard the sheep." (1972, p. 156) A possible alternative to both torts and no-fault is a govenment-operated insurance system along the lines of workmen's compensation for work-related injuries. This, of course, would have its own set of costs as well as benefits.

Medical Malpractice

Some physicians bury their errors (Jacobs, 1978, Ch. 3). Although malpractice claims have grown considerably in recent years, the universe of medical injuries and the universe of medical negligence are far larger (Lander,

1978, pp. 5–6). A 1972 study found that 40 percent of those interviewed had a "negative medical care experience." Of these more than 85 percent believed that a medical failure of some sort was involved. Yet, only 8 percent even considered seeking legal assistance. Many problems can lead to a malpractice claim (Jacobs, 1978, pp. 15–17). For example, there may have been an error or delay in diagnosis or treatment of a problem. Despite the mystique of modern medicine, doctors and tests are necessarily fallible and medicine is defective. A great irony in medical malpractice is that claims have grown more likely in recent years even as medicine has achieved great advances. The irony can be understood, however. Two important problems involved in contemporary medicine are an increased amount of risk from new treatments and the impersonal character of specialists and hospitals (Lander, 1978, Ch. 1). Patients have come to have high expectations from medicine. When a doctor fails them—and particularly if the doctor has acted in an alien manner or abruptly—their anger may result in a malpractice claim.

Medical malpractice suits generally revolve around the tort doctrine known as negligence (Institute of Medicine, 1978). This doctrine argues that when losses result from someone's action or failure to act, the injured individual should not bear all the losses. Instead, the party who caused the injury is held financially accountable. Negligence law does not attempt to make physicians guarantee successful treatment. Rather, it tries to make a physician liable if the plaintiff can prove by "the preponderance of the evidence" that the physician has failed to perform in a way consistent with accepted modes of medical practice. The injured party must demonstrate that the doctor's conduct was unreasonably negligent and that this was the cause of the specific injury which occurred (Law and Polan, 1978, p. 7). The precise meaning of "acceptable practice" varies from state to state and is resolved by the courts on a case-by-case basis. However, there is a customary presumption that the conduct of professionals, including doctors, was reasonable in nature. In general, an injured party will need the testimony of an expert witness stating that the physician's conduct was not reasonable (Law and Polan, 1978, p. 8).

Malpractice litigation increased substantially during the 1970s (Institute of Medicine, 1978, p. 9). This reflects not only problems in the medical profession but also an increased amount of litigation for all types of personal injury cases. During a period of 14 months from January 1974 to March 1975, some 1,010 of the 7,100 physicians in Cook County, Illinois, were sued for malpractice (Cohen, 1979, p. 4). Of course, few cases reached the trial stage. Yet, settlements averaged $8,000 higher than they were in 1970. The threat of a malpractice suit has led many doctors to practice a sort of "defensive medicine," which involves more tests, consultations, and diagnostic procedures than were used in the past, as well as to show more concern for patients. One malpractice insurance carrier advises its physician-customers: "Warm up to your patients—if you show a genuine interest in their problems, they're far more likely to forgive and forget when there's a bad medical result." (Eisenberg, 1973, p. 163)[10]

From 1969 to 1975 insurance companies increased premiums for liability insurance to an unprecedented degree (Lander, 1978, Ch. 8; Institute of Medicine, 1978, p. 8). They began to think of medical malpractice as a rather risky enterprise and responded by raising rates or even canceling their service. The Insurance Services Offices (ISO), which is an actuarial advisor to malpractice insurers, recommended premium increases for 1974 of 70.1 percent for doctors and surgeons and 56.5 percent for hospitals (Institute of Medicine, 1978, p. 8). In 1975 ISO recommendations were for increases of 110.8 percent and 87 percent respectively. The malpractice/insurance crisis prompted an enormous amount of legislative activity at the state level (Institute of Medicine, 1978, p. 9; Lander, 1978, p. 144). New legislation created insurance mechanisms to deal with the availability of insurance and altered the procedures and substance of relevant tort law. For example, stricter limitations were placed on recovery of damages by patients. Tort law concerning patients' right to recover was altered. Mandatory pretrial screening panels were established. The American Medical Association characterized these changes as "a remarkable record of achievement." (Lander, 1978, p. 143) Still, the threat of legal action remains a very real concern for physicians and hospitals.

Changes in tort law governing medical malpractice have not silenced all calls for further reform. Social welfare advocates suggest moving to a government-sponsored medical injury compensation system, much like workmen's compensation. The Institute of Medicine has provided an analysis of the advantages and disadvantages of litigation and social insurance (1978, pp. 33–34). On the positive side, litigation protects the rights of those who gain access to the system. It also carefully controls unreliable or prejudicial testimony through formal rules of evidence. Finally, the litigation process is relatively impartial, favoring neither providers nor patients. At the same time, the Institute cites four problems associated with the use of litigation in malpractice cases. First, the need for a lawyer hinders accessibility to compensation. Second, many injuries receive no compensation, since it is necessary to prove that the provider was at fault. Third, compensation is unpredictable, with frequent overcompensation or undercompensation. Fourth, professional liability insurance may reduce somewhat the injury avoidance incentives established by tort liability.

Social insurance for medical injuries has a different set of advantages and disadvantages. One benefit is that the access of injured patients to compensation would be enhanced. In addition, a greater number of medical injuries would be compensated, albeit at a lower level per claim than in litigation. Last, the amount of the award for a given injury would be predictable. At the

---

[10] Quoting Richard D. Hall, president, Empire Casualty Co.

same time, the Institute notes three disadvantages inherent in a system of social insurance for medical injuries. First, the budgetary cost would be quite high. Second, the claimant would gain predictability of benefits only by sacrificing individualized valuation of loss. Finally, certain social insurance plans would eliminate provider accountability and would offer no incentives for providers to avoid medical injuries. Whatever the balance of pros and cons between torts and social insurance, it is clear that we are in an age where the utility of torts for particular injuries, such as those produced by physicians, is being seriously questioned.

DOMESTIC RELATIONS

Domestic relations is another major area of civil law (Krause, 1977; Strickman, 1981). In regulating domestic relations, the civil courts may touch deeply into our everyday lives. The creation of the marital relationship is one broad area where legal guidelines exist. For example, there are laws stating the substantive requirement for entering into marriage (see *Loving v. Virginia,* which declared laws banning intermarriage invalid), laws dealing with heterosexual relationships,[11] minimum age,[12] mental condition,[13] health, a waiting period, and bans on polygamy (*Reynolds v. United States*) and incestuous marriages.[14] The types of marriage contracts, and any antenuptual agreements, are also the subject of legal guidelines. The ongoing marriage is another basic concern of the law. There are legal guidelines regulating family support and property rights within the marital relationship. The law also contains special rules for tort liability between husband and wife. The parent-child relationship is also a major concern of civil law. Concerning the creation of that relationship, laws focus on abortion (*Roe v. Wade*), illegitimacy of children, establishing paternity, adoption, and artificial insemination. Laws touching on the ongoing parent-child relationship focus on parental authority, child support (for example, *Stanton v. Stanton*), child neglect, child abuse, and the custody of children in a divorce.[15] The termination of marriage is also the subject of legal guidelines. Indeed, in many states a veritable metamorphosis of divorce law has taken place. Apart from the rules governing divorce, the law also regulates its economic effects, including alimony (see *Orr v. Orr,* which holds that al-

---

[11] The Supreme Court has chosen not to deal with the constitutionality of same-sex marriages. See *Baker v. Nelson,* 409 U. S. 810 (1972), "dismissed for want of substantial federal question."

[12] Typically, the age is sixteen or eighteen or higher without parental consent.

[13] Mental incompetents are generally forbidden to enter into marriage, although in practice this is very difficult to enforce.

[14] Note that there is variation from state to state in the affinity of relationships seen as incestuous.

[15] Custody decisions are generally made in accordance with "the best interests of the child."

imony awards may not be limited to a single gender by a state), the division of property, and separation agreements. Finally, the mental competence of family members is another important area of domestic relations law. Most notably, the law spells out procedures and criteria for civil commitments.

The following discussion of domestic relations will concentrate on two key areas of the law—civil commitment and divorce.

Civil Commitment

Civil commitment is the process through which an individual is institutionalized, having been found mentally ill. Commitment may occur on a voluntary basis or without the individual's consent. When involuntary, it is much like preventive detention, enabling society to confine people for conditions or behaviors we do not wish to criminally outlaw (for example, senility, manic behavior, strange desires) (Livermore, Malmquist, and Meehl, 1968). Obviously, commitment involves a serious abridgment of personal liberty. Through commitment you can be denied your freedom even if you are guilty of no crime. In many states commitment proceedings can be initiated by a broad group of individuals, including relatives, physicians, and the police. (Warning: Do not allow the ease of civil commitment to upset you emotionally, or someone may become convinced that you need to be committed.)

The merits of the civil commitment procedure have been hotly contested (Scheff, 1964, pp. 21–22). Still, considerable support for the commitment procedure can be found. As Seymour Halleck observes: "While there are many people in our country who are wary of the psychiatrist's power to control behavior, there are also many who would encourage psychiatrists to use their power to shape citizens in such a way that they are more conforming." (1974, p. 385) Advocates note that civil commitment is an important mechanism by which society can prevent disorderly conduct and ensure the public safety. Many of those committed would be a nuisance if allowed to roam free, while others would be outright dangerous. It is also stressed that civil commitment is really beneficial to those committed. The procedure sets the stage for medical expertise to be applied to resolve the mental illness of the patient. Lacking such treatment, the condition of the mentally ill individual might rapidly deteriorate.

Critics, however, have raised a number of provocative questions about the commitment procedure. The issue of personal liberty is a special concern. Thomas Szasz characterizes involuntary commitment as "a deprivation of liberty that violates basic human rights, as well as the moral principles of the Declaration of Independence and the U. S. Constitution." (1969, p. 55) A concern for liberty seems to demand restraint in confining people against their will. Aside from this normative assault, critics make some empirical claims as well. On the basis of his investigation, Eugene Du Bose, Jr., concludes that it is not appropriate for the state to confine a nondangerous, mentally ill person for the purpose of treatment (1976). According to Du Bose, the benefits of confinement are too uncertain and the dangers not inconsiderable. Critics note that the common practice of equating mental illness with dangerousness is quite mistaken (Halleck, 1969; Scheff, 1964, p. 22). Those housed in mental institutions may be no more dangerous than the general population. Further, there is a social stigma attached to commitment that is often highly detrimental to the future opportunities of those who have been committed (Scheff, 1964, p. 21).

Perhaps the most compelling problem noted by the critics of commitment is our inability at this time to accurately determine who is or is not mentally ill (Livermore et al., 1968; Dix, 1976). Leaving aside the difficulty of defining mental illness, it may be true that many clear-cut cases of mental health or mental illness can be found. Yet, there are also a great number of marginal cases over which a group of "experts" would surely disagree. In this regard, even a test which was 95 percent accurate might be viewed as seriously inadequate.[16] Assuming that 100 people were insane in a group of 100,000, a 95 percent accurate test would commit not only 95 insane people (that is, 95 percent of 100 insane) but also 4,995 sane people (that is, 95 percent of 99,900 sane). The consequences for those mistakenly declared to be insane are enormous. Even at that, there is no reason to believe that we now have an insanity test which even approaches 95 percent accuracy. Further, the problems inherent in trying to predict mental illness are compounded by the weak relationship between mental illness and dangerousness. Psychiatrists have not only been unsuccessful in developing the means to predict the presence of mental illness but also dangerousness (Morse, 1978; Cocozza and Steadman, 1976).

Given the perils of civil commitment, it is not surprising that many are concerned about the rights of those alleged to be mentally ill.[17] Those believed to be mentally ill possess a number of legal rights. Among these rights are the presumption of sanity, notification of the charges, the right to be present at a formal hearing, the right to counsel and a jury trial, and individual consideration of the case on its merits (Eisenstein, 1973, pp. 130–135). Nevertheless, in some states many of these rights are commonly abridged. Seeing the individual involved as a "patient" rather than as a "defendant," courts have often given short shrift to rights in order to avoid traumatizing a person who already seems severely upset. In countless cases hearings have been held without the accused being present. Jury trials and the right to counsel have also been denied.

[16] Typists, stenographers, and keypunchers work at enormous speeds and yet are highly accurate—perhaps 99.95 percent or more. Yet, such work involves virtually no ambiguity or discretion. By contrast, assessing someone's mental health necessarily involves considerable ambiguity and discretion. We cannot expect the effectiveness of psychiatrists in their work to ever approach the effectiveness of typists, stenographers, and keypunchers in theirs.

[17] However, for an argument against the legal rights perspective see Harvey J. Shwed, "Protecting the Rights of the Mentally Ill," *American Bar Association Journal,* 1978, *64,* 564–567.

Of late, civil commitment procedures have gone through a period of transition. The federal judiciary has strengthened the rights of the individual against the state and the physician (Hiday, 1977). The Supreme Court entered the fray in its decision in *O'Connor v. Donaldson*. The case concerned a claim by Kenneth Donaldson, who was confined as a mental patient in 1957 and kept in custody against his will for nearly fifteen years. Requests for release were rejected numerous times by the hospital's superintendent, Dr. J. B. O'Connor. Despite evidence that he was dangerous neither to himself nor to others, O'Connor refused to release Donaldson, believing that he benefited from custodial care by the state. Ruling for the former mental patient, Justice Stewart spoke for a unanimous Supreme Court (at 575):

> A finding of "mental illness" alone cannot justify a State's locking a person up against his will and keeping him indefinitely in simple custodial confinement. Assuming that that term can be given a reasonably precise content and that the "mentally ill" can be identified with reasonable accuracy, there is still no constitutional basis for confining such persons involuntarily if they are dangerous to no one and can live safely in freedom.

The Court's decision was narrowly defined, avoiding issues such as whether those confined by the state have a right to treatment and whether a nondangerous, mentally ill individual can be compulsorily confined for treatment. However, many states have responded to the activity in the federal judiciary by rewriting statutes regarding admission to, care in, and discharge from mental hospitals.

Despite this activity, the simple announcement of a new statute or court decision regarding civil commitment will not in itself change very much. To be effective, a policy must be implemented. The evidence from several states suggests that reformed commitment procedures have achieved little or no results (Bartol, 1981). The focus of legislation and major court decisions has been on the ancient doctrine of parens patriae. This doctrine holds that if a person cannot or will not take action in his or her own best interests, then the government should do so. Recent changes in the law have tried to limit the role of parens patriae in civil commitment decisions. Various procedural safeguards have been introduced by many states so that only those who are dangerous will be committed. However, despite these statutory changes, involuntary parens patriae commitments persist at virtually the same levels. The new statutes have failed to specify clearly defined criteria based on the actual behavior of people. This failure has been compounded by the continued deference shown by judges to the opinions of psychiatrists at civil commitment hearings. Thus, the new statutes have not been effective in eliminating or reducing the power of psychiatrists to successfully recommend involuntary commitments based on parens patriae rationales. In reviewing these legislative failures, Curt Bartol calls for the adoption of "clearly defined, behavior-based criteria for commitment proceedings. . . ." (1981, p. 195) Such an approach

would presumably limit civil commitments to people who have actually be-
haved in a dangerous manner, rather than those who have simply been eval-
uated as being mentally ill (or dangerous) by one or more psychiatrists.

Oddly, many of those who lose their liberty at commitment proceedings
may have no more mental illness than those who escape with their freedom
intact. The defendant's demeanor at the commitment proceeding, which may
be quite unrelated to mental illness or health, seems to be highly important.
Dorothy Miller and Michael Schwartz studied the relationship between defendants' behavior at the proceedings and their success in securing a fair hearing
and a release (1966). Essentially, Miller and Schwartz found that defiant defendants received longer hearings and were far more likely to be released. Those
who were defiant varied in intensity from silent disdain to verbal protest even
to assaultive violence. Resisters were generally more aware than other defendants. They were concerned about their rights and tried to fight the "injustice" of the hearing. Judges showed more personal interest in these cases.
An especially effective tactic was to question the validity of the complainants'
case rather than to question the validity of doctors' testimony. Half of those
who resisted were either released or held over for further study. Evidently, the
civil commitment process is one type of dispute where being congenial (as per
Dale Carnegie's advice) (1936) is not a very effective approach.

When dealing with people having mental problems, there is something
to be said for using "the least burdensome treatment." (Bezanson, 1975) Recent legislation in many states has stressed this goal. As a result, full-time
hospitalization is increasingly used only as a last resort. While the average stay
in a state hospital in 1950 was more than twenty years, by 1975 it was no more
than seven months (Scull, 1981, p. 741). The total number of residents in state
hospitals has dropped from a peak of 558,922 in 1955 to less than 200,000.
Today there is a strong preference for alternatives to state hospitals, such as
outpatient care or sheltered care in community-based facilities. The new alternatives are made possible in large part by the discovery of new psychotropic
drugs, particularly the phenothiazines. Outpatient care greatly enhances the
liberty of the individual (Allan and Parris, 1967). The individual lives at home,
may be employed, and is inconvenienced only moderately by periodic conferences with a psychiatrist. The patient is free to come and go at will.

Of course, many families regard the "homecoming" as a burden rather
than a blessing—particularly where drug treatment has proven ineffective. For
those who lack a family with whom to live, an approach with some promise
is community life in sheltered care facilities (Fairweather et al., 1969; Segal
and Aviram, 1978). Residents of such facilities are usually incapable of full
integration into the mainstream of society or of achieving complete economic
independence (Segal and Aviram, 1978). Yet, their success on both counts can
be greatly enhanced under the right circumstances, such as a positive neighborhood response and an ideal psychiatric environment. Unfortunately, these
conditions are rarely met. Area residents want a facility for the mentally ill

located in their neighborhood about as much as they want a nuclear power plant built there. Even more serious is the poor quality of care within most sheltered care facilities (Scull, 1981; Warren, 1981). To a large extent it has been out of a desire to save money that state governments have encouraged the movement of the mentally ill from state hospitals to community-based facilities. While the concept of sheltered care facilities is a good one, it cannot work effectively without adequate financing.[18]

Divorce

Divorce law in the United States has undergone an enormous transformation. Two competing ideologies have been influential in determining its content (Rheinstein, 1972, Ch. 2). The Christian-conservative principle suggests that marriage is indissoluble, except by death. Adherents contend that the state has a valid interest in promoting family stability. The eudemonistic-liberal principle implies that marriage may be terminated at any time by either party. Supporters believe that if either spouse wants to terminate a marriage, the state should not stand in the way. Traditionally, the written law in most states has been conservative. A state-imposed obstacle course stood in the way of obtaining a divorce. For example, until 1967 there were only three limited conditions under which a marriage could be legally terminated in New York State (O'Gorman, 1963, pp. 11–12). These include divorce if adultery was committed, an "Enoch Arden" decree if a spouse had been absent for five years and was presumed dead, and an annulment under unusual conditions, such as if one party was underage or insane. In addition, a separation could be obtained, but this did not terminate the marriage or relieve the entire range of marital obligations. For decades divorce laws underwent few revisions, and in most states the laws were quite restrictive. Until 1949, in fact, no divorce at all could be obtained in South Carolina (Rheinstein, 1972, p. 9).

In the face of highly restrictive divorce laws, evasion was a widespread response by spouses who wished to terminate their marriage. Studying the divorce process in New York, Hubert O'Gorman found four patterns of evasive behavior (1963, pp. 20–21). First, the law explicitly prevented divorce through mutual consent by the spouses. Nevertheless, it was quite common for mutual consent actually to be present in most of the divorces which took place. Second, collusion between the spouses was expressly forbidden. Yet, there was some collusion in nearly every divorce action. In fact, a courtroom

---

[18] Regarding the rights of the mentally retarded, Congress passed the Developmentally Disabled Assistance and Bill of Rights Act of 1975. Many argued that this law created broad rights for the retarded, including community living facilities. However, in *Pennhurst State School v. Halderman,* 451 U. S. 1 (1981), the Supreme Court disagreed. The Court ruled that the law did not require better facilities for the retarded but simply sought to encourage improvements. In a subsequent decision, *Youngberg v. Romeo,* 50 LW 4681 (1982), the Court ruled that the mentally retarded have the right to safe conditions of confinement, freedom from unreasonable bodily restraints, and whatever minimal training reasonably may be required to fulfill these rights.

script was often agreed upon by the spouses in which the husband accepted all responsibility and the wife appeared faultless. Third, the law assumed that matrimonial actions would be contested. Even so, spouses generally reached agreements prior to appearing in court. Finally, matrimonial actions were generally adjudged according to evidence presented in the courtroom. Yet, in general, such evidence was not consistent with the actual causes of the marital breakdown. Given such evidence, critics charge that restrictive divorce laws are unenforceable. Most couples who want a divorce will obtain it somehow—whether by traveling to a state with less restrictive divorce laws or by committing perjury to meet one of the available grounds for a divorce decree.

There has been a clear movement away from restrictive divorce laws and toward the concept of no-fault divorce (Robinson, 1978, p. 4). An initial step was the expansion of the allowable grounds for divorce. For example, in many states incompatibility was introduced as a legitimate ground for divorce. A strategy far more radical was initiated in 1970. At that time California acted to eliminate altogether the question of fault. The California law made "irreconcilable differences which have caused the irremediable breakdown of the marriage" an acceptable ground for divorce. No-fault divorce simply requires spouses to show that their marriage is no longer viable. The new California law resulted from a series of sweeping proposals made by the Governor's Commission on the Family (Wheeler, 1974, p. 19). This Commission, appointed by Governor Edmund Brown in 1965, was established to draft revisions in California's family laws. It included a bipartisan group of lawyers, judges, law professors, political officials, and other professionals. The California law not only enacted no-fault divorce but also focused on property division. In most cases it requires judges to split marital property equally, regardless of fault or need. Since 1970 more than one-third of the states have adopted a no-fault provision for divorce cases.

Some are concerned that no-fault divorce laws will encourage more divorces. For many a high divorce rate is symbolic of a society whose "moral fiber" is tearing apart. Critics suggest that divorce is a serious social problem, that the divorce rate is already too high, and that easy divorces will breed hasty divorces. Yet, one might argue that it is marital breakdown rather than divorce per se which is the real problem (Rheinstein, 1972, esp. Ch. 11). The breakdown of a marriage precedes efforts to obtain a divorce. Surely, strict divorce laws cannot force spouses to live together in harmony. Indeed, such laws cannot force spouses to live together at all. Of course, few would argue that as a matter of public policy, government ought to encourage divorces. One suggested approach is to couple no-fault divorce laws with mandatory marriage counseling for couples seeking a divorce (Rheinstein, 1972, pp. 429–443; Wheeler, 1974, p. 100). Such counseling could even be available as a government service for those with marital difficulties. As Michael Wheeler notes: "A court-connected counseling service could perform both a real and a symbolic function, by directly helping as many people as it could and by demonstrating to others that there is a larger social interest in preserving marriages." (1974, p. 100)

AN ASSESSMENT

An intricate body of procedural and substantive law exists in the civil courts. Civil cases are initiated by a party who feels injured in some way. Courts will not, in the interests of justice, initiate a legal case on behalf of some party—not even a party who clearly has been seriously wronged. The complexity of civil proceedings makes it virtually impossible to litigate a case without an attorney. Few others can intelligently navigate the course of a civil suit—choosing a forum, filing a complaint, arguing preliminary motions, undertaking discovery, handling negotiations, and perhaps going to trial. It might be argued that some types of civil cases should be simplified so that litigants would be freed from the burden of legal fees. However, any simplification of procedure must be mindful of the desire to ensure procedural and substantive justice.

We have examined a diverse body of civil law in the United States, concerning property, contracts, torts, and domestic relations. The diversity of civil law renders it very difficult to offer any general observations. For example, what can we say about civil justice and social equality? Certainly, it is true that disadvantaged people routinely lose in some kinds of cases, such as replevins, garnishments, and liens. Significantly, such debt actions are very common in the civil courts, and the poor almost always emerge as the losing party. It is also significant that the disadvantaged rarely use the civil courts as plaintiffs to assert some legal right. Still, this does not mean that the full range of civil law is biased against the disadvantaged. In particular, there has been a transformation of bankruptcy law in the United States so that debtors (some of whom are disadvantaged) may now be relieved of many of their obligations and get a "fresh start."

However, while broad generalization about civil law is difficult, it is clear that much is at stake in the civil courtroom. In a wide assortment of cases an enormous amount of wealth is redistributed. In zoning cases land owners learn whether they will be permitted by zoning authorities to use their property as they wish. In civil commitment cases the very freedom of the individual is at stake. Throughout civil law there is a concern by some that certain values are not being adequately promoted. Thus, critics charge that easy divorces lead to social disorder and decline. Many of the value conflicts in the civil courts are inevitable. Because of the political nature of civil justice, we can expect that this subject will always involve controversy and will always merit our close attention.

QUESTIONS FOR DISCUSSION

1. What is meant by "economic due process"? How would you be affected if the Supreme Court were to reaffirm the principles of the Lochner era? Did the Supreme Court act appropriately in reversing its course in the late 1930s by sanctioning increased restraints on property rights? If the Supreme Court of the 1930s retreated on property rights, is there reason to fear that a future Court will retreat on other rights, such as freedom of speech, press, and religion?

2. What is a contract? What contractual obligations do you now have? When you make a purchase on credit, do you feel obliged to repay your debt? Under what circumstances would you most likely default on a debt? Should there be strict bankruptcy laws preventing you from escaping debts you find difficult to repay?

3. What is a tort? How do torts differ from crimes? Have you ever been involved in tort litigation? In retrospect, have you ever been involved in any disputes that should have been dealt with through tort litigation? From a public policy standpoint, what are the problems of relying on tort law? Do you believe that tort law should increasingly be replaced by no-fault or social welfare insurance?

4. How effective is psychiatry in assessing whether an individual is mentally ill? Under what circumstances is it appropriate to commit an individual to a mental institution against his or her will? What problems are involved, for both the individual and society, in using "the least burdensome treatment" when dealing with the mentally ill?

FOR FURTHER READING

CAPLOVITZ, DAVID. *Consumers in Trouble.* New York: Free Press, 1974. Debtor default is analyzed.

NOZICK, ROBERT. *Anarchy, State, and Utopia.* New York: Basic Books, 1974. A defense of property rights by a philosopher who opposes the use of law to redistribute income.

O'CONNELL, JEFFREY. *Ending Insult to Injury.* Urbana, Ill.: University of Illinois Press, 1975. A critic of tort law discusses the no-fault alternative.

ROBINSON, JOAN. *An American Legal Almanac.* Dobbs Ferry, N.Y.: Oceana Publications, 1978. A useful inventory of information on the state of the law.

WHEELER, MICHAEL. *No-Fault Divorce.* Boston: Beacon Press, 1974. A thoughtful look at our changing divorce laws.

SUPREME COURT RULINGS

Arlington Heights v. Metropolitan Housing Corp., 429 U.S. 252 (1977)
Charles River Bridge Co. v. Warren Bridge Co., 11 Pet. 420 (1837)
Dartmouth College v. Woodward, 4 Wheat. 518 (1819)
Fletcher v. Peck, 6 Cranch 87 (1810)

Lochner v. New York, 198 U.S. 45 (1905)
Loving v. Virginia, 388 U.S. 1 (1967)
Nectow v. City of Cambridge, 277 U.S. 183 (1928)
O'Connor v. Donaldson, 422 U.S. 563 (1974)
Orr v. Orr, 440 U.S. 268 (1979)
Reynolds v. United States, 98 U.S. 145 (1879)
Roe v. Wade, 410 U.S. 113 (1973)
Sniadach v. Family Finance Corporation, 395 U.S. 337 (1969)
Stanton v. Stanton, 421 U.S. 7 (1975)
Sturges v. Crowninshield, 4 Wheat. 122 (1819)
Village of Belle Terre v. Boraas, 416 U.S. 1 (1974)
Village of Euclid v. Ambler Reality Co., 272 U.S. 365 (1926)
West Coast Hotel Co. v. Parrish, 300 U.S. 379 (1937)

7
CRIMINAL LAW

PREVIEW

Chapter Seven discusses crime and criminal justice in the United States. The chapter includes four sections:

Nature of crime
Causes of crime
Criminal justice process
Penal justice

To begin with, we examine the nature of crime. Although public discussion usually centers on street crime, there are other significant forms of crime including victimless crimes, white-collar crime, organized crime, and political crime. The extent and costs of crime in America are also discussed in this section. The second unit focuses on the causes of crime. We look first at three general theories of causation—biological, psychological, and sociological. Our attention then turns to some additional factors, including victim precipitation, deterrence, social welfare programs, gun control, and defensible space.

The third section analyzes the criminal justice process. Among the major concerns here are due process of law, bail, plea bargaining, and juvenile justice. Some commentators are critical of the process because relatively few crimes result in convictions. Others attack the courts for impinging on the rights of defendants in expedited proceedings that seem more concerned with speed than justice. Finally, the chapter addresses penal justice. We will discuss prisons and the full range of alternatives to a prison sentence. Beyond that, we will examine the difficulties experienced by analysts in rationalizing our system of penal justice. Even as punishments are meted out to offenders, no one can seem to agree on the purposes these penalties are supposed to serve.

NATURE OF CRIME

Crimes and Criminals

Americans have long had a peculiar fascination with crimes and criminals. Notwithstanding their notorious deeds, we romanticize criminals such as Bonnie and Clyde, Billy the Kid, and Al Capone. There is a certain intrigue attached to stories of criminal wrongdoing even though most of us, most of the time, believe it is very wrong to break the law. Often it is the unusual crime or criminal that captures the public eye, such as the kidnapping of Patty Hearst or the bank robbery by Patty Hearst. Evidently in response to public preferences, local news reports and newspaper articles seem preoccupied with the latest murders, robberies, burglaries, and arsons in their area. A serious discussion of public issues (including crime) is often sacrificed in order to show film footage of a suspect masking his face from a television camera or fire-fighters spraying water at a burning building. Beneath the surface of the sensational is a massive number of additional criminal offenses. While much money is spent to counter criminality, the results of all this activity are rather questionable.

A crime is a violation of the criminal laws of government. We are most familiar with the seven offenses cited by the FBI, as "serious crimes." These include criminal homicide, forcible rape, robbery, assault, burglary, larceny, and auto theft (FBI, 1966).[1] Even so, lesser crimes such as drunkenness, disorderly conduct, and vagrancy are far more common. Underlying most crime is some kind of dispute between two parties. We often think of crime as being committed by someone who is a stranger to the victim. Yet, many crimes involve relatives, friends, and acquaintances. The situation may involve a minor dispute between two people which escalates into an assault with battery, menacing threats, or larceny (Palmer, 1974). Indeed, about two-thirds of all homicides involve people who know each other, and one-fifth involve relatives (Sheley, 1979, p. 45). The dispute may stem from a tense family situation, a

---

[1]For a summary of the substantive law of crimes see Allen Z. Gammage and Charles F. Hemphill, Jr., *Basic Criminal Law* (New York: McGraw-Hill, 1974), espec. Chaps. 10–20.

neighborhood squabble, a misunderstanding between friends, or the break-up of a love affair.

Because of inconsistency in the reporting of crime and the apprehension and conviction of violators, not all crimes produce criminals. A criminal is someone who has been labeled a violator of criminal laws. Being labeled a criminal is no small matter. As Jonathan Casper points out: "The application of the criminal sanction is perhaps the most serious and destructive measure that the government can take against a citizen." (1972a, p. 1) Nearly all Americans have at one time or another violated a law for which they could be incarcerated. Yet, only a small portion of violators have been labeled "criminal." Those who are so branded may suffer serious losses (Eisenstein, 1973, pp. 246–247). Aside from possible imprisonment, convicted felons can lose a number of legal rights, such as the right to vote. Their future career opportunities are placed in jeopardy. Their family lives may suffer. Also, they may face police questioning for years to come, since the police often focus on known criminals when investigating unsolved crimes.

Crime is often portrayed as a deviation from normal behavior in society. Yet, it has been suggested by Emile Durkheim that "crime is normal because a society exempt from it is utterly impossible." (1964, p. 67) In this light, it might be said that if a person threatens someone's life or property, we *want* to call the culprit a criminal. At the same time, it is at least possible to conceive of a society that deals with violations of the law without ever invoking the criminal label. Many harmful activities are already dealt with exclusively on the civil side through tort litigation. This procedure could be extended to areas now dealt with through criminal prosecutions. Yet, for certain offenses—notably, homicide—civil action seems inadequate to the harm that has been inflicted. Some offenses, we persuade ourselves, are so severe that they are insults to society as well as to the victim. Such offenses come to be backed by the criminal sanction.

Naturally, people regard some crimes as more serious than others. A fascinating survey by Peter Rossi and associates sought to learn which crimes are commonly regarded as most serious (1974). Some 200 adults in Baltimore were asked to rate the seriousness of a total of 140 crimes. The ten *most serious* crimes included: (1) planned killing of a police officer, (2) planned killing of a person for a fee, (3) selling heroin, (4) forcible rape after breaking into a home, (5) impulsive killing of a police officer, (6) planned killing of a spouse, (7) planned killing of an acquaintance, (8) hijacking an airplane, (9) armed robbery of a bank, and (10) selling LSD. Going to the bottom of the Rossi listing, the crimes regarded as *least serious* included: (131) joining a prohibited demonstration, (132) false advertising of headache remedy, (133) refusal to pay alimony, (134) refusal to pay parking fines, (135) disturbing the peace, (136) repeated truancy, (137) repeated running away from home, (138) loitering in public places, (139) refusal to answer a census taker, and (140) being drunk in public places.

Certain patterns emerge from the ranking of the 140 crimes in the Rossi study. It seems clear that the public rates crimes against persons as most serious. As noted, the single most serious crime is the planned killing of a police officer, in the view of those who were interviewed. Indeed, any crime perpetrated against a police officer rather than an ordinary citizen was regarded as more serious. Other crimes against persons rating as very serious included murder, rape, assault, kidnapping, and making sexual advances to young children. Few crimes against persons ranked low in seriousness, an exception being the killing of a suspected burglar in a home. It is also noteworthy that people were more accepting of crimes committed by persons known to the victim than crimes committed by strangers. Presumably, this reflects both a fear of strangers and a feeling that there is often a satisfactory explanation for crimes where the victim and offender know each other.

Usually regarded as less serious were crimes against property. Those property crimes seen as most serious generally involved some human contact. Thus, armed robbery of a bank (ranked 9) is rated as far more serious than breaking and entering a bank (ranked 52). Also regarded as relatively nonserious were crimes with no victims—such as public drunkenness, selling pornography, adult homosexuality, and prostitution. This suggests that reformers who wish to decriminalize victimless crimes may find some support among the general public. At the same time, those seeking to strengthen penalties for white-collar crimes may find the struggle rather lonely. In general, the public rates white-collar crimes (for example, false advertising, price fixing, income tax fraud, embezzlement) as less serious than most other offenses.

Types of Crime

"Thinking of 'crime' as a whole is futile," according to the President's Commission on Law Enforcement and Administration of Justice (President's Commission, 1967b, p. 3). Actually, there are many kinds of crimes and many kinds of criminals. Crime consists not only of murder but also of prostitution, embezzlement, gambling, and treason. Criminal offenders include not only the teenager who robs a liquor store but also the middle-class businessperson who embezzles from a company. In the following discussion we consider five general classes of crime: street crime, victimless crime, white-collar crime, organized crime, and political crime.

Street crimes include the sorts of offenses which normally come to mind when you consider the matter of criminality. They embrace each of the seven "serious crimes" cited earlier—criminal homicide, forcible rape, robbery, assault, burglary, larceny, and auto theft. Other common street crimes include arson, vandalism, and weapons offenses. It is these crimes that the police and the public seem most concerned about. Some street crimes are committed by professionals, others by relative novices. A disproportionate number of street crimes are committed by young people and the poor. As street crime escalated during the 1960s, it became an explosive political issue. In 1968, for example, both Richard Nixon and George Wallace ran on "law and order" platforms. Fundamentally, the "law and order" theme was a call for a crackdown on those accused of street crimes. Many concerned with social order felt that Warren Court decisions had "handcuffed" the police and that criminal court judges were "going easy" on those accused of street crimes. Still, it is not clear to what extent we can reduce street crime by abridging the legal rights of suspects or adopting stricter penalties.

Victimless crimes are offenses declared criminal by government, but in which the participants do not normally see themselves as victimized. Prominent examples include illegal abortions, the sale of illicit drugs, illegal gambling, the sale of hard-core pornography, prostitution, homosexuality, public drunkenness, and vagrancy (Schur and Bedau, 1974). Generally, although not always, a banned product or service is involved. Critics charge that government should decriminalize these offenses and allow the criminal justice system to focus its energies on more serious crimes. Norval Morris and Gordon Hawkins argue that criminal law should not invade the "spheres of private morality and social welfare," lest it become less effective at its primary tasks— the protection of persons and property (1970, p. 2). Morris and Hawkins indict this extension of the criminal law on three counts—it is expensive, ineffective, and criminogenic. There is much to be said in support of each of these three indictments (Schur, 1974). To begin with, enforcement of victimless crimes is highly expensive. After all, in victimless crimes, the police lack complainants. As a result, they must rely on unsavory and expensive techniques such as the use of informers and decoys, clandestine surveillance, wiretapping, and surprise raids. Also, police efforts against victimless crimes are not very effective. Occasionally, a "crackdown" occurs on prostitutes, drug sellers, or pornographers. Yet, victimless-crime laws are virtually unenforceable. Finally, victimless crimes are criminogenic—that is, they create criminals. Because these activities are labeled "criminal," a wide range of criminal occupations is created (for example, professional drug traffickers, illicit gambling operators, pornography dealers). Moreover, the price of a product or service skyrockets when it is illicit. As a result, many are forced into criminal acts and become immersed in supply networks with underworld connections. Victimless-crime laws generally represent less-than-successful efforts to legislate morality. Even so, those concerned with social order argue that no matter what the costs, society should not sanction such activities by legalizing them.

White-collar crime includes offenses which relate to the violator's occupational role (Newman, 1977, p. 52). In general, such crimes are committed by persons who are more affluent than street criminals. For example, a bank manager may embezzle funds, a repair person may make unnecessary repairs, a farmer may water down milk, or a doctor may engage in fee splitting. Most attention has focused on white-collar crimes committed by business people. Among these crimes are misrepresentation of corporate financial statements, bribery, misrepresentation in advertising and salesmanship, embezzlement, misgrading commodities, tax frauds, misapplication of funds, and fraudulent bankruptcies (Sutherland, 1977a, p. 40). The enormous extent of white-collar crime flies in the face of the common tendency to associate crime with poor people. It also calls into question the common hypothesis that "poverty breeds crime." While more poor people have committed street crimes, there may be few differences in criminality among economic groups when one looks at the full range of criminal violations.

Focusing on white-collar crimes, Edwin Sutherland examined violations of the law committed by the seventy largest industrial and commercial corporations in the United States (1977b, esp. pp. 72–73). He found that every corporation has a decision against it; the average number of decisions is fourteen; and 98 percent are recidivists (that is, have two or more decisions against it). It is extremely rare for a white-collar criminal to go to prison. Indeed, some white-collar offenses are actually handled by administrative agencies rather than by criminal courts. In general, white-collar crimes go unpunished or are handled with fines, warnings, orders to cease and desist, or occasionally, revocation of a license. Despite this, the economic and human costs to the nation from white-collar crime are greater than the costs of street crime (Douglas, 1971, pp. 15–16; Swigert and Farrell, 1980–81).

Organized crime is committed by thousands of criminals working within complex structures which conduct intricate criminal conspiracies (President's Commission, 1967b, Ch. 7). The President's Commission on Law Enforcement and Administration of Justice reports that some twenty-four groups operate in criminal cartels in large cities of the United States. The main source of income of La Cosa Nostra is derived from supplying illegal goods and services to the American people such as gambling, loan sharking, narcotics, and other forms of vice. Organized crime is also involved in legitimate business and labor unions, where it often employs illegitimate methods such as monopolization, terrorism, extortion, and tax evasion. In order to secure its activities from government interference, corruption of public officials is sometimes necessary. Clearly, organized crime now thrives in the United States. Henry Ruth points to several factors explaining this success (1967). To begin with, organized crime offers services that some people want, such as gambling, narcotics, and quick cash loans. La Cosa Nostra also induces fear in people for their lives, reputation, and property—partly through the selective fulfillment of threats. Moreover, despite the mass of La Cosa Nostra's activities, the problem is fragmented in people's minds because of a lack of knowledge about it. Indeed, even policymakers fail to recognize the large cost of organized crime to the nation. Further, law enforcement acts against gambling and public corruption on a "hit-and-run" basis. While this approach may satisfy the public, it also permits organized crime to continue to thrive. Finally, organized criminals obtain some official protection because of their alliance with respectable members of the community.

Political crime is the application of criminal law against radicals and other opponents of the administration in power. Some criminal laws are explicitly designed to deal with intolerable challengers and resisters to the regime in power (Turk, 1982, pp. 54–68). Political offenses include treason, sedition, subversion, and disloyalty. During John Adams's administration the Alien and Sedition Acts of 1798 were passed to provide a legal basis for prosecuting political opponents. Twentieth-century measures of this sort have included the Espionage Act (1917), the Sedition Act (1918), the Smith Act (1940), the McCarran Act (1950), and the Communist Control Act (1954). A famous political trial in early America was that of John Peter Zenger, who was charged with seditious libel.

It should be noted that political trials sometimes occur when the charges involved cannot rightly be called political crimes (Belknap, 1981, pp. 6–10). As Otto Kirchheimer notes, a trial of a common crime may take on political overtones because of "the motives or objectives of the prosecution, or by the political background, affiliation, or standing of the defendant." (1961, p. 52) Along these lines, some suggest that Nicola Sacco and Bartolomeo Vanzetti were really prosecuted and executed for their anarchism rather than for the formal charges of robbery and murder which were leveled against them. Trials may also take on political overtones if a defendant injects political considerations into a case, if the outcome was determined by political considerations, or if the trial's outcome greatly affects the politics of the era (Belknap, 1981, pp. 6–10). Political crimes, political trials, and political prisoners have been present throughout American history (Becker, 1971; Goodell, 1973). Most of this activity occurred when the status quo was facing serious challenge (Belknap, 1981, p. 14).

Extent of Crime

It is difficult to calculate the amount of crime present in society. For a long time sole reliance was placed on the *Uniform Crime Reports* of the FBI (1966). The basic defect with these data is that they represent only those crimes reported to the police. Yet, many crimes go unreported—particularly those that are less serious, those that are not covered by insurance, and those that involve a low-income person as victim (Ennis, 1967). One way to circumvent the crime-reporting problem is to survey citizens to determine how many times they were victimized in the past year. A startling lesson from such studies is that a large number of victimizations occur which are never reported to the police (Flanagan, Hindelang, and Gottfredson, 1980, p. 328). For example, an estimated 1,082,936 personal robberies occurred in 1977. Yet, only about 56 percent of these were reported to the police. Also evident from victimization evidence is that the more serious offenses tend to occur less frequently. Thus, the number of forcible rapes and attempted rapes (154,237) was far less than the number of household burglaries (6,766,010) or vehicle thefts

(1,296,759). Finally, the victimization surveys also demonstrate that some social groups are far more likely to be victimized than others (Hindelang, Gottfredson, and Garofalo, 1978, pp. 3–14). Those most likely to be victimized tend to be young, male, single, and of low income.

Costs of Crime

The costs of crime to the nation are both enormous and varied. Thus, the President's Commission on Law Enforcement and Administration of Justice argued: "There is much crime in America . . . far too much for the health of the Nation. Every American knows that. Every American is, in a sense, a victim of crime." (1967b, p. 1) Loss of life is, of course, the greatest cost of crime. It is true that the risks of being murdered are substantially less than other life-taking risks (for example, auto accidents). Still, over 20,000 homicides occur annually—clearly a substantial figure.

Further, the economic cost of crime is massive (Trojanowicz, Trojanowicz, and Moss, 1975, pp. 11–12). According to one estimate, organized crime takes in nearly $19.5 billion per year. Kickbacks—including bribes and extortion—cost some $5 billion annually. Businesses suffer $500 million in losses from shoplifting and $3 billion in employee thefts. Heroin trade amounts to $3.5 billion per year. In 1970 burglaries cost $672 million, robberies $82 million, and auto thefts $875 million. These staggering costs are paid for in many ways. Substantial losses are suffered by the individual victim. Many are insured, but high crime rates produce increased premium costs. Also, insurance companies may refuse coverage in areas having high levels of street crime. Beyond that, people may pay enormous sums for security systems, alarms, locks, safes, extra lighting, computerized credit systems, and the services of guards and detective agencies. Also, the costs of the police and of courtrooms and corrections agencies must be calculated.

Another substantial cost of crime in America is the widespread fear of crime (McIntyre, 1967). Violent crime causes the greatest concern. People are more tolerant and less fearful of crimes against property. The fear of crime appears to be related to a general fear of strangers. Ours is such an urbanized society that we rarely know the people we come across. Not surprisingly, increased city size is associated with a greater fear of crime (Clemente and Kleiman, 1977, p. 527). Jennie McIntyre notes that people "are afraid that some unknown person will accost them on the street or break into their homes and take their property or attack them personally." (1967, p. 40) These fears are somewhat exaggerated. For example, the risk of serious attack by a stranger is only about half as great as an attack by persons well known to the victim. Surprisingly, the fear of crime is not related to prior victimization. Those who have not been victimized at all are just as fearful as those who have been severely victimized. Fear is more diffuse in character—perhaps relating more closely to intensive press coverage of crime waves rather than to personal experience. As McIntyre suggests, the fear of being victimized by strangers "is impoverishing the lives of many Americans." (1967, p. 41) Because of the fear of crime, people stay behind locked doors at home rather than walking outdoors at night. Some restrict earning opportunities by ignoring job openings in neighborhoods with high rates of street crime. Many are genuinely afraid to stop and talk with people they do not know. By staying at home, people may lose valuable opportunities to enrich their lives.

THE CAUSES OF CRIME

What causes crime? This question has generated an enormous amount of attention among scholars, policymakers, and the public (Vold, 1979; Sheley, 1979, Ch. 4; McCaghy, 1980, Ch. 3; Fox, 1976). It is also a question that has led to some very diverse responses, many of them not very satisfactory. Part of the problem in understanding the causes of crime is the diversity of the offenses we choose to characterize as "crime." As George B. Vold has observed: "Crime must be recognized clearly as not being a single phenomenon, but as consisting of many kinds of behavior occurring under many different situations." (1979, p. 422) Given the diversity of the offenses we call crimes, it is not an especially easy task to formulate a useful, general theory of the causes of crime. The criminological theories that have been proposed to date are quite varied. General theories of crime have a biological, psychological, and sociological emphasis. A number of particularistic explanations have also been advanced, focusing on factors such as victim precipitation, deterrence, and social welfare programs. These explanations are discussed below. It must be stressed that it would be very useful to learn the causes of crime, since different explanations suggest different remedies. If we had a better understanding of the causes of crime, we might be able to reduce its rate by developing more effective crime prevention measures.

Biological Theories

Early explanations of crime were biological in character (Sheley, 1979, pp. 93–95; Hooton, 1931). It was suggested that persons with certain body types were more likely to commit crimes. In particular, early analysts argued that criminals tended to have thicker, straighter, and more reddish hair. Criminals were also said to have low, sloping foreheads, thinner lips, long necks, and sloping shoulders. Today these biological theories are in disrepute. However, a modern version which has achieved some notoriety is the allegation that if a man has XYY chromosomes instead of the usual XY complement, he will be more aggressive and more prone to commit a crime (Fox, 1971). Such a theory might be comforting to the general population, for it offers a clear-cut, qualitative distinction between "normal" and "abnormal" people.

If XYY chromosomes cause crime, we need only identify those afflicted and deal with them (for example, isolate them, keep them under surveillance, provide psychotherapy). Yet, there is evidence that XYY offenders have less violent records than XY offenders (Fox, 1971). If XYY chromosomes play any role in criminality, it is surely a very small role. Similarly, we must be skeptical of any possible role attributed to other hereditary defects, such as endocrine imbalance, learning disabilities, and nervous system functioning (Vold, 1979, Ch. 6).

Psychological Theories

Crime has also been attributed to mental and psychological problems (Sheley, 1979, pp. 95-98; Vold, 1979, Ch. 7). For example, *intellectual and mental impairment* has been cited as a cause of crime. It was once believed that criminals were less intelligent than the average person and were even retarded. Yet, the planning and execution of many crimes actually requires a high IQ. In general, there are probably few IQ differences between those who have committed a crime and those who have not. As George B. Vold concludes: "Certainly, adult criminals are not severely or mildly retarded; they are not feebleminded." (Vold, 1979, p. 97)

Psychoanalytic theories stress emotional or personality disorders as causes of criminal behavior. If accurate, we should be able to greatly reduce crime by providing psychological treatment to the criminal population. Even so, the relationship between psychological problems and criminal activity is quite problematic. Some analysts point in particular to psychopathic personalities as a leading factor in crime. Psychopaths are callous people who are amoral and unafraid of sanctions, with problematic social relationships, less purposeful behavior, and few ties to society. Yet, there is much crime in society and few psychopaths. It is likely that only a small proportion of crimes are committed by psychopaths. Other personality disorder theories stress over-aggression, insecurity, paranoia, emotional instability, immaturity, and ego-centrism. Yet, existing evidence is not very supportive of these theories.

Sociological Theories

There has also been much sociological investigation into the causes of crime (Sheley, 1979, pp. 98-109; Vold, 1979, Chaps. 8-14; Fox, 1976; Mc-Caghy, 1980, Ch. 3; Merton, 1957; Sutherland and Cressey, 1978, Ch. 4; Glaser, 1962; Quinney, 1980). A wide range of explanations have been offered. According to structural theories, modern society has created a sense of alienation and powerlessness among many people. This "anomie" has led some to seek out easy solutions (including crime) to their problems. It is also argued by structural theorists that the economic system leads to crime, both in times of prosperity and during a depression. While our social institutions promote materialistic values, the economic system has failed to enable people to achieve their economic goals. The implication of structural theories is that we need to open up opportunities for people, particularly the disadvantaged.

Marxist theories stress that crime is a manifestation of the struggle between the classes. Crimes such as price fixing are committed by owners to maintain the economic status quo. Other crimes, such as burglary, are committed by workers to deal with their deprivation. Still others, such as illegal strikes, are committed to disrupt and bring down the system. The implication of Marxism as regards crime is that a fundamental change in our current economic and political system is needed.

Finally, cultural transmission theories assert that people learn criminal behavior from those with whom they associate. Although some have characterized it as the "bad company" theory, this may be an oversimplification. As Vernon Fox notes: "Rather than just association, frequency, duration, priority, intensity, motives, drives, rationalization, attitudes, and many other factors influence the quality and effect of the association." (1976, p. 102) Taking all these factors into account may help to explain why all those who come into contact with criminals do not themselves become criminals.

Sociological theories steer us away from the notion that criminals are somehow abnormal people. Such theories suggest that criminals are not biologically bizarre or psychologically distressed. Structural theories see crime as basically caused by blocked opportunities. Marxist theories view crime as a normal and unavoidable response to oppression. Finally, cultural transmission theories portray crime as a normal response to the beliefs an individual has been taught. Still, there are difficulties with the sociological theories of the causes of crime. Structural theories generally portray crime as a lower-class phenomenon. Yet, this assertion is valid only if we focus narrowly, and rather arbitrarily, on street crimes. Marxist theory is generally criticized for "tunnel vision": It suggests that the economic system, and nothing else, determines crime rates. However, statistical evidence suggests that noneconomic factors are also important in causing crime (Vold, 1979, Ch. 8). Finally, cultural transmission theories seem to overstress the idea of a subculture of crime. One survey indicates that virtually every American admits to having committed at least one offense for which he or she might have received a jail or prison sentence (President's Commission, 1967b, pp. 43–44). It is neither useful nor accurate to suggest that over 90 percent of Americans are part of a subculture of crime.

Victim Precipitation

While the notion may contain a touch of irony, some analysts allege that it is the victim who is responsible for many of the crimes which take place. Victim-precipitated crimes are those which would not have taken place were it not for the precipitative actions of the victim (Gobert, 1977). The provocative act of the victim may be the sole cause of the offender's conduct or a minor triggering factor. Clearly, it is quite possible for a victim to provoke a crime (Curtis, 1974). For example, in the heat of a fight one party may hand a gun to an agitated adversary and accuse the latter of not having enough "guts" to shoot. Or, someone at a bar may flash a great deal of money and then stagger home alone on a dark street. Less obviously, social practices have made it easier to steal. As Leroy Gould observes: "With a proliferation of checks, credit cards, serve-yourself retail stores, inadequately protected banks, and unlocked and unprotected merchandise of all kinds, it is not surprising that property crime is increasing." (1971, p. 116) This suggests a need for better locks, alarms, and surveillance systems.

A clear implication of the victim precipitation concept is that to reduce crime, potential victims have a responsibility to take positive steps to reduce their risks of being victimized. With tongue-in-cheek, *The National Lampoon* humor magazine once called for a "bold new approach" to crime which includes prosecution of the victims of crime.[2] The *Lampoon* article pictures a frenzied female victim trying to avoid punishment by persuading detectives that no crime really took place: "I'm telling you, officer, you got the wrong gal. I didn't get robbed. Not me. I *threw* all my money away. Honest I did. You can ask anybody. . . ." While the criminal justice system in America does not punish victims for precipitating a crime, offenders may face lesser charges if their conduct was provoked by the victim (Curtis, 1974; Gobert, 1977). Homicide laws in the United States recognize precipitation by allowing mitigation of the offense from murder to excusable homicide. Similarly, a burglary generally requires breaking and entering. Those who steal after entering a home through an open window are guilty only of larceny—a crime which carries a lesser penalty. In other crimes as diverse as entrapment and rape, efforts are made to protect offenders from victim precipitation.

Deterrence

Crime also results from government failure to act adequately to deter it. Most discussions of deterrence focus on the certainty and severity of punishment. Some suggest that crime will decrease where the risk of detection, apprehension, and conviction is greater (Andenaes, 1966; Zimring and Hawkins, 1973). This has a ring of truth to it. Certainly, few would burglarize a home if a police officer was standing on every doorstep. More problematic is whether a marginal increase in policing would deter crime. Some crimes are committed impulsively without due consideration of the risks. In other cases the individual may accept possible penalties as a reasonable risk for the potential benefits of the illegal actions. Also, the effectiveness of deterrence undoubtedly varies with the type of crime committed. Yet, if we were to convince people that crime does not pay, violations would surely reduce somewhat.

---

[2]*National Lampoon* Inc. (January 1980), p. 21.

In an empirical analysis William Bailey and associates found that certainty, and not severity, of punishment is the chief deterrent for most crimes (1974). Homicide, however, is influenced by the severity of punishment, according to these findings. It is likely that we fail to deter many crimes because we are ethically opposed to taking the steps needed to substantially deter crime. The option of increasing the certainty of punishment implies serious sacrifices in our right to privacy, including increased reliance on electronic surveillance, secret police, and searches and seizures. Few would wish to increase the severity of punishment to the extent that might be needed to drastically curb crime—that is, not punishment that fits the crime, but rather punishment which far exceeds the severity of the crime committed.

Social Welfare Programs

Some authors stress that improved social welfare programs can diminish the degree of crime. If street crime is a product of blocked opportunities and relative deprivation, opening up opportunities and alleviating deprivation can reduce crime. For example, the President's Commission on Law Enforcement and Administration of Justice asserted (President's Commission, 1967b, p. 6):

> Warring on poverty, inadequate housing and unemployment, is warring on crime. A civil rights law is a law against crime. Money for schools is money against crime. Medical, psychiatric, and family-counseling services are services against crime. More broadly and most importantly every effort to improve life in America's "inner cities" is an effort against crime.

Such a claim is music to the ears of American liberals, who favor social welfare programs on purely ideological grounds. Liberals are highly equality-oriented. If social welfare programs also reduce crime, then so much the better. Yet, we lack any "hard" evidence supporting the claim that current programs—such as job training or food stamps—really have any impact on crime rates. To deal with the crime problem, Robert Trojanowicz and associates have called for stepped-up social welfare programs in the form of "community crime prevention." (1975, pp. 27–36, 162–164) This approach would involve community response teams composed of police officers and representatives of various community agencies (for example, Alcoholics Anonymous, crisis centers, drug centers, youth services, welfare, religious groups, and neighborhood representatives). These teams would respond to calls on a round-the-clock basis—much as the police do today. Their mission would be to deal with people's problems without invoking the criminal label. Trojanowicz contends that such a program can have an enormous effect, preventing crime by opening opportunities to people who have serious problems.

Gun Control

Gun control is often cited as a means of reducing the extent of violent crimes such as murder, assault, rape, and robbery (Dolan, 1978; Sheley, 1979, pp. 228–230; Cook, 1981). There are an estimated 150 million firearms in the

United States today, including about 25 million handguns. A 1975 FBI study found that two-thirds of the 20,510 people murdered that year were killed with a gun; 14,873 committed suicide with a gun; 2,700 died in gun accidents; and 200,000 were injured in gun-related accidents. Already some gun control laws are in operation in the United States. For example, some states require a permit to purchase a gun. Nationally, the Gun Control Act of 1968 set up regulations governing the manufacture, import, and sale of firearms. Harsh penalties may be imposed by the Bureau of Alcohol, Tobacco and Firearms for failing to register guns. Certain groups (for example, convicts, those indicted, fugitives from justice, drug users, mental defectives) are barred from buying, owning, or selling a gun. Gun control advocates believe that these laws are inadequate and seek far more stringent standards. At the same time, it should be noted that gun control advocates are not calling for confiscation of weapons but rather tighter regulations governing manufacture and purchase. In support of gun control, advocates note that foreign countries with gun control, such as Great Britain, have very few murders. Yet, opponents of gun control are concerned that people's right to bear arms ought not be abridged. Moreover, gun control opponents suggest that criminals will not abide by such legislation. (Hence, one popular bumper sticker reads: "If guns are outlawed, only outlaws will have guns.") It is likely that some violent crimes of passion would be prevented by stricter gun control laws. However, predatory violence by strangers probably would not diminish substantially as a result of the sort of gun controls that have been seriously considered.

Defensible Space

Increased crime will be produced if the physical design of residential areas encourages rather than inhibits the commission of crime. Oscar Newman, who developed the notion of "defensible space," calls for residential environments where the building layout and site plan encourage residents to play a primary role in ensuring their own security. Defensible space is of special importance because of the recent shift of crime from commercial to residential areas. The defensible space strategy seeks to deal with residential crime by releasing people's latent sense of territoriality and community. Newman argues: "It is possible, through physical design, to create a situation in which both inhabitant and stranger can perceive that a particular area is under the undisputed sphere of influence of a specific group of inhabitants." (1976, p. 5)[3]

Several design mechanisms are suggested by the notion of defensible space. First, different kinds of people must be assigned the specific residential environment they are best able to use and control. The most suitable type of environment will vary by age, lifestyle, socializing desires, background, income, and family structure. Second, buildings must be designed so as to sub-

[3]For a useful discussion of the limits to defensible space for crime prevention, see Sally E. Merry, "Defensible Space Undefended: Social Factors in Crime Control Through Environmental Design," *Urban Affairs Quarterly*, 1981, *16*, 397–422.

divide residential environments into zones. Through proper design the zones closest to or within the housing will come under the control of specific residents. Third, the housing must be positioned such that residents can look out of their windows to survey the area at all times. Fourth, the entries to the housing should be positioned along the city streets so as to incorporate the streets within the domain of the residential environment. Fifth, building forms and labels must not stigmatize or isolate the residents from the larger community.

Newman goes on to offer specific housing guidelines for different types of people (1972, pp. 193–195). For example, low-income families with children should not live in high-rise apartment buildings. Instead, such families ought to be housed in walk-up buildings which are no more than three stories tall. Entrances and interior corridors should be designed so that only a few families share a common lobby. Another set of guidelines is possible for the affluent. Affluent families who wish to live in apartments can hire a doorman and superintendent to oversee a single common entry and the building grounds. Finally, high-rise apartments for the elderly work well if the nonelderly are excluded and there is a single entry place with a tenant doorman and an alarm. It is incredible that so much housing continues to be built contrary to the principles of defensible space. While defensible space is only part of the solution to the crime problem, it does offer the prospect of a significant decline in residential crimes such as burglary, larceny, robbery, and even auto theft.

The Wright Explanation

A fundamental defect of most of the crime explanations we have touched upon is their limited scope. The diversity of criminal offenses makes it very difficult to produce a generalized theory of criminality. An interesting exception is a theory of crime formulated by Erik Olin Wright (1973, Ch. 1). Wright sees crime as a rational response to an individual's problems and options in life. According to Wright, social structure influences the pattern of crime in a society in three essential ways. First, social structure creates problems for people in various social positions. As Wright notes: "The problems which confront an individual are to a large extent the result of the society in which he lives and of his particular place in it." (1973, p. 7) Problems often focus on economic concerns. The consumption values of American society intensify many problems faced by individuals. Given the stress on consumption, many feel relatively deprived even if they do not suffer from abject poverty. Hence, the social structure induces embezzlement by a bank vice president as well as a liquor store robbery by a lower-class juvenile.

Second, the options which exist to deal with problems are also socially structured. As Wright points out: "The options available to a twenty-five-year-old unemployed black for solving his economic problems are more limited than those of a twenty-five-year-old wealthy doctor." (1973, p 8) The ghetto black may lack the opportunity to get a good paying job. Some options available to individuals are illegal. As with legal options, there is a close relationship between a person's social situation and the illegal options available to that person. Bank presidents never need consider the option of robbing a store or burglarizing a home. The options of embezzling cash or committing income tax evasion—not open to the poor, unemployed ghetto resident—are far more appealing. In general, the illegal options open to the poor are much more likely to involve violence. This suggests that the poor are not more innately violent than the affluent but are simply responding to the kinds of options the social structure has made available to them.

Finally, many factors are involved in the actual decision to choose an illegal option to deal with a problem. Four principal factors are the effectiveness of the crime for achieving personal goals, the risk involved, the ethical implications, and the intrinsic satisfaction provided by the crime. As to effectiveness, an illegal option may be the only viable alternative for dealing with a problem. However, most situations are more ambiguous. In some crimes the risk of being apprehended may play an important role. To be sure, some people are easily intimidated, while others are unrealistically undeterred. Yet, if we could increase the certainty of arrest, crime would probably be reduced somewhat.

Ethical implications are important to crime, since some believe it is immoral to break any law. Others feel that only certain crimes, such as murder or rape, are inherently immoral. Also, some may feel justified in committing a crime under certain circumstances (for example, stealing bread to feed a child). Lastly, an illegal option may be intrinsically satisfying. This is especially true in crimes without victims such as gambling or prostitution. Also, some may take pleasure in the excitement and challenge of street crimes such as theft, rackets, and drug pushing. To some extent government can alter an individual's perception of the costs and benefits of committing a crime. For example, it can open up more noncriminal opportunities, increase the risk of detection, and try to socialize people into believing that all lawbreaking is unethical.

To be sure, there are some problems with Wright's formulation of the causes of crime. For example, some criminal behavior may be basically irrational and due to psychological problems in the individual. Prominent examples may include rape, child molesting, and mass murders. Then too, some crimes may take place on impulse, without consideration of problems or options. Yet, as Wright suggests, most crime is probably as rational as the law-abiding efforts of people to deal with their personal problems. In support of this, we might note that nearly all crime is committed in the pursuit of property. Excluding robbery, only a small proportion of crimes involve violence or the threat of violence. Although refinements may be needed, Wright's formulation is clearly both a useful and general theory of the causes of crime.

CRIMINAL JUSTICE PROCESS

Courtroom Work Group

"Everyone has his or her day in court," according to popular mythology about the criminal justice process. When Americans think about their criminal justice system, they generally picture a trial setting where a prosecutor and defense attorney are combatants trying to persuade a judge and jury. Defendants are seen as protected by an "obstacle course" comprised of procedural safeguards (Packer, 1968, esp. Chaps. 8–12). The objective is to avoid ever convicting an individual for a crime he or she did not commit. Among these "due process" safeguards are a fair trial before a jury, the consideration of each case on its merits, a truly adversarial proceeding, and the right to call witnesses and confront adverse witnesses under strict rules of evidence. The "adversarial ideal" of criminal justice holds that the truth will emerge from a structured confrontation between the prosecution and defense.

The reality of the criminal justice process is quite different from the myth. In reality, there is far more administrative cooperation than adversarial conflict in most court proceedings. As Abraham Blumberg argues: "In the United States, the adversary system has always been an ideal; it has little if any validity." (1971, p. 74) Generally, a small group of the same people works together for several months or years. Regular participants in the criminal courtroom include judges, prosecutors, and defense counsel—as well as police officers, court clerks, bailiffs, psychiatrists, and probation officers (Eisenstein and Jacob, 1977; Jacob, 1978, pp. 173–181; Blumberg, 1967b). In time a certain cohesion develops among work group members. Standard operating procedures evolve for processing the common workload. Members of the work group increasingly come to know each other and the pressures they face. Work group members depend on one another. As a result, decisons and dispositions of cases become collective products. There is a spirit of bureaucratic cooperation rather than adversarial conflict. Few cases go to trial. Nearly all are dismissed or plea bargained.

It is the efficient processing of cases rather than the dispensing of justice that is the primary goal of a cohesive courtroom work group. The work group's formal leader is the judge, who has many formal powers. These include ruling on motions, ordering dismissals, determining guilt or innocence, and passing sentence. However, the judge does not completely dominate the work group. He or she does not select its other members, lacks detailed information about upcoming cases, and cannot control the defendant. Prosecutors also have important powers. It is the prosecutor who possesses most of the information about cases (for example, police reports, witness interviews, defendant's police record). Prosecutors decide whether to proceed with a case. They also decide the charges and the most appropriate penalty. Defense counsel may be either public defenders or private attorneys. Public defenders have a close, interdependent relationship with the prosecutor and judge. Given their large case-load, public defenders need the cooperation of the other work-group members to process cases efficiently. Rarely will a public defender insist on a trial for a client. Nonindigent defendants are represented by private attorneys. These private attorneys may be "regulars" or "occasionals" in a criminal court-room. Like public defenders, regulars become part of the courtroom work group. As we might expect, regulars are far less likely than occasionals to insist on a trial to dispose of a case.

Screening and Filtering

From arrest to infliction of penalty, there are many possible stages to a criminal case. These stages are noted in Figure 7-1. Misdemeanors, which are less serious offenses, are dealt with in special misdemeanor courts. Examples of such cases included drunkenness, disorderly conduct, vagrancy, prostitu-tion, petty theft, littering, simple assault, disturbing the peace, and traffic offenses (Eisenstein, 1973, pp. 121-122). Misdemeanor courtrooms are crowded, noisy, and hurried. Commonly, defendants are not informed of their rights or even told what is going on. They are unrepresented by counsel or receive only perfunctory representation. Shortcuts are necessary, given the enormous caseload which must be processed. As James Eisenstein points out: "In a sense, these judges are victims of circumstance. Given the work load, time constraints, and resources made available to them, there may be little else they could do no matter how noble their intentions." (1973, p. 129)

Misdemeanor courtrooms also do the preliminary work for felonies, which are more serious cases, generally punishable by a year or more in prison (Jacob, 1978, p. 173). Felony cases may include numerous stages such as arrest by the police, bond setting, arraignment, preliminary hearing, grand jury in-dictment, trial court arraignment, plea or trial, and sentencing. At any point a dismissal or acquittal may occur, returning the accused to full freedom.

Members of the courtroom work group engage in a process of screening and filtering. As a result of their discretion in dealing with cases, few of those who are arrested actually are sentenced or imprisoned. As Joseph Sheley notes: "The key to understanding the filtering effect of the criminal justice system is understanding the *discretion* inherent in the system—the ability to choose one option from among more than one in dealing with a situation or case." (1979, p. 166; McCaghy, 1980, pp. 42-44) As depicted in Figure 7-2, many cases evaporate between crime and punishment. For every 635 robberies oc-curring in Washington, D.C., only an estimated 400 are reported. In only 100 of these is an arrest made. Nearly two-thirds of these cases are not fully pros-ecuted or are dismissed by a judge. Some 26 of the 36 going to court are dealt with through plea bargaining, while in only 10 cases does a trial occur. A full 33 of the 36 defendants are found guilty, but many are fined or placed on probation. Thus, we are faced with the startling fact that for every 635 rob-

A general view of The Criminal Justice System

This chart seeks to present a simple yet comprehensive view of the movement of cases through the criminal justice system. Procedures in individual jurisdictions may vary from the pattern shown here. The differing weights of line indicate the relative volumes of cases disposed of at various points in the system, but this is only suggestive since no nationwide data of this sort exists.

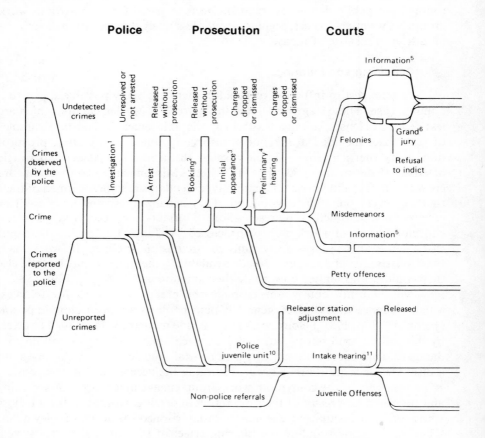

Police   **Prosecution**   **Courts**

1 May continue until trial.

2 Administrative record of arrest first stage at which temporary release on bail may be available.

3 Before magistrate, commissioner, or justice of peace, formal notice of charge, advice of rights, Budget Summary trials for party offenses usually conducted here without further processing.

4 Preliminary testing of evidence against defendent. Charge may be reduced. No separate preliminary hearing for misdemeanors in some systems.

5 Charge filed by prosecutor on basis of information submitted by police or citizens. Alternative to grand jury indictment often used in felonies, almost always in misdemeanors.

6 Reviews whether government evidence sufficient to justify trial. Some states have no grand jury system, others seldom use it.

Corrections

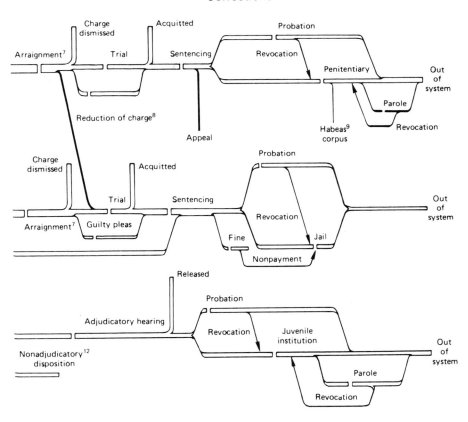

7 Appearance for plea. Defendent
   elects trial by judge or jury. If
   available counsel for indigent
   usually appointed here in felonies. Often not at all in other cases.

8 Charge may be reduced at any
   time prior to trial in return for
   plea of guilty or for other
   reasons.

9 Challenge on constitutional
   grounds to legality of detention. May be sought at any
   point in process.

10 Police often hold informal
   hearings, dismiss or adjust
   many cases without further
   processing.

11 Probation officer decides
   desirability of further court
   action.

12 Welfare agency, social services,
   counseling, medical care, etc.,
   for cases where judiciary
   handling not needed.

Source: President's Commission on Law Enforcement and Administration of Justice, *The Challenge
of Crime in a Free Society* (Washington, D.C.: U.S. Government Printing Office, 1967), pp. 8-9.

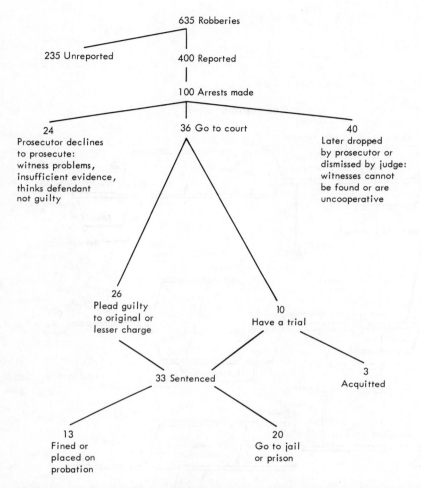

635 Robberies

235 Unreported   400 Reported

100 Arrests made

24
Prosecutor declines
to prosecute:
witness problems,
insufficient evidence,
thinks defendant
not guilty

36 Go to court

40
Later dropped
by prosecutor or
dismissed by judge:
witnesses cannot
be found or are
uncooperative

26
Plead guilty
to original or
lesser charge

10
Have a trial

33 Sentenced

3
Acquitted

13
Fined or
placed on
probation

20
Go to jail
or prison

FIGURE 7-2 **Estimations of Case Dispositions for Every 635 Robberies in Washington, D.C.**

From Charles H. McCaghy, *Crime in American Society* (New York: Macmillan, 1980), p. 43. Derived from National Criminal Justice Information and Statistics Service, *Criminal Victimization Surveys in 13 American Cities* (Washington, D.C.: U.S. Department of Justice, 1975), p. 250; and "'Revolving Door Justice' : Why Criminals Go Free," *U.S. News and World Report* (May 10, 1976), pp. 36–40.

beries only 33 individuals are sentenced and only 20 persons go to jail or prison.[4]

The evaporation of cases through the criminal justice process is rather disturbing. Such evidence makes the criminal justice system seem like the epitome of ineffectiveness. As James Eisenstein observes: "The extensive screening out that occurs is a far cry from the naive view that people committing

---

[4]Note that these 33 persons undoubtedly accounted for more than 33 robberies.

violations are typically arrested, tried, and imprisoned." (Eisenstein, 1973, p. 233) However, it is not clear that we should fault the criminal justice system for the serious deterioration of cases in the course of the process. Some point an accusatory finger at factors such as court congestion, the laxity of judges and prosecutors, or the understaffing of the criminal justice system. However, a study by the Vera Institute suggests that much of the fault for caseload deterioration is unrelated to any defects in the criminal justice system (1977). Much deterioration occurs because of the cases themselves. A prime factor is that the complainant knows the defendant and decides at some point not to cooperate with the prosecution. Beyond that, many other cases are dismissed because the defendant has no prior record. Thus, attrition of suspects during the course of the criminal justice process seems to be less of a problem than finding likely suspects for crimes that have taken place.

Due Process

When analyzing the criminal justice system, a primary concern is whether defendants are dealt with fairly. An important concept in criminal justice is that of "due process." The notion of due process relates to the procedures used by the criminal justice system. As Abraham Blumberg notes, due process "refers simply to the application of 'just' legal norms in the resolution of controversies between individuals and between the individual and the state, in a 'fair' and 'reasonable' manner." (1967b, p. 15) In short, due process demands that "fair" procedures be followed by the criminal justice system. The due process model contains a series of checkpoints designed to curb the state. The purpose of these checkpoints is to try to minimize the chances that an individual is punished for a crime he or she did not commit.

It is difficult to generate a comprehensive list of due process requirements. To begin with, many due process norms are vague. It is not always clear what due process requires in individual cases. In addition, due process norms regularly shift. Every year, in its written opinions on cases, the Supreme Court reinterprets some key aspects of due process, making the requirements looser or more rigid. Even so, it will be instructive to cite, at a general level, some twenty-two norms which are a part of the notion of due process (Casper, 1972b; Blumberg, 1967b). These rights include:

1. Definiteness of penal statutes and codes
2. Protection against police coercion
3. Protection of individual privacy
4. Protection from illegal searches and seizures
5. Representation by the counsel of one's choice
6. Presumption of innocence of the accused until proved guilty beyond a "reasonable doubt"

7. No discrimination based on "irrelevant" characteristics such as race, sex, and income
8. Notice of the specific charge
9. A preliminary hearing
10. Speedy arraignment so that charges may be reviewed to determine their propriety
11. Right to a reasonable bail
12. Indictment by a grand jury
13. Right to an impartial judge
14. No person acting simultaneously as prosecutor, judge, and jury
15. Open, public proceedings
16. Trial by an impartial jury of one's peers
17. The right to call witnesses
18. Privilege against self-incrimination
19. Confrontation by one's accusers
20. Any plea bargaining conducted freely and willingly
21. Protection against double jeopardy
22. Protection against cruel and unusual punishment

The specific requirements of these standards varies over time. (See Chapter Eight for Supreme Court decisions regarding due process.) Moreover, these norms—if they are to be more than mere words on paper—depend upon compliance by the members of the criminal justice system. This compliance may be voluntary, or it may occur at the urging of the accused and his or her lawyer. For those who value procedural justice and individual liberty, close adherence to the rules of due process is a special concern. Nevertheless, many of these standards are commonly abridged by the criminal justice system.

Bail

Bail is a sort of ransom in that the accused supposedly puts up a sum of money that can be forfeited for failure to appear for trial (Eisenstein, 1973, p. 234; Freed and Wald, 1964). Obviously, bail is extremely important to those accused of more serious crimes. It determines whether defendants spend their time awaiting disposition at liberty or confined in a pretrial detention facility. Formally, bail is set by the judge, although in many jurisdictions this responsibility is actually delegated to the prosecutor or arresting officer. In theory, the only criterion entering into the level of bail is supposed to be the amount needed to ensure that the accused will appear at future proceedings. This would seem to be most closely associated with the strength of the accused's ties to the community. In practice, bail is often set according to the seriousness of the offense and the prior record of the accused. However, these criteria are not closely related to the probability that the accused will subsequently appear in court. The result of restrictive bail policies is that some people who would appear for disposition of their case are nevertheless detained in jail. Some of these people are innocent of the charges against them.

Those who are not poor can almost always afford bail. As a result, they remain free throughout the time of disposition of their case. Yet, many disadvantaged defendants have traditionally been denied release because they are too poor to pay the level of bail that has been set. For those who are poor, bail bondsmen, in effect, hold the keys to the jailhouse. Bondsmen are private entrepreneurs who may offer to post bail in return for a fee of about 10 percent. They have enormous discretion in their activities. Ironically, while courts have often ignored the likelihood of appearance when setting bail, this is the major factor considered by bondsmen in deciding whether to post bail. Since the fees of the bondsmen are based on the amount of bail, there are some suspects who are offered bail but cannot afford the bondsmen's services.

As a result, there are large numbers of people who have not been found guilty of any crime yet are incarcerated while awaiting trial. Some of these people spend a substantial amount of time in jail, only to have the charges dismissed later. Even more disturbing is the fact that pretrial detention appears to increase one's chances of conviction and further imprisonment (Wald, 1964). This is true because individuals at liberty are more readily available to their lawyers, can locate witnesses and evidence, and can persuade witnesses to testify. Not surprisingly, therefore, pretrial detention has been seen by some as a serious inequity.

To deal with the problem of pretrial detention, the Manhattan Bail Project was initiated in 1961 by the Vera Foundation (Ares, Rankin, and Sturz, 1963). The purpose of this social experiment was to determine whether a substantial number of poor people can be successfully released on their own recognizance pending trial. The hypothesis of the experiment was that defendants with strong community roots could be released without posting any bail. Staff members interviewed defendants to determine whether or not to recommend that they be given a pretrial release. Questions were asked concerning employment history, family roots, residential ties, references from the community, current charges, previous record, and other factors. In the first year of operation only 3 of 250 defendants jumped pretrial release. This is actually a lower rate than that for those who had been released on bail. Charles Ares and associates conclude: "Available evidence at least suggests that the financial deterrent to flight has been overrated and that other factors—ties to the community—are really the effective deterrents." (1963, p. 90) Ares further suggests that those not qualifying for wholesale release be permitted liberty during the day but be required to return to detention at night. Others might gain pretrial release conditioned on strict supervision by the probation department. As a result of the Manhattan Bail Project, far more defendants are now released on their own recognizance pending disposition of their cases.

Plea Bargaining

Media accounts of the criminal justice system tend to emphasize the jury trial and the due process requirements articulated by the Supreme Court. Such a view of the criminal justice system is highly distorted. To be sure, the courts do conduct trials, many of them with juries, where possible due process violations are challenged by defense counsel. Yet, such cases are the exception rather than the rule. Like much of American society, contemporary criminal courts have come to be dominated by bureaucratic decision making. Faced with intense pressures to process a large number of cases, the criminal courts secure some 90 percent of convictions through plea bargaining. In plea bargaining, the defendant—often on the advice of counsel—pleads guilty in return for reduced charges, the dropping of some charges, or a promise of a lenient sentence. While due process demands a presumption of innocence, the bureaucratic justice embodied in plea bargaining invokes a presumption of guilt. In this regard Herbert Packer notes: "Once a man has been arrested and investigated without being found to be probably innocent, . . . then all subsequent activity directed toward him is based on the view that he is probably guilty." (1968, p. 160) While courts are supposed to dispense justice, the primary goal of plea bargaining is the quick, efficient processing of cases.[5] Packer observes: "The image that comes to mind is an assembly-line conveyor belt down which moves an endless stream of cases, never stopping, carrying the cases to workers who stand at fixed stations and who perform on each case. . . ." (1968, p. 159)

This is not to suggest that the criminal justice system operates in a random or haphazard manner. Certainly, those involved in the criminal justice process make some effort to dispense justice. In trying to be efficient, however, the criminal justice process is "telescoped" by its participants. Many shortcuts are made and, in the process, some defendants may suffer unjustly. Based upon his investigation, W. Boyd Littrell concludes that several factors enter into the process of plea bargaining (1979). A key factor is the seriousness with which officials view the action of the defendant. Officials perceive violence or the threat of violence as being most serious. Defendants guilty of such behavior are likely to be dealt with harshly. Second, officials also consider the degree to which the defendant may be sinister in character. The "really bad guy" receives a more severe penalty than the "basically good guy in trouble."

Third, insofar as their bureaucratic procedures permit, officials also attempt to fit the penalty to the crime. There is an effort among criminal justice personnel to evaluate how much time the defendant should serve for the action committed. Fourth, there is a presumption of guilt rather than of innocence.

---

[5]Some who have studied plea bargaining stress that sincere efforts are made within the bargaining process to ensure just results. See David W. Neubauer, *Criminal Justice in Middle America* (Morristown, N.J.: General Learning Press, 1974); Arthur Rosett and Donald R. Cressey, *Justice By Consent* (Philadelphia: Lippincott, 1976).

Criminal justice personnel are rather confident that the fact-finding activities of the early stages have sorted out the guilty from the innocent. In the course of bargaining, officials select the crime which would, in all probability, effect a fair punishment for the defendant's actions. Surely, it is true that most of those charged with a crime really did commit the offense. Yet, a minority of innocent people may get caught up in this "telescoped" system of justice with no reasonable escape other than pleading guilty to a lesser offense.

There is an enormous literature on plea bargaining, with both supporters and detractors. Several justifications for plea bargaining have been offered (President's Commission, 1967b, p. 135). To begin with, it is argued that if most defendants were to go to trial, the criminal justice system would be unable to handle the immensely increased demands for court time. Second, supporters of plea bargaining note that the system would feel enormous strain even if court personnel could be increased. It is said, therefore, that the system would produce an inferior quality of justice if most cases went to trial. Third, some suggest that if the facts of a crime are uncontested, a trial is an exceedingly cumbersome and time-consuming process. Fourth, defendants are said actually to benefit from plea bargaining because the procedure eliminates the possibility of losing a case entirely. Finally, supporters argue that truly innocent defendants would find it more difficult to prove their innocence if all cases were brought to trial. The idea here is that if trials were used in all cases, judges would be more skeptical of defendants than they are now.

At the same time, many criticisms have been leveled against plea bargaining (President's Commission, 1967b, p. 135; Eisenstein, 1973, pp. 118, 243). For example, it is noted that the primary aims of plea bargaining are expediency, economy, and efficiency. It is feared that in the process of trying to achieve these goals, justice suffers. Second, critics point out that the plea closes a case to any kind of judicial review. As a result, the defendant loses the opportunity to be vindicated, and all types of possible illegalities in law enforcement and court practices are concealed. Indeed, prosecutors may offer defendants especially attractive bargains to avoid public exposure of damaging or embarrassing information. Third, there is no guarantee that the "bargain" agreed to by prosecutor and defense will be implemented by the judge. After a defendant has entered a plea of guilty, the judge may sentence the defendant to a harsher penalty than that agreed upon. Fourth, the process induces the defendant to plead guilty to a lesser charge and forfeit the right to a trial.

Theoretically, guilty pleas should be made voluntarily and without any promises made to induce them (*Brady v. United States; McMann v. Richardson; Parker v. North Carolina*).[6] Instead, there is only the facade of freely made guilty pleas. Typically, the defendant has been overcharged by the police

---

[6]In the *Brady* case, while the Court ruled against Brady, it did argue: "Of course, the agents of the State may not produce a plea by actual or threatened physical harm or by mental coercion overbearing the will of the defendant." (at 750) However, the Court has not recognized overcharging as a form of subtle coercion.

and prosecutor for the unlawful act supposedly committed. The overcharging is a form of subtle intimidation to induce a guilty plea. Finally, it has also been suggested that overburdened prosecutors may relieve their workload by offering excessively lenient bargains in some cases. Considerations of justice may be overwhelmed by the need to manage the caseload.

Despite its shortcomings, plea bargaining may be with us for many years to come.[7] Plea bargaining meets four significant needs of the criminal justice system (Eisenstein, 1973, p. 110; Littrell, 1979, p. 214). First, it is efficient enough to dispose of all cases with current resources. Second, it gives the appearance of meeting all the due process tenets. Third, the state may get a bargain on weak cases.[8] Finally, it permits both prosecutors and defense counsel to satisfy the demands placed on them. Plea bargaining is seen as a welcome necessity by judges, prosecutors, and defense attorneys. Judges gain a relatively current docket while formally meeting due process requirements. Prosecutors gain some easy convictions, albeit with fewer and reduced charges. Defense attorneys get cases processed quickly and can use the concessions won through plea bargaining to help in client control. Meanwhile, defendants may gain little from plea bargaining. The evidence from some cities indicates that those who plea bargain do not receive significantly lower sentences than those who go to trial (Eisenstein and Jacob, 1977, p. 277, 283).[9] Evidently, in some cities defendants are being misled into believing that their guilty plea will give them a lighter sentence. In other cities genuine "bribes" in the form of lower sentences may be offered to induce a guilty plea.

Still, some critics have not given up the hope of reducing or even eliminating the practice of plea bargaining. Herbert Packer suggests two reforms to move away from plea bargaining and toward the due process model (1968). According to Packer, we need more resources put into the operation of the criminal justice process (for example, police officers, prosecutors, judges, public defenders, and other supporting services). In addition, we need to reduce the uses of the criminal sanction, perhaps decriminalizing victimless crimes and some other offenses. By focusing more resources on a narrower

[7]On the difficulties of eliminating plea bargaining see Howard C. Daudistel, "On the Elimination of Plea-Bargaining: The El Paso Experiment," William F. McDonald and James A. Cramer, ed., *Plea-Bargaining* (Lexington, Mass.: Lexington Books-Heath, 1980). However, see also Michael L. Rubinstein and Teresa J. White, "Alaska's Ban on Plea-Bargaining."

[8]However, for evidence that prosecutors do not engage in unethical bluffing when they have no case against a defendant, see William F. McDonald, James A. Cramer, and Henry H. Rossman, "Prosecutorial Bluffing and the Case Against Plea-Bargaining," William F. McDonald and James A. Cramer, ed., *Plea-Bargaining* (Lexington, Mass.: Lexington Books-Heath, 1980).

[9]However, see also David Brereton and Jonathan D. Casper, "Does It Pay to Plead Guilty?: Differential Sentencing and the Functioning of Criminal Courts," *Law and Society Review,* 1981–1982, *16,* 45–70; Thomas M. Uhlman and N. Darlene Walker, "'He Takes Some of My Time; I Take Some of His': An Analysis of Judicial Sentencing Patterns in Jury Cases," *Law and Society Review,* 1980, *14,* 323–341.

range of crimes, the full-dress adversary system could be employed more regularly. Even so, it is unlikely that tinkering with the current system will permit us to eliminate plea bargaining. With current caseloads even a 10 percent increase in jury trials would require nearly twice as many judges, prosecutors, defense counsel, and courtrooms (Jacob, 1978, p. 191). An alternative suggested by Jack Douglas is the abandonment of the current system in favor of a system of administrative justice (1971, pp. 20–22). Under this scheme guilt and sentencing decisions would be made by a board of jurists who would hear all the evidence and reach collective judgments.

Juvenile Justice

The juvenile justice system has a critical impact upon a large number of young people (Eisenstein, 1973, pp. 247–250). One out of four nontraffic arrests involve juveniles. This means that nearly two million youths are arrested annually. Each year nearly one million young people appear in juvenile court to face charges. A significant portion of appearances are for nonadult offenses such as drinking, curfew violations, truancy, and running away. Many other juveniles, however, are accused of adult offenses such as auto theft, robbery, and burglary. The key question in the history of juvenile justice in the United States has been whether juvenile offenders ought to be treated like adults or given special treatment to facilitate their rehabilitation (Leepson, 1979). As late as the Industrial Revolution, children past infancy were treated as little adults. However, the concept of juvenile delinquency began to emerge in the 1800s. Increasingly, the concern was for reforming and rehabilitating youths rather than for deterring and punishing them.

The juvenile justice system was established to protect youths who break the law. Unlike adult courts juvenile courts are supposed to be treatment-oriented. The typical disposition in delinquency cases is probation. However, a significant number of youths are sent to juvenile homes, which have an average daily attendance of nearly 63,000. Despite the lofty goals of the juvenile justice system, a key missing element has been constitutional due process of law (Leepson, 1979, p. 551). Commonly, juvenile suspects were not given notice of the charges against them, did not have a right to legal counsel, could not refuse to testify, and could not cross-examine witnesses or challenge evidence. The Supreme Court sought to rectify this situation with its 1967 decision *In re Gault.* Here the Court ruled that due process must be provided in juvenile cases.

Still, the controversy over how to deal with juvenile offenders continues (Leepson, 1979, pp. 553–554). The goal of rehabilitation was stressed in the Juvenile Justice and Delinquency Act (PL 93–415) passed by Congress in 1974. Federal grants were provided to improve state juvenile justice systems. The program stressed diversion of juveniles from criminal incarceration to less severe forms of supervision such as halfway houses. The law also provided funds to assist states in providing shelter, counseling, and medical services to run-away children, truants, and uncontrollable children. These federal grants served as a catalyst for changing the circumstances under which juveniles are incarcerated. While the success of rehabilitation programs is questionable, the evidence suggests that more punitive handling of juveniles is no more effective than diverting juveniles from the criminal justice system (Clarke, 1974). Some theorists note that most children engage in delinquent actions at one time or another. They suggest, however, that those labeled as delinquent are likely to alter their behavior to conform with their new status and self-image, that is, "no good." If this theory is correct, then in diverting juveniles from the criminal justice system, we may be following the least destructive policy for dealing with their offenses.

PENAL JUSTICE

Penal justice involves the application of some form of punishment to those convicted of a crime (Wright, 1973, Ch. 2; van den Haag, 1975). In the course of human history a variety of sanctions have been applied against criminal offenders. These sanctions include fines, pillory, flogging, mutilation, and the death penalty. Even for an identical violation of the law, penalties have varied enormously. For example, in medieval Europe a traditional punishment for theft was public amputation of the thief's right hand. Today corporal punishment is regarded as inhumane. It is now common to deal with serious violations through a prison sentence. Yet, it can be debated whether the loss of a right hand through corporal punishment is truly any more harsh than the loss of ten years of liberty through imprisonment. Perhaps penal justice in America has been too unimaginative in the kinds of penalties imposed. For example, in China today theft is generally punished by placing the thief under community surveillance. While this specific penalty may be impractical in our own society, there ought to be some methods of penal justice which are equitable and yet not as disruptive of an individual's everyday life as is prison.

Justification

The subject of penal justice is suffering from something of an intellectual crisis. Having convicted someone of a crime, we are at a loss as to what to do with that individual. Some wish to take vengeance against the offender. Others would prefer rehabilitation. Still others have different ideas. Somehow, civil justice is more easily rationalized than criminal justice. In a civil case injured parties bring suit against the parties who have violated their rights. The goal of the proceedings is clear-cut, generally involving some kind of money for restitution. In a criminal case, however, it is government rather than the victim who brings suit. The goals of government in taking the action are murky. Rarely is restitution for the victim sought. Rather, a defendant who is found guilty is simply penalized in some way. However, our reasons for imposing this penalty are shrouded in mystery. In fact, six possible goals for penal justice have been identified—retribution, rehabilitation, incapacitation, deterrence, restitution, and reintegration (Leiser, 1979, Ch. 7; Holten and Jones, 1978, pp. 317–325). At this juncture there is no consensus as to the proper goal(s) of penal justice in America.

Retribution proclaims: "Let us inflict punishment on offenders to match the injuries which they have caused the victims." By exacting retribution, government acts as the agent of vengeance for the victim and society. In a more positive sense, government ensures through retribution that the seriousness of the crime will be matched by the severity of the punishment. The terminology of punishment is filled with references to retribution. For example, it is said that individuals who have committed a crime must "pay their debt to society" and that "the punishment must fit the crime." Punishment is essentially "a deprivation, or suffering, imposed by law." (van den Haag, 1975, p. 8) People regard crime as an affront to society. Acting through government, society may seek vengeance on the violator of the law. As Ernest van den Haag has said, punishment "vindicates the social order by branding crime as antisocial, the criminal as outcast. The moral solidarity of those who live within the law is reaffirmed by casting out those who break it." (1975, p. 63) By placing criminals in prison, we curtail their liberty, expose them to prison conditions, and stigmatize them for life. However, while prison imposes great hardships on the prison population, it does so only at an enormous expense to society. Moreover, some reformers have sought to direct society away from the quest for retribution.

Rehabilitation proclaims: "Let us apply a treatment to offenders to cure them of the desire to break the law." The rehabilitation model sees criminals as sick or maladjusted rather than evil (Allen, 1959; Wright, 1973, Ch. 3). Given accurate diagnosis and appropriate therapy, the criminal would be cured. The rehabilitation model came into vogue at the turn of the century and had a resurgence in the late 1950s. With rehabilitation, the terminology of punishment was changed. Prisons became "correctional facilities," while guards became "correctional officers" or "counselors." Various educational, vocational, religious, and counseling services were instituted as tools of rehabilitation. Also, fixed sentences were replaced by the indeterminate sentence: Prisoners would be released as soon as they were "cured."

Nevertheless, most experts consider in-prison treatment to be a failure. Some feel that this failure is due to a lack of adequate effort, given that rehabilitation programs are severely underfinanced (Schnur, 1958). Others call for wholesale changes in the rehabilitation approach, including the use of brainwashing techniques. James McConnell argues: "I believe that the day has come when we can combine sensory deprivation with drugs, hypnosis and astute manipulation of reward and punishment to gain almost absolute control over an individual's behavior.'' McConnell would have us use this control "to make dramatic changes in a person's behavior and personality.'' (1970, p. 74) There is some question as to the effectiveness and propriety of such an approach. The rehabilitation strategy is grounded on the faith that criminals are sick. Yet, crime is often a rational act committed in pursuit of economic gain. In these cases therapy would have questionable value. Moreover, McConnell's suggestions seem sorely at odds with our notions of individual liberty. We might wonder whether we really want the American government to be in the business of using psychotherapy and brainwashing on those who commit burglary (or income tax evasion).

Incapacitation proclaims: "Let us confine offenders so that it is impossible for them to commit more crimes in the community.'' When someone is a threat to a community, its members feel that they have a right to protect themselves from that person. Clearly, a person who is locked in prison cannot victimize those outside. Although it is a difficult task, David Greenberg attempted to determine empirically the amount of serious crime prevented by prisons today (1975). He found that no more than 8 percent of the total crime rate is prevented through the physical restraint of the present prison population. If we were to increase the average sentence by one year to a term of three years of prison, the crime rate would drop another 4 percent. While this is some gain, it is probably less than most people would expect. Greenberg's findings call into question the utility of making increased use of prison for purposes of incapacitation. Given the costs of incapacitation, the gains are problematic.

The incapacitative effect of prison is especially limited by three factors cited by Greenberg. First, it is very difficult for correctional officers to predict which inmates are likely to commit violent crimes in the future and therefore should be incapacitated. Among inmates there is little relationship between past commission of a violent crime and commission of another such crime after being released (Greenberg, 1975, p. 543). Second, the rate of return to serious crime by parolees is relatively low. Recidivism of parolees is high, but much of this is due to technical violations of parole regulations (Greenberg, 1975, p. 572). This suggests that by the time they are sent to prison, most criminals are already nearing the end of their crime career. Finally, the rate of imprisonment for serious crimes is fairly low (Greenberg, 1975, p. 572). This reflects (1) the low rates for apprehending culprits of crime; (2) prosecutorial discretion to drop charges or reduce them to misdemeanors; and (3) judicial reluctance to impose prison sentences, particularly for juvenile defendants. Incapacitation could make a more substantial dent in crime rates if we "throw away the key" and confine those imprisoned for life terms. However, this would greatly expand the prison population and mean extended confinement for those convicted of less serious crimes. There is also the possibility that if more people were placed in prison, other members of the general population would decide to take advantage of opportunities to commit crimes.

The application of the incapacitation approach to penal justice produces some ironic policy implications. Essentially, meeting the goal of incapacitation does not always square with our sense of "just dessert." For example, a ghetto youth who robs a liquor store is probably far more likely to commit another crime than the jealous husband who murders his unfaithful wife in a moment of anger. Does this mean that the person who took someone's property should get a longer prison sentence than the person who took someone's life? If the goal of penal justice we accept is incapacitation of likely recidivists, the answer would appear to be in the affirmative. Yet, there are those who would question the equity of a system of penal justice that imposed a less severe penalty for a more serious crime simply because an expert believes the offender is unlikely to commit additional offenses.

Deterrence proclaims: "Let us punish the offenders such that they will not commit another crime and so that other possible violators will be persuaded not to break the law." Deterrence theory suggests that if people hear of penalties inflicted on lawbreakers, or if they themselves are once punished for an offense, they will be persuaded not to risk similar penalties by breaking the law. Discussions of deterrence focus on the certainty and severity of punishment. Presumably, people are more likely to park their cars illegally if the risk of punishment is 1 in 1,000 rather than 1 in 10. Likewise, people will be more likely to park illegally if the fine imposed is only $1 rather than $1,000. As Robert Martinson notes: "It is possible that there is indeed something that works . . . something that deters rather than cures, something that does not so much reform convicted offenders as prevent criminal behavior in the first place." (1974) There is some evidence suggesting that the certainty of punishment is a more effective deterrent than the severity of punishment. If so, a mild fine imposed universally on all criminal activities would be more effective than even the death penalty if the latter is imposed on only a handful of violators. However, a basic problem, as identified earlier, is how to increase the certainty of punishment without creating a police state atmosphere.

Restitution proclaims: "Let us force offenders to repay the victims for the injuries suffered." While restitution is not a primary goal of penal justice today, many reformers would like it moved to the forefront (Barnett, 1977). Restitution focuses narrowly on the individual who has been victimized. The offender is obligated to make restitution to the victim, under court order. This carries us away from the notion that it is society, rather than a specific victim, who has been offended by the commission of a crime. Currently, restitution is rarely imposed upon offenders in sentencing by a judge. Occasional exceptions are largely for minor offenses such as passing worthless checks, minor property offenses, and vandalism by juveniles. A serious complication is that many offenders are poor and lack the means to pay damages. Obviously, the more serious the offense, the more difficult it will be to make restitution. Yet, if restitution is narrowly confined to cases having small losses, we have the paradoxical result of compensating only those victims who have been hurt least. Moreover, there are times when our sense of justice would be violated if restitution were the only goal of penal justice. If a bank robber is captured but returns the stolen funds, should that be the end of the matter? And what payment would be adequate restitution to a rape victim or surviving family members in a murder case? Still, this leaves open the possibility of including restitution as one of several goals of the penal justice system. At the same time, however, if restitution is most attractive for minor offenses, perhaps these offenses ought to be decriminalized and treated as torts.

Reintegration proclaims: "Let us ensure that an individual will have a successful return to society." Many reformers would like the penal justice system to focus on reintegration as the fundamental feature (Holten and Jones, 1978, p. 325). It is largely because of the failure of rehabilitation that reintegration has emerged as a possible function of penal justice. According to reintegrationists, the rehabilitation rationale falsely assumes that offenders are sick and need to be cured by the application of some treatment. Advocates of reintegration see the basic problem as one of the relationship between society and the offender. Reintegration involves dealing not only with the problems of offenders (for example, lack of job skills) but also with the problems of people on the outside (for example, prejudice against convicts). It generally involves a phased reentry of offenders into society. The reintegration rationale is most consistent with the use of alternatives to prison confinement, such as furloughs and work releases. There is an effort in reintegration to ensure that offenders will establish and maintain ties with the community at large.

Methods of Punishment

Prison   Sing Sing, Soledad, and San Quentin have never been confused with Disneyland, Disneyworld, or Darien Lake Fun Country. Prison is a very painful experience, involving a number of serious deprivations (Sykes, 1958). Most obviously, prisoners suffer a loss of liberty. They are confined to a few acres and their freedom of movement within prison grounds is seriously restricted. The loss of liberty also entails an involuntary seclusion from family, relatives, and friends—with all the loneliness and boredom which that represents. In addition, prison involves a deprivation of goods and services. The basic material needs of prisoners—such as food, shelter, and heat—are met, but the standard of living in prison is hopelessly monotonous.

In most prisons inmates are deprived of regular heterosexual relationships. When prisoners do see their spouses or intimate friends, it may be from separate sides of a plate glass window, communicating by phone, under the scrutiny of a guard. This atmosphere of involuntary celibacy often produces severe frustration, self-doubts, and homosexual attacks. Loss of personal autonomy is another deprivation associated with imprisonment. Prison inmates must abide by an elaborate system of rules established by their captors. These rules are not consented to but rather are imposed upon inmates. Moreover, some of the rules—such as the one forbidding inmates to take food from the mess hall to their cells—often seem very arbitrary to the prisoner. Finally, prison also deprives inmates of a sense of security. As one inmate of the New Jersey State Prison commented: "The worst thing about prison is you have to live with other prisoners." (Sykes, 1958, p. 77) Clearly, even the hardened criminal may feel very anxious about being in close daily contact with large numbers of people who have a long history of violent, aggressive behavior.

Many of the pains of imprisonment have been exacerbated by the problem of overcrowding. Large numbers of Americans are experiencing the pains of imprisonment. For every 1,000 civilians in America, there are 1.2 people in prison (U.S. Bureau of the Census, 1978, Table 328, p. 197). From 1950 to 1976 the number of prisoners increased from 166,123 to 263,291. The mounting prison population has led to a deterioration of living conditions at some institutions. Overcrowding is a complaint expressed by many inmates. While some call for construction of more prisons and others suggest reduced reliance on the prison sentence (or shorter sentences), the "double celling" of inmates is a common response today. In *Rhodes v. Chapman,* decided in 1981, the Supreme Court refused to characterize "double celling" in the Southern Ohio Correctional Facility as "cruel and unusual punishment," in violation of the Eighth Amendment. The effect of the decision, unless reversed, would be to give states greater leeway in dealing with (or not dealing with) the problem of prison overcrowding.

Those concerned with social equality have pointed to a deeper problem with prisons in America. It is noted that prisons in the United States are used disproportionately to punish crimes committed by poor people (Wright, 1973, pp. 25–26). Although only 17 percent of the total labor force are manual laborers or service workers, 43 percent of the prison population comes from these occupations. This is in spite of the fact that the crimes committed by the affluent pose a far greater economic cost to the nation. The offenses of the affluent are generally dealt with less harshly, rarely involving use of a prison sentence. When an affluent person is sent to prison, it is more likely to be a minimum security facility, where living conditions are more tolerable. Jack Douglas concludes: "Imprisonment creates a thorough sense of injustice because it is invoked erratically, arbitrarily, and unfairly. Imprisonment is the most depersonalizing, dehumanizing, and cruel practice in our society." (1971, p. 40)

The extent to which the federal government and the states will continue to rely upon prisons in the years to come is uncertain. Some forces in society have called for greater use of alternatives to prison. At the same time, other forces call for large social investments to construct new prison facilities that will house an even larger population of criminal offenders. Still others suggest a wholesale change in the nature of prisons and the prison experience. The "prison of the future" identified by Daniel Glaser would house fewer than 100 inmates (Glaser, 1970). It would try to lead offenders to identify with anticriminal individuals and make it more likely that released prisoners would be satisfied with legitimate postrelease activities. Glaser suggests that in the future, prisons will be located in metropolitan areas. This will enable prisoners to be near their homes and be released on a conditional basis. In addition, labor legislation affecting prisons will be changed. Industries and services will be operated in prison, similar to those existing on the outside. Inmates will receive financial compensation for work and schooling. According to Glaser, future prisons will also have extensive links with community organizations such as churches and service groups. No one knows whether Glaser's vision of the "prison of the future" will ever come to pass. We do know that this vision is quite unlike the "prison of the present."

Alternatives to Prison   Some analysts, dissatisfied with the penalty of imprisonment, have searched for alternatives (Sutherland and Cressey, 1978, esp. Ch. 13; Sheley, 1979; van den Haag, 1975). In fact, alternatives to prison as a means of dealing with convicts do exist. In some cases these alternatives are less costly, less brutal, and less restrictive of personal freedom. Here we will consider eight alternatives: diversion, fines, restitution, supervision, halfway houses, release, furlough, and the death penalty. This is truly an unsettled age in the history of penal justice. It cannot be predicted which, if any, of these alternatives will be more commonly utilized in the future.[10]

Diversion attempts to avoid stigmatizing those who have violated the criminal law. In prearrest diversion, disputants confront each other and work out the problem in a controlled setting (Palmer, 1974). This was the philosophy of the Night Prosecutor Program of Columbus. Private citizens coming to file a warrant were diverted into the Night Prosecutor's Program. Rather than processing an affidavit for the courts, complaints were taken and an administrative hearing scheduled. Some 98 percent of cases were settled without criminal charges being filed. The most common sanction imposed was "prosecutor's probation," which simply emphasized to the respondent that a criminal affidavit would be filed if the latter bothered the complainant during the following sixty days. No criminal record was made, although information about the case was retained. In pretrial diversion, people are diverted at their arraignment from the rest of the criminal justice process. Criminal prosecution is suspended to give the accused an opportunity to get a job, schooling, or

---

[10]Three additional forms of punishment are social degradation, corporal punishment, and banishment. Social degradation involves the use of shame and humiliation as a criminal penalty. Early forms included the open use of the ducking stool. Today some states degrade felons by forbidding them from voting, holding public office, or practicing certain professions or occupations. Corporal punishment involves physically hurting a person as punishment for the crime committed. Flogging, pillorying, and mutilation were common in bygone times. Finally, banishment consists of the forced removal of a person from a jurisdiction. Many of the early settlers in America were actually criminals who had been banished from England. In the United States today aliens found guilty of a crime are sometimes banished. See the discussion in Sutherland and Cressey (1978) and van den Haag (1975).

training. Charges are dropped if the person successfully completes the program. Diversion is used most often where the accused has little or no prior criminal record. It is used to give the individual another chance. Diverted defendants are no more likely to be rearrested than those fully processed through the entire criminal justice system (Zimring, 1974).

Fines are another important way of dealing with those who violate the law (van den Haag, 1975, pp. 229–240). In the United States today fines are frequently used for the least serious crimes, such as parking violations, traffic offenses, and littering. In some European countries a wide range of serious offenses are punished through fines. Of course, affluent people are more able than poor people to pay a fine of $50. Yet, this inequity can be dealt with by fining people in terms of days of income. Fines permit those convicted to resume a relatively normal life. Where it is desirable to stigmatize the offender, other sanctions can be invoked in conjunction with the fine. An added advantage to fines is that if the person should later be found to have been innocent, the fine can easily be remitted. The fine is the most easily and thoroughly remissible form of punishment. (That person who discovers a means of remitting the penalty of death is likely to make the front page of more than one daily newspaper.)

Restitution is a third way of dealing with lawbreakers (Barnett, 1977). Implicit in restitution is a perception of crime as an offense by one person against the rights of another person. According to this view, justice consists of offenders making good the losses that they caused. Once found guilty, the court would sentence the criminal to make restitution to the victim. If unable to pay immediately, the offender would be permitted to do so from future wages. Failure to pay might result in garnishment of wages or some new type of confinement. Criminals who were deemed not trustworthy would be confined to an employment project where they could earn money to make restitution. Some view restitution as an alternative to other forms of punishment. Others believe that victim compensation should be provided by government, with lawbreakers getting more traditional forms of punishment (Jones, 1979). One problem with the notion of restitution is that victims would have an incentive to identify someone as a suspect even when they had doubts as to who really victimized them.

Supervision consists of releasing guilty parties into the community but keeping them under watchful eyes. Major forms of supervision are probation and parole.[11] Probation tries to supervise and rehabilitate offenders through use of a probation officer (Sheley, 1979, p. 210). Nearly 75 percent of all felony and misdemeanor convictions result in probation (Chamelin, Fox, and Whisenand, 1975, p. 329). The judge suspends offenders' prison sentences and places them under the supervision of a government employee. Offenders are

---

[11] Another form of supervision is community surveillance, in which the criminal is watched by all residents of a locality. This is not very feasible in large cities, since few know each other. Its use of informants is also questionable from a civil liberties standpoint.

given liberty, conditioned by good behavior. Conditions of probation generally include keeping regular hours, being employed, avoiding public drunkenness, and not leaving the jurisdiction (Chamelin et al., 1975, p. 330). During the period of probation, which averages about three years, the state maintains some personal supervision of the offenders to help them maintain good behavior (and help detect violations). Under parole prison inmates are released into the community after serving only part of their sentence. Larger numbers of those released from prison leave under some type of conditional release such as parole. Those paroled are monitored by a parole agent. Although probation and parole involve some expense, the costs are far less than those involved in incarceration. Unfortunately, states almost uniformly underfinance their probation and parole departments, making adequate supervision impossible. Evidence suggests that it is no more dangerous to the community to release offenders on probation or parole than to release them after they have completed a full prison sentence.

Halfway houses are another alternative to imprisonment (Chamelin et al., 1975, pp. 398–440; Keller and Alper, 1970). Although a halfway house is a correctional facility, residents are free to come and go to work, to shop, to go to school, or to find recreation. The facility more closely resembles a home than a prison. Programs in halfway houses vary greatly. Some focus almost exclusively on supervision, while others engage in counseling and therapy. In those with a therapeutic orientation constructive peer pressure is used to bring about conforming behavior among participants. Newer members of the halfway house are socialized by those who have been there for a longer period of time. Halfway houses offer criminals far more freedom than prisons, permitting them to carry on relatively normal lives. Some halfway houses function as guidance centers prior to the release of a prisoner into the community. Others house offenders who have been sent there as an alternative to a prison sentence. Perhaps the greatest obstacle to increased use of halfway houses in dealing with offenders is community resistance.

Release and furlough are two methods which may be used to minimize the need for incarcerating offenders (Sheley, 1979, pp. 211–212; Chamelin et al., 1975, pp. 396–397). In a release program the inmate is permitted to leave the prison during the day in order to work or attend classes in the community. When these activities have been completed for the day, the offender must return immediately to prison. The release program enables inmates to make contacts with the free community and help support their families. The furlough provides the inmate with a leave of absence for a longer period of time. Furloughs allow an offender to leave prison in order to deal with family or business problems or to prepare either for parole or final release. Both the release and furlough methods may be used more often in the future for minimum- and medium-security prisoners.

The death penalty is a final (very final) alternative to prison. The philosopher Montesquieu argued that a person deserves death who has violated the security of another person to the extent of taking that person's life or attempting to do so (Montesquieu, 1949, p. 187). According to Montesquieu, the punishment of death may serve as a cure for such sickness in society. Many techniques have been used for inflicting death—burning, boiling in oil, breaking at the wheel, the iron coffin, drowning, and impaling (Sutherland and Cressey, 1978, p. 310). In the United States electrocution was introduced in 1890, supposedly as a more humane method than hanging (Holten and Jones, 1978, p. 315). Public executions have been abandoned, the last one occurring in 1936. The Supreme Court dealt with the death penalty in 1972 in the case of *Furman v. Georgia*. In this case the Court ruled that existing capital punishment laws in the states were unconstitutional, since they represented "cruel and unusual punishment." The Court focused its objections on the inconsistent way that death penalty laws were being administered. In response to this decision, many states revised their capital punishment laws. In 1976 the Supreme Court upheld the new death penalty laws of Georgia, Florida, and Texas (*Gregg v. Georgia; Proffitt v. Florida; Jurek v. Texas; Woodson v. North Carolina; Roberts v. Louisiana*). Still, there are many vocal critics of capital punishment. For example, Thorsten Sellin suggests that the penalty of death is invoked in a highly inequitable way, placing poor black males at highest risk (1980, pp. 55–68). Moreover, many—including the Economic and Social Council of the United Nations—have branded capital punishment as inhumane (Sutherland and Cressey, 1978, p. 311). There is also the concern that people will be executed by the state, only later to be proven innocent. Finally, while the death penalty is a "can't miss" approach for dealing with recidivism, many wonder whether it really deters others from committing crimes (Leiser, 1979, Ch. 8).

AN ASSESSMENT

Our discussion of criminal justice has uncovered a number of important concerns. First, it should be apparent that crime is a significant social phenomenon. It takes people's lives and their property, and it causes them considerable anxiety. People have a sense of outrage about street crime. This outrage is understandable given that street crime may involve direct contact with someone who wants to or is willing to hurt others. Even when there has been no direct contact, victims may feel a sense of violation if their home or business has been burglarized. At the same time, people's sense of outrage about crime seems rather narrow in scope. Despite popular indifference, enormous costs to society are caused by white-collar crime and organized crime. There is much to be said for increasing our national commitment to deal with such offenses. In a very different sense, perhaps Americans should feel a sense of outrage about victimless crimes and political crimes. Decriminalization of the various victimless crimes has been called for by some reformers. We have been too willing to brand certain kinds of actions as "criminal" in character. In addition, it would appear that during some points in our nation's history, government officials have been far too willing to use the criminal sanction to punish dissidents.

For all the talk about and testing of the causes of crime, there remains much misunderstanding. This misunderstanding can be traced in large part to our preoccupation with the crimes of the poor. "Poverty breeds crime" is an easy conclusion if we refuse to look beyond street crimes for evidence of criminality. By focusing only on street crimes, liberals are able to advocate more social welfare spending while conservatives can speak of the "undeserving poor." Yet, criminal behavior is not limited to disadvantaged people. At one time or another, nearly all people have violated a criminal law. Ours is a highly materialistic society where few of us can afford all that we want. At some point many decide to break the rules a bit (or a lot) to get a little (or a lot) more. The affluent may seem more law-abiding than the poor, but this is largely because they need not take to the streets to commit a property offense. From a sociological standpoint, however, "crime in the suites" may be just as important as "crime in the streets." If crime is largely a rational pursuit of economic gain, this suggests that we must make it irrational to attempt to commit a crime. Presumably, this could be accomplished only by vastly increasing the risks of detection and punishment. Unfortunately, this would require a degree of surveillance that is inconsistent with our love of liberty and privacy as well as a penal justice policy which violates our sense of just dessert.

The criminal justice process of America provides critics with an easy target. If the chief mission of criminal justice is to convict criminals, it has been far less than effective. Very few crimes produce suspects; even fewer produce defendants, convicts, or prisoners. On the other hand, if the primary goal of criminal justice is to provide procedural justice for defendants, this aim is not being achieved either. An elaborate set of procedural rights has been articulated by the Supreme Court. However, many of these paper rights are rarely put into practice. Instead, defendants are commonly persuaded to relinquish their rights and plead guilty. While criminal justice personnel make some effort to devise an equitable plea, there is a presumption of guilt rather than of innocence. Although the process produces savings in time and money, justice may suffer in many cases. A serious effort to ensure due process for every defendant would cost an enormous amount of money. Our society has not been willing to pay the price to achieve procedural due process at the level of implementation.

America's system of penal justice is in considerable turmoil. When we do manage to identify, indict, and convict a suspect, we do not seem to know what penalty should be inflicted or for what purposes. For example, the penalty of imprisonment has been criticized as being too expensive for society while violating the liberty of the individual. There are alternatives to prison, such as diversion, fines, and restitution. Yet, we have been unable to settle upon a penal justice policy which makes careful, coherent choices among these alternatives. To some extent our difficulties stem from an inability to justify penal justice in philosophical terms. While many simply wish to take retribution on offenders, others prefer more subtle uses of penal justice, such as rehabilitation, incapacitation, deterrence, restitution, and reintegration. Perhaps, we will eventually decide what we want our system of penal justice to accomplish.

QUESTIONS FOR DISCUSSION

1. Why do people commonly regard street crime as the most serious kind of crime? Is the seriousness of white-collar crime underrated? Is it wise social policy to deal with victimless crimes through criminal law? Should juveniles who break the law be dealt with as harshly as adult offenders?
2. How do different perspectives on the causes of crime suggest different remedies for reducing crime? To what extent is crime the result of defects in people? To what extent is crime due to problems in the social environment?
3. Does the criminal justice system use fair procedures when processing those accused of a crime? If you were charged with a crime that you did not commit, would you agree to plea bargain?
4. How well could you withstand the "pains" of imprisonment? Should we make greater or lesser use of prison to deal with offenders who are convicted of a crime? If someone seriously victimized you, would you want that person to be sent to prison?

FOR FURTHER READING

CASPER, JONATHAN D. *American Criminal Justice: The Defendant's Perspective.* Englewood Cliffs, N.J.: Prentice-Hall, 1972. Looks at criminal defendants in the throes of the criminal justice system.

PACKER, HERBERT. *The Limits of the Criminal Sanction.* Stanford, Calif.: Stanford University Press, 1968. Concludes that we can provide due process of law by decriminalizing the less serious offenses and concentrating our resources on the remaining offenses.

VAN DEN HAAG, ERNEST. *Punishing Criminals.* New York: Basic Books, 1975. One scholar's view of the proper varieties and degrees of punishment.

VERA INSTITUTE OF JUSTICE. *Felony Arrests: Their Prosecution and Disposition in New York City's Courts.* New York: Vera Institute of Justice, 1977. Discusses why so few of those arrested actually get convicted and punished.

VOLD, GEORGE B. *Theoretical Criminology.* New York: Oxford University Press, 1979. A comprehensive survey of perspectives on the causes of crime.

SUPREME COURT RULINGS

Brady v. United States, 397 U.S. 742 (1970)
Furman v. Georgia, 408 U.S. 238 (1972)
Gregg v. Georgia, 428 U.S. 153 (1976)
In re Gault, 387 U.S. 1 (1967)
Jurek v. Texas, 428 U.S. 262 (1976)
McMann v. Richardson, 397 U.S. 759 (1970)
Parker v. North Carolina, 397 U.S. 790 (1970)
Proffitt v. Florida, 428 U.S. 242 (1976)
Rhodes v. Chapman, 49 L.W. 4677 (1981)
Roberts v. Louisiana, 428 U.S. 325 (1976)
Woodson v. North Carolina, 428 U.S. 280 (1976)

8

CONSTITUTIONAL LAW

PREVIEW

Chapter Eight focuses on constitutional law in America. Because of the vastness of this subject area, we will paint our portrait in rather broad strokes. The chapter contains three major sections:

Constitution and courts
Supreme Court decisions
The impact of courts

The first section examines the relationship between Constitution and courts. The power of judicial review enables the courts to declare any law or executive action unconstitutional. This is a power of great importance, though it is constrained by the self-restraint of judges and the constitutional system of checks and balances. The second section of this chapter discusses the substance of Supreme Court decisions. We will look at several areas of Supreme Court adjudication, including separation of powers, freedom of expression, due process of law, and equal protection. The final section investigates the burgeoning literature on the impact of courts. We will see that the mere announcement of Supreme Court doctrine does not necessarily produce tangible changes in people's attitudes or behavior. However, we will also argue that the judiciary can be an important source of both social change and social stability.

CONSTITUTION AND COURT

Limited Government

The United States Constitution was born of a fear of tyrannical rule and a sense of frustration at the ineffectiveness of the Articles of Confederation (McLaughlin, 1962). Following the Peace of Paris in 1763, Great Britain was determined to exercise increased control over its colonies. However, after suffering the imposition of burdensome regulations under King George III of England, American colonists grew increasingly dissatisfied with this arrangement. Taxes were unilaterally imposed; colonists were required to house British troops in their homes; colonial legislatures were even dissolved. Hostilities broke out in 1775 between the colonists and Great Britain. A peace treaty was finally signed in 1783. During the course of the Revolutionary War national affairs were managed by the Continental Congress. The Articles of Confederation, proposed in 1777 and approved in 1781, gave this government constitutional standing. Under the Articles national government was quite weak. It did not have the constitutional authority to collect taxes, regulate interstate commerce, or enforce orders. Finally, the Continental Congress authorized a convention in Philadelphia for "the sole and express purpose of revising the Articles of Confederation." The delegates, meeting for four months in 1787, decided instead to exceed their mandate and write an entirely new constitution. Their intention was to establish a more powerful national government, but not a national government of unlimited powers. Both the tyranny of King George III and the weakness of the Articles somehow had to be avoided. The success of the framers' efforts is suggested by the fact that our Constitution, drafted nearly 200 years ago, is the oldest written constitution in the world today. Further, this document, amended only twenty-six times, remains the basis for the actual workings of American government.

The United States Constitution overcame the weaknesses of the Articles by lodging potentially far-reaching powers in the national government. The Articles had created a confederation in which authority over individuals was under the aegis of the states. Under a confederation only the states have direct control over individual citizens. The national government possesses only those powers expressly delegated by the states. Normally, states delegate only those powers which they believe must be handled by a larger unit of government. In the case of the Articles very few powers (apart from conducting foreign relations) were delegated to the national government. The framers who met in Philadelphia rejected government by confederation. However, they did not go so far as to opt for a unitary system in which only the national government would have direct control over individuals. Rather, the framers invented a new system of government, which has come to be known as federalism. Under federalism political power is constitutionally divided between a national government and the states. Both levels of government simultaneously exercise authority over individuals. While the framers left a substantial role for the states, many important powers were granted to the national government. These include exclusive authority over foreign relations, interstate commerce, and coining money. Under the new Constitution the national government could impose taxes on individuals, spend money for the general welfare, and enforce its laws directly without the intervention of the states.

Given the substantial increase in national authority under the new Constitution, there was a real possibility for the abuse of power. In view of this, the framers incorporated within the Constitution two methods for avoiding tyrannical rule. First, the framers created a system of separated institutions sharing power. National powers would not be placed in the hands of either a dictator or an all-powerful legislature. Following the philosophy of Montesquieu, power would be divided among a bicameral legislature, a president, and a judiciary. Moreover, the personnel of each institution would be selected in a different manner, giving each institution a unique constituency. This arrangement would make it difficult for a popular majority to seize control of the government and trample on minorities. An intricate system of checks and balances was also set in place. These checks and balances were designed to prevent any institution of government from gaining a monopoly of power. For example, Congress can pass a law, but the president has the power to veto. However, Congress may then override the veto if it can muster a two-thirds majority in each chamber. The authority to carry out the laws of Congress resides with the president and the executive bureaucracy. However, if the president is grossly negligent in fulfilling executive duties, Congress may take the extreme step of impeaching and removing the president from office. The framers believed that by dividing the powers of government and setting each institution of government against the other, the abuse of power could be prevented.

At the same time, the framers also introduced a second method to avoid the abuse of power. This involved establishing certain constitutional rights. We may define a right as "a legal or moral claim on some benefit." (Weissberg, 1980, p. 520) All Americans automatically enjoy certain rights simply because of their citizenship. A right must also be regarded as "a claim asserted against or through public authorities." (Friedman, 1971, p. 193) By invoking a right, we demand that government protect us in some way. Privileges stand in contrast to rights. Rights *must* be granted—public officials do not have the authority to withhold a right. Privileges may be granted and then easily withdrawn, but rights are meant to be guarantees which can be abridged only under extreme circumstances.

The framers included within the text of the original Constitution several personal rights. For example, the Constitution provides for a writ of habeas corpus. This guarantees that an imprisoned person can go to federal court and be released if the confinement is found to be unlawful. Second, the Constitution forbids the passage of a bill of attainder. As a result, no legislature may enact a special law declaring that someone has committed a crime and specifying a punishment. Ex post facto laws are likewise forbidden by the Constitution. This means that no law may declare some action to be a crime after that action has already taken place. In addition, individuals expressing unpopular views are given some protection by the original Constitution. Because treason is defined narrowly, people have more freedom to speak out without fear of being prosecuted as traitors. Also, the original Constitution provides for the right to trial by jury for federal crimes and trial location in the state where the crime was committed. It also contains a ban on religious tests or vows for employment by government and a ban on the granting of titles of nobility.

Nevertheless, most of the rights we normally associate with the Constitution are not found in the original seven articles, which contain 6,000 words. At the convention the delegates decided that a broad listing of rights would not be very meaningful. The feeling was that the liberties of the people could best be safeguarded through the Constitution's institutional restraints—the system of separated institutions with checks and balances. However, the delegates' decision to exclude a broad bill of rights from the Constitution proved to be quite unpopular. During the ratification process, one of the main objections voiced by Antifederalist opponents of the Constitution concerned the absence of a bill of rights. Although ratification was secured, some states approved the Constitution only after assurances were made that amendments would soon be offered. The result was quick passage of ten amendments to the new Constitution. The First Amendment focuses on personal liberty—freedom of religion, speech, press, assembly, and petition. Many of the other ten amendments deal with procedural justice issues, such as protection against self-incrimination.

Judicial Review

It was not immediately clear whether the Constitution would be just another historical document and nothing more. After all, what was to prevent Congress from passing a law that was contrary to the words or spirit of the Constitution? If Congress had the power to pass any law, then the Constitution would be little more than a piece of paper, with no living application. The so-called "rights" of citizens might become only "paper rights" that were sometimes upheld and sometimes withheld, depending on short-term changes in the composition of the nation's leadership. In Great Britain, in fact, there is no one document that can be called the Constitution. Civil liberties are simply entrusted to the British Parliament. Of course, British courts do have the power to interpret the law, and sometimes this is an important power. However, the courts of England do not have the authority to strike down legislation and declare it void. It seems certain that the framers intended the Constitution to have some living application. Indeed, various proposals were debated at the Constitutional Convention for establishing a mechanism of judicial review. However, even though most delegates seem to have favored judicial review, none of the proposed mechanisms were actually approved and written into the text of the Constitution. At best, the Constitution only implies that courts can declare laws and actions to be unconstitutional.[1]

It was in 1803, in the celebrated (and scorned) case of *Marbury v. Madison,* that the Supreme Court claimed for itself and the entire judiciary the power of judicial review.[2] It was a complex case, with far-reaching implications for the status of the Supreme Court. In his bid for reelection in 1800 President John Adams had been defeated by Thomas Jefferson. Determined to aid his forsaken Federalist Party, Adams sought to pack the federal judiciary with partisan supporters. In this effort Adams enjoyed the active assistance of the lame-duck Federalist Congress. Before leaving office on March 3, 1801, Adams was able to nominate and win confirmation of the commission of sixteen new circuit judges, forty-two new justices of the peace, and a new Chief Justice of the Supreme Court—his own secretary of state, John Marshall. Adams worked on these appointments to the very end of his term, but left seventeen undelivered commissions to the incoming secretary of state, James Madison. Upon assuming the presidency, Thomas Jefferson was understandably upset at the packing of the judiciary with Federalists. At the same time, he was delighted to find that some of the commissions had not been formally delivered. Mischievously, Jefferson ordered Madison not to deliver the promised commissions.

The actions of Jefferson and Madison did not sit very well with William Marbury, who was looking forward to serving as justice of the peace. Marbury opted to hire an attorney, who in turn looked to Section 13 of the Judiciary Act of 1789 for legal relief. This provision of the act, as passed by Congress, seemed to extend to the Supreme Court the power to issue a writ of mandamus under its original jurisdiction.[3] This power had not been included in the Constitution. If the Supreme Court agreed to invoke the writ—and the Court was

---

[1]For example, Article III states: "The judicial power shall extend to all cases, in law and equity, arising under this Constitution, the laws of the United States and treaties made or which shall be made. . . . " To some this implies the authority of the Court to review constitutional questions as they arise in live disputes.

[2]For an excellent review of the politics surrounding this case, see Henry J. Abraham, *The Judicial Process* (New York: Oxford University Press, 1980a), pp. 327–332.

[3]A *writ of mandamus* is a court order to a public official directing that official to perform a legal duty. The Supreme Court has original jurisdiction over some cases and appellate jurisdiction over others. *Original jurisdiction* is the authority to hear a case for the first time. *Appellate jurisdiction* is the power to hear cases on appeal from lower courts.

literally loaded with Federalists—Madison would be under court order to issue the commission to Marbury. For the Supreme Court, however, the case of *Marbury v. Madison* posed a tactical dilemma of serious dimensions. The very status of the Supreme Court as a coequal branch of government may very well have been in jeopardy. On the one hand, if the Court refused to grant the writ, Jefferson would triumph and the Court would appear rather meek. Even worse, if the Court were to grant the writ, Madison would almost surely disobey and the Supreme Court of the United States would be rendered a powerless institution.

Remarkably, the Supreme Court managed to emerge from this case with its credibility intact and its powers enhanced. In his written opinion for the Court, Chief Justice Marshall shrewdly manipulated this case, using it as the occasion to declare for the Supreme Court the power of judicial review. Marshall's opinion asserted that Marbury did indeed have a right to the commission and that a legal remedy did exist. However, Marshall wrote that a writ of mandamus issued under Section 13 of the Judiciary Act of 1789 was definitely not an appropriate remedy, for *it was unconstitutional*. Section 13 was unconstitutional, according to a unanimous Court, because in passing this provision, Congress had added to the Supreme Court's original jurisdiction through legislation—something that is nowhere sanctioned by the Constitution and is in apparent violation of Article III. In essence, the Supreme Court was refusing to accept a rather trivial power granted to it by Congress some fourteen years earlier. However, in denying its right to this power, the Supreme Court was laying claim to a far more significant power— the power of judicial review. Henceforth, the judiciary would have the ultimate authority to interpret the meaning of the Constitution. This is an awesome power, for it can be used to invalidate any law by any American legislature and any action by any executive officer in the nation.

Activism and Restraint

Few today question the authority of the Supreme Court to exercise judicial review. Nevertheless, there is much ongoing debate over how activist or restrained the Court ought to be. Given that federal judges are not elected and serve for life, many equate an activist judiciary with the undermining of democratic rule. While judicial restraint is a tricky concept, it seems to imply two general characteristics. A restrained Court will impose stringent limits on itself as to the kinds of cases it will hear and how a judgment will be reached (Lamb, 1982, pp. 14–22). For example, a restrained Court accepts for review only live disputes between parties who have a genuine stake in the outcome (that is, cases and controversies, standing). A Court that is restrained neither issues advisory opinions nor answers "political" questions. Judges adhering to judicial restraint address only "legal" questions and answer them in accordance with prior Court decisions. On a restrained Court judges abide by the intent of the Constitution and statutes rather than read their own policy preferences into the law. Restrained judges normally base their decisions on statutory grounds rather than on provisions of the Constitution. Finally, and perhaps most critically, a restrained Court pays deference to the legislature and executive by overruling their policies only rarely.

Two points of confusion are common with regard to the notions of judicial activism and restraint. First, judicial activism is emphatically not the same as liberalism. Clearly, the Warren Court was active in promoting liberal values such as liberty, equality, and procedural justice. However, an activist Court may instead expand rights related to conservative values such as social order and private property. Indeed, until recent decades the Supreme Court's history has largely been the fairly active pursuit of conservative values. Beyond that, it is also important that "activism" not be equated with "rights-consciousness." Normally, we think of an activist Court as one that expands the list of individual rights. However, an activist Court need not be protective of constitutional rights. Recall that an activist Court, as traditionally defined, is one that permits the easy access of litigants to address constitutional questions. In addition, activism also implies a strong willingness to depart from stare decisis and go against legislative and executive desires. Clearly, however, this can mean the use of judicial review to erode the extent of our rights. The direction that Supreme Court activism takes is largely a function of the backgrounds, attitudes, and other attributes of the justices on the Court.

It is often argued that the extent of judicial activism has increased in recent decades (Halpern, 1982; Winter, 1979). The maxims of judicial restraint are said to have eroded, so that concerns such as legal standing no longer present an obstacle to obtaining access to the Court. The widened scope of Supreme Court activism is also noted, with the Court addressing such issues as school desegregation, sexual morality, and abortion on demand. New activism has occurred in these areas even though, in recent history, there have been no relevant changes in the United States Constitution. Moreover, the decisions of the Supreme Court increasingly involve an "affirmative activism" in which the Court goes beyond simply voiding legislation or executive actions. Decisions may also specify—sometimes in elaborate detail—the affirmative steps required to remedy illegalities. To some the Court is behaving like a "super-legislature" that ignores the intent of the framers and legal precedents when rendering decisions. Some even believe that the Supreme Court has become the dominant institution of government, upsetting the traditional balance of powers between the branches and levels of government. To some extent judges have come to see their decisions as binding, not only on the parties to the dispute but also on other individuals and institutions that are similarly situated. The fear has also been expressed that this new activism is a permanent feature rather than a fleeting phenomenon. It must be emphasized, however, that other observers believe that this perception of an overly extended Court is quite exaggerated (Halpern, 1982).

Supreme Court activism is viewed with much trepidation in some quarters. As Eugene Rostow noted: "A theme of uneasiness, and even guilt, colors the literature about judicial review." (Rostow, 1952, p. 193) From the standpoint of social values, a primary fear is that Supreme Court activism undermines democracy (Graglia, 1982). It is noted that judges are not elected and that they serve for life terms. Thus, the exercise of judicial review can be seen as redistributing authority away from the people's elected representatives.[4] Henry Steele Commager has argued that when a legislature approves a bill, it "is not only a majority vote for its wisdom but a majority vote for its constitutionality." (1943, p. 418) According to Commager, there have been few clear-cut instances where majorities wilfully attempted to ride down constitutional barriers. Given the ambiguity of the Constitution, an activist Court may be seen as simply substituting its values for those of the people's representatives. In this regard Lino Graglia notes that there is no reason to believe that the values of judges will be superior to those of elected officials (1982, pp. 161–162). Along these lines, it has been observed that throughout most of American history, the record of the Supreme Court on civil liberties was actually rather poor (Commager, 1943, p. 422). Critics of the Court also suggest that judicial policies tend to be less effective than those of other government institutions (Winter, 1979, pp. 54–63; Horowitz, 1977). It is said that there are defects in the adversarial process that tend to make for poor policy decisions. In addition, it is noted that judges are generalists rather than experts. Hence, Court decisions may fail to meet their intended goals and may produce unintended negative effects.

Still, there is much to be said in defense of the exercise of some activism by the judiciary. To begin with, it is not fair to cast judicial review in the role of villain in a democracy. Critics of judicial review have failed to notice the myriad of institutional practices throughout our government which constrain majority rule (Rosenblum, 1955, pp. 73–74). For example, nonmajoritarian practices in Congress include seniority, the committee system, bicameralism, the Senate filibuster, malapportionment, adoption of the "trustee" rather than "delegate" style,[5] low voter turnout in elections, and issueless campaigns. It must also be remembered that while democracy is an important social value, it is but one of many significant values. Among the other values which must be considered are liberty, equality, procedural justice, social order, and effectiveness. A central aim of the Constitution is to ensure that, irrespective of majority sentiment, other significant values (that is, those expressed as rights)

---

[4]Under the Constitution of 1787 there was direct election only of members of the House of Representatives. Direct election of senators came in 1913 through the Seventeenth Amendment. This replaced selection by the respective state legislatures. The president is still chosen by the electoral college, but the electors do not normally exercise the independent judgment that the framers intended.

[5]The Congress member who endorses the "delegate" role attempts to follow constituent desires in roll call votes and other policy actions. "Trustees" opt to use their own best judgment of constituents' interests or of the national interest.

will be achieved in substantial measure. Hence, even if there were some wholly democratic institution in our national government, we might well wish to impose external restraints, such as judicial review, upon it. While rights are always at risk (Scheingold, 1974), Court members have the independence and institutional obligation to uphold the basic rights expressed in the Constitution. Certainly, the Court cannot be an eternal guardian of Constitutional rights. A new, longstanding majority that gains power can pass constitutional amendments and, through new appointments, can even remake the membership of the judiciary. However, our rights have some protection from short-term swings in public opinion that run counter to the thrust of the Constitution.

Limits on Courts

If judges actively uphold rights, they may interpret the Constitution in ways that are highly offensive to us. It must be remembered that the provisions of the Constitution are very vague and are subject to differing interpretations. Judging is not merely the application of preexisting rules to cases before the Court. Some policymaking is almost inevitable. While the Supreme Court does not nullify a law as unconstitutional every day of the week, it does exercise judicial review often enough to be a matter of concern. By the fall of 1979 the Supreme Court had declared a total of approximately 122 provisions of federal laws unconstitutional (out of a total of over 85,000 laws passed) (Abraham, 1980a, pp. 296–297). Also, since 1789, 950 state laws or provisions of state constitutions have been declared invalid by the Supreme Court—850 of these since 1870. Those who fear "judicial imperialism" wonder who can constrain the courts. Nevertheless, there are a number of constitutional and extraconstitutional limits on the American judiciary.

Self-Restraints   A recurring theme in legal literature is that judges restrain themselves (Abraham, 1980a, pp. 346–351). Judicial self-restraint occurs out of a desire for consistency in court rulings (that is, stare decisis), a deference to the legislation of elected representatives, considerations of equal treatment, and recognition of social and political realities. Supreme Court justices may exercise restraint not only in the substance of their decisions but even in deciding what cases they will address. Based upon his examination of Supreme Court practices, Henry Abraham has identified a series of "maxims of judicial self-restraint." (1980a, pp. 373–397) The Supreme Court will not even issue a ruling in a case that does not meet certain criteria. For example, a genuine controversy must exist between two parties, the initiator must have legal standing, and the issue must not raise a "political" question that should be decided by a legislature or executive. Justices are not free agents if, by virtue of their role orientation, they feel obliged to limit the exercise of their authority.

Some have questioned the usefulness of the notion of judicial restraint. Certainly, there have been many instances where judges manipulated the rules of self-restraint in a self-serving manner (Murphy, 1964, pp. 29–31). If enough justices wish to use a case to alter public policy, the maxims of self-restraint will not impose an absolute bar. Sometimes the Court has eased the rules of granting review, as by accepting a case for review despite strong evidence of collusion between the parties and, thus, no real dispute. On occasion the justices have also discovered and ruled upon issues which counsel did not raise or argue. Also, judges have manipulated norms of stare decisis—either stretching or narrowing the implications of precedents in order to suit their policy designs. Nevertheless, judging is not simply a raw exercise of power. In deciding what cases to consider, surely the maxims of self-restraint play some role in the choices made by judges. As Walter Murphy concludes: "It would be false to think of judicial use of technical rules as a game of legal charades. These rules are not infinitely malleable. They provide flexibility but not total freedom of choice." (1964, p. 31) Judges do not aspire to be dictators. While there is a mixture of role orientations on the bench most judges agree that some restraint is desirable. Because judges believe that they ought to be constrained, the Constitution, the law, and the maxims of self-restraint pose some real limitations on the judiciary.

Congress   Limits are also imposed on the Supreme Court by the other major institutions of government. For example, Congress has a number of weapons in its arsenal to counter an activist Court (Murphy, 1964, p. 26; Abraham, 1980a, pp. 351–354). To begin with, Congress may propose constitutional amendments which would either reverse particular court decisions or curtail the power of the judiciary. The Eleventh, Thirteenth, Fourteenth, Fifteenth, Sixteenth, and Twenty-sixth Amendments were each designed to overcome some Supreme Court decision.[6] A stunning number of other amendments have been introduced in Congress but failed to win approval.[7] To some extent the mere proposing of constitutional amendments may tend to moderate subsequent Court decisions. A second Congressional limit on the courts is legislation which has the effect of reversing a court ruling. If, in the new legislation, Congress has removed the unconstitutional defect, the Supreme Court will usually sustain the validity of the new law. Third, all appointments of judges to the federal courts must be confirmed by the Senate. While confirmation usually occurs with relative ease, there have been noteworthy ex-

[6]The Eleventh Amendment concerned lawsuits against state governments. The Thirteenth, Fourteenth, and Fifteenth Amendments were the post-Civil War actions in behalf of the newly freed slaves. The Sixteenth Amendment gave Congress the power to levy an income tax. The Twenty-Sixth Amendment gave eighteen-year-olds the right to vote.

[7]For example, between 1963 and 1964 164 amendments were introduced in an effort to reverse the Court on school prayer. See Charles H. Sheldon, *The American Judicial Process* (New York: Dodd, Mead, 1974), p.146; *Engel v. Vitale,* 370 U.S. 421 (1962); *Abington School District v. Schempp,* 374 U.S. 203 (1963).

ceptions. For example, the Senate refused to confirm two of President Nixon's Supreme Court nominees—Clement Haynsworth and Harrold Carswell. The confirmation power gives the Senate some ability to influence the kinds of people who serve on the judiciary. Fourth, Congress may also impeach and remove federal judges, though only one Supreme Court justice has ever been impeached—Samuel Chase in 1801. This was largely a political battle waged by Jeffersonians against Federalist domination of the judiciary. The failure to convict Chase set a standard for use of the impeachment power only under extreme circumstances. Beyond that, Congress also has the authority to curb the Court by increasing the number of justices, regulating judicial procedure, abolishing or adding a tier of courts, and cutting off the funding needed to implement a decision.

There is some dispute as to whether Congress possesses yet another check on Supreme Court activism. In Article III, section 2, the Constitution states that Congress has the authority to make "exceptions" and impose "regulations" on the appellate jurisdiction of the Supreme Court. The meaning of this language is unsettled (Kaufman, 1981). Through the course of American history many bills have been proposed seeking to use Article III, section 2, to limit the cases that the Supreme Court can accept on appeal (Murphy, 1962a; Pritchett, 1961).[8] Some of these "divestiture bills" have actually been adopted. In *ex parte McCardle* the Supreme Court seemed to acknowledge Congressional authority to limit its appellate jurisdiction. In 1868 Congress repealed a law passed one year earlier that had granted the Supreme Court the jurisdiction to hear on appeal from the circuit courts a petition for a writ of habeas corpus. The Supreme Court had already heard oral argument in *ex parte McCardle,* which was one such case. However, after Congress passed the restrictive legislation, the Supreme Court responded by dismissing the case on grounds that it lacked jurisdiction.

Nevertheless, some constitutional scholars believe that too much has been made of the Court's decision in *McCardle.* It is argued that the decision did not give Congress the authority to prevent the Supreme Court from upholding constitutional rights. It is noteworthy that in the *McCardle* case the petitioner still had the option of applying for a writ of habeas corpus under the Court's original jurisdiction. Thus, the Congressional legislation did not really prevent the Supreme Court from protecting people's constitutional right to habeas corpus relief. Moreover, in *United States v. Klein* in 1872 the Supreme Court actually struck down an attempted limitation on its appellate jurisdiction. The Court ruled that it is unconstitutional for Congress to interfere with the Court's duty to interpret and give effect to a provision of the Constitution. In light of this decision, Irving Kaufman concludes: "As *Klein* demonstrates, Congress does not have the power to subvert established constitutional principles

---

[8]In 1982 similar consideration was given to divestiture bills regarding federal court-ordered busing, abortion, and school prayer.

under the guise of regulating the Court's appellate jurisdiction.'' (1981, p. 98) It is not clear how a contemporary Court would respond if Congress sought to limit its appellate jurisdiction over some key area involving constitutional rights.

The President   Supreme Court activism may also be constrained by the president (Pritchett, 1978, p. 104; Murphy, 1964, p. 26). Most notably, the president is in an excellent position to alter court policy through the power to appoint judges. Between 1937 and 1942 Franklin Roosevelt chose a Chief Justice and appointed eight other justices to the Supreme Court. More recently Richard Nixon was able to appoint four justices during his abbreviated tenure as president. Few presidential decisions have the long-range effects of a Supreme Court appointment. For example, William O. Douglas, a Roosevelt appointee, remained on the Court for thirty years after Roosevelt's death. Through careful use of their appointive powers both Roosevelt and Nixon had considerable success in remolding the ideological make-up of the Court. Presidents may also attempt to increase the size of the Supreme Court or mount a political atack against it. Frustrated by the opposition of the Supreme Court to his New Deal programs, President Roosevelt proposed to pack the Court with additional justices. Although this effort was rebuffed by Congress, the Supreme Court ultimately yielded to the pressure exerted by Roosevelt. Beyond that, the president may also order executive officials to refuse to enforce Supreme Court decisions, pardon those convicted of contempt of court for defying judicial decisions, and urge Congress to impeach a judge. Less formally, as our nation's ''chief opinion leader,'' the president may attempt to move public opinion against the Court as a means of exerting pressure upon it. Informally as well, presidents may quietly ''drag their feet'' on the implementation of a Court decision.

States   Through a variety of means state governments may also limit Supreme Court impact (Murphy, 1964, pp. 27–28). From a constitutional standpoint states have the sole authority to ratify constitutional amendments. This power can be used to circumvent a Supreme Court decision that Congress and three-quarters of the states do not like. This power can also be used to protect the place of the states in our federalist system. Less formally, state officials may refuse to cooperate in carrying out Court decisions, throw their prestige against the Court, and bring pressure to bear against national politicians. State influence was felt early in our nation's history in response to the Court's ruling in *Chisholm v. Georgia.* Here the Supreme Court ruled that a state could be sued in federal court by a citizen of another state. The unpopularity of this decision with the states prompted Congress to propose the Eleventh Amendment, which was ratified by the states in 1798. Quite simply, the purpose of this amendment was to nullify the Court's *Chisholm* decision.

During the 1950s, anti-Court action by the states became even more intense (Ebenstein et al., 1980, pp. 62–63). In response to desegregation decisions by the Supreme Court, most Southern legislatures drafted declarations of interposition. These resolutions claimed that states had the constitutional authority to interfere with the implementation of Supreme Court decisions. Such a claim was brought before the Supreme Court in *Cooper v. Aaron* in 1958. However, the Court flatly and unanimously rejected the argument in the only opinion ever handed down by the Court which was signed individually by each of the nine justices. However, while the states do not have the constitutional authority to exercise interposition, they certainly can "drag their feet" and otherwise thwart the edicts of the Supreme Court. Indeed, "foot-dragging" was virtually the universal reaction in Southern states to the Supreme Court's school desegregation decisions.

Lower Courts   The lower courts are in an excellent position to limit the impact of Supreme Court activism (Murphy, 1962b; Murphy, 1964, pp. 24–25). Indeed, in many cases the lower courts can even reverse the thrust of Supreme Court decisions. The Supreme Court rarely makes the first or final decision in a case. When the Supreme Court reverses a decision on appeal, it remands (sends back) the case to the lower courts for final action. Thus, the "last word" in a court case normally comes from a lower court judge. Significantly, the Supreme Court's remand formula is quite vague and noncompelling. Usually, it simply states that the lower court decision should be handled in a way "not inconsistent with this opinion." This can give great leeway to lower court judges, permitting them to discover some new grounds on which to justify their original decision.

As we might expect, lower court discretion is even wider in subsequent cases on some legal issue. A Supreme Court decision applies only in the case immediately before it. The ruling may or may not apply to other cases, depending on the facts involved in these cases. It is always possible for lower courts to somehow distinguish the facts of cases before them from the facts in the case adjudicated by the Supreme Court.[9] In this way a contrary verdict can be rendered without being directly disobedient to the Supreme Court. Lower court judges are well aware that few of their decisions are reviewed—and even fewer reversed—by the Supreme Court or the circuit courts of appeals.

The character of federal court recruitment and tenure also contributes to the independence of lower-court judges. It is significant that lower-court judges are appointed by the president and Senate rather than by the justices of the Supreme Court. Equally significant is that Supreme Court justices cannot fire lower-court judges for failing to conform with the doctrines of the

[9]There is evidence that federal trial courts do tend to move in the direction of Supreme Court decisions. See Ronald Stidham and Robert A. Carp, "Trial Courts' Responses to Supreme Court Policy Changes: Three Case Studies," *Law and Policy Quarterly,* 1982, *4,* 215–234.

High Court. Only Congress can remove federal judges, and only then for failing to maintain "good behavior." These processes of judicial recruitment and tenure serve to insulate the lower courts from the Supreme Court. It is true that some Chief Justices, notably William Howard Taft, have sought to promote a sense of teamwork among judges at all levels. The fact that Taft, as president, had appointed many federal judges may have helped him in this effort. Still, many lower-court judges may remain unimpressed by such efforts and may opt to adhere to their own consciences when issuing decisions.

Majority Coalition   Finally, judicial activism may also be influenced by the character of the nation's majority coalition (Dahl, 1957; Casper, 1976). A look at the history of national elections indicates the dominance of a single party for long stretches of time. As Robert Dahl argues, judicial decisions will not be oblivious to this pattern of one-party dominance. Federal judges, after all, are appointed by the president and confirmed by the Senate. On the average, a new Supreme Court justice has been appointed every two years. This means that the ideological composition of the Court will not long be at odds with the rest of the political elite. Given that the Supreme Court will usually be ideologically similar to the other branches of government, Court activism will rarely oppose the wishes of an established majority coalition. Most of the time, according to Dahl, the bulk of the Supreme Court's work involves legitimating, rather than invalidating, the policies of the president and Congress.

This does not mean that clashes never occur between the Supreme Court and the other branches of government. Dahl suggests, however, that the most severe clashes occur during the period of transition, when one majority coalition is being replaced by another. For example, the election of Franklin Roosevelt in 1932 marked a transition in national leadership from conservatism to big government liberalism. However, differences in recruitment patterns (namely, elections versus lifetime appointment) meant that the composition of the federal judiciary did not change so quickly. Indeed, part of President Roosevelt's early difficulties with the judiciary stemmed from his inability to make a Supreme Court appointment for some four years. However, Court activism in opposition to the New Deal was ultimately constrained by the growing force of the new majority coalition. Under pressure the Supreme Court finally relented and upheld the constitutionality of the New Deal legislation. This "switch in time that saved nine" may have reflected an acceptance by some Court members that a new majority coalition had emerged. In time the process of judicial recruitment enabled President Roosevelt (who was elected to four terms) to remake the Supreme Court in his own image. In the four years that followed, the Supreme Court did not prove to be a roadblock preventing the nation's movement to a welfare state.

No one is suggesting that the Supreme Court is a mere puppet of the presidential-Congressional majority coalition. After all, the caseload of the Supreme Court includes some critical policy questions. By using its powers of judical review and statutory interpretation, the Supreme Court can make some momentous decisions. These powers can be used to block the policy goals of a temporary majority coalition or constrain the efforts of a new majority coalition. Even when acting within the ideological framework of the majority coalition, the Supreme Court has substantial institutional powers and can use this authority to play a leading policymaking role. Notwithstanding the restraints on the Supreme Court, the decisions it has made are worthy of intense study.

SUPREME COURT DECISIONS

Our attention now turns to the substance of Supreme Court decisions that were grounded in the provisions of the Constitution (Chase and Ducat, 1979; Funston, 1978; Mason and Beaney, 1972; Ebenstein et al., 1980, Chaps. 13–15; Abraham, 1980b; Gunther, 1980; Cusham, 1979; Mendelson, 1980). If we want to know the state of constitutional law, it is not enough simply to examine the text of the Constitution. Given the vagueness of many of its provisions, it is necessary that we turn to the actual decisions made by the judiciary in cases before it. Such an analysis reveals a variation in the nature of constitutional law throughout the history of the United States. This suggests that the Supreme Court has considerable discretion in the way it interprets our rather ambiguous Constitution.

The following discussion focuses on four main areas of constitutional law. We begin by examining the powers of various institutions of government. Here we consider the status of constitutional law with respect to Congress, the executive branch, the judiciary, and the states. Second, our attention turns to a discussion of personal liberty. Our analysis will include such forms of personal liberty as freedom of expression, religion, and implied rights. Third, we examine due process of law. This will include an analysis of the rights of suspects, defendants, and those convicted of a crime. Finally, we will consider the constitutional requirement of equal protection under the law. Throughout this discussion certain questions will be relevant. For example: Is the Court's decision a reasonable interpretation of the Constitution? Has the Court gone beyond the bounds of the Constitution in declaring rights? Has the Court been too timid in not declaring additional rights? Is the Court giving appropriate weight to the social values of importance to us?

Institutional Powers

The Constitution, as interpreted by judges, grants certain powers to each institution of government and limits other powers. In *The Federalist Papers* #51, James Madison observed: "In framing a government which is to be administered by men over men, the great difficulty lies in this: you must first enable the government to control the governed; and in the next place oblige it to control itself." (Hamilton, Madison, and Jay, 1961, pp. 320–325) The Constitution sought to achieve both of these objectives. Important powers are granted to various institutions of government, but significant constraints are imposed as well. The powers of Congress are listed in Article I. In Article II the executive powers are invested in the president. Article III grants the judicial powers to the Supreme Court and any other courts that Congress may establish.

No institution of government may encroach upon the fields of the others except as the Constitution provides. For example, the president has some legislative powers, being able to veto Congressional legislation. National powers are limited in Article I, section 9 and in the Bill of Rights, while states are restrained in Article I, section 10 and in the Fourteenth Amendment. Various other provisions of the Constitution also promote or impinge upon the authority of government institutions. These provisions are given meaning through the decisions of the Supreme Court in cases which come before it. No one should underestimate the significance of its decisions in determining the amount of power exercised by each of the branches and levels of government.

Congress   In Article I, section 8 of the Constitution, most of the powers of the national government are assigned to Congress. These powers are not unlimited. In Article I, section 1, Congress is limited to "all legislative powers herein granted." Still, the powers granted to Congress are a far cry from those allocated to the Continental Congress under the Articles of Confederation. Among the Article I, section 8 powers are levying taxes, spending for national defense and general welfare, borrowing money, regulating interstate and foreign commerce, establishing national naturalization and bankruptcy rules, coining and regulating money, establishing post offices and roads, granting patents and copyrights, establishing lower federal courts, exercising war powers, and governing the District of Columbia and other federal enclaves. There are also additional provisions of the Constitution that grant powers to Congress. Some of these powers include admitting new states to the union, proposing constitutional amendments, imposing an income tax, and enforcing various rights through legislation. As a result of Supreme Court decisions, Congress also has the power to delegate authority to the executive branch *(The Aurora v. United States; Field v. Clark; United States v. Grimaud)* and conduct legislative investigations (*Kilbourn v. Thompson*).

The commerce clause of Article I, section 8 deserves special attention. This provision states that Congress shall have the power "to regulate commerce with foreign nations, and among the several states. . . . " Surely, regulation of the economy has come to be one of the most important functions of the national government. The constitutional authority for this activity comes from the commerce clause. Initially, the scope of national regulatory powers was unclear. An early test came in the case of *Gibbons v. Ogden*. Significantly, the Marshall Court announced a very broad interpretation of national regulatory powers. These powers were extended to a wide range of commercial activities. The decision also stated that national regulation could reach into the interior of states to protect the flow of interstate commerce. For a long time the Supreme Court resisted efforts by Congress to regulate production, as evidenced by its decision in *United States v. E. C. Knight Co.* It was this laissez-faire attitude, in fact, that led to Franklin Roosevelt's attack on the Supreme Court. Ultimately, the Court did relent in *National Labor Relations Board v. Jones and Laughlin Steel Corp.* and subsequent cases. Thus, the commerce clause has enabled Congress to exercise enormous powers over the national economy.

Over the course of American history a broad range of national action has been validated through the commerce clause. For example, in *Champion v. Ames* the Supreme Court cited the commerce clause as validating Congressional laws which punished illicit activity of an interstate character. Through this decision the Court circumvented the absence of Congressional police powers in the Constitution.[10] In addition, the Court allowed the use of the commerce clause to validate the nation's sweeping assault on racial discrimination in public accommodations *(Heart of Atlanta Motel, Inc. v. United States)*. Of course, this does not mean that "anything goes" as far as the commerce clause is concerned. Most noteworthy is the decision of the Burger Court in *National League of Cities v. Usery*. In this decision the Court forbade the federal government from placing regulations on the minimum wages that can be paid by state governments. The effect is to limit Congressional authority in this area in favor of state prerogatives.

Also critical to Congressional powers is the "necessary and proper" clause contained in Article I, section 8. The clause itself states that Congress shall have the ability "to make all laws which shall be necessary and proper" for executing its constitutional powers. Clearly, the phrase is subject to various interpretations. A broad interpretation has the effect of expanding the powers of the national government. The Marshall Court confronted this issue in 1819 in the case of *McCulloch v. Maryland*. The federal government had established a national bank even though no such authority is explicitly delegated in the Constitution. The constitutionality of the national bank created by Congress was tested when the state of Maryland imposed a $15,000 tax on the Baltimore branch of the bank. The cashier of the Baltimore branch, James McCulloch, refused to pay, so the state of Maryland sued. In *McCulloch v. Maryland,* the Court took a broad interpretation of the "necessary and proper" clause. According to the Court, Congress could establish the national bank, and the state of Maryland could not tax it. Thus, the powers of Congress were not rigidly tied to those specifically cited in the Constitution. Con-

---

[10]The "police power" held by state governments enables them to protect the safety and welfare of the general public by regulating individuals and property. See *Lemieux v. Young,* 211 U.S. 489 (1908).

gress could fulfill its constitutional mandates through any convenient means. Today the Supreme Court rarely challenges the validity of Congressional legislation unless the legislation impinges on some other constitutional right. At the same time, the Court has found some limits to the delegated powers of Congress, as witnessed in its decision in *Oregon v. Mitchell.*

The President   The framers of the Constitution feared that the presidency would ultimately succumb to an all-powerful legislature. Despite this fear, the history of the American presidency has been one of expanding authority. A number of powers are granted to the president in the text of the Constitution. These include the power to act as commander-in-chief of the military, the power to recommend and to veto legislation, the power to grant reprieves and pardons, extensive powers over foreign affairs, and the role of chief executive. In exercising official duties, the president enjoys absolute immunity from liability for civil damages, even if these damages result from violations of the Constitution (*Nixon v. Fitzgerald*). The exercise of presidential power has grown along with the need for effective action in dealing with war, economic crises, and complex problems. While the president is no dictator, a persuasive president has the constitutional authority to act effectively.

Article II provides: "The executive power shall be vested in a president. . . ." Generally, the executive power of the president has been given broad interpretation by the courts. For example, in *In re Neagle* in 1890 the Supreme Court suggested that the president's duties to execute the laws need not be supported by specific statutes. Thus, there appears to be some inherent executive powers under the Constitution. Subsequently, in *In re Debs* the Supreme Court ruled that the president may even use military force or other necessary means to fulfill the obligations of chief executive. The president also has the authority to declare martial law to restore order, as decided in *Martin v. Mott*. The notion of executive privilege came before the Supreme Court in *United States v. Nixon*. According to Nixon, the White House tapes were privileged communications, which he did not have to release, even to a criminal prosecutor. While the case represented a defeat for Nixon (he was ordered to release the tapes), it was not a defeat for the presidency. The Court ruled that executive privilege did indeed have some constitutional basis, but it did not extend to withholding evidence of a crime.

Broad powers of appointment are granted to the president in the text of the Constitution. It is the president who makes the key appointments in the national executive branch. Even so, the Constitution is unclear as to whether the president also has the authority to remove executive officers. In 1867 Congress passed the Tenure of Office Act, under which department heads could be removed only with Senate consent. The impeachment and near removal of Andrew Johnson resulted from his violation of this act. Subsequently, the act was amended and ultimately repealed. The president's removal powers were finally adjudicated by the Supreme Court in *Myers v. United States*. Here the Court granted the president broad powers to remove executive officials. The decision implied that Congress could not limit the president's control over executive personnel. However, in *Humphrey's Executor v. United States* the president's removal powers were whittled down substantially with regard to independent regulatory agencies. The effect of the decision has been to insulate these regulatory agencies from presidential dominance.

Presidential powers are far more extensive in foreign affairs than in domestic affairs. While military powers are constitutionally divided between the president and Congress, modern technological realities have tended to concentrate such powers in the presidency. For example, in *United States v. Curtiss-Wright Export Corp.* the Supreme Court refused to nullify the delegation of Congressional foreign policy powers to the president. The decision also suggested that the power of the federal government to conduct foreign relations was not limited to the affirmative grants of power contained in the Constitution. The president's substantial powers over foreign affairs are also demonstrated by *United States v. Belmont*. Here the Court ruled that executive agreements would be enforced in American courts as being legally analogous to treaties. This means that a president who wishes to enter into agreements with foreign nations need not resort to treaties, which require the approval of two-thirds of the Senate. On the domestic side, by contrast, there are stronger constitutional limits on presidential power. For example, in the course of the Korean War President Truman seized American steel mills in order to avert a strike. This action was invalidated by the Supreme Court in *Youngstown Sheet and Tube Co. v. Sawyer*. The Supreme Court ruled that Truman's action was an unconstitutional usurpation of legislative authority. The decision helped to limit the powers of the domestic presidency and sustain the operation of checks and balances.

Judiciary   Considerable powers are also exercised by the judiciary. First, it is the task of the courts to interpret the meaning of federal statutes. Statutory interpretation by the courts, even when said to be based on "legislative intent," may be quite different from the apparent aims of Congress and the president. Notably, the Supreme Court's decision in *Weber* upholding affirmative action rested on what critics have called a rather unnatural reading of Title VII of the Civil Rights Act of 1964.[11] Even when the judiciary simply interprets a federal law, it can make significant policy choices. Second, the Supreme Court is also involved in assessing the constitutionality of state laws

---

[11]For example, see the dissenting opinion of Justice Rehnquist in *United Steelworkers v. Weber,* 443 U.S. 193 (1979). At one point Rehnquist writes (p. 222): "Thus, by a *tour de force* reminiscent not of jurists such as Hale, Holmes, and Hughes, but of escape artists such as Houdini, the Court eludes clear statutory language, 'uncontradicted' legislative history, and uniform precedent in concluding that employers are, after all, permitted to consider race in making employment decisions."

and provisions of state constitutions. As indicated by the supremacy clause of Article VI, the Constitution was meant to stand above state constitutions and state laws.

The Supreme Court first claimed the power to review the constitutionality of state laws in *Fletcher v. Peck.* In *Martin v. Hunter's Lessee,* in 1816 the Court ruled that it had the authority to review the corrections of decisions by state supreme courts. Clearly, there are extraordinary ramifications to the use of this power. In some cases the result may be to impose uniform national standards (that is, those enunciated by the federal judiciary) to supersede the variety of standards that may be present in the fifty states. Finally, another power of the Supreme Court is judicial review over the laws and actions of Congress and the executive. First exercised in *Marbury v. Madison* in 1803, the Supreme Court did not declare another federal law unconstitutional until 1857 in *Dred Scott v. Sandford.* While judicial review is exercised only rarely, any use of this power may have important policy consequences. Moreover, the mere threat of judicial review may well act as a powerful constraint on the activities of other government institutions.

States   The replacement of the Articles of Confederation with the United States Constitution clearly weakened the position of the states. In the Constitution no effort is made to itemize the powers to be exercised by the states. Consequently, many functions previously controlled by the states may be subsumed under the powers of the national government. Moreover, certain powers are explicitly denied to the states, such as taxing imports and exports, coining money, and entering into treaties. Yet, the framers did not intend to relegate the states to an inconsequential role. It was the intention of the framers to reserve to the states all powers not granted to the national government. Indeed, the Tenth Amendment was added to make this aim explicit.[12]

More important than the absence of delegated powers is the presence of many powers held concurrently by the federal government and the states. Thus, the states as well as the federal government have the constitutional authority to tax and spend for the general welfare. State governments may act in an area unless the activity is expressly forbidden by the United States Constitution or by their own state constitution. Although national powers and expenditures have greatly expanded in the course of American history, state governments have surely not become impotent. In our nation some important policy choices are made by state governments. Indeed, most of the laws respecting civil and criminal justice are adopted and enforced at the state level. At the same time, recent decades have seen the increased imposition of national standards upon

---

[12]Note, though, that in *McCulloch v. Maryland* the Supreme Court adjudged a broad interpretation of the powers granted to the national government.

state governments. (See the discussion below on the application of the Bill of Rights to the states through the Fourteenth Amendment.)

Personal Liberty

Personal liberty is given some protection by the Constitution. The First Amendment was designed to prevent Congress from imposing controls that limited freedom of religion, speech, press, and assembly. According to the First Amendment, "Congress shall make no law" limiting these several freedoms. This constitutional language suggests that these liberties must not be sacrificed, regardless of the effect on other social values. As a result, the language of the First Amendment has stirred a debate among the justices as to whether "no law" should really mean *"no* law."

Justice Hugo Black has stated: "It is my belief that there are 'absolutes' in our Bill of Rights, and that they were put there on purpose by men who knew what words meant. . . ." (1963, p. 45) Even so, there has been little sympathy on the Court (or among the general public) (Zellman, 1975) for this absolutist position. As a result, some restrictions on First Amendment rights have been permitted in order to safeguard other values. Various criteria falling short of absolutism have been employed to assess whether a particular law is constitutional. Indeed, Justice Black himself voted in favor of certain restraints on personal liberty while serving on the High Court. At the same time, First Amendment freedoms have been extended by the Supreme Court in that the restrictions now apply to the states as well as to the national government. The First Amendment was "incorporated" into the Fourteenth Amendment in a series of cases (Heberie, 1972). The Fourteenth Amendment reads (in part) that no state shall "deprive any person of life, liberty, or property, without due process of law. . . ." The result is that the Constitution, as now interpreted by the Supreme Court, also forbids the states from imposing certain controls on First Amendment rights.

Freedom of Expression   A major aspect of personal liberty is freedom of expression, or the right to communicate orally or in writing. Also of relevance are the rights of picketing, assembly, petition, and spending money to support a candidate. The language of the First Amendment seems unequivocal: "Congress shall make no law . . . abridging the freedom of speech, or of the press; or the right of the people peaceably to assemble, and to petition the Government for a redress of grievances." (Note that in *Gitlow v. New York* the Supreme Court applied the constitutional requirement of free expression to the states.) Despite the sweeping character of this language, the Supreme Court has not accepted all forms of expression as constitutionally protected. At some point the Court must "draw the line" between instances of free expression which are constitutionally protected and instances which are not. A number of tests have been used by the justices to assist them in determining where to draw the line.[13] Each test provides a different degree of protection for various forms of expression.

The Supreme Court has upheld some limits on free expression where its exercise may slander, libel, or otherwise injure someone. However, prior restraint of the press was forbidden in *Near v. Minnesota.* In this case an anti-Semitic newspaper had been enjoined from publishing under a Minnesota statute which provided that "malicious, scandalous, and defamatory" newspapers could be treated as public nuisances and forbidden to publish. The Supreme Court invalidated the statute as an infringement on freedom of the press. If prior censorship is generally unconstitutional, those who are guilty of slandering or libeling others may still be punished after the fact. While we do not want someone's reputation to be falsely besmirched, neither do we wish to silence free expression by threatening to punish people for what they say or write.

In *Beauharnais v. Illinois* the Supreme Court upheld the constitutionality of a criminal libel law that allowed for the punishment of those who portray groups of people as depraved, criminal, or unchaste. In the Beauharnais case the Supreme Court sanctioned the right of the state of Illinois to punish Beauharnais, of the White Circle League, for publishing a racist leaflet. In other cases the desire to safeguard freedom of expression has sometimes been seen as overriding. For example, in *New York Times v. Sullivan* the police commissioner of Montgomery, Alabama, sued *The New York Times* for printing a paid advertisement which falsely criticized police treatment of blacks in Montgomery. A decision against the *Times* could have silenced some controversial reporting. However, the Supreme Court ruled against Sullivan, arguing that a public official may not recover damages for libel unless the official is able to prove that the statement was made with knowledge of its falsity or with reckless disregard of whether or not it was false.

Restrictions have also been placed on free expression where it endangers social order. In general, the Supreme Court will not interfere with what people, in the course of their everyday lives, say to one another (excluding the conveying of threats). On the other hand, the Court has been more willing to limit free expression when it takes a more organized or symbolic form, such as communicating ideas by marching, picketing, or demonstrating. Such forms of expression have been termed "speech plus conduct." The Court has upheld limitations on the nonspeech element if a sufficiently important governmental interest is involved: In *United States v. O'Brien* the Court upheld the constitutionality of a federal law prohibiting the destruction or mutilation of draft registration cards. Free expression was a central issue here, since O'Brien had

[13]Among the tests have been "clear and present danger," *Schenck v. United States,* 249 U.S. 47 (1919); "bad tendency," *Gitlow v. New York,* 268 U.S. 652 (1925); "imminence," *Whitney v. California,* 274 U.S. 357 (1927); and "redeeming social value," *Chaplinsky v. New Hampshire,* 315 U.S. 568 (1942).

burned his registration card as part of a demonstration against the Vietnam War. In a separate case, however, the Supreme Court upheld the right of school children to wear black armbands as a protest against the Vietnam War (*Tinker v. Des Moines School District*). Since the aim of symbolic speech is to attract attention, it will almost always entail the use of a public place. In *Hague v. CIO* the Supreme Court recognized a right of access to "the public forum."[14] However, the Court has been mindful of the fact that demonstrations on streets and other public areas may interfere with normal uses. As a result, the Supreme Court has sanctioned laws requiring demonstrators to obtain a permit. (There is no right to hold a sit-in at Times Square, New York City, during rush-hour traffic.) At the same time, the Court has also ruled that a permit system may not be administered in a discriminatory fashion.

Limits on free expression are also allowed where it undermines community morality. In an early case, *Roth v. United States,* the Supreme Court declared that obscenity was "utterly without redeeming social importance" and therefore was not protected by the First Amendment. The Court sustained the validity of the obscenity law and upheld the conviction of Roth under that law. The test that the justices applied was "whether to the average person, applying contemporary community standards, the dominant theme of the material taken as a whole appeals to prurient interest." This test, and others that developed, were generally applied by the justices so as to ban only "hard core pornography." In 1973 the Supreme Court set on a new course in *Miller v. California.* In its decision the Court permitted findings of obscenity when the material lacked serious literary, artistic, political, or scientific value. Most critically, the Court stated that *local* rather than *national* standards were to be used in evaluating whether the material was obscene. Since then the Court has upheld a New York criminal statute which outlaws producing, directing, or promoting child pornography *(New York v. Ferber).* In the area of obscenity the Supreme Court has also sanctioned the use of zoning laws to restrict the number and concentration of adult film theatres, bookshops, and massage parlors *(Young v. American Mini-Theatres).*

It appears that there are also some circumstances under which the Supreme Court might permit prior restraint of the press to protect national security. This is suggested by the Court's decision in *New York Times Co. v. United States.* The case concerned the publication of *The Pentagon Papers—* a classified study of American policy in the Vietnam War (The New York Times, 1971). The United States government sought to enjoin publication of the study through prior censorship. As discussed above, in its *Near* decision in 1931 the Supreme Court had recognized national security as a possible justification for prior restraint. In the *New York Times Co.* case the Court did decide to dissolve the lower court injunction that had interrupted publication

---

[14]Moreover, in *NAACP v. Claiborne Hardware Company,* 50 LW 5122 (1982), the Supreme Court held that the NAACP, which had held a peaceful boycott of white merchants in Claiborne, Mississippi, could not be made liable for the resulting economic loss to the merchants.

of *The Pentagon Papers.* However, a look at the separate opinions of the nine justices suggests that the Court would have been willing to permit prior restraint had the government been able to make a stronger argument on national security grounds.

    Freedom of Religion   Freedom of religion is also given constitutional protection by the First Amendment. A portion of that amendment reads: "Congress shall make no law respecting an establishment of religion, or prohibiting the free exercise therof. . . ." Thus, freedom of religion is protected by two clauses—the "establishment clause" and the "free exercise clause." These clauses are given meaning by the decisions of the Supreme Court. The establishment clause has served to protect religious freedom by preventing government from promoting any particular religion. The free exercise clause seeks to prevent government from interfering with an individual's practice of religious beliefs. Like other First Amendment rights, freedom of religion has been made applicable to the states *(Cantwell v. Connecticut).*

    The meaning of the "establishment clause" has engendered a great deal of debate. At one extreme the clause can be narrowly interpreted to mean that Congress is merely forbidden from establishing an official, publicly supported religion of the kind that had existed in England. If we accept this view, then many kinds of governmental activities relevant to religion are constitutionally permissible. Congress could, under this interpretation, provide aid to parochial schools and other religious institutions as long as no preference was shown for one religion over another. At the other extreme, however, the "establishment clause" can be interpreted as barring any government support whatsoever to religion. According to this view, the Constitution demands that there be a "wall of separation" between church and state. In practice the Court has tended toward the "wall of separation" interpretation but has not been rigidly bound to it. In *Engel v. Vitale* the Court struck down the practice in New York State public schools of reciting a prayer that had been approved by the State Board of Regents. The Court held that such a prayer placed the state in a nonneutral position. Similarly, Bible reading and the recitation of the Lord's Prayer in class have been held unconstitutional *(Abington School District v. Schempp).* However, in *Zorach v. Clauson* the Court upheld a New York program permitting public school students to be released from classes to attend religious institutions off school grounds. Similarly, in *Walz v. Tax Commission* the Supreme Court upheld state tax exemptions for real property owned by religious organizations and used for religious purposes. In some cases certain forms of indirect aid to parochial schools have been disallowed, as in *Lemon v. Kurtzman;* other forms have been approved, however, as benefiting the child rather than the religious institution *(Everson v. Board of Education).*

    The "free exercise" of religion is also constitutionally protected by judicial interpretation of the First Amendment. Yet, again, the precise meaning of the constitutional language is not self-evident. It is possible to interpret the clause as meaning that individuals are free to practice the tenets of their religion without interference from government. In *Pierce v. Society of Sisters* the Supreme Court ruled unconstitutional an Oregon statute compelling attendance in a public school between ages eight and sixteen. The Court reasoned that if parents wanted to send their children to a parochial or other private school, this was within their rights. Similarly, in *Wisconsin v. Yoder* the Court ruled that a child may not be compelled to attend school beyond the eighth grade, if this is contrary to a legitimate religious belief. In addition, in *Sherbert v. Verner* the Supreme Court reversed a state denial of unemployment benefits to a Seventh Day Adventist who refused to accept a job which would have required her to work on Saturdays, contrary to her religious beliefs.

Notwithstanding cases such as these, however, the High Court has not always upheld the right of an individual to put religious beliefs into practice. Instead, the Court has enforced a "secular regulation rule." According to this rule, people may believe what they want to believe, but they may not always put their beliefs into practice. Religion may not be used as an excuse for breaking laws that have a valid secular purpose which outweighs (that is, in the minds of the justices) any concerns based on religion. Thus, despite the approval of polygamy by Mormons, it is not a right protected by the "free exercise" clause and may be criminally punished *(Reynolds v. United States)*. Similarly, in *Jacobson v. Massachusetts* the Supreme Court upheld compulsory vaccination laws despite objections based on religious convictions. In addition, the Court denied a "free exercise" claim which argued that freedom of religion includes the right to exhibit poisonous snakes in a church *(Thompson v. Lawson)*.

Implied Rights   Most of our individual rights, as articulated by the Supreme Court, refer to some clause in the text of the Constitution. Nevertheless, there are also a number of "implied rights." These are rights that have been given constitutional protection by the Supreme Court even though they are not explicitly mentioned in the Constitution (Davis, 1980–1981). For example, the Court has long recognized that people have a right to travel. In *Crandall v. Nevada* the Supreme Court negated a state tax imposed on every person leaving the state by common carrier.

Several implied rights are associated with the First Amendment. While the following rights are not included in the express language of that amendment, the Supreme Court has declared that people have a right to engage in symbolic expression *(Stromberg v. California);* to use public property as a forum *(Hague v. CIO);* and to associate with others to promote ideas *(NAACP v. Alabama)*. In addition, the Supreme Court has declared some things as rights because they are "fundamental." For example, in *Reynolds v. Sims* the Supreme Court ruled that people have a fundamental right to vote in state elections. Beyond that, constitutional protection has been assigned to the right to marry *(Loving v. Virginia),* to procreate *(Skinner v. Oklahoma),* to avoid procreation *(Griswold v. Connecticut),* and to have rights associated with child rearing *(Meyer v. Nebraska; Pierce v. Society of Sisters).* Finally, in the momentous decision of *Roe v. Wade* the Supreme Court invalidated restrictive abortion laws on the grounds of an implied right to privacy.

There are some who object to the judiciary's unilateral declaration of implied rights. Critics note that the vehicle of implied rights can be used by the Court to go well beyond the rights contained in the Constitution. In so doing, the Court may seem to be arbitrarily overruling the policies enacted by elected representatives. At the same time, the language of the Ninth Amendment states that citizens have constitutional rights beyond those specifically enumerated in the Constitution. In the language of the Ninth Amendment: "The enumeration in the Constitution, of certain rights, shall not be construed to deny or disparage others retained by the people." The Ninth Amendment provides some justification for those who wish to establish additional rights beyond the discretion of elected representatives.

Due Process

Due process is the area of constitutional law directly concerned with procedural justice. Various provisions of the Constitution address the treatment of suspects, defendants, and convicts. The courts have the task of interpreting the meaning of these provisions as applied to particular cases. Since the 1960s the courts have come under sharp criticism for being overly concerned with the rights of those accused of a crime. These criticisms are based largely on a series of procedural justice decisions by the Warren Court. The members of the Warren Court defended their decisions as being consistent with provisions of the Constitution. It seems likely that many Warren Court decisions went beyond majority sentiment in declaring rights of suspects, defendants, and convicts. Still, many would argue that it was the purpose of the Bill of Rights to ensure that certain values, including procedural justice, were protected, regardless of prevailing majority sentiment. To some extent the judiciary may be able to apply the provisions of the Constitution to fulfill this mission.

The protection of due process rights can, at times, interfere with the criminal justice system's quest for obtaining the conviction of likely offenders. It is noteworthy, however, that the Supreme Court has sought to limit this possibility. In the case of *Harrington v. California* in 1969 the Warren Court held that some violations of procedural justice may be regarded as only "harmless error." In other words, the Supreme Court will not automatically overturn a conviction on some technicality. Instead, the Court will attempt to determine how much of an impact the error would have on an average jury. Thus, if there is overwhelming evidence pointing to the guilt of a defendant, a technical violation of due process will not necessarily bring about reversal of a conviction.[15]

When discussing procedural justice, a key concern is the application of the Bill of Rights to state courts. After all, it is in the state courts that nearly all criminal cases are prosecuted. In *Barron v. Baltimore* in 1833 the Supreme Court ruled that the Bill of Rights imposed limits only upon the federal government. This meant that the multitude of procedural safeguards contained in the Constitution were not applicable to the state courts. While most state constitutions contained a bill of rights, state courts were not highly protective of due process rights. With the adoption of the Fourteenth Amendment in 1868, however, a new constitutional basis existed for asserting that national standards of procedural justice were now applicable to the states. The Fourteenth Amendment provides, in part, that no state may deprive a person "of life, liberty, or property, without due process of law. . . ." Total incorporation of the Bill of Rights into the Fourteenth Amendment was advocated by Justice John Harlan Sr. and later by Justice Hugo Black. This would entail the application of the entire Bill of Rights, including the provisions pertaining to procedural justice, to the states.

The notion of total incorporation was not embraced by the Supreme Court. In *Palko v. Connecticut* in 1937 the Court ruled that states were free to adopt any standards which did not conflict with "the concept of ordered liberty" and did not violate "fundamental principles" of justice. However, what ultimately transpired was a "selective incorporation" of the Bill of Rights on a case-by-case basis. During the 1930s and 1940s procedural safeguards were incorporated into the Fourteenth Amendment in a few cases. These protections included the right to a fair trial and the right to counsel in capital cases *(Powell v. Alabama);* the right to a public trial *(In re Oliver);* and the right which protects against unreasonable searches and seizures *(Wolf v. Colorado).* Even so, the great thrust for incorporation of procedural safeguards did not come until the era of the Warren Court. Beginning with *Mapp v. Ohio* in 1961, the Warren Court incorporated into the Fourteenth Amendment various provisions of the Fourth, Fifth, Sixth, and Eighth Amendments. This involved an enormous change in Supreme Court doctrine regarding procedural justice. Those who sympathized with these decisions feared that with the coming of the Burger Court, there would be a repudiation of this jurisprudence. However, while the Burger Court has chipped away at some procedural rights, its main thrust has been one of consolidation.[16]

[15]However, the "harmless error" rule is limited by the Court's doctrine of "fruit of the poisonous tree." See *Wong Sun v. United States,* 371 U.S. 471 (1974) and *Taylor v. Alabama,* 50 LW 4783 (1982).

[16]For example, see the Burger Court's decisions in *Adams v. Williams,* 407 U.S. 143 (1972); *Brown v. Texas,* 443 U.S. 47 (1979); *Pennsylvania v. Mimms,* 434 U.S. 106 (1977); *Delaware v. Prouse,* 440 U.S. 648 (1979).

Rights of Suspects   Suspects are granted a number of important rights under the Constitution. For example, the Fourth Amendment protects individuals "in their persons, houses, papers and effects, against unreasonable searches and seizures." *(Boyd v. United States)* A series of court decisions have set the bounds for permissible and unlawful searches and seizures. Thus, in *Brown v. Texas* the Supreme Court ruled that the police may "stop and frisk" a person only when circumstances justify a reasonable suspicion that the person was involved in criminal conduct. Additionally, places can be searched without a warrant only under certain circumstances. In *Boyd v. United States* in 1886, the Supreme Court refused to permit the government to force an individual to produce papers that might lead to his conviction. Supreme Court decisions also touch on the circumstances under which electronic surveillance, such as wiretapping, is unlawful or unconstitutional *(Olmstead v. United States; Silverman v. United States)*. Also dealing with the rights of suspects was the highly significant decision of the Court in *Miranda v. Arizona*. Here the Supreme Court laid out a stiff code of police conduct. Prior to interrogating suspects, an officer must inform the suspects of their rights, including the right to remain silent and to see an attorney. These rules were designed to give meaning to the Fifth Amendment protection against self-incrimination which states that no one "shall be compelled in any criminal case to be a witness against himself." *(Malloy v. Hogan; Murphy v. Waterfront Commission of New York)* According to Court doctrine, confessions must be voluntary *(Rogers v. Richmond)* and must result from a free and rational choice *(Spano v. New York)*.

Rights of Defendants   Under the Constitution defendants are protected by numerous procedural safeguards.[17] The Fifth Amendment provides that a person must be indicted by a grand jury for capital crimes. However, the Supreme Court has not applied this federal requirement to state courts *(Hurtado v. California)*. In addition, the Fifth Amendment protects against double jeopardy for the same offense. A defendant who is acquitted in a federal trial court cannot be retried for the same offense. The double jeopardy rule was applied to the states in *Benton v. Maryland*.[18] The Eighth Amendment, meanwhile, prohibits excessive bail *(Stack v. Boyle)*. Trial by jury in criminal cases is required by Article II of the Constitution as well as by the Sixth Amendment. In the federal courts a trial by twelve jurors is required in criminal cases. However, the Burger Court has held that in the states juries may have as few as six members *(Williams v. Florida)*, and they need not reach a verdict unanimously *(Johnson v. Louisiana)*. The Sixth Amendment also speaks of the right of defendants to legal counsel *(Johnson v. Zerbst)*. Initially, state courts were

[17]Note that procedural rights as expressed in Court doctrine may, in practice, be abridged by criminal justice personnel. See Abraham S. Blumberg, *Criminal Justice* (Chicago: Quadrangle Books, 1967b).

[18]However, see also the Burger Court's ruling in *Tibbs v. Florida,* 50 LW 4607 (1982).

required to provide an attorney only under special circumstances *(Powell v. Alabama; Betts v. Brady)*. Not until 1963, in the celebrated case of *Gideon v. Wainwright* (and later in *Escobedo v. Illinois)*, did the Court hold that an attorney is constitutionally required in felony cases. This was extended nine years later in *Argersinger v. Hamlin* to misdemeanor cases which might be punished by imprisonment. In the courtroom the exclusionary rule makes illegally obtained evidence inadmissible. The exclusionary rule is a means of enforcing the due process rights of the Fourth and Fifth Amendments. It was incorporated into the Fourteenth Amendment by the Court's decision in *Mapp v. Ohio*. However, in *Harris v. New York* the Burger Court chipped away at the exclusionary rule as it pertains to a defendant who, when questioned, is not given *Miranda* rights. According to this ruling, if a defendant takes the witness stand, any statements made to the police may be introduced as evidence (that is, even though the defendant was not given *Miranda* rights) in order to help the jury assess the defendant's credibility.

Rights of Convicts   Those convicted of a crime are also afforded various constitutional safeguards. Most notable is the Eighth Amendment protection against the infliction of "cruel and unusual punishments." This was incorporated into the Fourteenth Amendment in 1962 by *Robinson v. California*. Perhaps the most widely publicized case concerning rights of convicts was *Furman v. Georgia*. Here the Supreme Court held that the death penalty in the state of Georgia was unconstitutional. However, the case left open the possibility that a less arbitrary statute calling for the death penalty might be declared valid. Numerous criminal statutes underwent revision as a result of the *Furman* decision. Ultimately, the Court did uphold a death penalty statute in *Gregg v. Georgia*. However, the Court ruled that imposing the death penalty in rape cases is not constitutional *(Coker v. Georgia)*. Further, the Court has held that in applying the death penalty to juveniles, their background and emotional and mental development must be considered *(Eddings v. Oklahoma)*. Also, the Court has ruled that persons who participated in a robbery where a killing took place may not be put to death if they themselves did not kill or intend to kill *(Enmund v. Florida)*.

Convicts also have other constitutionally protected rights. For example, the Constitution provides for a writ of habeas corpus. This may allow imprisoned persons to be released if they have been arrested arbitrarily or punished unlawfully. A law of Congress passed in 1867 permitted those convicted in state courts to have their case reviewed by a federal court through issuance of a writ. This caseload grew substantially in the 1960s and 1970s; in response, the Burger Court decided in *Stone v. Powell* to limit access to federal habeas corpus if the defendant was provided a full opportunity to air Fourth Amendment grievances in the state courts. Beyond that, the Supreme Court has also ruled that prisoners must be granted certain civil rights. Various decisions have limited censorship of a prisoner's mail *(Procunier v. Martinez),* required attentiveness to a prisoner's illness or injury *(Estelle v. Gamble),* and provided that prisoners receive assistance in preparing legal claims *(Bounds v. Smith).*

Equal Protection

It is in the very nature of laws to make distinctions of one kind or another (Chase and Ducat, 1979, p. 728). A law may specify that different groups of people should receive some kind of distinct treatment. Thus, the law may provide that certain people are entitled to receive government benefits such as unemployment compensation, while others are not. Also, state law may prevent people under a certain age (for example, sixteen or eighteen) from driving a car. In both cases government is discriminating—that is, the law is making distinctions between people. In most instances such distinctions are usually regarded as reasonable. It is necessary for government to set eligibility rules for determining who may receive unemployment benefits and who may drive an automobile. However, while some distinctions in the law are either necessary or acceptable, there may be certain distinctions that are somehow offensive. Indeed, some distinctions may be so offensive that we would want to constitutionally forbid legislators or executives from ever making them. For example, we can appreciate the need to prevent the very young from driving an automobile. Yet, a law that barred black people from driving a car would be inherently objectionable. Modern constitutional theory argues that it is desirable to constitutionally forbid the creation of classifications in the law that are unreasonable, arbitrary, or invidious. A key question for any Court, however, is where to draw the line between legislative classifications which are or are not constitutional.

The notion of equal protection of the law, as embodied in the Fourteenth Amendment, seeks to prevent legislators from making distinctions among Americans which are objectionable. The equal protection clause of the Fourteenth Amendment asserts: "No state shall . . . deny to any person within its jurisdiction the equal protection of the laws." Since 1868, when the amendment was ratified, various interpretations have been offered by the Supreme Court. Some argue that the original intention of the Fourteenth Amendment was quite limited in scope (Perry, 1979, p. 1027; Berger, 1977). From this perspective the aims of the amendment were to protect the safety of blacks, ensure their free movement, and provide them with basic property rights. In the *Civil Rights Cases* in 1883 the Supreme Court ruled that the Fourteenth Amendment provided no restrictions on discrimination by private citizens. This interpretation held that the Fourteenth Amendment was a bar only on state action of a discriminatory nature and not on "private discrimination."[19] With

---

[19]Not until 1948 in *Shelley v. Kraemer,* 334 U.S. 1 (1948), did the Supreme Court offer a broader interpretation of "state action."

regard to discrimination by the states, however, an early Supreme Court decision interpreted the Fourteenth Amendment with some force. In *Strauder v. West Virginia* in 1880 the Court reversed the conviction of a black man as a violation of the equal protection clause because state law had prevented blacks from serving on the jury. *Strauder* might have served as a precedent for use of the Fourteenth Amendment to bar a wide range of distinctions made by state governments discriminating against blacks.

But state discrimination against blacks would not soon dissipate. Despite *Strauder,* the Court soon reversed gears and placed a rather narrow interpretation on the intended meaning of the equal protection clause. Of enormous significance was the Court's decision in *Plessy v. Ferguson* in 1896. Here the Court upheld a Louisiana statute mandating separate but equal railway accommodations for whites and blacks. This decision provided support for a whole system of segregation that had developed in many states and cities following the Civil War. Legislation was enacted permitting or requiring segregation of all manner of facilities—buses, drinking fountains, schools, hospitals, housing, theaters, hotels, restaurants, and the like. In *Plessy* the Court held that legislatures must have "large discretion" in determining what is "a reasonable regulation." According to the Court, a legislature "is at liberty to act with reference to the established usages, customs and traditions of the people, and with a view to the promotion of their comfort, and the preservation of the public peace and good order." (at 550) By this "minimal scrutiny" approach the Supreme Court allowed legislatures wide discretion in selecting statutory classifications. A classification would be held valid if it simply were rationally related to some legitimate state interest.[20]

Finally, in the 1950s and 1960s the content of the equal protection clause was recast by the Warren Court. In *Brown v. Board of Education* the Court renounced the doctrine of "separate but equal" as advanced in *Plessy*. Writing for the Court, Chief Justice Warren argued: "We conclude that in the field of public education the doctrine of 'separate but equal' has no place." (at 495) The *Brown* decision was followed by a number of other rulings which invalidated objectionable distinctions in the law. These included the segregation of beaches *(Mayor of Baltimore v. Dawson),* buses *(Gayle v. Browder),* golf courses *(Holmes v. City of Atlanta),* and parks *(New Orleans City Park Imp. Ass'n v. Detiege).* Similarly, the Warren Court invalidated a state law which required that the race of every candidate appear on the ballot *(Anderson v. Martin).* Under the Warren Court the traditional "minimal scrutiny" approach was replaced by a "two-tiered" approach. A statutory classification would receive "strict scrutiny" if it involved an inherently "suspect category" or touched upon a "fundamental interest." While strict scrutiny did not al-

---

[20]For example, see *Lindsley v. National Carbonic Gas Co.,* 220 U.S. 61 (1911).

ways mean that the justices would invalidate the law in question, invalidation would occur unless the classification advanced some compelling state interest. Thus, the Fourteenth Amendment was used by the Warren Court to substantially curtail legislative discretion to make certain distinctions in the law.

Significantly, the Warren Court extended the scope of the equal protection clause beyond racial classifications. Most notably, political equality was held to be within the bounds of the Fourteenth Amendment *(Baker v. Carr; Wesberry v. Sanders; Reynolds v. Sims)*. Severe malapportionment of legislative districts had made the value of one person's vote far greater than that of another. After finally agreeing that legislative apportionment was a justiciable issue, the Court set a standard of "one person, one vote." In *Reynolds v. Sims* the Court ruled: "Since the achieving of fair and effective representation for all citizens is concededly the basic aim of legislative apportionment, we conclude that the Equal Protection Clause guarantees the opportunity for equal participation by all voters in the election of state legislators." (at 565–566) Many analysts felt that the equal protection clause would soon be extended by the Court to cover additional "suspect categories" and "fundamental interests." As Gerald Gunther notes: "The Warren Court left a legacy of anticipations as well as accomplishments. Its new equal protection was a dynamic concept, and the radiations encouraged hopes of further steps toward egalitarianism." (1972, p. 8)

The work of the Warren Court could have served as the beginnings for a broad base of equal protection rights. As events unfolded, however, Chief Justice Earl Warren retired and was replaced in 1969 by Warren Earl Burger. As president, Richard Nixon appointed four justices to the High Court; his accidental successor, Gerald Ford, replaced another. In general, the Burger Court has sought to restrain the domain protected under the Fourteenth Amendment by the criterion of strict scrutiny. Indeed, the sustained effort made to pass an Equal Rights Amendment for women reflects the Court's continuing refusal to recognize sex as a "suspect classification" under the Fourteenth Amendment *(Geduldig v. Aiello; Reed v. Reed; Frontiero v. Richardson; Craig v. Boren)*. Similarly, the Burger Court has refused to recognize wealth as a "suspect classification" or education as a "fundamental interest" *(San Antonio v. Rodriguez)*. Beyond that, the Burger Court has held a wavering position with regard to equal protection for aliens *(Graham v. Richardson; Foley v. Connelie)* and illegitimates *(Levy v. Louisiana; Mathews v. Lucas)*. Rather than extending the criterion of "strict scrutiny" to new areas, the Burger Court has required only that legislative classifications be "substantially related" to legislative purposes *(Craig v. Boren)*. While this has more bite than the original criterion of "minimal scrutiny," it still represents a rather restrained approach to equal protection claims. Institutionally, the effect is to limit Supreme Court activism in favor of legislative discretion. From the standpoint of social values, the effect is to fail to guarantee more equality to women and the poor as a matter of "right."

THE IMPACT OF COURTS

Examining Impact

In the previous section we focused on the principal areas of Supreme Court doctrine. While this is a critical area of concern, it is hardly the last word on the subject of Court policy. Jonathan Casper has offered a useful distinction between three levels of law—doctrinal, attitudinal, and behavioral (1972b, pp. 3–10). Doctrinal law consists of the formal rules enunciated by the legal system. It includes the United States Constitution and state constitutions, the laws of Congress and other legislatures, treaties, executive actions, administrative rules, and the decisions of courts. As we have already seen, the Supreme Court plays a very important part in setting the nation's doctrinal law. In areas such as institutional powers, freedom of expression, due process of law, and equal protection, the voice of the Court is quite powerful.

However, despite the significance of doctrinal law, the nature of law at the attitudinal and behavioral levels must also be considered. It must be realized that Court doctrine is not always implemented. While the voice of the Court is powerful, it is not always heard, accepted, or obeyed. Hence, written opinions of judges will not invariably alter the attitudes or behavior of people—certainly not precisely as the Court desires. Attitudinal law refers to the perceptions of people with regard to doctrinal law. Our concern is with how people perceive the law as it is and as it ought to be. Often we wish to learn whether a change in doctrinal law has produced a similar change in the attitudes of citizens. Both the attitudes of the general population and those of the people directly affected by a law need to be understood. Behavioral law concerns "the living law," or law as it is practiced in daily life. In the 1920s doctrinal law outlawed the consumption of alcohol. Yet, there was so little compliance and such spotty enforcement that one can truly say that behavioral law was quite divergent from doctrinal law. Perhaps the major test of the effectiveness of a law is its ability to produce the desired changes at the behavioral level.

The problems of translating doctrinal law into attitudinal and behavioral law are illustrated by our nation's experience with school desegregation (Shank and Conant, 1975, pp. 370–379). It was in 1954 in *Brown v. Board of Education* that the Supreme Court declared "separate but equal" schools to be unconstitutional. The Court ordered that schools be desegregated "with all deliberate speed." However, the pace of desegregation proved to be imperceptibly slow. In 1967, thirteen years after *Brown,* the U. S. Commission on Civil Rights reported that most students were still attending segregated schools (1967). The Commission noted that in seventy-five cities, 75 percent of black students attended schools which were more than 90 percent black. Similarly, 88 percent of the white students attended schools that were over 90 percent white. It was more difficult to achieve desegregation in the North than in the South. Outside the South schools were segregated largely because of housing patterns and school district boundaries rather than through legally enforced dual school systems *(Keyes v. School District No. 1)*. By 1974 the Court had become divided over further desegregation of schools, having encountered obstacles such as residential patterns, white suburbs, and increasing presidential and Congressional resistance *(Milliken v. Bradley; Pasadena City Board of Education v. Spangler)*. While the judiciary is still heavily involved in school desegregation efforts, the phenomenon of segregated schools persists in our nation. Compliance has been neither swift nor assured.

Many observers were astonished at the widespread failure of school districts to comply with the *Brown* decision and related litigation. Most Court analysts failed to recognize that judicial decisions are not automatically translated into social reality. In retrospect, however, the absence of immediate compliance with the *Brown* decision should not have been so surprising. As James Levine notes, we should not expect a written opinion of a court to "create the instantaneous and drastic effects of a nuclear explosion. . . ." (1970, p. 589) The Supreme Court may, under some circumstances, be powerful. However, it is not an omnipotent institution. As Levine adds: "The Supreme Court is *not* a Supreme Being." (1970, p. 592) Recognition of the failure of Court doctrine to become translated into living law leads inescapably to a concern for impact.

In addressing Court impact, it should be clear that we are dealing with a highly complex subject. Impacts may be rather inconsequential, or they may deeply affect the lives of countless Americans. It is the litigants to a case who feel the immediate impact of a court case. Indeed, a court ruling is, in a formal sense, only applicable to the parties in a case. Even here, however, impact is problematic. It is always possible that a losing party will attempt to evade the implications of a court ruling. Compliance with a court decision is far from automatic. Beyond that, there is always doubt as to whether "similarly situated" individuals will voluntarily adhere to the apparent implications of court rulings. Failing voluntary compliance, it would be necessary for new lawsuits to be filed by injured parties in order to bring noncompliers into line. Problems arise here, however, since the Supreme Court does not have the time to hear every follow-up case in areas it has already ruled upon. Further, as we have seen, the lower courts do not uniformly adhere to Supreme Court doctrine.

In discussing court impact, we must look beyond the degree of compliance with court decisions (Wasby, 1970, pp. 3–15, 27–56). In any Supreme Court case there may be an abundance of unanticipated consequences. For example, a clear aim of the Court's desegregation decisions was to benefit black schoolchildren in some way. However, there are serious questions as to whether this intended effect has been realized. Notably, some have argued that cross-town busing is associated with white flight to the suburbs (Coleman, Kelly, and Moore, 1975).[21] If white middle-class families really do move to the

[21]But see also Christine H. Rossell, "School Desegregation and White Flight," *Political Science Quarterly*, 1975–1976, *90*, 675–695.

suburbs to escape busing, this may leave blacks in a worse situation than before. Housing segregation will have increased; the fiscal hardship of central cities will have worsened; central city schools might be no less segregated than before the issuance of the busing edict. It is also argued that the educational achievement scores in desegregated schools do not appreciably improve (Armor, 1972).[22] Indeed, any gains may be far outweighed by the social disruption engendered and the huge financial costs involved in cross-town busing. More deeply, school busing may have contributed to a climate of opinion opposing an activist national government. Such sentiment makes it far more difficult for the government to engage in other, perhaps more effective, social programs. In any event this discussion of possible impacts should illustrate the enormous difficulties involved in assessing the impact of a court decision.

Correlates of Compliance

The decisions of the Supreme Court are likely to have a greater impact if certain conditions prevail (Wasby, 1970, pp. 243–268; Levine, 1970; Sheldon, 1974, pp. 127–163; Grossman, 1970). Because this is a concern of recent vintage, there is much uncertainty as to the correlates of court impact. Hypotheses abound, but the evidence is spotty or nonexistent. We might expect that judicial impact will vary with factors such as the formal powers of the Court, the activism of its members, and the procedures used by the Court (Grossman, 1970). Given that these characteristics are constants (that is, unchanging) at any given time, most attention has focused on other factors. The three basic sets of variables which have been examined relate to the internal characteristics of the Court, various external governmental conditions, and a number of environmental influences. In the following discussion we narrow our field of inquiry to the matter of compliance with Supreme Court decisions. Given the "right" set of circumstances, compliance with a Supreme Court decision is considerably more likely.

To begin with, certain internal characteristics of the Supreme Court may be of importance in achieving compliance. It has been argued, for example, that a clearly announced decision is more likely to have a substantial impact. After all, if the litigants and similarly situated parties are not given clear instructions, they may not be certain as to how they are expected to act. Other internal factors of possible relevance include the degree of consensus on the Supreme Court, the craftsmanship of the written opinion, whether the decision has a constitutional or statutory basis, whether the decision overrules a precedent, the completeness of a decision, release of the decision simultaneously with other decisions, and whether the Court periodically repeats its doctrine in follow-up cases.

[22]But see also Thomas F. Pettigrew et al., "Busing: A Review of 'The Evidence,' " *The Public Interest, 1973, 30,* pp. 88–118, and Nancy H. St. John, *School Desegregation: Outcomes for Children* (New York: Wiley-Interscience, 1975).

Various external governmental conditions may also have a bearing on compliance with a Court decision. For example, presumably it is significant whether the president and Congress support the Court's ruling. Simultaneous opposition by the other two branches would seriously jeopardize full compliance. Other relevant factors may include whether a decision has been adequately transmitted to relevant government officials, whether responsibility for compliance is federal rather than state or local, whether compliance involves changing existing bureaucratic policy, the number of government officials or institutions that must comply, the nature of the reaction by public attorneys, a commitment by relevant public officials to obey court decisions, low fiscal costs of compliance, the security of public officials in their jobs, and the coordination of effort among affected officials.

A final set of correlates of compliance with court decisions relate to environmental conditions. For example, public support of a decision may be expected to have some positive effect on compliance. Among the other relevant factors may be low intensity of sentiment among the opposition, sympathetic treatment of decisions by the media, whether the decision was expected, favorable commentary by opinion leaders, substantial related litigation, whether the decision is regarded as authoritative; stronger political resources among beneficiaries of a decision as compared with losers, the belief that the Supreme Court has applied the provisions of the Constitution neutrally, and the perception that the Supreme Court is a legitimate decision maker.

It must be kept in mind that these hypothesized relationships have yet to be confirmed through empirical research. Existing research suggests that we may be in for some surprises. An excellent case in point is Charles Johnson's statistical analysis of lower court decisions (1979). His study investigated the well-known proposition that "the greater the original support for a decision at the Supreme Court level, the greater the subsequent compliance with the decision by the lower courts." (1979, p. 792) Johnson found, however, that degree of support on the Supreme Court has little or no relationship with the eventual treatment of that case by lower court judges. Thus, the preoccupation by many justices (including Chief Justice Warren in the *Brown* case) with achieving unanimity on the Court may be misplaced. It is possible that a very forceful opinion supported by only five justices will have a greater impact than a 9–0 decision which has been made ambiguous by virtue of a need for compromise. Social science research on compliance with Supreme Court decisions may help the Court to increase the impact it has upon society. Of course, there are those who would not welcome a more potent judiciary (Levine and Becker, 1970).

The Competence of the Courts

The judiciary has come under fire as lacking the institutional capacity to deal with social problems (Horowitz, 1977; Lamb, 1978; Cavanagh and

Sarat, 1980; Wasby, 1978b). According to this view, judges should become more cognizant of their limitations and exercise far more restraint. Some even wish to see judicial authority sharply curtailed. The basic argument is that courts "can't or shouldn't hear certain types of cases because they lack the resources, expertise, procedures, or time necessary to comprehend what is really at issue, provide a wise and fair resolution, and insure that their decisions are enforced." (Cavanagh and Sarat, 1980, p. 377) Such an argument has been developed by Donald Horowitz and effectively analyzed by Charles Lamb and others (Horowitz, 1977; Lamb, 1978). In *The Courts and Social Policy,* Horowitz discusses the institutional limitations of the judiciary and illustrates these limitations through discussion of two Supreme Court cases and two cases from lower federal courts.[23]

Critics of the judiciary's institutional capacity have focused on a number of problems. One problem identified by Horowitz is the case-by-case approach of the judicial process. It is argued that because of this process, court policies are decided in a piecemeal fashion and apply only to the case at hand. In addition, because courts are reactive, judges lack control over the sequencing of judicial decisions. The case-by-case method also means that judges cannot know whether the litigants are faithfully representing the dimensions of a social problem or if the litigants are representative of the whole class of parties that may be affected by a decree. Consequently, courts may base legal decisions on special, highly atypical situations.

Courts may also lack the informational resources needed to make effective policies. A basic difficulty here is that judges are generalists rather than experts. They deal with a broad range of legal disputes and therefore do not have intensive knowledge in any one area. The result may be decisions that are far more naive than those that would have been made by a bureaucracy or a Congressional committee. According to Horowitz, the judiciary has been unable to tap the specialized information of others effectively for help in making decisions. Generally, judges simply rely on the expert testimony supplied by litigants. However, these expert witnesses are paid by the parties involved and may be highly unrepresentative of the state of knowledge in the field. Relying on these witnesses also makes the judge a prisoner of the parties' definition of the issues involved in the case. Moreover, adjudication does not adequately review the effects of past judicial decisions. As a result, courts may fail to abandon policies that are ineffective or are producing severe spillover effects.

Finally, Horowitz is also critical of the judiciary's focus on rights as a means of resolving social problems. According to this argument, many problems are best dealt with through compromises that may not be easily defended through reasoned argument. Moreover, when courts identify a right, they may

[23]*Mapp v. Ohio,* 367 U.S. 643 (1961); *In re Gault,* 387 U.S. 1 (1967); *North City Area-Wide Council, Inc. v. Romney,* Civil No. 69-1909 (E. D. Pa. Nov. 12, 1969); *Hobson v. Hansen,* 269 F. Supp. 401 (D. D. C. 1967).

fail adequately to address the costs that will be involved in enforcing that right. In principle, if a right exists, cost is no bar to its full enforcement. Court decisions may also seriously distort spending patterns by states and localities. For example, a court order to increase spending at mental institutions may lead to a transfer of funds previously allocated to the prevention and relief of alcoholism. Hence, a decision supporting the rights of some people in need may be detrimental to others in need. Moreover, courts may be seen as defective in that it is difficult for them to reverse their course of action. Having identified a right possessed by a class of people, courts find it very difficult to take that right away, even after it is apparent that the policy is producing very negative results.

Despite the multitude of arguments attacking the capacity of the courts, there are those who believe strongly that the judiciary is no less competent than the other institutions of government (Lamb, 1978; Cavanagh and Sarat, 1980; Wasby, 1978b). It seems likely that the criticisms of court competence have been highly overstated. First, there is much to be said in support of the judicial process. Horowitz himself concedes that there are some attractive elements to the judicial method. For example, the adversary process tries to place all relevant legal arguments before judges.[24] In a real dispute both plaintiff and defendant have a vested interest in making the best possible case for their position. Judges are then expected to review the merits of these arguments, apply the relevant law or constitutional provision, and justify their decision through reasoned argument. Thus, the judicial process may be conducive to a thoughtful evaluation of a problem. This is in contrast to the processes of the executive and legislature, which are often dominated by interest group pressures or a concern about short-term swings in public opinion.

Any serious evaluation of the competence of the courts must, moreover, be made alongside similar analyses of alternative institutions. In this regard, there have been some very critical evaluations of the effectiveness of Congress (Burns, 1949; Clark, 1964; Bolling, 1965), the president (Reedy, 1970; Cronin, 1980), the bureaucracy (Pressman and Wildavsky, 1973; Fried, 1976; Schultze, 1977), state governments (Sundquist, 1972) and the private sector (Thurow, 1980). Indeed, many problems reach the judiciary as a result of a failure by other social and governmental institutions to deal with these problems adequately. Surely this may be said of the problem of racial injustice. In addition, many disputes reach the courts because our nation lacks a well-developed system of dispute-processing mechanisms. It is not entirely fair to criticize an

---

[24]Note, however, that there may be some nonlegal arguments which courts fail to consider despite their societal significance. Thus, the Supreme Court's decisions on contraception and abortion were based on a woman's constitutional right to privacy rather than on a concern about overpopulation. In this regard the Court has never mentioned any "right" to live in a nation that is not overpopulated. See *Griswold v. Connecticut* and *Roe v. Wade.* On the other hand, the issue of overpopulation has not been effectively addressed by Congress or by the executive, despite the willingness of these other branches of government to consider nonlegal arguments. On overpopulation see Paul R. Ehrlich and Anne H. Ehrlich, *Population, Resources, Environment* (San Francisco: W. H. Freeman and Company, Publishers, 1972).

overburdened court system when lawmakers have failed to make adequate provision for mediation, arbitration, or other means of dispute processing. Moreover, while the judicial process is criticized for dealing with issues on a piecemeal basis, the policies of the other branches of government are also generally set in an incremental fashion (Wildavsky, 1979). On the other hand, judicial decisions are not always ad hoc. Sometimes judges think openly about the implications of their rulings for related litigation. It is true that litigants may supply judges with imperfect information. Yet, the other branches of government are also rather unsure of their informational sources. Critics are correct in noting that courts are reactive institutions that depend on litigants to raise an issue. Still, much of the work of legislatures and bureaucracies is also done in response to citizen complaints.

There is an absence of clear-cut evidence indicating that courts are inherently less effective than the other branches of government. It is true that courts may fail to address new subject areas adequately. However, similar problems are also faced by the other branches of government. Perhaps legal reasoning is not the most effective path for resolving certain kinds of problems. Yet, compromise and log rolling may not be inherently superior. Indeed, interest group activity may so overwhelm the legislature and executive that the result may be stalemate or conflicting policy (Lowi, 1979). While the existing judiciary is not without defects, some of its problems can be dealt with through modest reforms, such as ready access to social science knowledge. Nor is it true that judges are as blind to the effects of past judicial decisions as Horowitz seems to believe. Plainly, judges are generalists (except for the few in specialized courts). Surely, there is far more expertise on technical issues in Congressional committees and bureaucracies than in the judiciary. Nevertheless, much policymaking is little more than a choice among competing values. We cannot say that courts are inherently less effective than other institutions in making such value choices. If it is desirable to protect some things as rights, then courts may well be the most appropriate institution to fulfill this task.

AN ASSESSMENT

The Supreme Court is clearly an important policymaker in our country.[25] Since claiming the power of judicial review in 1803, the Court has served as the ultimate interpreter of the Constitution. In this capacity the Court has declared unconstitutional a large number of federal laws, state laws, and provisions of state constitutions. Moreover, the Court has also played an active

---

[25]The fifty state judiciaries can also play a very important role in safeguarding the rights of Americans. Significantly, there are some rights under state constitutions which are not given constitutional protection in the United States Constitution. On this see William J. Brennan, Jr., "State Constitutions and the Protection of Individual Rights," *Harvard Law Review,* 1977, *90,* 489–504; and Peter J. Galie, "The Pennsylvania Constitution and the Protection of Defendants' Rights, 1969–1980: A Survey," *University of Pittsburgh Law Review,* 1981, *42,* 269–311.

role in statutory interpretation. At the same time, there are many restraints upon the American judiciary. Apart from judicial self-restraint, the Court is also constrained by Congress, the president, states, lower courts, and the majority coalition. Despite these internal and external restraints, the Supreme Court plays a significant policy role in areas such as institutional powers, personal liberty, due process, and equal protection. While Supreme Court decisions do not always have the intended impact, some decisions have had a momentous impact upon society.

It is not easy to say whether the Supreme Court exercises too much, too little, or just the right amount of power. Naturally, there have been some very poor judicial decisions, which seems to indicate that more restraint is needed. Yet, other, more positive, decisions can be found that tend to bolster one's faith in the efficacy of the judiciary. Moreover, the other institutions of government—and those in the private sector—have also experienced both stunning successes and extraordinary failures. In order to assess the efficacy of the judiciary, we need a careful, sensitive analysis of the characteristics of the American judiciary and the qualities it brings into the American political process. Such an analysis can help us assess whether we want the judiciary to be more activist or more restrained.

A highly significant bias of judicial activism is toward the protection of constitutional rights from a short-term shift in majority opinion. The primary reason for this bias lies in the nature of judicial recruitment. Federal judges in our nation are appointed by the president and confirmed by the Senate. Those appointed may serve for life terms. As a result of this, there is more stability as regards the personnel of the judiciary than there is in either the presidency or the Congress. This means that a newly elected president—even with the support of Congress—may have some policy preferences rebuffed by the judiciary. In areas such as institutional powers, personal liberty, due process, and equal protection, the judiciary has the capacity to protect certain values as rights. In this regard, should a repressive president and Congress assume power, the commitment of the federal government to civil liberties would not immediately evaporate. While repressive legislation might be adopted and even implemented, those adversely affected could (and presumably would) take their grievances to the judiciary. Given that the judiciary was selected by previous administrations, we can expect that federal judges would be unsympathetic to repressive legislation and would affirm the constitutional rights of individuals. Of course, it would take a certain amount of fortitude for a Court to oppose a coalition that had taken control of the other branches of government.[26] Still, the nature of the recruitment and tenure of federal judges suggests that in many cases this is precisely what would occur.

---

[26]Along these lines, Stephen L. Wasby notes that it is not necessarily politically realistic for the Supreme Court to take a strongly activist position in defense of civil liberties. Such a posture may lead to widespread noncompliance, disenchantment, political attacks, and even loss of Court power. See Stephen L. Wasby, *The Supreme Court in the Federal Judicial System* (New York: Holt, Rinehart and Winston, 1978a), p. 22.

This does not mean that in the face of a long-lasting majority coalition of a repressive character, the judiciary can continue to serve as a vigilant guardian of civil liberties. On the contrary, given the nature of judicial recruitment, the judiciary could ultimately be recast by a majority coalition. Even our most cherished rights may ultimately yield if that is the wish of a new and durable majority coalition.[27] It is also important to note that many areas of American public policy are not protected as constitutional rights. Much of what the federal government does is in the nature of privileges rather than rights. These privileges can be withdrawn at the discretion of Congress and the president. Thus, should a new administration have a different hierarchy of values than those that preceded it, the new administration may alter much of American policy if it can marshal the support of Congress. For the judiciary one implication of this situation is that to the extent it is desirable to protect new areas as rights beyond legislative discretion, further judicial activism is desirable. Of course, the possibilities for such activism is itself limited by the nature of our political system, including the method of judicial selection and the other checks on the judiciary.

Clearly, this picture of American politics is quite different from that of simple majority rule. If we truly wanted public policy to be representative of public desires at any given time, we could find a fairly effective way of accomplishing it. For example, we might opt to hold regular referendums on major policy questions. We could also enforce the results of these referendums by imposing criminal sanctions on public officials who failed to carry out the wishes expressed by the majority. Plainly, our complex system of government was not invented as a means of maximizing majority rule. Instead, a system of separated institutions sharing power was put in place, partly to place institutional limits in the way of majority sentiment. Throughout this book we have emphasized the conflict of values that is inherent in politics. Among the values of enduring significance are procedural justice, liberty, equality, democracy, effectiveness, and social order. This history of public policy in America can be written in terms of differing degrees of commitment over time to each of these social values. Through its decisions in constitutional law the Supreme Court is able to promote some of these values beyond the wishes of majority sentiment. The judiciary is also able to remove itself from the ebbs and flows of public opinion—at least to a greater extent than the other institutions of government. As a result, a measure of stability and protection is provided in certain areas of American public policy. There is a good deal of merit in these policy consequences, which seem to flow from an activist judiciary.

[27]Note that through new appointments a longstanding majority coalition would be able to remake the federal judiciary into a repressive body. Should a libertarian majority coalition finally assume power, it could not immediately restore the rights of citizens (that is, the repressive judges would have life tenure). The traditional response to this concern is that democracy will tend to produce libertarian and egalitarian results. If this is true, the most serious threat to liberty or equality is short-term swings in the character of public opinion or government leadership. The argument here is that the judiciary will tend to protect us from short-term changes of this sort.

QUESTIONS FOR DISCUSSION

1. Should the courts be activist or restrained? How does a concern for democracy enter into the judicial activism controversy?. A concern for effectiveness? Equality? Social order?
2. Do Supreme Court justices really restrain themselves from exercising "too much" activism when deciding cases? How effective are the external restraints on the Supreme Court?
3. How have the decisions of the Supreme Court affected your life?
4. Under what circumstances will Supreme Court decisions be especially effective? Are Supreme Court justices doing all they can to enhance the impact of their decisions? Is it irresponsible for social scientists to conduct and report research which would inform the Supreme Court how to maximize its effectiveness?

FOR FURTHER READING

CHASE, HAROLD W., and DUCAT, CRAIG R. *Constitutional Interpretation*. St. Paul, Minn.: West Publishing Co., 1979. A full-length analysis of constitutional law, including excerpts from leading cases.

FUNSTON, RICHARD. *A Vital National Seminar: The Supreme Court in American Political Life*. Palo Alto, Calif.: Mayfield Publishing Co., 1978. A concise overview of constitutional law and the exercise of power by the Supreme Court.

HALPERN, STEPHEN C., and LAMB, CHARLES M., eds. *Supreme Court Activism and Restraint*. Lexington, Mass.: Lexington Books, 1982. Activism and restraint are analyzed in a series of articles.

SCHEINGOLD, STUART A. *The Politics of Rights*. New Haven, Conn.: Yale University Press, 1974. A pessimistic view of the ability of the courts to protect rights.

WASBY, STEPHEN L. *The Impact of the United States Supreme Court: Some Perspectives*. Homewood, Ill.: Dorsey Press, 1970. A ground-breaking inventory of the conditions under which Supreme Court decisions will have greater or lesser impact.

SUPREME COURT RULINGS

Abington School District v. Schempp, 374 U.S. 203 (1963)
Anderson v. Martin, 375 U.S. 399 (1964)
Argersinger v. Hamlin, 407 U.S. 25 (1972)
Baker v. Carr, 369 U.S. 186 (1962)
Barron v. Baltimore, 7 Pet. 243 (1833)
Beauharnais v. Illinois, 343 U.S. 250 (1952)
Benton v. Maryland, 395 U.S. 784 (1969)
Betts v. Brady, 316 U.S. 455 (1942)
Bounds v. Smith, 430 U.S. 817 (1977)
Boyd v. United States, 116 U.S. 616 (1886)
Brown v. Board of Education, 347 U.S. 483 (1954)

Brown v. Texas, 443 U.S. 47 (1979)
Cantwell v. Connecticut, 310 U.S. 296 (1940)
Champion v. Ames, 188 U.S. 321 (1903)
Chisholm v. Georgia, 2 Dall. 419 (1793)
Civil Rights Cases, 109 U.S. 3 (1883)
Coker v. Georgia, 433 U.S. 584 (1977)
Cooper v. Aaron, 358 U.S. 1 (1958)
Craig v. Boren, 429 U.S. 190 (1976)
Crandall v. Nevada, 6 Wall 35 (1868)
Dred Scott v. Sandford, 19 How. 393 (1857)
Eddings v. Oklahoma, 50 LW 4161 (1982)
Engel v. Vitale, 370 U.S. 421 (1962)
Enmund v. Florida, 50 LW 5087 (1982)
Escobedo v. Illinois, 378 U.S. 478 (1964)
Estelle v. Gamble, 429 U.S. 97 (1976)
Everson v. Board of Education, 330 U.S. 1 (1947)
Ex parte McCardle, 7 Wall. 506 (1869)
Field v. Clark, 143 U.S. 649 (1892)
Fletcher v. Peck, 6 Cranch 87 (1810)
Foley v. Connelie, 435 U.S. 291 (1978)
Frontiero v. Richardson, 411 U.S. 677 (1973)
Furman v. Georgia, 408 U.S. 238 (1972)
Gayle v. Browder, 352 U.S. 903 (1956)
Geduldig v. Aiello, 417 U.S. 484 (1974)
Gibbons v. Ogden, 9 Wheat. 1 (1824)
Gideon v. Wainwright, 372 U.S. 335 (1963)
Gitlow v. New York, 268 U.S. 652 (1925)
Graham v. Richardson, 403 U.S. 365 (1971)
Gregg v. Georgia, 428 U.S. 153 (1976)
Griswold v. Connecticut, 381 U.S. 479 (1965)
Hague v. CIO, 307 U.S. 496 (1939)
Harrington v. California, 395 U.S. 250 (1969)
Harris v. New York, 401 U.S. 222 (1971)
Heart of Atlanta Motel, Inc. v. United States, 379 U. S. 241 (1964)
Holmes v. City of Atlanta, 350 U.S. 879 (1955)
Humphrey's Executor v. United States, 295 U.S. 602 (1935)
Hurtado v. California, 110 U.S. 516 (1884)
In re Debs, 158 U.S. 564 (1895)
In re Neagle, 135 U.S. 1 (1890)
In re Oliver, 333 U.S. 257 (1948)
Jacobson v. Massachusetts, 197 U.S. 11 (1905)
Johnson v. Louisiana, 406 U.S. 356 (1972)
Johnson v. Zerbst, 304 U.S. 458 (1938)
Keyes v. School District No.1, 413 U.S. 189 (1973)
Kilbourn v. Thompson, 103 U.S. 168 (1881)
Lemon v. Kurtzman, 403 U.S. 602 (1971)
Levy v. Louisiana, 391 U.S. 68 (1968)
Loving v. Virginia, 388 U.S. 1 (1967)
Malloy v. Hogan, 378 U.S. 1 (1964)
Mapp v. Ohio, 367 U.S. 643 (1961)
Marbury v. Madison, 1 Cranch 137 (1803)
Martin v. Hunter's Lessee, 1 Wheat. 304 (1816)
Martin v. Mott, 12 Wheat. 19 (1827)

Walz v. Tax Commission, 397 U.S. 664 (1970)
Wesberry v. Sanders, 376 U.S. 1 (1964)
Williams v. Florida, 399 U.S. 78 (1970)
Wisconsin v. Yoder, 406 U.S. 205 (1972)
Wolf v. Colorado, 338 U.S. 25 (1949)
Young v. American Mini-Theatres, 427 U.S. 50 (1976)
Youngstown Sheet and Tube Co. v. Sawyer, 343 U.S. 579 (1952)
Zorach v. Clauson, 343 U.S. 306 (1952)

REFERENCES

ABRAHAM, H. J. *Justices and presidents.* New York: Penguin Books, 1975.

ABRAHAM, H. J. *The judicial process.* New York: Oxford University Press, 1980a.

ABRAHAM, H. J. *The judiciary.* Boston: Allyn and Bacon, 1980b.

ADAMS, T. F. Field interrogation. *Police,* March-April 1963.

Administrative Office of the United States Courts. *1978 annual report of the director.* Washington, D.C.: Administrative Office of the United States Courts, 1978.

ALKER, H. R., HOSTICKA, C., & MITCHELL, M. Jury selection as a biased social process. *Law and Society Review,* 1976, *11,* 9–41.

ALLAN, S., & PARRIS, D. Civil commitment of the mentally ill. *UCLA Law Review,* 1967, *14,* 822–878.

ALLEN, F. A. Criminal justice, legal values and the rehabilitative ideal. *Journal of Criminal Law, Criminology and Police Science,* 1959, *50,* 226–232.

ALSCHULER, A. W. Sentencing reform and prosecutorial power: A critique of recent proposals for "fixed" and "presumptive" sentencing. *University of Pennsylvania Law Review,* 1978, *126,* 550–577.

American Bar Association. *Standards relating to the urban police function.* Chicago: American Bar Association, 1972 (and 1973 supplement).

American Bar Association. *Standards relating to court organization.* Chicago: American Bar Association, 1974.

American Bar Association. *Federal government legal career opportunities 1976.* Chicago: American Bar Association, 1976.

American Bar Association. *Standards relating to appellate courts.* Chicago: American Bar Association, 1977.

American Bar Association. *A review of legal education in the United States—Fall, 1978.* Chicago: American Bar Association, 1979.

American Bar Association. *Model code of professional responsibility and code of judicial conduct.* Chicago: American Bar Association, 1980.

American Bar Association. *American Bar Association Journal,* 1981a, *67,* 142.

American Bar Association. *American Bar Association Journal,* 1981b, *67,* 1450-1451.

American Bar Association. *American Bar Association Journal,* 1981c, *67,* 414.

American Bar Association. *American Bar Association Journal,* 1982, *68,* 38-39.

ANDENAES, J. The general preventive effects of punishment. *University of Pennsylvania Law Review,* 1966, *114,* 949-983.

ANDERSON, J. E. *Public policy-making.* New York: Holt, Rinehart and Winston, 1979.

ARES, C. E., RANKIN, A., & STURZ, H. The Manhattan bail project: An interim report on the use of pre-trial parole. *New York University Law Review,* 1963, *38,* 67-95.

ARMOR, D. J. The evidence on busing. *The Public Interest,* 1972, *28,* 90-126.

ASHMAN, A., & ALFINI, J. J. *The key to judicial merit selection.* Chicago: American Judicature Society, 1974.

AUERBACH, J. S. *Unequal justice: Lawyers and social change in modern America.* New York: Oxford University Press, 1976.

AUSTIN, W., & WILLIAMS, T. A., III. A survey of judges' responses to simulated legal cases: Research note on sentencing disparity. *Journal of Criminal Law and Criminology,* 1977, *68,* 306-310.

AUTEN, J. The domestic disturbance: A policeman's dilemma. *The Police Chief,* 1972, *39,* (10), 16-17, 20, 22.

BAHN, C. The reassurance factor in police patrol. *Criminology,* 1974, *12,* 338-345.

BAILEY, W. C., MARTIN, J. D., & GRAY, L. N. Crime and deterrence: A correlation analysis. *Journal of Research in Crime and Delinquency,* 1974, *11,* 124-143.

BAKER, J. H. *Urban politics in America.* New York: Scribner's, 1971.

BALL, H. *Judicial craftsmanship or fiat?* Westport, Conn.: Greenwood Press, 1978.

BALL, H. *Courts and politics.* Englewood Cliffs, N.J.: Prentice-Hall, 1980.

BARKER, T., & ROEBUCK, J. *An empirical typology of police corruption.* Springfield, Ill.: Chas. C. Thomas, 1973.

BARNETT, R. E. Restitution: A new paradigm of criminal justice. *Ethics,* 1977, *87,* 279-301.

BARTOL, C. R. Parens patriae: Poltergeist of mental health law. *Law and Policy Quarterly,* 1981, *3,* 191-207.

BAUM, L. The judicial gatekeeping function: A general analysis. In S. Goldman & A. Sarat (Eds.), *American court systems.* San Francisco: W. H. Freeman, 1978.

BAUM, L. *The Supreme Court.* Washington, D.C.: Congressional Quarterly Press, 1981.

BAUMAN, Z. *Socialism: The active utopia.* New York: Holmes and Meier, 1976.

BEARD, C. A. *An economic interpretation of the Constitution of the United States.* New York: Macmillan, 1913.

BECKER, L. C. The moral basis of property rights. In J. R. Pennock & T. W. Chapman (Eds.), *Property.* New York: New York University Press, 1980.

BECKER, T. L. *Political behavioralism and modern jurisprudence.* Chicago: Rand McNally, 1964.

BECKER, T. L. (Ed.). *Political trials.* Indianapolis: Bobbs-Merrill, 1971.

BELKNAP, M. R. *American political trials.* Westport, Conn.: Greenwood Press, 1981.

BENN, S. I. Justice. In P. Edwards (Ed.), *The encyclopedia of philosophy* (Vol. 4). New York: Macmillan, 1967.

BENT, A. E. *The politics of law enforcement.* Lexington, Mass.: Lexington Books-Heath, 1974.

BENT, A. E., & ROSSUM, R. A.   *Police, criminal justice, and the community.* New York: Harper and Row, 1976.

BERGER, R.   *Government by judiciary: The transformation of the fourteenth amendment.* Cambridge, Mass.: Harvard University Press, 1977.

BERKSON, L., CARBON, S., & NEFF, A.   *A study of the U.S. circuit judge nominating commission.* Chicago: The American Judicature Society, 1979.

BEZANSON, R. P.   Involuntary treatment of the mentally ill in Iowa: The 1975 legislation. *Iowa Law Review,* 1975, *61,* 261–396.

BLACK, D. J.   Production of crime rates. *American Sociological Review,* 1970, *35,* 733–748.

BLACK, H.   The bill of rights. In E. Cahn (Ed.), *The great rights.* New York: Macmillan, 1963.

BLAUSTEIN, A. P., & PORTER, C. O.   *The American lawyer.* Chicago: University of Chicago Press, 1954.

BLUMBERG, A. S.   *Criminal justice.* Chicago: Quadrangle, 1967b.

BLUMBERG, A. S.   The practice of law as a confidence game: Organizational cooptation of a profession. *Law and Society Review,* 1967a, *1,* 15–39.

BLUMBERG, A. S.   Criminal justice in America. In J. D. Douglas (Ed.), *Crime and justice in American society.* Indianapolis: Bobbs-Merrill, 1971.

BOLLING, R.   *House out of order.* New York: Dutton, 1965.

BONSIGNORE, J. J. Law as a hard science: On the madness in method. *The ALSA Forum,* 1977, *2* (2), 47–74.

BONSIGNORE, J. J. et al.   Note on the history of the jury trial. In J. J. Bonsignore et al. (Ed.), *Before the law.* Boston: Houghton Mifflin, 1979a.

BONSIGNORE, J. J. et al.   Note on the use of expert testimony in jury trials. In J. J. Bonsignore et al. (Eds.), *Before the law.* Boston: Houghton Mifflin, 1979b.

BORDUA, D. J., & HAUREK, E. W.   The police budget's lot. *American Behavioral Scientist,* 1970, *13,* 667–680.

BORDUA, D. J., & TIFFT, L. L.   Citizen interviews, organizational feedback, and police-community relations decisions. *Law and Society Review,* 1971, *6,* 155–182.

BORKIN, J.   *The corrupt judge.* New York: Clarkson N. Potter, 1962.

BOTEIN, B., & GORDON, M. A.   *The trial of the future.* New York: Simon and Schuster, 1963.

BRAITHWAITE, W. T.   *Who judges the judges?* Chicago: American Bar Foundation, 1971.

BRAKEL, S. J.   Legal aid in mental hospitals. *American Bar Foundation Research Journal,* 1981, 21–93.

BREITEL, C. D.   Controls in criminal law enforcement. *University of Chicago Law Review,* 1960, *27,* 427–435.

BRENNER, S.   Fluidity on the United States Supreme Court: A reexamination. *American Journal of Political Science,* 1980, *24,* 526–535.

BROWDER, O. L., CUNNINGHAM, R. A., & JULIN, J. R.   *Basic property law.* St. Paul, Minn.: West Publishing Co., 1966.

BROWN, E. L.   *Lawyers, law schools and the public service.* New York: Russell Sage Foundation, 1948.

BUCHANAN, J. M.   *The limits of liberty.* Chicago: University of Chicago Press, 1975.

BULLOCK, C. S., III, & RODGERS, H. R., JR.   Coercion to compliance: Southern school districts and school desegregation guidelines. *Journal of Politics,* 1976, *38,* 987–1011.

BURNS, J. M.   *Congress on trial: The legislative process and the administrative state.* New York: Harper, 1949.

CANON, B. C. The impact of formal selection processes on the characteristics of judges—reconsidered. *Law and Society Review,* 1972, *6,* 579–593.

CAPLOVITZ, D. *Consumers in trouble.* New York: Free Press, 1974.

CARBON, S. B. Judicial retention elections: Are they serving their intended purpose? *Judicature,* 1980, *64,* 210–233.

CARDOZO, B. N. *The nature of the judicial process.* New Haven, Conn.: Yale University Press, 1921.

CARDOZO, B. Introduction. In Committee of the Association of American Law Schools (Ed.), *Selected readings on the law of contracts from American and English legal periodicals.* New York: Macmillan, 1931.

CARLIN, J. E. *Lawyers on their own.* New Brunswick, N.J.: Rutgers University Press, 1962.

CARLIN, J. E. *Lawyers' ethics.* New York: Russell Sage Foundation, 1966.

CARLIN, J. E., HOWARD, J., & MESSINGER, S. L. *Civil justice and the poor.* New York: Russell Sage Foundation, 1967.

CARLSON, R. J. Measuring the quality of legal services: An idea whose time has not come. *Law and Society Review,* 1976, *11,* 287–317.

CARNEGIE, D. *How to win friends and influence people.* New York: Simon and Schuster, 1936.

CARP, R. A. The behavior of grand juries: Acquiescence or justice? *Social Science Quarterly,* 1975, *55,* 853–870.

CARP, R., & WHEELER, R. Sink or swim: The socialization of a federal district judge. *Journal of Public Law,* 1972, *21,* 359–393.

CASEY, G. The Supreme Court and myth: An empirical investigation. *Law and Society Review,* 1974, *8,* 385–419.

CASEY, G. Popular perceptions of Supreme Court rulings. *American Politics Quarterly,* 1976, *4,* 3–45.

CASPER, J. D. *American criminal justice.* Englewood Cliffs, N.J.: Prentice-Hall, 1972a.

CASPER, J. D. *The politics of civil liberties.* New York: Harper and Row, Pub., 1972b.

CASPER, J. D. The Supreme Court and national policy making. *American Political Science Review,* 1976, *70,* 50–63.

CAVANAGH, R., & SARAT, A. Thinking about courts: Toward and beyond a jurisprudence of judicial competence. *Law and Society Review,* 1980, *14,* 371–420.

CHAMELIN, N. C., FOX, V., & WHISENAND, P. M. *Introduction to criminal justice.* Englewood Cliffs, N.J.: Prentice-Hall, 1975.

CHASE, H. W. *Federal judges: The appointing process.* Minneapolis, Minn.: University of Minnesota Press, 1972.

CHASE, H. W., & DUCAT, C. R. *Constitutional interpretation.* St. Paul, Minn.: West Publishing Co., 1979.

CHEVIGNY, P. *Police power.* New York: Pantheon Books, 1969.

CHRISTIE, G. C. Lawful departures from legal rules: "Jury nullification" and legitimated disobedience. *California Law Review,* 1974, *62,* 1289–1310.

CHURCH, T. W., et al. *Pretrial delay.* Williamsburg, Va.: National Center for State Courts, 1978.

CLAPP, C. L. *The Congressman.* Washington, D.C.: Brookings Institution, 1963.

CLARK, J. S. *Congress: The sapless branch.* New York: Harper and Row, Pub., 1964.

CLARKE, S. H. Juvenile offender programs and delinquency prevention. *Crime and Delinquency Literature,* 1974, *6,* 377–399.

CLAUDE, R. *The Supreme Court and the electoral process.* Baltimore: Johns Hopkins University Press, 1970.

CLEARY, E. W., & STRONG, J. W.   *Evidence: cases, materials, problems.* St. Paul, Minn.: West Publishing Co., 1979.

CLEMENTE, F., & KLEIMAN, M. B.   Fear of crime in the United States: A multivariate analysis. *Social Forces,* 1977, *56,* 519–531.

COCOZZA, J. J., & STEADMAN, H. J.   The failure of psychiatric prediction of dangerousness: Clear and convincing evidence. *Rutgers Law Review,* 1976, *29,* 1084–1101.

COFFIN, F. M.   *The ways of a judge.* Boston: Houghton Mifflin, 1980.

COHEN, M.   Lawyers and political careers. *Law and Society Review,* 1969, *3,* 563–574.

COHEN, R. J.   *Malpractice.* New York: Free Press, 1979.

COLEMAN, J. S., KELLY, S. D., & MOORE, J. A.   *Trends in school segregation, 1968–73.* Washington, D.C.: The Urban Institute, 1975.

COMMAGER, H. S.   Judicial review and democracy. *Virginia Quarterly Review,* 1943, *19,* 417–428.

Commission on Revision of the Federal Court Appellate System. *Structure and internal procedures: Recommendations.* Washington, D.C.: U.S. Government Printing Office, 1975.

Congressional Quarterly Service. *Weekly Report.* January 24, 1981; January 20, 1979.

COOK, P. J.   The effect of gun availability on violent crime patterns. *Annals, American Academy of Political and Social Science,* 1981, *455,* 63–79.

COULSON, R.   Forward. In C. Gold & S. Mackenzie (Eds.), *Wide world of arbitration.* New York: American Arbitration Association, 1978.

Council of State Governments, The. *The book of the states 1978–1979.* Lexington, Ky.: The Council of State Governments, 1978.

COUND, J. J., FRIEDENTHAL, J. H., & MILLER, A. R.   *Civil procedure.* St. Paul, Minn.: West Publishing Co., 1980.

CRONIN, T.   *The state of the presidency.* Boston: Little, Brown, 1980.

CULVER, J. H., & CRUIKSHANKS, R. L.   Judicial discipline at the federal level: A new response to an old problem. In P. L. Dubois (Ed.), *The analysis of judicial reform.* Lexington, Mass.: Lexington Books-Heath, 1982.

CURRAN, B. A.   Survey of the public's legal needs. *American Bar Association Journal,* 1978, *64,* 848–852.

CURTIS, L. A.   *Criminal violence: National patterns and behavior.* Lexington, Mass.: Lexington Books, 1974.

CUSHAM, R. F.   *Cases in civil liberties.* Englewood Cliffs, N.J.: Prentice-Hall, 1979.

DAHL, R. A.   *A preface to democratic theory.* Chicago: University of Chicago Press, 1956.

DAHL, R. A.   Decision-making in a democracy: The role of the Supreme Court as a national policy-maker. *Journal of Public Law,* 1957, *6,* 279–295.

DAHL, R.   *Pluralist democracy in the United States.* Chicago: Rand McNally, 1967.

DANELSKI, D. J.   *A Supreme Court justice is appointed.* New York: Random House, 1964.

DANELSKI, D. J.   The influence of the chief justice in the decisional process of the Supreme Court. In S. Goldman, & A. Sarat (Eds.), *American court systems.* San Francisco: W. H. Freeman, 1978.

DANZIG, R., & LOWY, M. J.   Everyday disputes and mediation in the United States. *Law and Society Review,* 1975, *9,* 675–694.

DAVID, E. M., & KNOWLES, L.   An evaluation of the Kansas City patrol experiment. *The Police Chief,* 1975, *42,* (6), 22–27.

DAVIS, A.   Implying constitutional rights. *Black Law Journal,* 1980–1981, *6,* 198–210.

DAVIS, A. L. *The United States Supreme Court and the uses of social science data.* New York: MSS Information Corporation, 1973.

DAVIS, F. J. Law as a type of social control. In F. J. Davis et al., *Society and the law.* New York: Free Press, 1962.

DAVIS, R. R., JR. The Chandler incident and problems of judicial removal. *Stanford Law Review,* 1967, *19,* 448–467.

DIETZE, G. *In defense of property.* Chicago: Henry Regnery Co., 1963.

DIX, G. E. "Civil" commitment of the mentally ill and the need for data on the prediction of dangerousness. *American Behavioral Scientist,* 1976, *19,* 318–334.

DOLAN, E. F., JR. *Gun control: A decision for Americans.* New York: Franklin Watts, 1978.

DOLBEARE, K. M. The public views the Supreme Court. In H. Jacob (Ed.), *Law, politics, and the federal courts.* Boston: Little, Brown, 1967b.

DOLBEARE, K. M. *Trial courts in urban politics.* New York: John Wiley, 1967a.

DORF, M. C. Disbarment in the United States: Who shall do the noisome work? *Columbia Journal of Law and Social Problems,* 1975, *12,* 1–75.

DOUGLAS, J. D. *Crime and justice in American society.* Indianapolis: Bobbs-Merrill, 1971.

DOWNS, A. *Opening up the suburbs.* New Haven, Conn.: Yale University Press, 1973.

DRUCKMAN, D. Social-psychological approaches to the study of negotiations. In D. Druckman (Ed.), *Negotiations: Social-psychological perspectives.* Beverly Hills, Calif.: Sage Publications, 1977.

DUBOIS, P. L. *From ballot to bench.* Austin, Tex.: University of Texas Press, 1980.

DUBOSE, E. Z., JR. Of the parens patriae commitment power and drug treatment of schizophrenia: Do the benefits to the patient justify involuntary treatment? *Minnesota Law Review,* 1976, *60,* 1149–1218.

DUNNE, F. P. *Mr. Dooley in peace and in war.* Boston: Small Maynard, and Co., 1898.

DUNNE, F. P. *Mr. Dooley's opinions.* New York: Harper and Brothers, 1906.

DURKHEIM, E. *The rules of sociological method.* New York: Free Press, 1964.

EBENSTEIN W. et al. *American democracy in world perspective.* New York: Harper and Row, Pub., 1980.

EDMUNDS, E. F., JR., Disparity and discretion in sentencing: A proposal for uniformity. *UCLA Law Review,* 1977, *25,* 323–364.

EISENBERG, H. New light on the costliest malpractice mistakes. *Medical Economics,* August 20, 1973, pp. 146–163.

EISENSTEIN, J. *Politics and the legal process.* New York: Harper and Row, Pub., 1973.

EISENSTEIN, J., & JACOB, H. *Felony justice.* Boston: Little, Brown, 1977.

ELKINS, S. M. *Slavery: A problem in American institutional and intellectual life.* Chicago: University of Chicago Press, 1976.

ENGSTROM, R. L., & GILES, M. W. Expectations and images: A note on diffuse support for legal institutions. *Law and Society Review,* 1972, *6,* 631–636.

ENNIS, P. H. *Criminal victimization in the United States,* Field Surveys II, The president's commission on law enforcement and the administration of justice. Washington, D.C.: U.S. Government Printing Office, 1967.

ERLANGER, H. S. Lawyers and neighborhood legal services: Social background and the impetus for reform. *Law and Society Review,* 1978, *12,* 253–274.

ERLANGER, H. S., & KLEGON, D. A. Socialization effects of professional school: The law school experience and student orientations to public interest concerns. *Law and Society Review,* 1978, *13,* 11–35.

ETZIONI, A. Science: Threatening the jury. *The Washington Post,* May 26, 1974.

EULAU, H., & SPRAGUE, J. D. *Lawyers in politics.* Indianapolis: Bobbs-Merrill, 1964.

FAIRCHILD, E. S. Organizational structure and control of discretion in police operations. *Policy Studies Journal,* 1978, *7,* 442–449.

FAIRWEATHER, G. W. et al. *Community life for the mentally ill.* Chicago: Aldine, 1969.

Federal Bureau of Investigation. *Uniform crime reporting handbook.* Washington, D.C.: U.S. Government Printing Office, 1966.

Federal Judicial Center. *Report of the study group on the caseload of the Supreme Court.* Washington, D.C.: U.S. Government Printing Office, 1972.

FEELEY, M. M. *The proces is the punishment: Handling cases in a lower criminal court.* New York: Russell Sage Foundation, 1979.

FELSTINER, W. L. F. Influences of social organization on dispute processing. *Law and Society Review,* 1974, *9,* 63–94.

FINSTERBUSCH, K., & MOTZ, A. B. *Social research for policy decisions.* Belmont, Calif.: Wadsworth, 1980.

FITZGERALD, P. J. *Criminal law and punishment.* Oxford: Clarendon Press, 1962.

FLANAGAN, T. J., HINDELANG, M. J., & GOTTFREDSON, M. R. (Eds.). *Sourcebook of criminal justice statistics—1979.* Washington, D.C.: U.S. Government Printing Office, 1980.

FLYNN, W. J., JR. Public preference for the jury. *New York State Bar Bulletin,* 1960, *32,* 103–110.

FOLLEY, V. L. *American law enforcement.* Boston: Holbrook Press, 1976.

Ford Foundation. *Law and justice.* New York: Ford Foundation, 1974.

FORD, S. D. *The American legal system: Its dynamics and limits.* St. Paul, Minn.: West Publishing Co., 1970.

FORKOSCH, M. D. The nature of legal evidence. *California Law Review,* 1971, *59,* 1356–1383.

FOX, R. G. The XYY offender: A modern myth. *Journal of Criminal Law, Criminology and Police Science,* 1971, *62,* 59–73.

FOX, V. *Introduction to criminology.* Englewood Cliffs, N.J.: Prentice-Hall, 1976.

FRANK, J. A plea for lawyer-schools. *Yale Law Journal,* 1947, *56,* 1303–1344.

FRANK, J. *Courts on trial: Myth and reality in American justice.* Princeton, N.J.: Princeton University Press, 1949.

FRANKEL, M. E. *Partisan justice.* New York: Hill and Wang, 1980.

FRANKFURTER, F. *The case of Sacco and Vanzetti.* Boston: Little, Brown, 1927.

FREED, D., & WALD, P. *Bail in the United States: 1964.* Washington, D.C.: U.S. Government Printing Office, 1964.

FREEMAN, H. A. *Legal interviewing and counseling.* St. Paul, Minn.: West Publishing Co., 1964.

FREEMAN, H. A. *Counseling in the United States.* Dobbs Ferry, N. Y.: Oceana Publications, 1967.

FREUND, J. C. *Lawyering: A realistic approach to legal practice.* New York: Law Journal Seminars-Press, 1979.

FRIED, M., KAPLAN, K. J., & KLEIN, K. W. Juror selection: An analysis of voir dire. In R. J. Simon (Ed.), *The jury system in America.* Beverly Hills, Calif.: Sage Publications, 1975.

FRIED, R. C. *Performance in American bureaucracy.* Boston: Little, Brown, 1976.

FRIEDMAN, L. M. *Contract law in America.* Madison, Wis.: University of Wisconsin Press, 1965.

FRIEDMAN, L. M. The idea of right as a social and legal concept. *Journal of Social Issues,* 1971, 27 (2), 189–198.

FRIEDMAN, L. M.   *A history of American law.* New York: Simon and Schuster, 1973.

FRIEDMAN, L. M.   *The legal system.* New York: Russell Sage Foundation, 1975.

FRIENDLY, A., & GOLDFARB, R. L.   *Crime and publicity: The impact of news on the administration of justice.* New York: Twentieth Century Fund, 1967.

FROMSON, D.   Let's be realistic about specialization. *American Bar Association Journal,* 1977, *63,* 74–77.

FULLER, L. L.   *The morality of law.* New Haven, Conn.: Yale University Press, 1969.

FUNSTON, R.   The double standard of constitutional protection in the era of the welfare state. *Political Science Quarterly,* 1975, *90,* 261–287.

FUNSTON, R.   *A vital national seminar: The Supreme Court in American political life.* Palo Alto, Calif.: Mayfield Publishing Co., 1978.

GALANTER, M.   Why the "haves" come out ahead: Speculations on the limits of legal change. *Law and Society Review,* 1974, *9,* 95–160.

GALLAGHER, B. M.   *How to hire a lawyer.* New York: Dell, 1979.

GARBUS, M., & SELIGMAN, J.   Sanctions and disbarment: They sit in judgment. In R. Nader & M. Green (Eds.), *Verdicts on lawyers.* New York: Thomas Y. Crowell, 1976.

GARDNER, D. S.   The perception and memory of witnesses. *Cornell Law Quarterly,* 1933, *18,* 391–409.

GARMIRE, B. I.   The police role in an urban society. In R. F. Steadman (Ed.), *The police and the community.* Baltimore: Johns Hopkins University Press, 1972.

GAY, W. G.   *Issues on team policing: A review of the literature.* Washington, D.C.: U.S. Government Printing Office, 1977.

GELLHORN, W.   *Ombudsmen and others.* Cambridge, Mass.: Harvard University Press, 1966.

GENTEL, W. D., & HANDMAN, M. L.   *Police strikes: Causes and prevention.* Gaithersburg, Md.: International Association of Chieves of Police, 1979.

GERSTEIN, R. E., & ROBINSON, L. O.   Remedy for the grand jury: Retain but reform. *American Bar Association Journal,* 1978, *64,* 337–340.

GETMAN, J. G.   Labor arbitration and dispute resolution. *Yale Law Journal,* 1979, *88,* 916–949.

GIBSON, J. L.   Judges' role orientations, attitudes, and decisions: An interactive model. *American Political Science Review,* 1978, *72,* 911–924.

GIBSON, J. L.   Environmental constraints on the behavior of judges: A representational model of judicial decision making. *Law and Society Review,* 1980, *14,* 343–370.

GIBSON, J. L.   The role concept in judicial research. *Law and Policy Quarterly,* 1981, *3,* 291–311.

GILLESPIE, P., & KLIPPER, M.   *No-fault: What you save, gain, and lose with the new auto insurance.* New York: Praeger Publishers, 1972.

GLASER, D.   The differential-association theory of crime. In A. M. Rose (Ed.), *Human behavior and social processes.* Boston: Houghton Mifflin, 1962.

GLASER, D.   The prison of the future. In D. Glaser (Ed.), *Crime in the city.* New York: Harper and Row, Pub., 1970.

GLAZER, N.   Should judges administer social services? *The Public Interest,* 1978, *50,* 64–80.

GOBERT, J. J.   Victim precipitation. *Columbia Law Review,* 1977, *77,* 511–553.

GOFFMAN, E.   *Asylums.* Garden City, New York: Anchor, 1961.

GOLDBERG, A. J.   One Supreme Court: It doesn't need its cases "screened." *The New Republic,* February 10, 1973, 14–16.

GOLDING, M. P.   *Philosophy of law.* Englewood Cliffs, N.J.: Prentice-Hall, 1975.

GOLDMAN, S.   Characteristics of Eisenhower and Kennedy appointees to the lower federal courts. *Western Political Quarterly,* 1965, *18,* 755–762.

GOLDMAN, S.   Voting behavior on the United States courts of appeals 1961–64. *American Political Science Review,* 1966, *60,* 374–383.

GOLDMAN, S.   Judicial appointments to the United States courts of appeals. *Wisconsin Law Review,* 1967, 186–214.

GOLDMAN, S.   American judges: Their selection, tenure, variety and quality. *Current History,* 1971, *61,* 1–8.

GOLDMAN, S.   Judicial backgrounds, recruitment, and the party variable: The case of the Johnson and Nixon appointees to the United States district and appeals courts. *Arizona State Law Journal,* 1974, 211–222.

GOLDMAN, S.   Voting behavior on the United States courts of appeals revisited. *American Political Science Review,* 1975, *69,* 491–506.

GOLDMAN, S.   Should there be affirmative action for the judiciary? *Judicature,* 1979, *62,* 488–494.

GOLDMAN, S.   Carter's judicial appointments: A lasting legacy. *Judicature,* 1981, *64,* 344–355.

GOLDMAN, S., & JAHNIGE, T. P.   *The federal courts as a political system.* New York: Harper and Row, 1976.

GOLDMAN, S., & SARAT, A. (Eds.).   *American court systems.* San Francisco: W. H. Freeman and Co., Publishers, 1978.

GOLDSTEIN, A. P. et al.   *Police crisis intervention.* Kalamazoo, Mich.: Behaviordelia, 1977.

GOLDSTEIN, H.   Police discretion: The ideal versus the real. *Public Administration Review,* 1963, *23,* 140–148.

GOODELL, C.   *Political prisoners in America.* New York: Random House, 1973.

GOULD, L. C.   Crime and its impact in an affluent society. In J. D. Douglas (Ed.), *Crime and justice in American society.* Indianapolis: Bobbs-Merrill, 1971.

GRAGLIA, L. A.   *Disaster by decree.* Ithaca, N. Y.: Cornell University Press, 1976.

GRAGLIA, L. A.   A case for judicial restraint. In S. C. Halpern, & C. M. Lamb (Eds.), *Supreme Court activism and restraint.* Lexington, Mass.: Lexington Books-Heath, 1982.

GRAHAM, F.   Cameras in the courtroom: Yes, bring them in. *American Bar Association Journal,* 1978, *64,* 545–548.

GRAHAM, H. D., & GURR, T. R. (Eds.).   *The history of violence in America.* New York: Praeger Publishers, 1969.

GREACEN, J. M.   The role of the police: Should it be limited to fighting crime? In R. A. Staufenberger (Ed.), *Progress in policing: Essays on change.* Cambridge, Mass.: Ballinger, 1980.

GREEN, E.   *Judicial attitudes in sentencing.* New York: St. Martin's Press, 1961.

GREEN, MARK J.   *The other government: The unseen power of Washington lawyers.* New York: Grossman, 1975.

GREENBERG, D. F.   The incapacitative effect of imprisonment: Some estimates. *Law and Society Review,* 1975, *9,* 541–580.

GREENBERG, E. S.   *Serving the few.* New York: John Wiley, 1974.

GREENWOOD, P. W., CHAIKEN, J. M., & PETERSILIA, J.   *The criminal investigation process.* Lexington, Mass.: Heath, 1977.

GREY, D. L.   *The Supreme Court and the news media.* Evanston, Ill.: Northwestern University Press, 1968.

GREY, T. C.   The disintegration of property. In J. R. Pennock, & J. W. Chapman (Eds.), *Property.* New York: New York University Press, 1980.

GRODZINS, M.   *Americans betrayed: Politics and the Japanese evacuation.* Chicago: University of Chicago Press, 1949.

GROSSMAN, J. B.   *Lawyers and judges: The ABA and the politics of judicial selection.* New York: Wiley, 1965.

GROSSMAN, J. B.   Social backgrounds and judicial decision-making. *Harvard Law Review,* 1966, *79,* 1551–1564.

GROSSMAN, J. B.   The Supreme Court and social change. *American Behavioral Scientist,* 1970, *13,* 535–551.

GULLIVER, P. H.   Negotiations as a mode of dispute settlement: Towards a general model. *Law and Society Review,* 1973, *7,* 667–691.

GUNTHER, G.   Foreword: In search of evolving doctrine on a changing court: A model for a newer equal protection. *Harvard Law Review,* 1972, *86,* 1–48.

GUNTHER, G.   *Constitutional law.* Mineola, N. Y.: Foundation Press, 1980.

HALL, C. W., JR.   In the public interest. *The Center Magazine,* January/February 1977, 29–32.

HALLECK, S.   The reform of mental hospitals. *Psychology Today,* March 1969, 50–51.

HALLECK, S. L.   Legal and ethical aspects of behavior control. *American Journal of Psychiatry,* 1974, *131,* 381–385.

HALPERN, S. C.   *Police-association and department leaders.* Lexington, Mass.: Lexington Books, 1974.

HALPERN, S. C.   On the imperial judiciary and comparative institutional development and power in America. In S. C. Halpern and C. M. Lamb (Eds.), *Supreme Court activism and restraint.* Lexington, Mass.: Lexington Books-Heath, 1982.

HAMANN, A. D., & BECKER, R.   The police and partisan politics in middle-sized communities. *Police,* 1970, *14* (4), 18–23.

HAMILTON, A., MADISON, J., & JAY, J.   *The federalist papers.* New York: Mentor, 1961.

HANDLER, J. F.   *The lawyer and his community.* Madison, Wis.: University of Wisconsin Press, 1967.

HARNO, A. J.   American legal education. *American Bar Association Journal,* 1960, *46,* 845–851.

HARPER, F. V., & ETHERINGTON, E. D.   Lobbyists before the court. *University of Pennsylvania Law Review,* 1953, *101,* 1172–1177.

HARRIS, R. N.   *The police academy: An inside view.* New York: Wiley, 1973.

HART, H. L. A.   *The concept of law.* Oxford: Clarendon Press, 1961.

HAYEK, F. A.   *The constitution of liberty.* Chicago: University of Chicago Press, 1960.

HAYEK, F. A.   *Law, legislation, and liberty: Vol. 1, rules and order.* Chicago: University of Chicago Press, 1973.

HAYS, S. W.   *Court reform.* Lexington, Mass.: Lexington Books-Heath, 1978.

HEBERLE, K. H.   From Gitlow to Near: Judicial "amendment" by absent-minded incrementalism. *Journal of Politics,* 1972, *34,* 458–483.

HERNDON, J.   Appointment as a means of initial accession to elective state courts of last resort. *North Dakota Law Review,* 1962, *38,* 60–73.

HEUSSENSTAMM, F. K.   Bumper stickers and the cops. *Transaction,* 1971, *8,* 32–33.

HIDAY, V. A.   Reformed commitment procedures: An empirical study in the courtroom. *Law and Society Review,* 1977, *11,* 651–666.

HINDELANG, M. J., GOTTFREDSON, M. R., & GAROFALO, J.   *Victims of personal crime.* Cambridge, Mass.: Ballinger-Lippincott, 1978.

HODGE, R. W., SIEGEL, P. M., & ROSSI, P. H.   Occupational prestige in the United States, 1925–1963. *American Journal of Sociology,* 1964, *70,* 286–302.

HOGAN, R., & HENLEY, N.   Nomotics: The science of human rule systems. In S.

Krislov et al. (Eds.), *Compliance and the law.* Beverly Hills, Calif.: Sage Publications, 1972.

HOLLAND, K. M. The federal rules of civil procedure. *Law and Policy Quarterly,* 1981, *3,* 209–224.

HOLTEN, N. G., & JONES, M. E.   *The system of criminal justice.* Boston: Little, Brown, 1978.

HONORÉ, A. M.   Ownership. In A. G. Guest (Ed.), *Oxford essays in jurisprudence.* Oxford: Clarendon Press, 1961.

HOOTON, E. A.   *Crime and the man.* Cambridge, Mass.: Harvard University Press, 1931.

HOROWITZ, D. L.   *The courts and social policy.* Washington, D.C.: Brookings Institution, 1977.

HOWARD, C. G., & SUMMERS, R. S.   *Law: Its nature, functions, and limits.* Englewood Cliffs, N.J.: Prentice-Hall, 1965.

HOWARD, J. W., JR.   On the fluidity of judicial choice. *American Political Science Review,* 1968, *62,* 43–56.

HOWARD, J. W., JR.   Role perceptions and behavior in three U.S. courts of appeals. *Journal of Politics,* 1977, *39,* 916–938.

HOWARD, J. W., JR.   *Courts of appeals in the federal judicial system.* Princeton, N.J.: Princeton University Press, 1981.

HUDSON, J. R.   Organizational aspects of internal and external review of the police. *Journal of Criminal Law, Criminology, and Police Science,* 1972, *63,* 427–433.

HUGHES, C. E.   Foreword. *Yale Law Journal,* 1941, 50, 737–738.

HUNTINGTON, S. P.   *Political order in changing societies.* New Haven, Conn.: Yale University Press, 1968.

Institute of Judicial Administration. *Judicial education in the United States.* New York: Institute of Judicial Administration, 1965.

Institute of Medicine. *Beyond malpractice: Compensation for medical injuries.* Washington, D.C.: National Academy of Sciences, 1978.

International City Management Association. *The municipal yearbook 1979.* Washington, D.C.: International City Management Association, 1979.

JACKSON, R. H.   *The struggle for judicial supremacy.* New York: Random House-Vintage, 1941.

JACOB, H.   The effect of institutional differences in the recruitment process: The case of state judges. *Journal of Public Law,* 1964, *13,* 104–119.

JACOB, H.   Judicial insulation—elections, direct participation, and public attention to the courts in Wisconsin. *Wisconsin Law Review,* 1966, 801–819.

JACOB, H.   *Debtors in court.* Chicago: Rand McNally, 1969.

JACOB, H.   Black and white perceptions of justice in the city. *Law and Society Review,* 1971, *6,* 69–89.

JACOB, H.   *Urban justice: Law and order in American cities.* Englewood Cliffs, N.J.: Prentice-Hall, 1973.

JACOB, H.   *Justice in America.* Boston: Little, Brown, 1978.

JACOBS, H. B.   *The spectre of malpractice.* New York: Nationwide Press, 1978.

JAMES, D. B.   Role theory and the Supreme Court. *Journal of Politics,* 1968, *30,* 160–186.

JEFFERY, C. R.   Criminal justice and social change. In F. J. Davis et al., *Society and the law.* New York: Free Press, 1962.

JENKINS, I.   *Social order and the limits of law.* Princeton, N.J.: Princeton University Press, 1980.

JOHNSON, C. A.   Lower court reactions to Supreme Court decisions: A quantitative examination. *American Journal of Political Science,* 1979, *23,* 792–804.

JOHNSON, R. T.   *Managing the white house.* New York: Harper and Row, Pub., 1977.

JOHNSTONE, Q., & HOPSON, D., JR. *Lawyers and their work.* Indianapolis: Bobbs-Merrill, 1967.

JONES, E. D., III. The costs of victim compensation. In C. M. Gray (Ed.), *The costs of crime.* Beverly Hills, Calif.: Sage Publications, 1979.

KAIRYS, D., KADANE, J. B., & LEHOCZKY, J. P. Jury representativeness: A mandate for multiple source lists. *California Law Review,* 1977, *65,* 776–827.

KALVEN, H., JR. The dignity of the civil jury. *Virginia Law Review,* 1964, *50,* 1055–1075.

KALVEN, H., JR., & ZEISEL, H., *The American jury.* Boston: Little, Brown, 1966.

KANT, I. *The metaphysics of morals.* Indianapolis: Bobbs-Merrill, 1965.

KAPLIN, W. A. *The law of higher education.* San Francisco: Jossey-Bass, 1978.

KAUFMAN, I. R. Congress v. the court. *The New York Times Magazine,* September 20, 1981, 44–56, 96–104.

KELLER, O. J., & ALPER, B. S. *Halfway houses.* Lexington, Mass.: Lexington Books-Heath, 1970.

KELLING, G., et al. *The Kansas City preventive patrol experiment: Summary report.* Washington, D.C.: Police Foundation, 1974.

KELLING, G. L., & FOGEL, D. Police patrol—Some future directions. In A. W. Cohn (Ed.), *The future of policing.* Beverly Hills, Calif.: Sage Publications, 1978.

KELSEN, H. *Pure theory of law.* Berkeley, Calif.: University of California Press, 1978.

Kerner Commission. *Report of the national advisory commission on civil disorders.* Washington, D.C.: U.S. Government Printing Office, 1968.

KHARASCH, R. N. *The institutional imperative.* New York: Charterhouse Books, 1973.

KING, M. L., JR. Letter from Birmingham city jail [April 16, 1963]. In T. R. Dye & B. W. Hawkins (Eds.), *Politics in the metropolis.* Columbus, Ohio: Chas. E. Merrill, 1967.

KIRCHHEIMER, O. *Political justice.* Princeton, N.J.: Princeton University Press, 1961.

KLEE, K. N. The new bankruptcy act of 1978. *American Bar Association Journal,* 1978, *64,* 1865–1867.

Knapp commission report on police corruption. New York: George Braziller, 1976.

KNAUSS, R. L. Developing a representative legal profession. *American Bar Association Journal,* 1976, *62,* 591–595.

KRATCOSKI, P. C., & WALKER, D. B., *Criminal justice in America.* Glenview, Ill.: Scott, Foresman, 1978.

KRAUSE, H. D. *Family law in a nutshell.* St. Paul, Minn.: West Publishing Co., 1977.

KRISLOV, S. The amicus curiae brief: From friendship to advocacy. *Yale Law Journal,* 1963, *72,* 694–721.

KRISLOV, S. *The Supreme Court and political freedom.* New York: Free Press, 1968.

KUBIE, L. S. Implications for legal procedure of the fallibility of human memory. *University of Pennsylvania Law Review,* 1959, *108,* 59–75.

LADINSKY, J. Careers of lawyers, law practice, and legal institutions. *American Sociological Review,* 1963, *28,* 47–54.

LA FAVE, W. R. *Arrest.* Boston: Little, Brown, 1965.

LAKOFF, S. *Equality in political philosophy.* Cambridge, Mass.: Harvard University Press, 1964.

LAMB, C. M. Book review: The courts and social policy. *UCLA Law Review,* 1978, *26,* 234–252.

LAMB, C. M. Judicial restraint on the Supreme Court. In S. C. Halpern & C. M. Lamb (Eds.), *Supreme Court activism and restraint.* Lexington, Mass.: Lexington Books-Heath, 1982.

LANDAU, J. C.   The challenge of the communications media. *American Bar Association Journal,* 1976, *62,* 55–59.

LANDER, L.   *Defective medicine.* New York: Farrar, Straus & Giroux, 1978.

LARSON, R. C.   What happened to patrol operations in Kansas City? *Journal of Criminal Justice,* 1975, *3,* 267–297.

LASSWELL, H.   *Politics: Who gets what, when, how.* Cleveland, Ohio: Meridian Books, 1958.

LAW, S., & POLAN, S.   *Pain and profit: The politics of malpractice.* New York: Harper and Row, 1978.

LEEPSON, M.   Juvenile justice. *Editorial research reports.* Washington, D.C.: Congressional Quarterly, July 27, 1979.

LEFKOWITZ, J.   Psychological attributes of policemen: A review of research and opinion. *Journal of Social Issues,* 1975, *31* (1), 3–26.

LEFLAR, R. A.   The appellate judges seminar at New York University. *Journal of Legal Education,* 1956, *9,* 359–365.

LEFLAR, R. A.   The quality of judges. *Indiana Law Journal,* 1960, *35,* 289–305.

LEIBOWITZ, A., & TOLLISON, R.   Earning and learning in law firms. *Journal of Legal Studies,* 1978, *7,* 65–81.

LEISER, B. M.   *Liberty, justice, and morals.* New York: Macmillan, 1979.

LEUBSDORF, J.   The contingency factor in attorney fee awards. *Yale Law Journal,* 1981, *90,* 473–513.

LEVINE, J. P.   Methodological concerns in studying Supreme Court efficacy. *Law and Society Review,* 1970, *4,* 583–611.

LEVINE, J. P., & BECKER, T. L.   Toward and beyond a theory of Supreme Court impact. *American Behavioral Scientist,* 1970, *13,* 561–573.

LEVY, B.   Cops in the ghetto: A problem of the police system. In L. H. Masotti & D. R. Bowen (Eds.), *Riots and rebellion: Civil violence in the urban community.* Beverly Hills, Calif.: Sage Publications, 1968.

LEWIS, A.   *Gideon's trumpet.* New York: Random House, 1964.

LIEBERMAN, J. K.   *The litigious society.* New York: Basic Books, 1981.

LINDBLOM, C. E., & COHEN, D. K.   *Usable knowledge: Social science and social problem solving.* New Haven, Conn.: Yale University Press, 1979.

LIPSET, S. M.   Why cops hate liberals—And vice versa. *The Atlantic,* March 1969, 76–83.

LITTRELL, W. B.   *Bureaucratic justice.* Beverly Hills, Calif.: Sage Publications, 1979.

LIVERMORE, J. M., MALMQUIST, C. P., & MEEHL, P. E.   On the justifications for civil commitment. *University of Pennsylvania Law Review,* 1968, *117,* 75–96.

LOCHNER, P. R., JR.   Some limits on the application of social science research in the legal process. *Law and the Social Order,* 1973, 815–848.

LODGE, E. T.   Regulation of private police. *Southern California Law Review,* 1967, *40,* 540–549.

LOEVINGER, L.   Jurimetrics: Science in law. In W. A. Thomas (Ed.), *Scientists in the legal system.* Ann Arbor, Mich.: Ann Arbor Science Publishers, 1974.

LOFTUS, E.   Reconstructing memory: The incredible eyewitness. *Psychology Today,* December 1974, 116–119.

LORCH, R. S.   *Democratic process and administrative law.* Detroit, Mich.: Wayne State University Press, 1980.

LOUISELL, D. W., & HAZARD, G. C., JR.   *Cases and materials on pleading and procedure.* Mineola, N. Y.: Foundation Press, 1979.

LOWI, T.   *The end of liberalism.* New York: W. W. Norton, 1979.

MACAULAY, S.   *Law and the balance of power: The automobile manufacturers and their dealers.* New York: Russell Sage Foundation, 1966.

MACAULAY, S., & WALSTER, E. Legal structures and restoring equity. *Journal of Social Issues,* 1971, *27* (2), 173–188.

McBRIDE, J., WACHTEL, I., & TOUHEY, T. J. *Government contracts.* New York: Matthew Bender, 1976.

McCAGHY, C. H. *Crime in American society.* New York: Macmillan, 1980.

McCOID, J. C., II. *Civil procedure.* St. Paul, Minn.: West Publishing Co., 1974.

McCONNELL, J. V. Criminals can be brainwashed—Now. *Psychology Today,* April 1970, 14–18, 74.

McINTYRE, J. Public attitudes toward crime and law enforcement. *Annals, American Academy of Political and Social Science,* 1967, *374,* 34–46.

MACKENZIE, S. Introduction. In C. Gold & S. Mackenzie (Eds.), *Wide world of arbitration.* New York: American Arbitration Association, 1978.

McKNIGHT, R. N., SCHAEFER, R., & JOHNSON, C. A. Choosing judges: Do the voters know what they're doing? *Judicature,* 1978, *62,* 94–99.

McLAUCHLAN, W. P. *American legal processes.* New York: John Wiley, 1977.

McLAUGHLIN, A. C. *The confederation and the constitution.* New York: Collier Books, 1962.

MALLEN, R. E., & LEVIT, V. B. *Legal malpractice.* St. Paul, Minn.: West Publishing Co., 1977.

MANNING, P. K. The police: Mandate, strategies, and appearances. In J. D. Douglas (Ed.), *Crime and justice in American society.* Indianapolis: Bobbs-Merrill, 1971.

MARTINSON, R. What works?—Questions and answers about prison reform. *The Public Interest,* 1974, *35,* 22–54.

MASON, A. T., & BEANEY, W. M. *American constitutional law.* Englewood Cliffs, N.J.: Prentice-Hall, 1972.

MATHEWS, H. L. *Causes of personal bankruptcies.* Columbus, Ohio: Ohio State University Bureau of Business Research, 1969.

MATTHEWS, D. R. *The social backgrounds of political decision-makers.* Garden City, N. Y.: Doubleday, 1954.

MAYER, M. *The lawyers.* New York: Harper and Row, 1967.

MAYERS, L. *The machinery of justice.* Totowa, N.J.: Littlefield, Adams, & Co., 1973.

MAYHEW, D. R. *Congress: The electoral connection.* New Haven, Conn.: Yale University Press, 1974.

MAYHEW, L. H. Institutions of representation: Civil justice and the public. *Law and Society Review,* 1975, *9,* 401–429.

MAYHEW, L., & REISS, A. J., JR. The social organization of legal contacts. *American Sociological Review,* 1969, *34,* 309–318.

MAYO, H. B. *An introduction to democratic theory.* New York: Oxford University Press, 1960.

MEADOR, D. J. *Appellate courts: Staff and process in the crisis of volume.* St. Paul, Minn.: West Publishing Co., 1974.

MEDALIE, R. J., ZEITZ, L., & ALEXANDER, P. Custodial police interrogation in our nation's capital: The attempt to implement Miranda. *Michigan Law Review,* 1968, *66,* 1347–1422.

MENDELSON, W. The neo-behavioral approach to the judicial process: A critique. *American Political Science Review,* 1963, *57,* 593–603.

MENDELSON, W. *The American constitution and the judicial process.* Homewood, Ill.: Dorsey Press, 1980.

MERTON, R. K. *Social theory and social structure.* Glencoe, Ill.: Free Press, 1957.

MILL, J. S. *On liberty.* London: Oxford University Press, 1912.

MILLER, D., & SCHWARTZ, M. County lunacy commission hearings: Some observations of commitments to a state mental hospital. *Social Problems,* 1966, *14,* 26-35.

MONTESQUIEU, C. L. DE SECONDAT.   *The spirit of the laws* (T. Nugent, trans.). New York: Hafner Pub. Co., 1949.

MOORE, M. S.   The semantics of judging. *Southern California Law Review,* 1981, *54,* 151-294.

MORRIS, N.   The judge's declining role in the criminal justice system. *Law and the Social Order,* 1972, 373-381.

MORRIS, N., & HAWKINS, G.   *The honest politician's guide to crime control.* Chicago: University of Chicago Press, 1970.

MORSE, S. J.   Crazy behavior, morals, and science: An analysis of mental health law. *Southern California Law Review,* 1978, *51,* 527-654.

MUIR, W. K., JR.   *Prayer in the public schools.* Chicago: University of Chicago Press, 1967.

MURPHY, W. F.   Chief Justice Taft and the lower court bureaucracy: A study in judicial administration. *Journal of Politics,* 1962b, *24,* 453-476.

MURPHY, W. F.   *Congress and the court.* Chicago: University of Chicago Press, 1962a.

MURPHY, W. F.   *Elements of judicial strategy.* Chicago: University of Chicago Press, 1964.

MURPHY, W. F., & TANENHAUS, J.   *The study of public law.* New York: Random House, 1972.

MURPHY, W. F., TANENHAUS, J., & KASTNER, D. L.   *Public evaluations of constitutional courts: Alternative explanations.* Beverly Hills, Calif.: Sage Publications, 1973.

NADER, L.   Disputing without the force of law. *Yale Law Journal,* 1979, *88,* 998-1021.

NAGEL, S.   Political party affiliation and judges' decisions. *American Political Science Review,* 1961, *55,* 843-850

NAGEL, S.   Off-the-bench judicial attitudes. In G. Schubert (Ed.), *Judicial decision-making.* New York: Free Press, 1963.

NAGEL, S.   *Comparing elected and appointed judicial systems.* Beverly Hills, Calif.: Sage Publications, 1973b.

NAGEL, S. S.   Effects of alternative types of counsel on criminal procedure treatment. *Indiana Law Journal,* 1973a, *48,* 404-426.

NAHSTOLL, R. W.   Observation and memory of witnesses. *American Bar Association Journal,* 1962, *48,* 68-70.

National Center for State Courts.   *State court caseload statistics: Annual report, 1976.* Washington, D.C.: U.S. Government Printing Office, 1979.

NEUBAUER, D. W.   *Criminal justice in middle America.* Morristown, N.J.: General Learning Press, 1974.

NEUSTADT, R. E.   *Presidential power.* New York: Wiley, 1960.

New York Times, The.   *The Pentagon Papers.* New York: Bantam Books, 1971.

NEWLAND, C. A.   Legal periodicals and the United States Supreme Court. *Midwest Journal of Political Science,* 1959, *3,* 58-74.

NEWMAN, D. J.   White-collar crime: An overview and analysis. In G. Geis & R. F. Meier (Eds.), *White-collar crime.* New York: Free Press, 1977.

NEWMAN, O.   *Defensible space.* New York: Macmillan, 1972.

NEWMAN, O.   *Design guidelines for creating defensible space.* Washington, D.C.: U.S. Government Printing Office. 1976.

NIEDERHOFFER, A.   *Behind the shield.* New York: Doubleday, 1967.

NOZICK, R.   *Anarchy, state, and utopia.* New York: Basic Books, 1974.

OAKS, D. H., & LEHMAN, W.   Lawyers for the poor. *Trans-action,* July-August 1967, 25-29.

O'CONNELL, J. *Ending insult to injury.* Urbana, IL: University of Illinois Press, 1975.

O'GORMAN, H. J. *Lawyers and matrimonial cases.* New York: Free Press, 1963.

OKUN, A. M. *Equality and efficiency: The big tradeoff.* Washington, D.C.: Brookings Institution, 1975.

OPPENHEIM, F. E. Freedom. In D. L. Sills (Ed.), *International encyclopedia of the social sciences* (Vol. 5). New York: Macmillan, 1968.

ORREN, K. Standing to sue: Interest group conflict in the federal courts. *American Political Science Review,* 1976, *70,* 723–741.

PACKER, H. L. *The limits of the criminal sanction.* Stanford, Calif.: Stanford University Press, 1968.

PALMER, J. W. Pre-arrest diversion: Victim confrontation. *Federal Probation Quarterly,* 1974, *38,* 12–18.

PARTRIDGE, P. H. Freedom. In P. Edwards (Ed.), *The encyclopedia of philosophy* (Vol. 3). New York: Macmillan, 1967.

PELTASON, J. W. *Federal courts in the political process.* Garden City, N. Y.: Doubleday, 1955.

PELTASON, J. W. *Fifty-eight lonely men.* New York: Harcourt, Brace, and World, 1961.

PENNOCK, J. R. Thoughts on the right to private property. In J. R. Pennock & J. W. Chapman (Eds.), *Property.* New York: New York University Press, 1980.

PERRY, M. J. Modern equal protection: A conceptualization and appraisal. *Columbia Law Review,* 1979, *79,* 1023–1084.

PETTIGREW, T. F., et al. Busing: A review of "the evidence." *The Public Interest,* 1973, *30,* 88–118.

POMPER, G. M., et al. *The performance of American government.* New York: Free Press, 1972.

POUND, R. The causes of popular dissatisfaction with the administration of justice. *Journal of the American Judicature Society,* 1937, *20,* 178–187.

President's Commission on Law Enforcement and Administration of Justice. *The challenge of crime in a free society.* Washington, D.C.: U.S. Government Printing Office, 1967b.

President's Commission on Law Enforcement and Administration of Justice. *Task force report: The police.* Washington, D.C.: U.S. Government Printing Office, 1967a.

PRESSMAN, J., & WILDAVSKY, A. *Implementation.* Berkeley, Calif.: University of California Press, 1973.

PRINGLE, H. F. *Theodore Roosevelt: A biography.* New York: Harcourt, Brace, 1931.

PRITCHETT, C. H. *Congress versus the Supreme Court.* Minneapolis, Minn.: University of Minnesota Press, 1961.

PRITCHETT, C. H. Judicial supremacy from Marshall to Burger. In M. J. Harmon (Ed.), *Essays on the constitution of the United States.* Port Washington, N. Y.: Kennikat Press, 1978.

PROSSER, W. L. *Handbook of the law of torts.* St. Paul, Minn.: West Publishing Co., 1964.

PROUDHON, P. J. *What is property?* New York: Howard Fertig, 1966.

QUINNEY, R. *The social reality of crime.* Boston: Little, Brown, 1970.

QUINNEY, R. *Class, state, crime.* New York: Longman, 1980.

RADELET, L. A. *The police and the community.* Encino, Calif.: Glencoe Press, 1977.

RAINWATER, L. (Ed.). *Social problems and public policy: Inequality and justice.* Chicago: Aldine, 1974.

RAMSEY, R. C.   The role of the judge in civil settlements. *Law and the Social Order,* 1973, 109–118.

RAWLS, J.   The justification of civil disobedience. In T. Beauchamp (Ed.), *Ethics and public policy.* Englewood Cliffs, N.J.: Prentice-Hall, 1975.

REAVES, R. D.   Training Florida judges. *The Florida Bar Journal,* 1981, *55,* 522–525.

REEDY, G.   *The twilight of the presidency.* New York: World, 1970.

REICH, C. A.   The new property. *Yale Law Journal,* 1964, *73,* 733–787.

REISS, A. J., JR.   Police brutality—Answers to key questions. *Trans-action,* 1968, *5,* 10–19.

RHEINSTEIN, M.   *Marriage stability, divorce, and the law.* Chicago: University of Chicago Press, 1972.

RICHARDSON, R. J., & VINES, K. N.   *The politics of federal courts.* Boston: Little, Brown, 1970.

RINGER, R. J.   *Winning through intimidation.* Greenwich, Conn.: Fawcett, 1974.

RIVLIN, A. M.   *Systematic thinking for social action.* Washington, D.C.: Brookings Institution, 1971.

ROBINSON, J.   *American legal almanac.* Dobbs Ferry, N. Y.: Oceana Publications, 1978.

RODGERS, H. R., JR., & BULLOCK, C. S., III.   *Law and social change: Civil rights laws and their consequences.* New York: McGraw-Hill, 1972.

ROELKE, D. P.   Discipline and removal of the judiciary in Arizona. *Law and the Social Order,* 1973, 85–94.

ROHDE, D. W., & SPAETH, H. J.   *Supreme Court decision making.* San Francisco: W. H. Freeman, 1976.

ROJEK, D. G.   Private justice systems and crime reporting. *Criminology,* 1979, *17,* 100–111.

ROLOFF, M. E., & MILLER, G. R. (Eds.).   *Persuasion: New directions in theory and research.* Beverly Hills, Calif.: Sage Publications, 1980.

ROPER, R. T.   Jury size: Impact on verdict's correctness. *American Politics Quarterly,* 1979, *7,* 438–452.

ROSEN, P. L.   *The Supreme Court and social science.* Urbana, Ill.: University of Illinois Press, 1972.

ROSENBERG, M.   Anything legislatures can do, courts can do better? *American Bar Association Journal,* 1976, *62,* 587–590.

ROSENBLUM, V. G.   *Law as a political instrument.* New York: Random House, 1955.

ROSENBLUM, V. G.   A place for social science along the judiciary's constitutional law frontier. *Northwestern Law Review,* 1971, *66,* 455–480.

ROSENTHAL, D. E.   *Lawyer and client: Who's in charge?* New York: Russell Sage Foundation, 1974.

ROSENTHAL, D. E.   Evaluating the competence of lawyers. *Law and Society Review,* 1976, *11,* 257–285.

ROSNOW, R. L., & ROBINSON, E. J. (Eds.).   *Experiments in persuasion.* New York: Academic Press, 1967.

ROSS, H. L.   *Settled out of court.* Chicago: Aldine, 1970.

ROSS, H. L., CAMPBELL, D. T., & GLASS, G. V.   Determining the social effects of a legal reform. *American Behavioral Scientist,* 1970, *13,* 493–509.

ROSSI, P. H., et al.   The seriousness of crimes: Normative structure and individual differences. *American Sociological Review,* 1974, *39,* 224–237.

ROSTOW, E. V.   The democratic character of judicial review. *Harvard Law Review,* 1952, *66,* 193–224.

RUBIN, H. T.   *The courts.* Pacific Palisades, Calif.: Goodyear, 1976.

RUBIN, J.   Police identity and the police role. In R. F. Steadman (Ed.), *The police and the community*. Baltimore: Johns Hopkins University Press, 1972.

RUESCHEMEYER, D.   Lawyers and doctors: A comment on the theory of the professions. *Canadian Review of Sociology and Anthropology, 1964, 1,* 17–30.

RUMBLE, W. E., JR.   *American legal realism*. Ithaca, N. Y.: Cornell University Press, 1968.

RUTH, H. S., JR.   Why organized crime thrives. *Annals, American Academy of Political and Social Science, 1967, 374,* 113–122.

RYAN, J. P., et al.   *American trial judges*. New York: Free Press, 1980.

ST. JOHN, N. H.   *School desegregation: Outcomes for children*. New York: Wiley-Interscience, 1975.

SALERNO, C. A.   *Police at the bargaining table*. Springfield, Ill.: Chas. C. Thomas, 1981.

SARAT, A.   Alternatives in dispute processing: Litigation in a small claims court. *Law and Society Review, 1976, 10,* 339–375.

SARAT, A.   Judging in trial courts: An exploratory study. *Journal of Politics, 1977a, 39,* 368–398.

SARAT, A.   Studying American legal culture: An assessment of survey evidence. *Law and Society Review, 1977b, 11,* 427–488.

SARAT, A., & GROSSMAN, J. B.   Courts and conflict resolution: Problems in the mobilization of adjudication. *American Political Science Review, 1975, 69,* 1200–1217.

SAYRE, W. S., & KAUFMAN, H.   *Governing New York City*. New York: Russell Sage Foundation, 1960.

SCAGLION, R., & CONDON, R. D.   Determinants of attitudes toward city police. *Criminology, 1980, 17,* 485–494.

SCHATZ, D.   The trials of a juror. *New York State Bar Journal, 1977, 49,* 198–237.

SCHEFF, T. J.   Social conditions for rationality: How urban and rural courts deal with the mentally ill. *American Behavioral Scientist, 1964, 7,* (7) 21–24.

SCHEFLIN, A. W.   Jury nullification: The right to say no. *Southern California Law Review, 1972, 45,* 168–226.

SCHEINGOLD, S. A.   *The politics of rights*. New Haven, Conn.: Yale University Press, 1974.

SCHLESINGER, J. A.   Lawyers and American politics: A clarified view. *Midwest Journal of Political Science, 1957, 1,* 26–39.

SCHMID, G., & MACMILLAN, B.   *Tort reform: Evolution of the automobile accident compensation system*. Menlo Park, Calif.: Institute for the Future, 1976.

SCHMIDHAUSER, J. R.   *The Supreme Court: Its politics, personalities, and procedures*. New York: Holt, Rinehart & Winston, 1961.

SCHNAPPER, E.   The myth of legal ethics. *American Bar Association Journal, 1978, 64,* 202–205.

SCHNUR, A. C.   The new penology: Fact or fiction? *Journal of Criminal Law, Criminology and Police Science, 1958, 49,* 331–334.

SCHUBERT, G.   *The judicial mind revisited*. New York: Oxford University Press, 1974b.

SCHUBERT, G.   *Judicial policy making*. Glenview, Ill.: Scott, Foresman, 1974a.

SCHULTZE, C. L.   *The public use of private interest*. Washington, D.C.: Brookings Institution, 1977.

SCHUR, E. M.   *Law and society*. New York: Random House, 1968.

SCHUR, E. M.   The case for abolition. In E. M. Schur & H. A. Bedau, *Victimless crimes*. Englewood Cliffs, N.J.: Prentice-Hall, 1974.

SCHUR, E. M., & BEDAU, H. A.   *Victimless crimes*. Englewood Cliffs, N.J.: Prentice-Hall, 1974.

SCHWARTZ, B.   *The law in America: A history.* New York: McGraw-Hill, 1974.

SCHWARTZ, V. E.   *Comparative negligence.* Indianapolis: Allen Smith, 1974.

SCOTT, T. M., & McPHERSON, M.   The development of the private sector of the criminal justice system. *Law and Society Review,* 1971, *6,* 267–288.

SCULL, A.   A new trade in lunacy: The recommodification of the mental patient. *American Behavioral Scientist,* 1981, *24,* 741–754.

SEGAL, S. P., & AVIRAM, U.   *The mentally ill in community-based sheltered care.* New York: Wiley, 1978.

SELLIN, T.   *The penalty of death.* Beverly Hills, Calif.: Sage Publications, 1980.

SHAFFER, T. L.   Lawyers, counselors, and counselors at law. *American Bar Association Journal,* 1975, *61,* 854–856.

SHANK, A., & CONANT, R. W.   *Urban perspectives.* Boston: Holbrook, 1975.

SHAPIRO, M.   Appeal. *Law and Society Review.* 1980, *14,* 629–661.

SHAPO, M. S.   *The duty to act.* Austin, Tex.: University of Texas Press, 1977.

SHELDON, C. H.   *The American judicial process.* New York: Dodd, Mead, 1974.

SHELDON, C. H.   Influencing the selection of judges: The variety and effectiveness of state bar activities. *Western Political Quarterly,* 1977, *30,* 397–400.

SHELEY, J. F.   *Understanding crime.* Belmont, Calif.: Wadsworth, 1979.

SIMON, C. K.   The juror in New York City: Attitudes and experiences. *American Bar Association Journal,* 1975, *61,* 207–211.

SIMON, R. J.   *The jury: Its role in American society.* Lexington, Mass.: Lexington Books-Heath, 1980.

SKOLNICK, J.   *Justice without trial.* New York: Wiley, 1966.

SKOLNICK, J. H., & GRAY, T. C. (Eds.)   *Police in America.* Boston: Little, Brown, 1975.

SMITH, P. E., & HAWKINS, R. O.   Victimization, types of citizen-police contacts, and attitudes toward the police. *Law and Society Review,* 1973, *8,* 135–152.

SMITH, W. H.   *A political history of slavery.* New York: Ungar, 1966.

SPECTOR, M.   The rise and fall of a mobility route. *Social Problems,* 1972, *20,* 173–185.

SPOHN, C., GRUHL, J., & WELCH, S.   The effect of race on sentencing: A re-examination of an unsettled question. *Law and Society Review,* 1981–1982, *16,* 71–88.

STACEY, F.   *Ombudsmen compared.* Oxford: Clarendon Press, 1978.

STAMPP, K. M.   *The peculiar institution.* New York: Knopf, 1967.

STANG, D. P.   The police and their problems. In J. S. Campbell, J. R. Sahid, & D. P. Stang (Eds.), *Law and order reconsidered.* Washington, D.C.: U.S. Government Printing Office, 1969.

STANLEY, D. T., & GIRTH, M.   *Bankruptcy: Problem, process, reform.* Washington, D.C.: Brookings Institution, 1971.

STEELE, E. H., & NIMMER, R. T.   Lawyers, clients, and professional regulation. *American Bar Foundation Journal,* 1976, 917–1019.

STEIN, D.   *Judging the judges.* Hicksville, N. Y.: Exposition Press, 1974.

STERN, D. N.   How to avoid being sued—Special problems of the lawyer engaged in the litigation process. In American Bar Association (Ed.), *Professional liability of trial lawyers: The malpractice question.* Chicago: American Bar Association, 1979.

STERN, G.   Public drunkenness: Crime or health problem. *Annals, American Academy of Political and Social Science,* 1967, *374,* 147–156.

STRICKMAN, L. P.   Marriage, divorce, and the constitution. *Family Law Quarterly,* 1981, *15,* 259–348.

STRODTBECK, F. L., JAMES, R. M., & HAWKINS, C.   Social status in jury deliberations. *American Sociological Review,* 1957, *22,* 713–719.

STUMPF, H. P.   *Community politics and legal services.* Beverly Hills, Calif.: Sage Publications, 1975.

SUMMERS, M. R.   Analysis of factors that influence choice of forum in diversity cases. *Iowa Law Review,* 1962, *47,* 933–940.

SUNDQUIST, J.   *Making federalism work.* Washington, D.C.: Brookings Institution, 1972.

SUTHERLAND, E. H.   Crime of corporations. In G. Geis & R. F. Meier (Eds.), *White-collar crime.* New York: Free Press, 1977b.

SUTHERLAND, E. H. White-collar criminality. In G. Geis & R. F. Meier (Eds.), *White-collar crime.* New York: Free Press, 1977a.

SUTHERLAND, E. H., & CRESSEY, D. R.   *Criminology.* Philadelphia: Lippincott, 1978.

SWIGERT, V. L., & FARRELL, R. A.   Corporate homicide: Definitional processes in the creation of deviance. *Law and Society Review,* 1980–1981, *15,* 161–182.

SYKES, G.   *The society of captives.* Princeton, N.J.: Princeton University Press, 1958.

SZASZ, T.   The crime of commitment. *Psychology Today,* March 1969, 55–57.

TATE, C. N.   Personal attribute models of the voting behavior of U.S. Supreme Court justices: Liberalism in civil liberties and economic decisions, 1946–1978. *American Political Science Review,* 1981, *75,* 355–367.

TAWNEY, R. H.   *The acquisitive society.* New York: Harcourt, Brace, and Howe, 1920.

TESITOR, I. A.   *Judicial conduct organizations.* Chicago: American Judicature Society, 1978.

TEWKSBURY, W. J.   The ordeal as a vehicle for divine intervention in medieval Europe. In P. Bohannan (Ed.), *Law and warfare.* Garden City, N. Y.: Natural History Press, 1967.

THUROW, L. C.   *The zero-sum society.* New York: Basic Books, 1980.

TIEN, J. M., SIMON, J. W., & LARSON, R. C.   *An alternative approach in police patrol: The Wilmington split-force experiment.* Washington, D.C.: U.S. Government Printing Office, 1978.

TOCQUEVILLE, A. DE.   *Democracy in America* (H. Reeve, trans.). London: Longmans, Green, and Co., 1875.

TROJANOWICZ, R. C., TROJANOWICZ, J. M., & MOSS, F. M.   *Community based crime prevention.* Pacific Palisades, Calif.: Goodyear, 1975.

TRUMAN, D.   *The governmental process.* New York: Knopf, 1951.

TURK, A. T.   *Political criminality.* Beverly Hills, Calif.: Sage Publications, 1982.

Twentieth Century Task Force on Justice, Publicity, and the First Amendment. *Rights in conflict.* New York: McGraw-Hill, 1976.

U.S. Bureau of the Census.   *Statistical abstract of the United States: 1978.* Washington, D.C.: U.S. Government Printing Office, 1978.

U.S. Bureau of the Census.   *Statistical abstract of the United States: 1981.* Washington, D.C.: U.S. Government Printing Office, 1981.

United States code: 1976 edition.   Washington, D.C.: U.S. Government Printing Office, 1977.

U.S. Commission on Civil Rights.   *Racial isolation in the public schools.* Washington, D.C.: U.S. Government Printing Office, 1967.

U.S. News and Wold Report.   *What everyone needs to know about law.* Washington, D.C.: U.S. News and World Report, 1973.

U.S. News and World Report. *1978 study of American opinion.* Washington, D.C.: U.S. News and World Report, 1978.

VAGO, S.   *Law and society.* Englewood Cliffs, N.J.: Prentice-Hall, 1981.

VAN DEN HAAG, E.   *Punishing criminals.* New York: Basic Books, 1975.

VAN DYKE, J. M.　The jury as a political institution. *The Catholic Lawyer,* 1970, *16,* 224–241.

VAN MAANEN, J.　Working the street: A developmental view of police behavior. In H. Jacob (Ed.), *The potential for reform of criminal justice.* Beverly Hills, Calif.: Sage Publications, 1974.

VAN MAANEN, J.　The asshole. In P. K. Manning, & J. Van Maanen (Eds.), *Policing: A view from the street.* Santa Monica, Calif.: Goodyear, 1978.

Vera Institute of Justice.　*Felony arrests: Their prosecution and disposition in New York City's courts.* New York: Vera Institute of Justice, 1977.

VINES, K. N.　The role of circuit courts of appeals in the federal judicial process: A case study. *Midwest Journal of Political Science,* 1963, *7,* 305–319.

VOLCANSEK-CLARK, M.　Why lawyers become judges. *Judicature,* 1978, *62,* 166–175.

VOLCANSEK, M. L.　Codes of judicial ethics: Do they affect judges' views of proper off-the-bench behavior? *American Business Law Journal,* 1980, *17,* 493–505.

VOLCANSEK, M. L.　The effects of judicial-selection reform: What we know and what we do not. In P. L. Dubois (Ed.), *The analysis of judicial reform.* Lexington, Mass.: Lexington Books-Heath, 1982.

VOLD, G. B.　*Theoretical criminology.* New York: Oxford University Press, 1979.

VOLLRATH, D. A., & DAVIS, J. H.　Jury size and decision rule. In R. J. Simon (Ed.), *The jury: Its role in American society.* Lexington, Mass.: Lexington Books, 1980.

VOSE, C. E.　Litigation as a form of pressure group activity. *Annals, American Academy of Political and Social Science,* 1958, *319,* 20–31.

VOSE, C. E.　*Caucasions only.* Berkeley, Calif.: University of California Press, 1959.

WALD, P.　Pretrial detention and ultimate freedom: A statistical study. *New York University Law Review,* 1964, *39,* 631–640.

WALD, P. M.　The right to bail revisited: A decade of promise without fulfillment. In S. S. Nagel (Ed.), *The rights of the accused in law and action.* Beverly Hills, Calif.: Sage Publications, 1972.

WALKER, D.　*Rights in conflict.* Washington, D.C.: U.S. Government Printing Office, 1968.

WANNER, C.　The public ordering of private relations; part one: Initiating civil cases in urban trial courts. *Law and Society Review,* 1974, *8,* 421–440.

WANNER, C.　The public ordering of private relations; part two: Winning civil court cases. *Law and Society Review,* 1975, *9,* 293–306.

WARREN, C. A. B.　New forms of social control: The myth of deinstitutionalization. *American Behavioral Scientist,* 1981, *24,* 724–740.

WASBY, S. L.　*The impact of the United States Supreme Court: Some perspectives.* Homewood, Ill.: Dorsey Press, 1970.

WASBY, S. L.　Book review: *The courts and social policy* by Donald L. Horowitz. *Vanderbilt Law Review,* 1978b, *31,* 727–761.

WASBY, S. L.　*The Supreme Court in the federal judicial system.* New York: Holt, Rinehart and Winston, 1978a.

WATSON, R. A., & DOWNING, R. G.　*The politics of the bench and the bar.* New York: John Wiley, 1969.

WECHSLER, H.　*Principles, politics, and fundamental law.* Cambridge, Mass.: Harvard University Press, 1961.

WEIL, R. I., & BOWER, W.　Where the earnings are. *Barrister,* 1980, *7,* 44–48.

WEISSBERG, R.　*Understanding American government.* New York: Holt, Rinehart and Winston, 1980.

WESTLEY, W. A.　Secrecy and the police. *Social Forces,* 1956, *34,* 254–257.

WHEELER, M.　*No-fault divorce.* Boston: Beacon Press, 1974.

WHISENAND, J. D.   Florida's experience with cameras in the courtroom. *American Bar Association Journal,* 1978, *64,* 1860–1864.

WIDISS, A. I.   Accident victims under no-fault automobile insurance: A Massachusetts survey. *Iowa Law Review,* 1975, *61,* 1–72.

WILDAVSKY, A.   *The politics of the budgetary process.* Boston: Little, Brown, 1979.

WILENSKY, H. L.   The professionalization of everyone? *The American Journal of Sociology,* 1964, *70,* 137–158.

WILSON, J. Q.,   *Varieties of police behavior.* Cambridge, Mass.: Harvard University Press, 1968.

WILSON, J. Q.   The police in the ghetto. In R. F. Steadman (Ed.), *The police and the community.* Baltimore: Johns Hopkins University Press, 1972.

WILSON, J. Q.   Do the police prevent crime? *The New York Times Magazine,* October 6, 1974, 18–19, 96–101.

WINTER, R. K., JR.   The growth of judicial power. In L. J. Theberge (Ed.), *The judiciary in a democratic society.* Lexington, Mass.: Lexington Books-Heath, 1979.

WOLKIN, P. A.   A better way to keep lawyers competent. *American Bar Association Journal,* 1975, *61,* 574–578.

WOOCHER, F. D.   Did your eyes deceive you?: Expert psychological testimony on the unreliability of eyewitness identification. *Stanford Law Review,* 1977, *29,* 969–1030.

WRIGHT, E. O.   *The politics of punishment.* New York: Harper and Row, 1973.

YARMEY, A. D.   *The psychology of eyewitness testimony.* New York: Free Press, 1979.

YEAROUT, M.   Federal wage garnishment: Inadequate protection for wage earners' dependents. *Iowa Law Review,* 1979, *64,* 1000–1018.

YNGVESSON, B., & HENNESSEY, P.   Small claims, complex disputes: A review of the small claims literature. *Law and Society Review,* 1975, *9,* 219–274.

YORK, J. C., & HALE, R. D.   Too many lawyers? *Journal of Legal Education,* 1973, *26,* 1–31.

ZANDER, M.   How to explain the unmet need for legal services? *American Bar Association Journal,* 1978, *64,* 1676–1679.

ZEISEL, H.   The waning of the American jury. *American Bar Association Journal,* 1972, *58,* 367–370.

ZEISEL, H., KALVEN, H., JR., & BUCHHOLZ, B.   *Delay in the court.* Boston: Little, Brown, 1959.

ZELLMAN, G. L.   Antidemocratic beliefs: A survey and some explanations. *Journal of Social Issues,* 1975, *31,* (2), 31–53.

ZEMANS, F. K., & ROSENBLUM, V. G.   Preparation for the practice of law—The views of the practicing bar. *American Bar Foundation Research Journal,* 1980, 1–30.

ZIEGLER, H.   *Interest groups in American society.* Englewood Cliffs, N.J.: Prentice-Hall, 1964.

ZIMRING, F. E.   Measuring the impact of pretrial diversion from the criminal justice system. *University of Chicago Law Review,* 1974, *41,* 224–241.

ZIMRING, F. E., & HAWKINS, G. J.   *Deterrence.* Chicago: University of Chicago Press, 1973.

INDEX

587- 8789